ASTROLOGY
FOR ADULTS

Joan
Quigley

ASTROLOGY
FOR ADULTS

HOLT, RINEHART AND WINSTON

NEW YORK   CHICAGO

SAN FRANCISCO

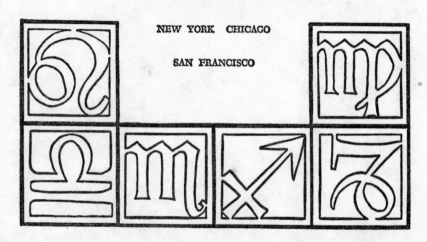

Contents

ASTROLOGY
FOR ADULTS

INTRODUCTION
Why Astrology Will Work for You

Have you ever wanted a complete, accurate and understanding analysis of your character? Did you ever wonder how two people in the family could be so very different even though their heredity and environment were the same? Do you understand yourself, your assets and liabilities well enough to make the most of your potential? Are you lucky in love?

To all these questions and many more, the stars have the answers. Knowing only your time and place of birth, astrology can, in fact, tell you more about yourself than a psychiatrist can tell you after many hours of consultations on his couch.

But how can astrology reveal so much with such scant information? It's very simple. Astrology is the oldest science. It is, in fact, as old as civilization itself and its roots are hidden in the mystery of man's earliest beginnings. No doubt the ancients noticed the correspondence of the phases of the Moon upon the tides, on crops, on all of life on earth. Later, as such observations were extended and codified, the influence of solar and planetary movements on human affairs became the astrologers' concern.

The earliest extant horoscope dates from 2767 B.C. It was cast by Imhotep, architect of the great Step pyramid at Saqqarah.* To our knowledge, astrology existed not only in Egypt but also in Babylon, India, Greece, China, Chaldea and in the Americas, North and

* Cyril Fagan, "Solunars," *American Astrology* (January, 1954), pp. 29–30.

South. The Bible of the ancient Hebrews contains frequent references to astrology. Stones with the various astrological symbols have been found the world over. Even the dolmens of Stonehenge were a primitive kind of observatory for the position of the Sun.

The early astronomers were also students of astrology. Ptolemy, Kepler, Copernicus were interested in the effect of the stars on mankind. The sixteenth-century French astrologer, Nostradamus, also a physician and philosopher, specialized in mundane astrology, the branch dealing with trends in world affairs rather than the destinies of individuals. In 1547, he began his famous work in which he predicted in rhyming verse events well into the twentieth century. Like many oracles, however, his references were somewhat equivocal and subject to various interpretations. William Lilly, a seventeenth-century mundane astrologer, was more specific in his predictions of the terrible plague of 1665 and the great fire of London the following year.

At the end of the seventeenth century most scientists rejected astrology as part of a superstitious past without thoroughly investigating it. Scientific prejudice continues into the present day, but no one who has given astrology a fair trial can dispute its psychological verities. Carl Jung was interested in astrology and wrote a study comparing the charts of married couples. Astrology is also of great value for understanding a person's physical make-up, and Dr. Heber J. Smith, who taught astrology to the famous Evangeline Adams, tried whenever possible to consult a patient's horoscope before seeing him.

Actually, though, modern scientific theory is an eloquent argument for belief in astrology. Science tells us that all matter vibrates, and it is through these vibrations that the stars influence all of human life—physical, mental, spiritual. Einstein's theory of relativity also provides the astrologer with an explanation for the reason the varying rates of time after birth refer to the various stages in the life of an individual.

It is well to remember, however, that astrology can best be compared to medical diagnosis. The astrologer relies on the computations of the astronomer in the same way a doctor bases his conclusions on the findings of the laboratory technician. In this sense astrology, like medical diagnosis, is an art. And, like the doctor, the astrologer can refer to case histories recorded from ancient times down to the present day to guide him in his work.

Now that we are on the threshold of the Aquarian Age, it is evident that astrology will again come into its own. Mankind has already experienced almost 2,000 years of the Age of Pisces, symbolized by two fish swimming in opposite directions and signifying the warring and separative elements of body and spirit and the philosophy of the Christian religion. It was a time of great art and high achievements, and of terrible persecutions and wars.

Pisces is the sign of both the highest types and the dregs of humanity. Although the hippies describe themselves as harbingers of the Aquarian Age, they are in reality remnants of the few remaining degrees of the Age of Pisces. Their irresponsibility and drug addiction are typical of Pisces at its worst. Nor is the current callous emphasis on the materialistic aspects of sex and the unprecedented rise in violence and crime Aquarian. Rather it can be attributed to the passage of Neptune, the deceptive planet, through the passionate and carnal sign of Scorpio. This began at the end of 1956 and will last roughly through 1971. One must keep in mind, however, that Neptune is also the planet of high ideals and Scorpio the sign of the dedicated doctor or scientist. For this reason, the higher vibrations of Neptune in Scorpio, in operation at the same time as the lower ones, have resulted in astounding advances in man's quest to solve the mysteries of the universe.

In reality, Aquarius is the best balanced of all the signs. Sex plays a part but only in proportion to the whole. A human sign, Aquarius is represented by the figure of a maiden pouring water onto the earth, and during the coming age, man's leaders, like the maiden, will pour out their good to all human kind. The common man will come into his own, aided rather than being exploited by people not of high birth but of unusual and outstanding achievements. Uranus, the planet ruling Aquarius, is the astrologers' planet, and in this age, astrology will regain its lost respectability. It will be taught in the schools and colleges and will be considered a profession on a par with medicine and law.

For in truth, astrology can be of the greatest benefit when constructively and rightly used. An astrologer knows that no one race or group of people has a monopoly on human joys and sorrows. There is no difference in the horoscopes of red or yellow, black or white. Each is in the eye of the astrologer a unique and separate human being. For we are not all born alike but with different characteristics and abilities, different capacities with which to meet our opportunities and troubles and the various other encounters with the forces that shape our human destinies.

To help each person to understand his essential nature and pattern of destiny is the role of the astrologer. A lot of it is up to the individual, of course. It is as though you were handed a road map of a journey you were about to take. Where the road is difficult, you can slow down and travel more cautiously, or go full speed ahead on a fine highway. How pleasant the trip will be depends on how well the vehicle in which you travel operates and how well it is fitted for the particular journey that is indicated for you. A badly put together vehicle might balk at the tiniest bump in the road, while a well-built engine could survive the toughest obstacle course; and even the frailest equipment is sometimes known to triumph when motivated by the indefinable power of human spirit.

It is the vehicle in which you make your life's journey that will be analyzed in this book. According to astrological theory, you are endowed with a certain character at the moment of conception and inhale the various planets' influences with your first breath. Indeed, an astrologer who charts the planetary influences at the moment of a person's birth can fully explain the nature of that person, even before he has had a chance to develop his character as an adult.

Why then are some people so skeptical about astrology? Perhaps you have been skeptical yourself. Perhaps you have wondered when you read your horoscope in the papers how what is said about your sign could also refer to everyone born during the same thirty-day period in any year. Obviously, it could not. Does that mean that astrology is a hoax? Not really. It means only that popular astrology can't possibly be accurate because it is incomplete.

According to popular astrology, your "sign" is the sign the Sun was in when you were born. If you were born under Aries, i.e., between March 21 and April 20, that means your Sun is in Aries. But a complete horoscope takes into consideration not only the sign position of the Sun but also that of the Moon and the eight planets. For this information you have to know the exact day, year, hour and place of birth. In every chapter of this book, your hour or date of birth will be mentioned. So look them up and read the descriptions that are written especially for you.

The Planets and the Ascendant in the Signs

The present work is divided into eleven chapters: one for the Sun which represents the individuality, one for the Moon, representing the personality, and one for the Ascendant. The latter is based on the hour of birth and has to do with the person himself, his physical body and temperament. The remaining eight are for the planets Mercury, Venus, Mars, Jupiter, Saturn, Uranus, Neptune and Pluto. From now on, for convenience, when the term "planets" is mentioned, it also includes the Sun and Moon.

Each of the planets is found in one of the twelve signs of the Zodiac, as is the Ascendant. Zodiac means animal, and the signs of the Zodiac are symbolized by animals except for Gemini, Virgo and Aquarius, the three human signs. The symbols of the twelve signs of the Zodiac are as follows: Aries, the Ram; Taurus, the Bull; Gemini, the Twins; Cancer, the Crab; Leo, the Lion; Virgo, the Virgin; Libra, the Scales; Scorpio, the Scorpion or Eagle; Sagittarius, the Centaur Archer; Capricorn, the Goat; Aquarius, the Water-bearer; and Pisces, two Fish swimming in opposite directions.

The first chapter of this book is devoted to the Sun. The Sun is the center of our planetary system, and it is one of the most important features in your horoscope. The Sun is in approximately the same position on the same day every year. For instance, if you had a friend born June 1, 1940, and you had a sister born June 1, 1934, and a father born June 1, 1901, they would all be Geminis because Gemini is the sign the Sun is in between May 21 and June 21 of any year.

But all people born between May 21 and June 21 are not alike. This is because one has to take the other planets into consideration. The other planets do not move regularly as does the Sun but can be in different signs on the same day in different years. A person might, for example, have his Sun in one sign and his Venus in another. Venus is the planet that has to do with a person's love nature. Two people born under the same sign can, for instance, have very different love natures depending on the sign their Venuses are in.

Take your friend born June 1, 1940. While his Sun is in the versatile and intellectual sign of Gemini, his Venus is in Cancer which would at the same time make him very sentimental and emotional in any romantic relationship. Your father born June 1, 1901, is another Gemini, but his Venus is also in Gemini, which would make him somewhat fickle and a great flirt; he would have an intellectual rather than an emotional approach to the opposite sex. Different still would be your sister born June 1, 1934. Although her Sun is in Gemini too, Venus in Aries would make her very fiery, headstrong and independent in love. So you can see how different your friend, father and sister will be in a romantic relationship even though they all have the same Sun sign and their birthdays are on the same day. If you want to know about your own love nature, look up your year and date of birth in the chapter entitled "Venus and Your Kind of Love."

If you would like to find out what the stars will say about your mind, look up Mercury; for physical strength and forcefulness, Mars. For luck, Jupiter; for will power, Uranus; for charm and illusions, Neptune; and for group involvement, Pluto.

But what about people born on the same day and year? Even they are not necessarily alike. Astrology has an explanation for this too. It is because the time of day can make such a difference in the position of the Ascendant and the Moon. The Ascendant goes through every sign of the Zodiac in the course of a single day, and on many days the Moon may be in either one of two signs. So you can see why people born on the same day and year but at different times of day can be very dissimilar because the Moon and/or the Ascendant have changed signs. We have on record cases of twins born only a few minutes apart who illustrate this point. Also, in a single sign, there are smaller divisions and a change of degree within the same sign can be significant.

The Aspects

Then there are the aspects or the relationships of the planets to one another. These can be good or bad, harmonious or inharmonious. From the descriptions in each chapter, you can guess which of these is most like you.

Usually each planet is in aspect to only a few of the others, so don't expect all of the aspects to apply to you. However, the more aspects a planet has, the greater its importance in your particular horoscope.

Some of the descriptions referring to the same individual may seem to be contradictory. For instance, a Virgo whose traits are intellectuality and a desire to serve might have Moon in Leo giving him a proud and noble personality. The Virgo trait of intellectuality would be there, but his Leo Moon would make it hard for him to be under another's authority, and he would tend to resent menial tasks and to leave them undone in a way a person with Moon in Virgo would never do.

Another example is a woman with the Sun in Taurus, indicating a plodding, conservative, stable character, but whose Moon is in the dashing, high-strung, aristocratic and often shy sign of Sagittarius, and whose Scorpio Ascendant would give her deep emotions and a forceful disposition.

Sometimes apparently contradictory traits are reconciled harmoniously within the same character. Sometimes they are continually at war. In other cases, traits will be dominant at certain periods of life and regressive at others. But they are all in the composition of the character and will reveal themselves in some way at some time.

Occasionally, you may find that one of your descriptions does not seem to refer to you at all but may instead resemble a person or persons intimately involved in your life. This may be because that planet is in the portion of your horoscope referring, for instance, to your mother, sister, friend, husband or wife.

If many of your planets are in the same sign, the traits described will be accentuated in your horoscope. If you have four planets in

Scorpio, for example, all of Scorpio's passion and dedication and many of the other typically Scorpio faults and virtues will be a major influence in your character. Virgo coupled heavily with Scorpio can be cold and detached and at the same time very passionate. A horoscope that is heavily Libran will stress partnership and justice, while one strongly Aquarian will have many friends and extensive and progressive interests. A predominately Piscean horoscope will be very sympathetic and charming.

If you have many planets in the air signs (Gemini, Libra or Aquarius), your approach tends to be mental; in water signs (Cancer, Scorpio and Pisces), emotional; in earth signs (Taurus, Virgo or Capricorn), practical; and in fire signs (Aries, Leo and Sagittarius), daring and ambitious. If you have most of your planets in cardinal signs (Aries, Cancer, Libra, and Capricorn), you are very active; if in the mutable signs (Gemini, Virgo, Sagittarius and Pisces), more passive or philosophical; in fixed signs (Taurus, Leo, Scorpio and Aquarius), you are sure of yourself and stable. People with an assortment of all the influences tend to be well balanced with a wide range of activities and interests, while people whose horoscopes are concentrated in only a few groups are more specialized in their outlook.

How Your Horoscope Will Relate to Someone Else's

It is also interesting to understand the relationships of your horoscope to those of other people. One of the finest indications of true compatibility between friends and between the sexes is for the Moon in one horoscope to be in the same sign as the Sun in another. The Moon person tends to be a foil to the Sun person, but generally they see eye to eye and their relationship is harmonious and full of understanding.

Venus in one horoscope in the same sign as the Sun in another is an excellent testimony of affection between friends or ideal love between the sexes. And if someone's Venus is in the same sign as your Moon or your Ascendant, you may also expect a bond of love between you. In these cases, often the Venus person is the one who loves or else is considered beautiful or pleasing in the eyes of the other.

Between the sexes, Mars in one horoscope in the same sign as Venus in another is the bond par excellence of physical passion. A man with Mars on a woman's Venus might easily seduce her, while a woman whose Mars is in the same sign as a man's Venus will play the siren with him. This is the kind of relationship that leads to affairs and flirtations rather than to marriage unless there are other more enduring bonds between the two horoscopes.

The Moon of one person in the same sign as Mars in another also results in sexual attraction but sometimes gives so much tension that the two will quarrel. The same is true when the Moon is three signs away or opposite Mars in another. This is similar to relationships between Mars and the Sun mentioned at the end of each description in Chapter 6.

A woman who would like to have a generous, indulgent husband should look for a man whose Jupiter is in the same sign as her Venus or Sun. Such a man will tend to impress her with his importance as well. In cases where Jupiter in a woman's horoscope is in the same sign as Venus, Sun or Ascendant in a man's, the benevolent role may be reversed. Jupiter and Moon relationships are somewhat similar. The Moon person will look up to and honor the Jupiter person who will in return treat him in the most magnanimous fashion.

While an admirer with Jupiter on a woman's Venus will shower her with presents, the man whose Saturn is in the same sign as her Sun or Venus will on the contrary be stingy with her and tend to use her for his own purposes. She will find that he weighs down her spirits and bores her as well. In the foregoing examples, the Jupiter benefits may be lessened if Jupiter is badly aspected or the Saturn defects modified if Saturn is well aspected, but in most cases, the general remarks will hold true.

There is often an attraction between a person whose Sun is opposite another's Saturn. The Sun person tends to buoy up the Saturn person's spirits and to shine in his eyes, while the Saturn person always needs cheering up and may at times be something of a drag on the Sun person's optimism and confidence. The Sun person usually puts up with him, however, as he enjoys being able to show off to so willing an audience. This is often true in the case of married couples who unconsciously have paired off, the one to compensate for the other's qualities.

Someone with Mercury in the same sign as your Sun tends to talk a blue streak when he is with you. This also makes for very effective teacher-student relationships. Venus in one horoscope in the same sign as Mercury in another leads to spontaneity, gaiety and aesthetic pursuits.

If you have Mars in the same sign as someone else's Mercury, you tend also to talk a lot and more often to argue and debate even the most commonplace issues. If these planets are badly aspected in the individual horoscopes, you may come to physical blows. The Mars person usually deals harshly with the Mercury person and is critical of his ideas. Often the Mars person is actively sadistic in this relationship.

Someone whose Sun is in the same sign as your Neptune can be charmed, confused, or misled by you. Or one of you may find the relationship embarrassing in some way. Mars-Neptune relationships are weird and dangerous, and if either planet is badly aspected can lead to scandal or crime. With Mercury and Neptune in the same sign, the Mercury person may clarify the Neptune person's hazy ideas. If well aspected, Venus-Neptune relationships can lead to an ideal love. If badly aspected, perversity in love may result.

Someone with Uranus in the same sign as your Sun will stimulate and amuse you or else may irritate you depending on the aspects. It is an exciting relationship, quite out of the ordinary. The unusual and unexpected almost always happens. Moon in one horoscope in the same sign as Uranus in another also describes a lively, scintillating relationship. Between a man and a woman, this often leads to romance. The Venus of one in the same sign as the Uranus of another spells a sudden attraction, even love at first sight. Mercury-Uranus relationships leads to mutual mental inspiration with the Uranus person displaying wit and originality.

Planets in the same sign as your Ascendant tend to react in a fashion similar to those in the same sign as your Sun. Then there are the relationships between people's Suns. It is generally true but in many cases an oversimplification to say that there is a natural affinity between Aries, Leo and Sagittarius; between Taurus, Virgo and Capricorn; between Gemini, Libra and Aquarius; and between Cancer,

Scorpio and Pisces. It is likewise correct to venture that in many but not all cases, there is an antipathy between Aries, Cancer, Libra and Capricorn; between Taurus, Leo, Scorpio and Aquarius; and between Gemini, Virgo, Sagittarius and Pisces. These generalizations must of course be modified. For instance, the intellectuality of Virgo and Gemini may be a bond between them, although it is evident that Virgo's practicality will conflict with Gemini's abstract reason. Other exceptions are people whose Suns are in opposite signs. Such persons are at opposite poles and therefore strike a balance in which one complements the other. For instance, an Aries' singlemindness and independence make him the exact opposite of the Libra, whose tendency is to see every side of a question and who desires above all union with others. But while they are at two extremes, each can in his way supply what the other lacks. Air and fire signs tend to get along as do water and earth signs.

There are naturally many other points of agreement and disagreement between horoscopes. The relationships between two horoscopes as between two people can be very complex. These are, however, among the simplest and most obvious ones to recognize.

1

Your Individuality and

THE SUN

Are you a rugged individual? Is your physical constitution vigorous and strong? Do others depend upon you for leadership and advice? These are important questions for everyone who must daily encounter all the challenges and responsibilites of adult life. And for the answers to these questions you must consult the Sun, that vital center of our universe. All the planets revolve around the Sun and could not exist but for its magnetism and life-giving light. And so it follows that you must look to the Sun for the most fundamental truths about your character and life.

The signs of the Zodiac were divided by the ancients into four elements: earth, air, fire and water. When the Sun is in the earthy signs (Taurus, Virgo and Capricorn), you are energetic, practical and stable, with the ability to put ideas to concrete, material use. The Sun in the airy signs (Gemini, Libra and Aquarius) gives intellectual force, sociability and an interest in the arts and sciences. The disposition is high-strung and sensitive, and such people have the ability to express themselves in writing and speech. Sun in fiery signs (Aries, Leo and Sagittarius) indicates ambition, courage and dignity with strong enthusiasms and great initiative, a love of action and the ability to lead or influence others. When the Sun is in watery signs (Cancer,

Scorpio and Pisces), you are sympathetic and emotional with strong passions and a great capacity for sex.

The signs are also divided into threes according to their natures. When the Sun is in the active or cardinal signs (Aries, Cancer, Libra and Capricorn), you are active and creative, conceiving plans, like an architect; you are not content until you have influenced those around you and expressed yourself and your ideas in the world at large. When the Sun is in the fixed or stable signs (Taurus, Leo, Scorpio and Aquarius), you are positive and reliable. You are constructive, like a builder, or you are a sustaining force, the person whose duty it is to keep the world running smoothly as it is. You tend to repeat the same experiences over and over either in your daily routine or in the important events of your life. When the Sun is in the mutable or variable signs (Gemini, Virgo, Sagittarius and Pisces), you tear down the old to make way for the new. You are interested in the meaning behind events and in gleaning wisdom from your experiences in this world.

Some planets affect you as an individual more than other planets. If the Sun is a strong influence in your particular horoscope, you are brave, positive, self-confident and bold, a leader in your field or circle of friends. You are the outstanding person, around whom the less-individual types revolve. A well-aspected Sun gives forcefulness, an indomitable will. The body is healthy and organically strong. The Sun rules the eyes, back, arteries and heart. Good eyesight in the right eye usually means a well-aspected Sun.

As the Sun represents the masculine force in nature, its position in a woman's horoscope tells a great deal about the men in her life—the father, suitors, or husband. If the Sun is well aspected, it means that they are helpful and well disposed toward her. In a man's horoscope, a well-aspected Sun means that men in positions of authority favor him and other men are helpful to him and are generally admirable. In both sexes, a well-aspected Sun is an excellent testimony of success in life. It makes up for other defects and will carry you far.

A badly aspected Sun, on the other hand, may indicate foolish pride, arrogance, and an intolerant attitude toward others. It is often the sign of a weak or unfortunate character, and no amount of favorable aspects from the other planets can counteract it. People with such a Sun in their horoscopes usually do not have the will power or endurance to succeed in life, and even when they do, health defects prevent them from realizing their life's ambitions or they suffer from the disapproval and opposition of those in positions of authority. In any event, they are bound to encounter many obstacles and difficulties. For a woman, a badly aspected Sun often causes her to come into contact with men who either have defective characters or who are unfavorable in their attitude toward her.

The Sun's relationships to the Moon are of the utmost importance. When they are both in the same sign at birth, the individual is inclined to be delicate in his early years, and certain parts of the body indicated by the sign tend to be vulnerable, especially if the Sun and Moon are badly aspected.

When the Sun and Moon are in opposite signs, i.e., Aries and Libra, Taurus and Scorpio, Gemini and Sagittarius, Cancer and Capricorn, Leo and Aquarius, Virgo and Pisces, a great deal of tension or extreme activity is experienced, sometimes even hysteria if the Sun and Moon are badly aspected.

Sun in good aspect to the Moon gives harmony with the opposite sex, the ability to communicate and get along with other people naturally and easily. Your innermost being and the self you show the world are in tune with each other. Sun in bad aspect to Moon, on the other hand, indicates inner conflict and difficulty in relationships with the opposite sex.

If your Sun is in good aspect to Mercury, you are able to express yourself easily in speech or writing. This adds to the intellect and sometimes also makes you clever with your hands. Sun in good aspect to Venus gives you an appreciation of beauty in all forms and artistic ability. The disposition is loving and romantic and very attractive to others as a result.

Sun in good aspect to Mars makes you energetic and forceful. It gives good co-ordination and athletic ability. You are a winner if you enter into a fight. Sun in bad aspect to Mars makes you quarrelsome and contentious. You are always ready to start a fight or else you lose fights you become involved in through no fault of your own. You may have scars on your body to prove it.

Sun in good aspect to Jupiter either makes you very fortunate in a material sense or contented with what you have. It gives a respect for law and order and, at its best, results in a religious or philosophical turn of mind. Jupiter being a benefic, even its adverse aspects to the Sun have their benefits. It makes a good salesman, for what these people have to sell always appears of exorbitant value in their own eyes. It also gives a boastful, extravagant nature. Such people are always in debt or overextended financially, and even when they can least afford it, they treat everyone else in the crowd. They rarely ever develop a serious philosophy of life and have a contempt for law and other rules.

Sun in good aspect to Saturn describes the true conservative, serious, trustworthy, diligent. These people have respect for their elders and when they themselves are older, command respect. You can always depend on them to put in the steady effort so necessary for success. They tend to benefit through older people. Sun in bad aspect to Saturn indicates hardships and obstacles in early life that often give rise to insatiable ambitions later on. These people are schooled in adversity, and they learn to make their own way in life. They usually do not benefit from the experience of their elders, and they are often hard on their young. They may be miserly even when they have enough money, and it takes real effort for them to spend. This aspect can also cause depression that results in too much alcohol.

Sun in good aspect to Uranus makes you strong-willed, magnetic and very musical. You have original ideas and are interested in new inventions and mechanical devices. Sun adversely aspecting Uranus makes you a revolutionary and iconoclast. You are an eccentric character, either in outlook or dress. You are noisy, a discordant note in society as a whole. You experience many sudden upsets and reversals in the course of a lifetime, or you may be the victim of an unforeseen accident.

Sun in good aspect to Neptune makes you idealistic and intuitive. You believe in a higher power, and you live your faith by your kindliness to your fellow man. You have vision and an otherworldly charm. Sun in adverse aspect to Neptune often makes people superficial or untrustworthy. They are never as they seem to be but are involved in a continual deception or masquerade. Con-men and speculators have this aspect as well as those who are bilked of their funds or who are in other ways deceived. Dope addicts and alcoholics often have this affliction in their horoscopes.

If your Sun is badly aspected now, don't be discouraged. Bad aspects show that you have a lesson to learn or a problem to solve. Practice to improve your character; determination to overcome obstacles often produces stronger people than those who have an easier time.

All the above is very general. You have to figure out for yourself which aspects apply to you. But the following describes quite accurately many of your traits of character. If Leo is the sign on your Ascendant (see Chapter 3), the Sun is your ruler, so pay particular attention to the description that refers to you.

If your date is mentioned twice, your Sun is at the end of one sign or the beginning of the next, and the characteristics of either or both apply to you.

SUN IN ARIES

March 21 to April 20

In Aries, the Sun is at its most splendid. You are fiery and brilliant with a great sense of adventure and an aggressive, pioneering spirit. You are original, seizing upon new ideas; you are ambitious, and have at the same time the daring and the practicality to realize your ambitions.

You may run into opposition with your ideas at first, because the average person is capable of recognizing only what has already been done and lacks the vision to appreciate the new. So you may need to find another Aries or else someone with strong Aries planets to give you the break you need.

Your only trouble is that if you aren't able to find a sympathetic ear or the chance to develop your ideas immediately, other ideas that you find equally interesting will take their place. For this reason, it is very hard for you, once you encounter obstacles, to persist in one course. Instead you tend to expend your energies in all directions. You need to learn to fix your eyes on a single goal and stick to it until you achieve success.

Even when you are successful, you need someone to follow after you. You are the trailblazing pioneer, the imperious leader. You leave it up to someone else to build the settlement and maintain order. It is seldom that those of you with Sun in Aries finish what you start.

You like to be at the head of things and in a position of authority. For this reason, you are apt to leave home early to establish a family of your own. Or else you may start your own business or go into a field where you can be the boss.

You are eternally optimistic and young in spirit. You inspire others; your enthusiasm is contagious, but you want everything your own way and should try not to be so imperious and domineering that others rebel. In private life Aries women particularly like to run the whole show, and they should guard against appearing too self-sufficient and being too dictatorial with men.

Sometimes you are independent to the point of rashness. You are also willful and impulsive, often flying headlong into a project or situation before you have investigated its dangers and possibilities sufficiently. You act on the spur of the moment and often this is cause for regret.

Aries rules the head, however, and in the final analysis you are guided by your intellect. With all your flaming energy, you don't control your passions. More often than not, you commit excesses, and there is a marked tendency to overwork your body. You are generally careless about your health. You place too much strain on the weakest part of your body or ignore the need to slow down when you are ill. In this way, you weaken yourself and aggravate your ailments. If the Sun is afflicted, you are prone to fevers, apoplexy or violent headaches.

The above remarks apply to the positive types of the sign of Aries, the ram. Sometimes, the negative side prevails and we find instead all the characteristics of the sheep.

People born under Leo (July 23 to August 23) Sagittarius (November 22 to December 22) or those with Moon in Aries are the most compatible and complementary to you. You would rapidly lose patience with Cancers (June 21 to July 23) for clinging to the past, and you might be at odds with Capricorns (December 22 to January 20) when their ambitions and positive natures conflict with your own. Libras (September 23 to October 23) might be somewhat complementary, but you would have to be careful not to ride over them roughshod.

Famous people with Sun in Aries

Doris Day	Warren Beatty
Gregory Peck	Virgil Grissom
Charlie Chaplin	Nathan Pusey
Eugene McCarthy	Henry Luce
Arturo Toscanini	Charlotte Ford Niarchos
Hayley Mills	Julie Christie
Thomas Jefferson	Robert Frost
Vincent Van Gogh	J. William Fulbright
Johann Sebastian Bach	Edward Steichen

SUN IN TAURUS

April 20 to May 21

People with Sun in Taurus are not so active mentally as their Aries friends, but they have a strong fund of good practical common sense. Neither the idealist nor dreamer, you are cautious, constructive and stable. You never expect a windfall, but rather the just rewards of good, steady application to your appointed task. Your motto is "one foot after another" until the goal is reached. And it is in the end responsible for your ultimate, solid success.

You are industrious, patient and practical. You are a conservative first and foremost, and you like to identify with the traditional, the tried and true. Once you have made up your mind, you stick quite stubbornly to a course of action. You are not afraid of hard work. In fact, you are dedicated to it. Obstacles only make you more persistent. For this reason, you are an excellent boss or a conscientious, devoted employee.

You have untold amounts of reserve energy, and you are capable of waiting a long time for your plans to mature. Sometimes you are overly tenacious, and when an appeal has been made to your feelings, you can stick to a losing cause long after others know it to be hopeless. You become obstinate, even violently enraged, when others try to drive you into doing something, but you are perfectly amenable if they appeal to you in the right way.

You are very sound and reliable when it comes to financial dealings, and you would make an excellent banker, fund manager or trustee. You are careful and saving with your own assets.

You like both money and the personal possessions it buys. You have an innate sense of beauty, but you tend to prefer the art objects that are useful as well as beautiful. You may also like jewelry: if a woman, to wear yourself; if a man, to give to your lady. Necklaces are likely to be your first choice.

You are placid, domestic and very affectionate. Your love affairs may be passionate in the beginning, but they develop into warm, friendly relationships that are ideal for being happily settled in the marriage state. You are usually a faithful and contented spouse.

Some of you may not communicate easily in speech or writing, although you have strong feelings to express. For this reason, you may appear stolid or phlegmatic to others. However, those of you with Mercury in Aries or Gemini usually do not have this difficulty.

The negative type of Taurus can be lazy, luxury-loving and self-indulgent. All types have to resist a tendency to overeat and over-imbibe. It is hard for you to deny yourself pleasures connected with the throat.

You have great physical endurance. However, once you have come down with a disease, you may be slow to recuperate. If the Sun is afflicted, you may be clumsy; if not, few better co-ordinated gymnasts exist. Taurus rules the throat, neck, shoulders and base of the brain, also the heart, sympathetically. If afflicted by the Sun, there can be trouble in any one of these. This is a better position for health than Sun in Aries, as Taurus people accept life more calmly and take better care of themselves.

Virgos (August 23 to September 23), Capricorns (December 22 to January 20) and those with Moon in Taurus are usually very compatible and sympathetic with the Taurus-born. If forced to come in close contact with Leos (July 23 to August 23), Taureans might stubbornly resist being dominated. They would find Aquarians (January 20 to February 19) too advanced in their thinking, and Scorpios (October 23 to November 22), while in some ways complementary, would be at opposite poles when it came to many essential points of view.

Famous people with Sun in Taurus

William Shakespeare	Robert Browning
Margot Fonteyn	Elizabeth II
Henry Fonda	J. Robert Oppenheimer
Barbra Streisand	Otto Klemperer
Shirley MacLaine	Perry Como
Audrey Hepburn	Bing Crosby
Harry Truman	Willem de Kooning
Benjamin Spock	Willie Mays
Nikolai Lenin	Yehudi Menuhin
Adolf Hitler	Eddie Arnold
Edmund Wilson	Carol Burnett
Peter Ilyich Tchaikovsky	

SUN IN GEMINI

May 21 to June 21

You are intellectual and many-sided. Your forces go into brain and nerve, not heart. And you have a very sensitive, high-strung disposition. Because of this, you need plenty of fresh air, rest and exercise. Your health is not robust, and there is danger of tuberculosis if the Sun is afflicted.

You have a fine mind and good memory, but unless there are other indications in the rest of the horoscope, you are not particularly creative or original. Nevertheless, your knowledge is accurate and you are very intuitive and receptive. You are capable of expressing in speech and writing a continual stream of ideas. You are very logical and adept at argument. You Geminis have the most versatile sign of the Zodiac, and you like variety in every facet of your existence. You are never so happy as when you are leading a double life. You are likely to have dual professions or two or more romantic interests at the same time. You often have several hobbies or other interests or diversions in your spare time.

In negative types, this bent can degenerate into a tendency to spread yourself too thin, to do a lot of things haphazardly and nothing especially well. You fritter your time away frivolously instead of concentrating your energies sufficiently to achieve excellence or success. You may become distracted and restless, unable to stick to any regular or repetitious occupation for long.

The positive type of Gemini is, however, a reminder that this is a masculine sign. These people display much force and initiative. They are very definite in their views, have a variety of talents and make excellent managers and executives. They are as firm and dependable as the negative type is irresolute and irresponsible.

Ordinarily, Geminis require more variety and change than other people. They need frequent vacations, and love to travel to many different places. They tend to work much more efficiently if there are changes in their schedules and breaks in their routines. They are adaptable to different people, situations and environments.

A Gemini usually puts up with domesticity but does not participate wholeheartedly in family life. He may have a somewhat superficial attitude toward his relationships with his relatives or spouse. He is ruled by mind, and unless other influences in his horoscope contradict this, his emotions are somewhat shallow. He tends to be a flirt, but this is a part of his nature and should not be taken seriously. His experience of love is rarely deep.

Gemini rules the hands and arms as well as the upper respiratory system, the nerves and the part of the brain controlling higher thought processes. You tend to be clever with your hands and like to use them constantly. If you are a chain smoker, it is not surprising because of your preoccupation with your lungs and hands, but if the Sun is afflicted, the danger of lung cancer is intensified.

People with Moon in Gemini are very sympathetic to Geminis, Libras (September 23 to October 23) and Aquarians (January 20 to February 19). Pisceans (February 19 to March 21) are too emotional to cope with the Gemini's pure logic. Virgos (August 23 to September 23), while equally intellectual, may conflict with Geminis by being more practical and down to earth. Sagittarians' qualities are complementary in some ways, but Geminis might find them excessively jovial.

Famous people with Sun in Gemini

Judy Garland	Igor Stravinsky
Prince Philip	Dean Martin
Jean-Paul Sartre	Leslie Uggams
Françoise Sagan	Robert McNamara
Richard Wagner	Bob Hope
John F. Kennedy	Paul McCartney
James Arness	David Rockefeller
William Styron	Laurence Rockefeller
John Wayne	Hubert Humphrey
Walt Whitman	Richard Strauss
Thomas Mann	Joe Namath

SUN IN CANCER

June 21 to July 23

There is more difference between active and passive types in Cancer than in any other sign. The active type is strong-willed and very persistent. Natives of this cardinal water sign have as corrosive effect on anything they set out to change or destroy as the milling waters that eat away an ocean cliff. These people are masterful in their approach to life and tirelessly active. Usually, they are very up to date and are interested in everything modern and current.

The passive type, on the other hand, is contented, lackadaisical and idle. He has no desire to bestir himself and make the effort necessary for accomplishment. He takes the line of least resistance, come what may. However, he is very tenacious and clings to what he already has.

Both types are the product of their environment and are very much influenced by their early training. You are usually very much attached to your home and mother. You absorb ideas and sense impressions from the world around you, and after digesting them, convert them to a new use. You are active in this way even though you may not be physically active.

You usually have an easygoing disposition and are faithful in love, a combination that makes for happiness in marriage. You are very sensitive, however, and can be deeply hurt by unkind criticism. You often feel very sorry for yourself when you do not get your own way, and if this happens often, you may take a kind of perverse pleasure in a martyr complex.

You are extremely sentimental about the past and rarely discard old ties and friendships, even when you have long ago outgrown them. You like all sorts of antiques, old books and art objects, and when these have historical interest, you can become an avid collector. You have a real knowledge of history; if your interest is mainly personal, of your own genealogy and the affairs of your relatives and friends or of some special period or periods of the general historical past. You are especially fond of anecdotes and love to reminisce. Unless the Sun is afflicted, you usually have an excellent memory.

Your interests are very domestic. If a woman, you are a devoted homemaker and mother; if a man, you like to help around the house and be mothered by your wife. You are especially interested in what goes on in the kitchen and may even cook yourself. This often gives an unwholesome appetite and love of rich food and sweets. Cancers are also likely to overindulge in alcohol.

You are very emotional and you respond to love, approval and sympathy. You like the adulation of the crowd and to feel popular. For this reason, even if you are only an amateur, you love to act. You like to receive publicity. You may also like the theater, or more commonly, TV.

Cancer rules the stomach, the breasts and lower lungs. Afflictions to the Sun can result in trouble to these parts, in indigestion, ulcers and other digestive disorders.

People with Moon in Cancer are naturally sympathetic to those with Sun in Cancer, as well as to the passionate, determined Scorpios (October 23 to November 22) and the emotional, self-sacrificing Pisces (February 19 to March 21). If forced to come into close contact with Aries (March 21 to April 20) or Capricorns (December 22 to January 20), the Cancer native will have to resist being dominated, and partnerships with Libras (September 23 to October 23) will ordinarily not be fortunate or enduring.

Famous people with Sun in Cancer

Phyllis Diller	Nelson Rockefeller
Ernest Hemingway	Van Cliburn
Leslie Caron	Louis Armstrong (Sachmo)
Ringo Starr	Paul Anka
Steve Lawrence	Marc Chagall
John Glenn	Luci Baines Johnson Nugent
Diahann Carroll	Tex Thornton
Merv Griffin	Franz Kafka
Rembrandt van Ryn	Helen Keller
Jean Jacques Rousseau	Arthur Ashe
Julius Caesar	Julie Nixon Eisenhower

SUN IN LEO

July 23 to August 23

You are proud, noble and magnanimous. You would not stoop to doing anything mean or underhanded and, for this reason, you find it hard to believe ill of other people. Even when they openly offend you, while you may retaliate swiftly, you forgive them easily and do not hold a grudge.

Just as you trust others, so you too want to be trusted absolutely. You will do anything to live up to the confidence that has been placed in you. You like to be responsible and in a position of authority. Otherwise, you will neglect your duties and look down upon your work.

You are a hard worker, but you don't like menial jobs. You might perform a menial task as an example to others, or if there is nobody else to do it, but you would not like it as a steady diet. If others would not do it for you, it would remain undone. You are bored by repetition and petty details.

You are strong, ambitious and masterful. You seem so ready for a fight that most people are wary of challenging you. Once you become involved in one, however, your tactics are fair and aboveboard. You would not consider using base or deceitful tactics. Your courage may seem reckless to less honorable types.

You have a great deal of self-confidence and a good opinion of yourself. But you require the adulation and approval of others. If you don't find it in the world at large, you retreat into a smaller circle where yours is the brightest light. You definitely prefer to be a big fish in a little pond. If your ambitions outside the home are thwarted, you can react by turning into a domestic tyrant and lording it over your immediate family.

Sometimes Leos can be very boastful. They tend to have the attitude that whatever is theirs is the best in the world, and as this is not always the case, they may incur the resentment of those who remain unconvinced.

You need more love and affection than the average person, and an emotional outlet is essential to you at all times. You love wholeheartedly and you give yourself unreservedly to your love. Because you are so convinced of your worth to others, you cannot conceive of being refused. Once you have sworn to love and protect someone, you tend to live up to your promises, no matter how unworthy the object of your affection may turn out to be.

You are very adventurous and can face any danger in the pursuit of your ideals. You are insatiably ambitious and no amount of success contents you. Because you refuse to accept limitations, you often attempt the impossible, and failure makes you very unhappy indeed.

You have an unusually magnetic personality, and if possible you should attend to important business in person because your enthusiasm is contagious and you are better able to influence others that way. You are a wonderful host or hostess and love to entertain.

Leo rules the heart, and the back and its afflictions can sympathetically affect the throat and generative organs. You have enormous vitality, and your great expenditure of energy can put too much strain on your heart if you are not careful. But your constitution is generally strong. You have great recuperative powers and easily throw off disease.

People with Moon in Leo are very compatible to you. So are the other fire signs, Aries (March 21 to April 20) and Sagittarius (November 22 to December 20). You would come to a conflict of wills with Scorpios (October 23 to November 22) and Taureans (April 20 to May 21). Aquarians might complement you in some ways but generally would not see eye to eye with you.

Famous people with Sun in Leo

Jacqueline Kennedy Onassis	Dr. Ralph Bunche
Princess Margaret Rose	Fidel Castro
Percy B. Shelley	James Baldwin
George Bernard Shaw	Ben Hogan
Napoleon Bonaparte	Casey Stengel
Jimmie Dean	Princess Anne
Eddie Fisher	Peter Duchin
Lucille Ball	Douglas Dillon
Mike Douglas	Paul Tillich
Dag Hammarskjold	Eero Saarinen
Julia Child	Benito Mussolini

SUN IN VIRGO

August 23 to September 23

You are practical and down to earth, a diligent worker with a competent, discriminating intellect. You gather knowledge from every conceivable source and have the ability to memorize and retain what you have learned. You are scientific, perceptive and very alert. You do not stop learning when you graduate from school, but keep it up throughout the rest of your life.

In human anatomy, Virgo rules the bowels, and just as they assimilate the food the body requires, so the mind of the Virgo assimilates food for thought. This process makes you very critical and discriminating. You analyze everything and to others less like yourself you may seem to be constantly finding fault. In reality, this is the way your mind works and no harm is intended. You simply have to categorize everything and see it for what it is in comparison with everything else.

You are clever at speech and writing, but unless there are redeeming influences from the planets, you may seem monotonous and dry. Mercury's influence makes you understand human emotion intellectually, but unless there are contrary indications in the rest of the horoscope, you rarely experience the gamut of human passions yourself. You can, however, be quite tactful when handling others because of your practicality and the way you analyze and observe. Generally, though, you haven't much sympathy for others.

You are usually very modest and unassuming. You are content to live in the background. You do not require the constant company of other people, but often want to be alone. You are so cool and evenly balanced that you almost never lose your temper. You are content to work quietly and unpretentiously at your chosen task. You are, however, very proud of your mental powers whether they happen to be extraordinary or not.

Because you are so shy and retiring, you often fail to inspire the confidence of others in the same way as more extroverted types. You may seem to be less reserved to those who know you, but your inner reserve never melts. However, you may be considered very interesting to the people who would be afraid of an aggressive Aries or Leo. And your innate humility and willingness to serve the rest of humanity may also endear you to gentler folk.

You lack inspiration, but you are very methodical and good at routine work. You like details, but need to be careful not to become so obsessed by them that you don't see the forest for the trees. You are usually clever at mathematics and might do well as a statistician or, if your other stars show more imagination, a businessman or an economist.

You would, however, normally prefer business to the professions, but might show an aptitude for law or medicine. You are very quick to see and take advantage of opportunities in commercial concerns. When it comes to money, you are thrifty and saving. And while you may not have the talents of a financier, your bank book is always balanced and accurate.

You are somewhat self-centered when it comes to love and do not like the idea either of conquest or self-sacrifice. However, you make a reliable spouse and the kind of parent who does not spoil a child but gives him the understanding and security that aid his development.

You have an instinctive sense of balance in diet and are also very sensible in taking care of your own health and that of others.

Virgos get along very well with those who have Moon in Virgo. They are also very compatible with other Virgos and natives of the two remaining earth signs, Capricorn (December 22 to January 20) and Taurus (April 20 to May 21). They will, however, tend to be at odds with emotional Pisceans (February 19 to March 21), and aristocratic Sagittarians (November 22 to December 22). Geminis (May 21 to June 21) are also ruled by Mercury, but are too airy and may seem either frivolous or too abstract for the earthy, concrete, practical Virgo.

Famous people with Sun in Virgo

Lyndon B. Johnson	Leonard Bernstein
Henry Ford II	Arnold Palmer
Sophia Loren	Alan Jay Lerner
Anne Bancroft	Cardinal Richelieu
Leo Tolstoi	Greta Garbo

SUN IN LIBRA

September 23 to October 23

You are sympathetic, affectionate and kind. You are very considerate of other people's feelings, and because you are basically so peace loving, you try to live in harmony with your fellow man. Social relationships are very important to you, but above all you need a partner for true fulfillment and happiness. For this reason, you are likely to be married, and if one marriage doesn't work out, you are swift to enter into another. Even when unmarried, you are not without an alter ego. You are very dependent on the approval of other people. You like to have someone around who appreciates everything you say and do.

You are unusually beauty-loving and artistic. Your sense of proportion, line and color are superb. You vibrate toward balance and harmony. You also tend to appreciate music and other cultured entertainments where aesthetic values are involved. You are very particular and beauty-loving in your dress. You are also very fastidious and dislike messy or dirty work.

One of your most outstanding characteristics is your love of justice. If you feel you have been treated unfairly, you will go to any lengths to oppose the wrong, or else you will react to the injustice by becoming resentful and cold.

When it is a matter of your own judgment, you are very careful to weigh all the factors and come up with a scrupulously considered opinion. You are, however, so subtle and finely balanced that you may tend to vacillate and fail to come to any conclusion at all. You want so much to be fair and to see both sides of a question that it is often hard for you to decide which course of action to follow.

Because you are so very considerate and sensitive to other people's feelings, you may appear to be overly dependent on them. You are grateful for favors and appreciate kindness shown to you. You have critical ability, but it is constructively and kindly meant.

You are very courteous and refined. Good manners are important to you. You exhibit them yourself and expect them of others. You love ritual when it is tastefully done. You are repelled by coarseness or vulgarity. If forced to live in an uncongenial environment, you would retire into your shell.

Libras tend to be very expert in love and have a distinct understanding of both the masculine and feminine roles. Their appreciation of the feelings of their partner makes of sex not so much an animal passion as an art. Most Libras tend to be highly developed on the sexual plane. Certain Libras are so delicately balanced between the sexes, however, that they are not distinctly either one, and homosexuality can be the result.

You have an excellent constitution, and while you may not seem to be exceptionally strong, you have great powers of endurance and recuperate quickly from any illness or disease. Libra rules the lower back and kidneys. Afflictions to your Sun can cause trouble in either of these.

People with Moon in Libra are most sympathetic to Librans—also other Librans, Geminis (May 21 to June 21) and Aquarians (January 20 to February 19). Aries (March 21 to April 20) tend to be too domineering for the Libra-born, and they will have to struggle for supremacy with Capricorns (December 22 to January 20) and Cancers (June 21 to July 23).

Famous people with Sun in Libra

Dwight D. Eisenhower	Pope Paul VI
William Faulkner	John Lennon
Ed Sullivan	Eleanor Roosevelt
Julie Andrews	Al Capp
Oscar Wilde	Vladimir Horowitz
Johnny Carson	Truman Capote
C. P. Snow	Le Corbusier
Helen Hayes	Juan Peron
Mohandas K. Gandhi	Giuseppe Verdi

SUN IN SCORPIO

October 23 to November 22

You are extremely forceful, and you exhibit tremendous strength of will. Your compelling personal magnetism fascinates others. Whether or not you are good looking doesn't matter. This is the sign par excellence for sex appeal.

There are two distinct types of Scorpio—the higher or noble type represented by the lofty soaring eagle; the lower type represented by the snake or scorpion. Both types are formidable adversaries, which is evident in their personal appearance. In better types, the expression may be stern but the disposition is kindly. In the others, the countenance may almost be ugly, but with a compelling attraction for the opposite sex.

The higher type has unassailable integrity. He is devoted and high-minded, using his ability to dominate people and situations for the universal good. He is dedicated unselfishly to the advancement of all mankind.

The lower type is sly, secretive and cunning, with diabolical passions and uncontrollable jealousies. Underhanded and treacherous when he feels he has been offended, he lusts after revenge. He flies into a rage at the smallest provocation. He is a dangerous opponent as he will take advantage of any weakness and will resort to any means at his disposal, however unfair, to wound his enemy. He is totally vindictive, having neither scruples nor compassion for human suffering.

Those of you who are Scorpios are generally shrewd and energetic, persistent and capable of hard work. You are indefatigable in pursuit of a tangible goal or an ideal. You are persevering and tenacious where others would tire and fall by the wayside. For this reason, you can be outstandingly successful, although the chances are you will have to fight uphill all the way. But you always use your wiles and wits to defeat your opponent. You are subtle, deadly and cool.

Your very subtlety coupled with intelligence, physical strength and the will to work are wonderful qualities for science and medicine. Crime detection can also be your forte, although the lower-type Scorpios make the most dangerous, wily criminals. The ability to keep secrets, dissimulate and deceive is important for excellent undercover agents and spies.

Domestically, the Scorpio can be something of a tyrant. If you do things his way, he is relatively peaceful. Heaven help you, however, if you go against him. He is easily offended, and he won't rest until the wrong has been avenged. He or she is never mistaken in his own eyes and never brooks the slightest dissent.

Scorpios love more passionately than any other sign in the Zodiac. In higher types, it is a noble emotion. The lower types are intensely selfish and possessive. There is a gross sexual appetite, as well as overindulgence in food and liquor, and once aroused, jealousy is all-consuming.

In religion, there is a combination of bigotry and self-righteousness. Although they are usually prolific, most Scorpios are too domineering to make the best parents, for they impose their wills relentlessly on their defenseless children.

You have a strong constitution if your Sun in unafflicted, and your powers of resistance can't be beaten. Scorpio rules the glands of the pelvis, the internal secretions of the body and the generative organs; this sign's afflictions are unfavorable for diseases of these parts and for cancer of the glands.

People with Moon in Scorpio are most compatible with the Scorpio-born. So are other Scorpios, Pisceans (February 19 to March

21) and Cancers (June 21 to July 23). If Scorpios do not want to engage in a contest of wills, they should usually avoid Leos (July 23 to August 23) and Taureans (April 20 to May 21). While higher types might co-exist with Aquarians (January 20 to February 19), the average type would not see eye to eye with them.

Famous people with Sun in Scorpio

Joan Sutherland	Richard Burton
Pablo Picasso	Petula Clark
Chiang Kai-Shek	Billy Graham
Robert Louis Stevenson	Rock Hudson
Marie Antoinette	Edward H. White 2nd
Martin Luther	Jonas Salk
Bobby Kennedy	Prince Charles
Eugene Ionesco	Leon Trotsky
Marie Curie	Felix Frankfurter

SUN IN SAGITTARIUS

November 22 to December 22

You are high-spirited, impetuous and refined. You resent coarseness in other people and are a born aristocrat in your tastes and tendencies. Your attitude is normally bright and cheerful. You are capable of great brilliance and daring. You are bold, brave and proud.

You are uncompromising in your love of freedom, and you grant everyone the same right. You are very democratic and have friends in every walk of life. You like the people around you to express themselves freely. You yourself tend to speak your mind with great independence and can at times be too direct and blunt.

Your intuition is unbeatable. If you go against your natural hunches and inclinations, it holds you back from the very actions that would ordinarily bring you success. You normally have high ideals and true vision. Your greatest luck in life comes from trusting yourself. You are also very trustworthy; your integrity is above reproach.

You would be embarrassed if someone were to doubt you. You

are also very thin-skinned and easily humiliated by the smallest slight. You are at the same time both proud and shy.

You tend to make sporadic thrusts at a variety of things rather than applying yourself steadily to one project. Once you put something down, it is hard for you to resume working on it again. You do, however, have great presence of mind in an emergency, and often what brings you to the fore is the way you solve situations that have arisen unexpectedly.

You love discussion and dialectic, and you are able to convert others to your viewpoint by holding a dialogue. You are usually a brilliant and amusing conversationalist. You may be skeptical about some facets of religion, but if you are not orthodox in your beliefs, you are nevertheless very philosophical.

You take a direct approach to business and are usually successful financially. However, you do not like routine work and are bored by petty details. Unless the Sun in afflicted, you have the good fortune to see the big picture and the future trend of events.

For you, sudden attractions often turn into lasting friendships. You are very loyal once you have entered into a friendship with someone. Sudden attractions to the opposite sex aren't always as fortunate, however. Your choices are more mental than emotional, but are often so impulsive they don't work out. Broken engagements and marriages often result. The men are true bachelor types. Even after marriage, they can't tolerate restraints. You are not in the least domestic and can become selfish and difficult to live with. You can be critical or sarcastic with relatives you have reason to resent or a spouse who bores or disillusions you.

You love outdoor life, especially sports such as hunting where dogs, horses and shooting are involved. You are very active and love to run or ride. You usually love the races.

You aren't particularly earthy and can have a strange attitude toward physical functions, as if by ignoring them they will go away. Sagittarius rules the thighs and hips and tendons. Afflictions to the Sun can cause lameness or trouble in these parts.

You are so high-strung that under prolonged strains you can be subject to nervous breakdowns; but you are generally healthy, and Sun in Sagittarius is the best sign for living to a ripe old age.

People with Moon in Sagittarius tend to be the most sympathetic to Sagittarians—also to Leos (July 23 to August 23) and Aries (March 21 to April 20). Virgos (August 23 to September 23) are too plodding and practical, and Pisceans (February 19 to March 21) too emotional to get along best with you. Geminis (May 21 to June 21), while in some ways complementary, might aggravate you and cause you to be impatient.

Famous people with Sun in Sagittarius

Frank Sinatra	Heinrich Heine
Mary Martin	Andy Williams
James Thurber	Connie Francis
Walt Disney	Jane Fonda
Winston Churchill	J. Paul Getty
Mark Twain	Sammy Davis, Jr.
Dick Van Dyke	Robert Vaughn
Patty Duke	Joe DiMaggio
John Lindsay	Charles de Gaulle
Margaret Chase Smith	Caroline Kennedy
Pope John XXIII	John F. Kennedy, Jr.
John Osborne	Ludwig van Beethoven

Willy Brandt

SUN IN CAPRICORN

December 22 to January 20

You have a towering practical ambition. Like your symbol, the goat, you leap over both adversaries and obstacles in your climb to the heights. Indeed, you have all the attributes necessary for success, since you are hard-working, punctilious and reliable, and you have tremendous initiative and drive.

You are both cautious and conservative, with a deep respect for authority. You have your own preconceived notions of what is right and wrong, and are stubborn in upholding them. You do not tend to be particularly original or creative, but stick to tried-and-true methods. This may limit your horizons and make you less adaptable to changing circumstances than you ought to be.

At best you have a healthy amount of self-respect and are decent and moral. But some of you have the less desirable trait of being obnoxiously self-righteous, certain in your own mind that you have always done exactly the correct thing at the proper time and in the right way.

Indeed, you take life seriously and have a strong sense of duty. You are very willing to assume responsibilities—in fact, you seek them out. But later you might complain about how many burdens have fallen on your shoulders and how much more than anyone else you have done. This is true from the time you are very young. And you are in fact very steady and faithful and conscientious in the extreme.

When it comes to money, Capricorns are usually thrifty, but some of them can be almost miserly with their funds. They can be trusted to make sound, conservative investments and to account for every nickel, but they are not likely to be brilliant speculators. They are usually too concerned with conserving smaller amounts to think in terms of making a grand coup.

You express yourself rather dryly in speech and writing and may tend to make classical allusions. You are very conscious of yourself, and are not likely to sacrifice yourself for others or to give yourself utterly in a relationship with the opposite sex. Basically you are too self-centered and too self-interested. You are, however, rarely subject to perversion, although afflictions to the Sun might make your sexual appetite somewhat gross.

You are often too domineering with your children, tending to squelch their desire for self-expression. You are not inclined to be especially affectionate or demonstrative, and should guard against being too strict and unyielding a disciplinarian with a high-spirited child. Because of your inborn respect for authority, you should also guard against a tendency to tell your child that the teacher is always right whether he is or not. With employees or inferiors, you are exacting and severe.

You accept the relatives you were born with and the circumstances of your life as a matter of course. While you are very ambitious, you usually operate within the hereditary framework rather than choosing a path very far afield. In many ways you tend to feel that what was good enough for your father is good enough for you.

You have an iron constitution, nerves of steel and terrific powers of endurance. Capricorn rules the knees, and afflictions can cause trouble to them. Afflictions can also cause colds, bad teeth, or bone deformity and may result in rheumatism later in life. Sometimes also, with an afflicted Sun in Capricorn, recurring moods of depression can give rise to chronic alcoholism. Capricorns tend to like highly seasoned food. This is, next to Sagittarius, the best sign for living to a ripe old age.

People with Moon in Capricorn tend to understand you best. Also other Capricorns, Taureans (April 20 to May 21) and equally practical Virgos (August 23 to September 23). You will tend to clash wills with Aries (March 21 to April 20) and to be somewhat tyrannical when in too close contact with Librans (September 23 to October 23) and Cancers (June 21 to July 23).

Famous people with Sun in Capricorn

Lady Bird Johnson	Joan Baez
Cary Grant	J. D. Salinger
Rudyard Kipling	Dr. Martin Luther King, Jr.
Sir Isaac Newton	Barry Goldwater
Louis Pasteur	Henri Matisse
Joan of Arc	Artur Rubinstein
Elvis Presley	Jule Styne
Danny Kaye	Pablo Casals
Everett Dirkson	Cassius Clay
Richard Nixon	Kit Carson
Benjamin Franklin	Joseph Stalin

SUN IN AQUARIUS

January 20 to February 19

You are noble, moderate and sound. You believe in helping others, but while you can be generous and self-sacrificing for your fellow man, even in this you do not go to extremes. You do not, however, like to see anyone suffer and will go to any lengths to avoid this.

You have an instinctive understanding of human nature coupled with great tolerance for human weakness. You know that the mistakes people make in the normal course of a lifetime are for their souls' growth and therefore for their own eventual good in the larger scheme. Your own character is usually well balanced and strong.

You are scientific and love new inventions and discoveries. You may even be the inventor or scientist yourself. Your powers of observation and ability to theorize often amount to real genius, and you are a profound student of human behavior.

You believe firmly in the brotherhood of man and in an eventual world order where race and nationality will be transcended by international unity. When it is a matter of reform or even revolution, you are neither the demagogue nor the visionary. Yours is the sound practical approach. In a downtrodden country, your first step would not be to hold a free election. You would be more concerned with seeing that everyone had some place to stay and enough food to eat. Your fault may lie in too much moderation. There are times when drastic action is necessary, and Aquarians are never liable to go to extremes.

You do not tend to be affected by your environment. You rely on your own spiritual and mental powers for your well-being and state of mind. You are in fact so well-balanced and you approach any problem with such a fair and open mind that you are the ideal person to consult for a safe, sane, well-considered judgment. You are aware of every factor and you see to the heart of a situation.

Your ideas may not always seem practical at the time you conceive them. You look so far ahead that for the short term they may not work out as planned. However, you base your conclusions on fundamentals, and although accidents may make you appear wrong for a time, in the long run what you predict always happens even though you may not live to see it. However, once you have settled on a course of action based firmly on fact, you go ahead with it, undaunted by disappointments along the way. You are not influenced by public opinion like the average person.

You do not make friends in a hurry, but once you do, you are extremely loyal. You are not especially subject to physical attractions. Your friendships are of the mind and spirit. You tend to have a wide circle of friends and acquaintances, and you are especially happy when advising and helping them.

You are an excellent conversationalist. You talk about worthwhile subjects and make pithy, interesting comments. You are intelligent, sensible and well educated at the same time. You are no doubt a firm believer in astrology and may even be interested in psychic research. You may also be very musical.

With money, an Aquarian is neither stingy nor profligate. He is always willing to spend for the benefit of others. He does not value money for its own sake, but rather as a means to an end.

Aquarians make excellent parents. They are very reasonable and understanding, but they rarely ever spoil a child. They give a child the freedom to develop as an individual, at the same time guiding him and gently correcting his faults.

Your health is basically sound, but you may have obscure nervous disorders. Your habits are temperate; you don't abuse your body. While you are mentally overactive, you don't like physical exercise. Aquarius rules the calves of the legs and ankles as well as the fluid-carrying vessels of the body, especially the lymph glands.

You find people with Moon in Aquarius most compatible, as well as other Aquarians, Geminis (May 21 to June 21) and Libras (September 23 to October 23). You may find Leos (July 23 to August 23) too aggressive, Scorpios (October 23 to November 22) too possessive and passionate, and Taureans (April 20 to May 21) too conservative and tradition bound.

Famous people with Sun in Aquarius

Leontyne Price	W. C. Fields
Lewis Carroll	Adlai Stevenson
Charles Dickens	Carol Channing
Lord Byron	Franklin Delano Roosevelt
Thomas Edison	Shelley Berman
Abraham Lincoln	John L. Lewis
Douglas MacArthur	Mia Farrow
Gertrude Stein	Ronald Reagan

Wolfgang Amadeus Mozart

SUN IN PISCES

February 19 to March 21

You are very considerate, sensitive and intuitive. You are so observant, and in so many subtle ways, that you may be considered psychic and, in fact, you often are. You have a vivid imagination and are suggestible and impressionable.

In negative types, this may take the form of illusions and delusions and in order to preserve them, you may be inclined to overindulgence in drugs or alcohol. These types can also be dreamy and impractical or detrimentally emotional.

There is a tremendous difference between the positive and negative Pisces, the one being able to rise to the top in every field, the other being at the very depths of degradation and despair. The vivid imagination that can be abused by negative types is a source of strength and direction to the positive ones.

Because you are so idealistic, you do not appear to be as practical as you often are. When you have to choose between common sense and theoretical idealism, you use down-to-earth methods. You usually manage to have the material things necessary for comfort.

If, however, there is a difference between your ideals and the real conditions of your life, you can become restless and discontented and, in order to compensate, can become obsessed by insignificant details.

You are very sympathetic to others, but you are usually modest and unassuming and lack confidence in yourself. You have a very agreeable love-nature and are quite domestic. You are so pleasant that you are often the pet of the family.

Undeveloped types tend to be lazy and attached to home mainly because it is the most comfortable place to be. They have to fight hard for stability and to resist the impulse of the moment. You are very much influenced by your environment and have a tendency to be molded by it. You are extraordinarily pliable and adaptable.

You are not so much concerned with superficial appearances, but with the inner being, the essence or spirit rather than the concrete physical fact. To you there is very little difference between the reality and the dream. You speak and write fluently. You are a mystic when it comes to religion, and may write about it with divine inspiration.

You are devoted to those you love, sometimes overly concerned about their welfare. You are, in fact, so self-sacrificing, and you do things so unselfishly for others and with so little fuss, that people may not fully appreciate what you do for them—apparently so effortlessly. And while you were not kind in hopes of a reward, ingratitude can hurt you deeply.

Physically, you are not particularly strong. Generally, your health is good, but you have little power to resist disease. Pisces rules the feet and the excretory fluids of the body. Afflictions to the Sun can cause tuberculosis or trouble in either of these areas.

People with Moon in Pisces are most compatible with you as well as other Pisceans, Cancers (June 21 to July 23) and Scorpios (October 23 to November 22). Virgos (August 23 to September 23), Geminis (May 21 to June 21) and Sagittarians lack the emotional responsiveness so necessary for a Piscean's happiness.

Famous people with Sun in Pisces

John Steinbeck	Tricia Nixon
Jackie Gleason	Sidney Poitier
Elizabeth Taylor	Rex Harrison
Albert Einstein	Thomas Schippers
Victor Hugo	Edward Albee
Nicolaus Copernicus	Samuel Barber
Frédéric Chopin	George Harrison
Luther Burbank	Lynda Bird Johnson Robb
George Washington	Rudolf Nureyev
Edward M. Kennedy	Pope Pius XII
Earl Warren	Prince Edward of England
Oliver Wendell Holmes	Prince Andrew of England
W. E. B. DuBois	Pierre Renoir

Pat Nixon

2

Your Personality and
THE MOON

Are you popular? Do you have an attractive personality? Do women play an important role in your life? Are your senses accurate and keen? For the answers to all these questions you must consult the Moon. And it is vital for every adult who is interested in what kind of an impression he makes on other people to know about the Moon's position in his particular horoscope.

Shakespeare calls the Moon "the inconstant Moon," and so it is. The Moon is the fastest moving heavenly body and the most sensitive, varying more than the Sun or any of the planets according to the sign in which it is found. It is also more influenced by the planets that aspect it.

The Moon moves so fast, in fact, that it passes through every sign in the Zodiac approximately every twenty-eight days. This explains why two children born only a few minutes apart can be so very different owing to the Moon changing signs.

Some planets affect you more than others. If the Moon is a strong influence in your particular horoscope and well aspected, you tend to be mild-mannered, even-tempered, peace-loving and kind.

The position of the Moon influences other people's opinion of you. If it is fortunate, people in general judge you favorably. The

Moon also represents the self you show the world. And a well-placed, well-aspected Moon is the best indication of a pleasing and popular personality.

The Moon's position shows what kind of a place ordinary people occupy in everyday life. With famous or outstanding people, it governs their public image. A well-aspected Moon can mean fame. It indicates great appeal for the masses and success in entertainment or politics.

Even when well aspected, the Moon gives a certain restlessness. If you are constantly moving from place to place or you frequently rearrange the furniture in your home, then quite likely the Moon is a dominant influence in your horoscope. This may even cause you to be a faddist in your taste—from the foods you eat to the clothes you wear. It can be an advantage where you need to be mobile and constantly adapt to changing conditions. Or it can be detrimental if you reverse your direction with every wind that blows.

A well-aspected Moon is good for the sight in the left eye. It indicates healthy body fluids and a good digestion. The Moon in fact rules all your sense impressions—taste, touch, sight, hearing and smell—and so provides food for your mind to function. If the Moon is well aspected, the senses are keen, accurate and acute. The Moon also affects all the body functions. Functional disorders mean some affliction to the Moon.

The Moon's position is of especial importance to a man because it represents the way he is affected by the women in his life. If favorable, his wife, his mother and his daughters will be beneficial to him. If favorable for a woman, the other women with whom she comes in contact will react to her favorably; it also carries the promise of a curvaceous, well-developed bosom.

If the Moon is badly aspected, on the other hand, you can be lazy, stupid, careless and overly fond of alcohol. Other people do not have a good opinion of you, and you are unpopular as a result. In extreme cases, the senses do not furnish food to the mind properly, and someone feeble-minded or idiotic can be the result. It is bad for sight in the left eye, the digestion and body fluids, and as the Moon also rules the water, it is prominently afflicted in the case of a person who drowns. It can also point to death in a public place or much unfavorable publicity. For a man, a badly aspected moon results in complexes associated with his early relationship with his mother and a bad adjustment to other women later on. Or women exert a detrimental influence in his life. For a woman, this kind of moon means that other women are antagonistic and tend not to be of benefit to her. If the Moon rules the Ascendant, such afflictions could ruin a person's entire character and life.

Moon in good aspect to the Sun gives harmony between the parents and sets an example you usually follow in your own life. The Moon in one horoscope in the same sign as the Sun in another gives great compatibility and understanding, particularly between people of the opposite sex. This is so in the case of Elizabeth Taylor and Richard Burton. Moon in adverse aspect to the Sun often gives incompatible parents as well as many inner tensions and conflicts. In some cases, however, it spurs you on to remarkable activity.

Moon in good aspect to Mercury is the best sign of a fluent linguist and also indicates that you can write and converse with ease. The mind and the senses are well co-ordinated and a competent intellect is the result. Moon adversely aspecting Mercury can give an actual defect in communication between the mind and the senses. Or it can mean a fuzzy thinker, the sort of person who talks too much and never takes into consideration the effect upon the listener. You may be glib, but you need mental discipline and your knowledge is superficial rather than being sound and deep.

Moon in good aspect to Venus gives a pleasant, agreeable, kindly personality. You are very affectionate and loving and your heart is in the right place. This may also make you beauty-loving and artistic, or you may be well dressed with a real flair for fashion. Moon aspecting Venus unfavorably usually makes a person heartless. You don't consider other people's feelings and are not sympathetic to them. If you observe them at all, it is to use them to your own advantage, for you tend to be unfeeling and cold in all your relationships. This may, on the other hand, have the opposite effect, and you may be the one whose feelings are hurt all too often.

If your personality is forceful and dynamic, if you are well co-ordinated and present a strong image to the public, chances are your Moon is in favorable aspect to Mars. If you are aggressive but do not persist in any policy long enough to win, if you are muscular as far as athletics are concerned but insufficiently trained, or if you are so competitive other people tend to resent your behavior, then no doubt your Moon is in adverse aspect to Mars.

Moon in good aspect to Jupiter indicates a genial, dignified manner. You are generous and at the same time provident. Other people just naturally have confidence in you. Moon adversely aspecting Jupiter indicates a florid, overexpansive personality. You are all show and braggadocio. You can be in debt up to your eyebrows, but you scoff at ways to save a dime.

Moon in good aspect to Saturn gives a sober, conservative personality. You impress other people as being serious and responsible, and you are careful with your money and want to receive value in return for what you spend. When the Moon is in bad aspect to Saturn, the senses are somewhat dulled. The hearing or eyes may be defective, and you will have more colds and have to take more trips to the dentist than the average person. You tend to be somewhat cold, selfish and ambitious. Or you may be pessimistic and easily depressed and repel other people with your personality.

Moon in good aspect to Uranus gives a magnetic personality compelling and almost electric in its impact. Your sense of sound and rhythm is well developed, and you may have an outstanding talent for music. You impress other people with your daring and originality. People with Moon in adverse aspect to Uranus, on the other hand, are rebellious and temperamental. They can also be unconventional in the extreme. You are sympathetic to the underdog and to causes that are unpopular in your own time. When it comes to music, you like it to be either discordant or amplified almost beyond endurance. You yourself are so careless and noisy that other people are delighted to have you leave.

If you have a charming personality, with the ability to weave spells and seem mysterious and elusive all at once, then no doubt your Moon is in good aspect to Neptune. If you are easily confused and impractical in your notions, if you daydream but rarely try to realize your dreams, if your moral fiber is not all it should be, chances are your Moon adversely aspects Neptune.

Do not be discouraged if some of your aspects are adverse. The so-called bad lunar aspects represent personality problems and other difficulties often found in people's lives, and you build character when you overcome them.

You will be able to locate the sign position of your planets in the dates after each description in the chapters that follow. However, the motion of the Moon is so rapid that you need to locate your date in the Moon sign Ephemeris at the end of the book to figure out the sign position of the Moon in your particular horoscope.

MOON IN ARIES

Because the senses are so sharp and brilliant, you have an unusually high-strung disposition. You are in fact keyed up and edgy, and because your temper is liable to flare up at the slightest provocation, you may say or do things on the spur of the moment that you regret later on. This is not because you are disagreeable, but because your impressions of the world around you are so swift and active that you experience intense nervous strain.

Sensations reach your mind so clearly and with such impact that you do not doubt them for an instant. You are in fact so convinced of them that you act on them immediately without giving the matter a second thought. On the slightest evidence, you go dashing off in any direction.

You are so sure of yourself in general that you don't like to listen to the conclusions of other people. In fact, you resent their advice. This may be a disadvantage in ordinary, everyday life, but in a field where making up your mind in a hurry is important, you can be very successful indeed, for you think quickly and have a very independent mind. Your most developed sense is your sense of sight.

Your mother was no doubt very ambitious for you and when you were younger, may have tried to dictate to you. You would have resented this as you resent all forms of authority, and you probably set out on an untried path of your own against her best advice. Depending on the Moon's aspects, the outcome would have been favorable or adverse. But despite opposition, you would have been determined to have your own way.

If a man, the women in your life are highly intelligent, passionate, willful and hard to manage. They are not at all domestic and are very independent and self-reliant. You are not inclined to be particularly faithful to them. If the Moon is well aspected, they can be very helpful to you. If not, you will tend to break off with them abruptly after having a fight. With a woman, this applies to the other females with whom she comes in close contact, whether they be relatives or friends.

Famous people with Moon in Aries

Charles de Gaulle	Mark Twain
Doris Day	Leonard Bernstein
James Thurber	Aleksei N. Kosygin
	Peter Duchin

MOON IN TAURUS

In Taurus, the restless nature of the Moon is steadied and stabilized. For this reason, the Moon in Taurus is said to be in her exaltation. This gives, above all, a conservative outlook and deep powers of concentration. You react very slowly to sense impressions but, at the same time, very fully. Once you make up your mind, you stick to your decision stubbornly right or wrong.

When any upsetting or unusual idea is presented to you, you do not get upset or act on the spur of the moment like people with Moon in Aries. Rather, your mind assimilates the new material quite deliberately, decides slowly and carefully, and then you surely and purposefully act.

You tend to accept only ideas that conform to your preconceived standards. And these are usually conservative. It is unlikely that anyone with the Moon in this position would ever do anything revolutionary. You accept the standards of your times and your upbringing. You are conventional in the extreme. You do not like anyone to take issue with you or contradict you. You have your fixed fundamental principles, and you are receptive only to ideas that conform to them.

Your mother was no doubt very affectionate, domestic and practical. She probably felt she knew what was best for you better than anyone else, and you may have resented the fact that she wanted to make all your decisions for you. Eventually you probably became obstinate and made it plain that you were a separate individual and were determined to stand on your own two feet. However, she had many wonderful qualities and was staunchly devoted to you.

If you are a man, all the women in your life will exhibit similar devotion. They will be faithful and domestic. Their loyalty will be unquestionable, and you can always be sure that they will stand by you, come what may. They are in fact so dedicated to you that, should you tire of their constant attentions, you would have a hard time breaking away. In a woman's chart, the same applies to her female friends and, in some cases, to her sisters and her own personality as well.

Taste and touch are your most developed senses.

Famous people with Moon in Taurus

Gregory Peck	Barry Goldwater
Mike Douglas	Sophia Loren
William Shakespeare	Ronald Reagan
Andy Williams	Hubert Humphrey
C. P. Snow	Helen Hayes
Joe Namath	Greta Garbo

MOON IN GEMINI

This sign agitates the Moon somewhat and makes it less stable. When it is afflicted, you can be frivolous, fickle and overly talkative. If it is well aspected, however, you tend to be lucid, brainy and intellectually stimulating. In some cases, you may have a real grasp of the fundamentals of mathematics or finance. If an artist, your technique would include a mastery of line.

You do not value your senses for the pleasure they give you but rather as a point of departure for your mind. Human passions and psychology may or may not interest you. But they do not distract you from your work. This is an asset for someone dedicated to making scientific experiments. It is also helpful where pure logic is required. Ordinarily, you are more at home in a field where you deal with abstractions rather than one where human emotions and sympathies are involved.

Your sense impressions are swift and accurate, but your judgments are apt to be superficial and you constantly change your mind. You learn rapidly, however, and you can teach what you have learned to others. You tend to half learn so many things that you may have mental indigestion, and you may not relate what you understand intellectually to the other facets of your life.

You tend to be high-strung and nervous. Travel is very beneficial to you, and you thrive best on a frequent change of scene. With you, variety is the spice of life as far as interests and people as well as places are concerned, and you also like frequent breaks if you are tied down to a daily routine.

You have a keen sense of smell, and your ear for music is very acute. You could be a first-rate critic, and if the Moon is well aspected you might want to make singing a career.

Your mother may have been very versatile and intellectual and provided you with much mental stimulation. Or if the Moon was afflicted, she could have been fickle and a flibbertigibbet. In no case would she have been a dedicated homemaker. Unless there are contrary indications in your horoscope, domesticity was not her forte, nor would she have been very sympathetic or affectionate.

If you are a man, the other women in your life may be like your mother, for they are likely to love change and to be frivolous and fickle, or else they may be highly intellectual. You women would be inclined to prefer a career of a mental nature to a purely domestic role in life.

Famous people with Moon in Gemini

Lady Bird Johnson	Jimmy Dean
Leontyne Price	Eddie Fisher
Rudyard Kipling	Jack Nicklaus
George Bernard Shaw	Casey Stengel
Louis Pasteur	Cassius Clay
Petula Clark	David Rockefeller
Albrecht Dürer	Adeline Patti
J. William Fulbright	Julie Nixon Eisenhower

MOON IN CANCER

With Moon in Cancer, your senses mirror impressions with great perfection and delicacy. But people with this position of the Moon do not react to their senses vigorously. Rather, they are placid and serene, content to contemplate the information they receive rather than going out and acting on it. You are basically so satisfied with what comes to you without your making any effort that, unless the rest of your horoscope shows activity and forcefulness, you tend to be too passive for your own best interests.

You do not go out of your way to garner new information, but once something sinks into your mind, it is indelibly impressed upon it. You therefore have, unless the Moon is sorely afflicted, an excellent memory. You can recall every detail of the past history of your acquaintances, relatives and friends. And you retain historical dates with surprising accuracy. You do not like anyone to spur you on mentally. You prefer to act at your own pace. Sometimes you are extremely psychic because your mind is so receptive and sensitive. But you need peace and quiet for your mind to operate. Any disturbance interferes with your acute sensibility.

Basically, you are very domestic, perhaps because you do not wish to exert yourself in activities outside the home. You are very attached to your home and your parents. You make a loving parent and spouse because you are gentle, romantic and very affectionate.

In women, this is not an especially favorable position for the Moon. Unless there are other indications in the rest of the horoscope, they tend to be so passive that they are unduly influenced by others, especially by the men in their lives.

With men, the women with whom they become involved will be very romantic, sympathetic and warm, loving them sometimes like a mother, sometimes like a sweetheart or wife. If the Moon is afflicted, women can be a disaster, expecting a great deal from a man and giving nothing to him in return.

Your mother was no doubt very devoted and maternal in her attitude toward you, and you possibly became so dependent on her that you never wanted to leave home. You men particularly can form such a strong attachment to her that you never marry at all or else wait to marry until after your mother's death.

Famous people with Moon in Cancer

Princess Margaret Rose	Bob Hope
Jean-Paul Sartre	Thomas Schippers
Phyllis Diller	Franklin Delano Roosevelt
Lord Byron	Alan Jay Lerner
Sir Isaac Newton	Charlotte Ford Niarchos
Benjamin Spock	Pat Nixon

MOON IN LEO

You have a noble, generous personality, and you are positive and very confident. Physically, you have great strength and vitality. Once you make a decision, you stick to it firmly and resolutely—so much so, that sometimes you fail to recognize a dead-end street.

Sight is your most developed sense, but your other senses are healthy and normal. You must, however, have some interest in and affection for a subject before you can learn. The first appeal must be made to your heart rather than to your head. Once your emotions have been aroused, no one learns faster or more accurately. What you believe, however, is irrevocably linked with your affections. You have very little natural curiosity and only in rare cases do you have a scientific turn of mind.

You are very independent; you love your freedom. You have a great deal of initiative and an optimistic approach to life. You make an inspiring, capable leader with great vigor and self-reliance, and you may even feel that you have a mission to perform.

You men tend to be quite conceited and are not only impressed by your own importance but by your mental and physical powers as well. You are often so egotistical that you don't take other people's feelings and reactions into consideration, and you are impervious to outside influences when you should be taking them into account. This is not true of the women who are modest in contrast to the men and have unusually fine, well-balanced personalities.

For a man with Moon in Leo the women in his life will be a wonderful influence. They are noble and big-hearted, but at the same time dignified and reserved. They have all the best qualities of Moon in Leo and will be of the greatest credit and benefit to him.

Your mother might have tried to decide everything for you, but she would have considered that the best was none too good for you. While she may not have been particularly interested in your physical needs or in taking care of you physically herself, she would have been very interested in your mental and moral training and development.

Famous people with Moon in Leo

Prince Philip   Martin Luther
Barbra Streisand   Ringo Starr
Oscar Wilde   Elizabeth II
Luther Burbank   Paul McCartney
          Margaret Chase Smith

MOON IN VIRGO

In this position, the Moon not only stabilizes but it also makes you very intelligent and practical. You have a fine mind, but you are not interested in intellect for its own sake. The minute you learn something new, you immediately try to figure out how it can be put to use. You are first and foremost down to earth and practical.

Your reaction to your sense impressions is to analyze them. You do this very meticulously. You are very discriminating and critical. You do not see the world through rose-colored glasses. You face life as it really is and go on from there.

Because Virgo is an earth sign and the Moon can influence growth, you may well have a green thumb. You are also naturally clever about medical matters and can make an excellent nurse or doctor. You are, in addition, very sensible about handling money, and if the Moon is well placed and aspected, may have a very profitable understanding of business affairs.

Women with this position of the Moon are never particularly romantic, but they are methodical and very well organized. They are gems in a business office and, when it comes to running a home, no one is more efficient or practical. Everything runs like clockwork, but while they make their home very serviceable and comfortable, they tend to calculate the fun out of ordinary, everyday life. Although they may take care of the material details with precision, the human emotion and happiness that go into real homemaking are outside their ken. Such women tend to come in contact with other women who are very bright and who are rarely jealous of them. Women with Moon in Virgo are cold and intellectual rather than warm and emotional with men. They tend to calculate every move.

Men with Moon in Virgo tend to attract the kind of woman just described. Their attraction isn't usually particularly romantic, but they can be very helpful in a practical, material way. Aspects of the Moon to Neptune or Uranus, however, would make them more exciting and passionate.

Your mother no doubt brought you up with excellent common sense, but she was not especially intimate in her relationship with you, nor was she particularly sympathetic or affectionate. Rather she tended to criticize you in an effort to help you eliminate your faults.

Famous people with Moon in Virgo

Lyndon B. Johnson	J. Pierpont Morgan
William Faulkner	Richard Burton
Shirley MacLaine	Patty Duke
Leo Tolstoi	Sammy Davis, Jr.
Edward M. Kennedy	Princess Anne
John F. Kennedy	Immanuel Kant
Alexander the Great	Richard Strauss

MOON IN LIBRA

Your highly accurate senses are an excellent point of departure for your mind. Intellectually, you have balance and you consider every problem that is presented to you with an eminently fair mind. Your function is to criticize and judge, but like the symbolic Libra scales, you often find yourself in perfect equilibrium. You try to be so just, in fact, that it is hard for you to decide on a course of action. You tend to make plans, but not necessarily to put them into practice.

Moon in Libra, unless grievously afflicted, gives a beauty-loving nature. You value your senses because of the aesthetic impressions that they give. You might either have a keen appreciation of art, music or the ballet, or you yourself may actually perform, compose, sculpt, paint or dance.

If an artist, you can create works that are extraordinarily beautiful. You have exquisite taste and a native grasp of the fundamentals of line, color and design. You could also be a very discriminating critic or collector. In fields that are not musical or artistic, however, you may not be especially original.

You have naturally beautiful manners, and even though your background may have been simple, you have an instinct for doing the right thing. You expect in return good manners from other people and are offended when they don't live up to your standards of politeness.

You like ritual for its aesthetic possibilities. In a religious service, the artistic accouterments would interest you far more than the religious content. At a meal, the tasteful presentation of the food and its appetizing appearance would interest you almost more than the flavor.

If a woman, you will be keenly observant, highly refined and have a somewhat aloof attitude. You have a very distinctive personality, and although you may or may not be beautiful, you are always attractive. Coarseness in any form is alien to your nature. You may be passionate; you are never earthy or crude.

If a man, you tend to attract the type of woman just described. Women are important to you and you have to be careful that they don't influence you unwisely. Your wife may want to go on with her artistic interests after marriage and to place greater importance on them than on your comfort and domestic needs.

You would like to have had a charming, beautiful mother and if you didn't, you would have replaced her in your affections with someone closer to your ideal. Usually, though, unless the Moon is very afflicted, your mother is attractive, fair-minded, and arranges her home artistically.

Famous people with Moon in Libra

Walt Disney	James Arness
Marie Antoinette	Louis Armstrong (Sachmo)
Frédéric Chopin	George Harrison
Joan of Arc	Anne-Marie of Denmark
Steve Lawrence	Rudolf Nureyev
Sidney Poitier	Arthur Ashe

MOON IN SCORPIO

You can be passionate, emotional and strong willed, or else you can be lax and sensual, throwing your life away in the pursuit of pleasure in every form. If the latter type, you do, in fact, value your senses for the pleasure they give you rather than the information for a constructive life.

If the Moon is afflicted, there is a tendency to dissipation and waste. These people are either too highly sexed or so jaded that they turn to perversions as a pastime. Or they may be naturally perverted. Their hedonistic tendencies lead them inevitably to destruction, and they may hasten the process by overindulgence in alcohol or drugs.

When the Moon is well aspected, on the other hand, the judgment is both shrewd and acute. You make excellent scientists, for your reaction to sense impressions is quite perfect—stable and neither too fast nor too slow. Your powers of observation are phenomenal, so sharp and accurate that your conclusions are based on the best possible material. The will power and determination this position of the Moon can give is tremendous if used constructively. Once you have conceived an idea, you do not rest until you have transformed it to give to the world at large.

There are two types of women that come under this influence. The one is possessive and highly sexed, shrewd, unscrupulous and jealous. The other has immense initiative, will power, ambition, high ideals and determination. The lower type is revengeful and treacherous when thwarted. The higher type, while admirable, has the courage of her convictions and is determined to have her own way.

With a man, the women in his life will be of either type depending on the Moon's aspects. He himself may be passionate and so strongly sexed that he throws his life away on ruinous associations with women. Or he may benefit emotionally and practically through relationships with the higher type. Sometimes, however, a man with this position may inexplicably have little to do with women, and they are a very weak influence in his life.

Your mother may have seemed to put her ambitions for you above her love for you. She would have been so domineering and positive that you would have been compelled to do as she dictated and might have had to do what she would have liked to have done herself, whereas you may have been more suited to a different path in life.

Famous people with Moon in Scorpio

John Steinbeck	Nelson Rockefeller
Elizabeth Taylor	J. Paul Getty
Julie Andrews	Carol Channing
Dick Van Dyke	Perry Como
Hayley Mills	John Wayne
Prince Andrew	Edmund Wilson
Tricia Nixon	

MOON IN SAGITTARIUS

You are blessed with great inspiration and what amounts to second sight. In its highest form, you have the rare ability to prophesy; at the least, you are keenly perceptive and intuitive. You know in a flash what will happen, and unless the Moon is sorely afflicted, you are almost always right.

In Sagittarius, the feminine, receptive nature of the Moon is made more positive and more masculine. Your senses are extraordinarily acute and present the sharpest, clearest impressions to your mind. You have a lucid, cold intellect and your judgment is superb, based as it is on such a perfect picture of the world around you.

Your reactions are rapid and accurate, which is excellent for any scientific pursuit, but you like to consider a problem free of any distracting influences. This tends to make your experiments narrower in scope than that of the scientist who evolves universal theories and takes even the side issues into consideration. You think quickly, but do not meditate deeply and for long periods of time unless favorable aspects modify this position of the Moon. Einstein and Copernicus, two of the greatest scientists who ever lived, had Moon in Sagittarius in combination with a Pisces Sun and Mercury in Aries.

If a woman, you will be idealistic, religious, ethereal and refined. You will attract the highest types when it comes to other women, and unless your Moon is badly aspected, they will not be envious or antagonistic. You will have few, if any, enemies among women. You will act with exquisite sensitivity in your relationships with the opposite sex. You are both gentle and shy and would never appeal to a coarse or common man.

In the case of a man, the women in his life will resemble the preceding description of women with Moon in Sagittarius. He will have to be careful how he approaches them, for they are so timid that the slightest misstep will cause them to flee from him. Unless there are other indications in the rest of the horoscope, they prefer their other interests to homemaking, and while their sensitivity and high spirits appeal to him, he won't be able to rely on them to attend to down-to-earth matters the way he could with Moon in Taurus or Virgo.

Your mother would have taken a real interest in your intellectual and religious training, and she would have instilled in you philosophical principles on which to base your life. She would not, however, have given you the warmth and affection necessary for your fullest emotional development.

Famous people with Moon in Sagittarius

Joan Sutherland	Nicolaus Copernicus
Anne Bancroft	Rock Hudson
Albert Einstein	Virgil Grissom
Lewis Carroll	Henri Matisse
Charles Dickens	Arnold Palmer
Victor Hugo	Bing Crosby

Artur Rubinstein

MOON IN CAPRICORN

This position of the Moon tends to somewhat dull the senses unless the Moon is especially well aspected. Although your response to sense impressions is quick, it is somewhat hostile. You are, however, alert and eager to learn. At its best, Moon in Capricorn gives the power of quick decision, and you are able to look at a problem and resolve it in a split second and still be quite correct.

You may have a certain coldness in your makeup and your self-sufficiency can make you a somewhat solitary soul. You tend also to fix all your hopes and fears on one idea, about which you can become obsessed, so much so that your imagination can play tricks on you. This leads to false illusions and even depression when things fail to go your way, and you have to be careful of an inclination to drown your sorrows in drink. At best, you are likely to look on the dark side of things. You have to guard against brooding over your disappointments and becoming dispirited and gloomy.

You may have responsibilities thrust upon you. However, even if you don't, you have a strong sense of duty and go out of your way to assume burdens others would avoid, and to feel put upon as a result. You are so busy fulfilling all these obligations that you do not have much free time left over to amuse yourself.

Women with this position of the Moon are very practical, and they want everything to be as they have planned. While they are not particularly warm and sympathetic, they are dependable and of the sternest moral fiber. Other women in general are not well disposed toward you usually. Even if they are, you are of benefit to them, not they to you.

A man with Moon in Capricorn tends to attract the type of women just described. Although they will be faithful to him, they won't be likely to contribute to his happiness. In many cases, the man remains a bachelor or women play a subsidiary role in his life.

Your mother was no doubt very practical and patient in her attitude toward you, but she would have wanted above all to be proud of you, and when this was not possible, she may have been very unsympathetic and cold.

Famous people with Moon in Capricorn

Margot Fonteyn	John Glenn
Mary Martin	Johnny Carson
Napoleon Bonaparte	Robert Vaughn
Thomas Edison	Geraldine Chaplin
Abraham Lincoln	Willie Mays
George Washington	Merv Griffin
Eugene Ionesco	Felix Frankfurter

MOON IN AQUARIUS

Unless the Moon is very afflicted, your senses operate to near perfection. They are not only accurate, but the mind's reaction to them is also altogether estimable, being unusually steady and neither too fast nor too slow.

This is an excellent position for being well balanced. You are neither too emotional nor too cerebral. You are rational without losing sight of human interests. You are religious, but never a bigot. And your sex instinct is well developed but not to excess and is in harmony with the rest of your character. Although you are visionary, you have none of the eccentricity that ordinarily goes with it, and you do not tend to go to extremes.

You are a delightful companion. Your conversation is stimulating: witty, easy, sensible and intelligent. What you have to say is inevitably worthwhile. Because of this, any number of people are attracted to you, and you can choose your friends from every calling and walk of life. While you are very democratic, you do not suffer fools gladly; even with them, however, you can understand and therefore forgive.

You would never be content to limit yourself to one person only. Your interests are so wide and varied that you require a large circle of people to satisfy the many facets of your being. You are therefore more satisfactory to your friends than they are to you, for you contribute something to each of them. It is, however, only very rarely that one of them has as much to offer as you do.

This is not a particularly good position for the Moon in a woman's horoscope. Unless there are other planets in water signs or in Leo, she tends to be too impersonal and to lack emotional warmth and responsiveness. Other women will, however, be very helpful and favorably disposed.

This is a much better position for a man. Not only will his own personality be admirable, but the women in his life will also be idealistic, faithful, intelligent and superior to the average. They will also tend to be of greatest benefit to him and to help further his career.

Your mother would have acted as a friend and comrade to you rather than as a strict disciplinarian. Unless the Moon is sorely afflicted, she would be tolerant, broad-minded and inclined to gratify your every whim.

Famous people with Moon in Aquarius

Cary Grant	Marc Chagall
Richard Wagner	Rita Tushingham
Richard Nixon	Mia Farrow
Adlai Stevenson	Diahann Carroll
Eugene McCarthy	Caroline Kennedy
John F. Kennedy, Jr.	Prince Edward

MOON IN PISCES

Your sense impressions create illusions rather than reflecting the world as it actually is. Their report to your mind is as hazy as some of the more extreme Impressionist paintings and equally unreal.

You tend to look at life through rose-colored glasses. You are a dreamer and mystic, the idealist who expects the best to happen in this best of all possible worlds. You are essentially so romantic that you rarely see life as it really is.

Generally, you are overly optimistic, and you can get into a lot of trouble through not coming to grips with reality and expecting the best to come out of the wrong situations and people. You want so much to believe that the world is fine and beautiful that you must guard against taking to drink or drugs to preserve the illusion.

You are neither analytical nor critical. To you, there is very little difference between the spiritual and material worlds, and you are therefore inclined to be extraordinarily psychic. If the Moon is well aspected, you may be a visionary of the first rank. If it is afflicted, you will be prey to unreliable and fantastic illusions. Your visions will be deceptive and misleading.

Women with Moon in Pisces are very romantic and feminine. They are tremendously unselfish, trusting and openhanded, and are generous to a fault, giving sympathy and whatever they happen to have on hand to anyone who asks. Others tend to impose upon them as a result. In love, they are emotional and voluptuous, but so passive that men all too often take advantage of them.

A man with this position of the Moon is apt to attract this type of woman. The women in his life will be charming, otherworldly and emotional, and will place love above all else. They may not be practical or realistic, but their sole aim in life will be to make him happy as his romantic inspiration and ideal.

Your mother would have been so self-sacrificing, loving and affectionate that she may have tended to spoil you—so much so, that unless there were some counterbalancing features in the rest of the horoscope, you may not have developed your best traits or the strongest aspects of your character.

Famous people with Moon in Pisces

Audrey Hepburn	Edgar Allan Poe
Frank Sinatra	Dr. Martin Luther King, Jr.
Percy B. Shelley	Jule Styne
Robert Louis Stevenson	John L. Lewis
Joe DiMaggio	Al Capp
Helen Keller	Johann W. von Goethe

Leon Trotsky

3

Your Ascendant

The horoscope figure is a circle divided into twelve parts. The first part, which begins with the eastern (lefthand) half of the horizontal line dividing the circle into two sections, is called the rising sign, or Ascendant. It represents your physical body, your temperament, or you yourself, and ranks with the Moon and Sun as a major influence in your horoscope. Horoscope means hour, and to calculate the Ascendant of the horoscope, you need to know the hour of your birth.*

The tables that follow will enable you to know the sign position of your Ascendant. These tables are calculated for every five days of the year at 39 degrees latitude, and you can figure out the exact degree by mathematical proportion. If you are not a great one for figuring things out, practice first on one of your friends. For instance, if your friend was born at 3:00 A.M. on March 22nd, turn to the Table of Ascendants to page 70 where you will find that at 3:00 A.M. on March 22nd, the Ascendant was in 25 degrees of Capricorn. He therefore has a Capricorn Ascendant. If another friend was born at 3:30 on the same day, you will know that his Ascendant was somewhere between Capricorn and Aquarius, the sign mentioned at 4:00 A.M. In this way, you can know that he either has a Capricorn or an Aquarius Ascendant.

* If you were born during daylight saving time, subtract an hour from your time of birth.

If you prefer to calculate more exactly, consider the following examples.

First, let's consider your same friend, born on March 22 at 3:30 A.M. Again, you would look up March 22nd on page 70. Now 3:30 is halfway between three and four o'clock. At 3:00 A.M., the Ascendant is 25 degrees of Capricorn. At 4:00 A.M., the Ascendant is 13 degrees of Aquarius. There are 30 degrees in every sign. From 25 to 30 degrees of Capricorn would be 5 degrees plus 13 degrees of Aquarius equals 18 degrees. Divide this by half and you get 9 degrees. Add 9 to 25 degrees of Capricorn and you get 4 degrees of Aquarius. This gives your friend an Aquarius Ascendant.

If you had another friend born at 3:00 A.M. on March 24th, you would look up March 22nd at 3:00 A.M. and March 27th at the same time. The difference between them is 5 degrees, or a degree a day. March 24th is 2 days after the 22nd. Add 2 degrees to 25 degrees of Capricorn and you have 27 degrees of Capricorn on the Ascendant. The degree, however, is not so important for the present purposes.

Once you have established the sign of your Ascendant, you will want to know what this means to you. For this, you must refer to the description of the Sun in that particular sign. For instance, if the Ascendant is in Leo, read the Sun in Leo description; if it is in Libra, the Sun in Libra description, etc. As your calculations can only be at best inexact, you may not be certain whether the Ascendant falls at the end of one sign or the beginning of the next. If so, read both descriptions and decide which one best fits you.

Pay special attention to the description of the planet ruling your Ascendant.

Sun	rules	Leo
Moon		Cancer
Mercury		Gemini and Virgo
Venus		Taurus and Libra
Mars		Aries
Jupiter		Sagittarius
Saturn		Capricorn
Uranus		Aquarius
Neptune		Pisces
Pluto		Scorpio

For instance, if you have a Virgo Ascendant, turn to the Mercury chapter (4) and locate the description of your Mercury. This will tell you more about your character than any of the other descriptions except those of the Ascendant, Sun and Moon.

TABLE OF ASCENDANTS

JANUARY 1

A.M.			P.M.		
12 Midnight	8 of Libra		12 Noon	17 of Aries	
1 o'clock	21 of Libra		1 o'clock	10 of Taurus	
2	3 of Scorpio		2	0 of Gemini	
3	15 of Scorpio		3	16 of Gemini	
4	27 of Scorpio		4	0 of Cancer	
5	9 of Sagittarius		5	14 of Cancer	
6	22 of Sagittarius		6	26 of Cancer	
7	5 of Capricorn		7	8 of Leo	
8	20 of Capricorn		8	20 of Leo	
9	8 of Aquarius		9	2 of Virgo	
10	29 of Aquarius		10	14 of Virgo	
11	23 of Pisces		11	26 of Virgo	

JANUARY 6

A.M.			P.M.		
12 Midnight	13 of Libra		12 Noon	25 of Aries	
1 o'clock	25 of Libra		1 o'clock	17 of Taurus	
2	7 of Scorpio		2	5 of Gemini	
3	19 of Scorpio		3	21 of Gemini	
4	1 of Sagittarius		4	5 of Cancer	
5	13 of Sagittarius		5	18 of Cancer	
6	26 of Sagittarius		6	0 of Leo	
7	10 of Capricorn		7	12 of Leo	
8	26 of Capricorn		8	24 of Leo	
9	15 of Aquarius		9	6 of Virgo	
10	7 of Pisces		10	18 of Virgo	
11	1 of Aries		11	0 of Libra	

JANUARY 11

A.M.		P.M.	
12 Midnight	17 of Libra	12 Noon	3 of Taurus
1 o'clock	29 of Libra	1 o'clock	23 of Taurus
2	11 of Scorpio	2	11 of Gemini
3	23 of Scorpio	3	26 of Gemini
4	5 of Sagittarius	4	9 of Cancer
5	17 of Sagittarius	5	22 of Cancer
6	1 of Capricorn	6	4 of Leo
7	15 of Capricorn	7	16 of Leo
8	2 of Aquarius	8	28 of Leo
9	22 of Aquarius	9	10 of Virgo
10	15 of Pisces	10	22 of Virgo
11	9 of Aries	11	4 of Libra

JANUARY 16

A.M.		P.M.	
12 Midnight	21 of Libra	12 Noon	10 of Taurus
1 o'clock	3 of Scorpio	1 o'clock	29 of Taurus
2	15 of Scorpio	2	16 of Gemini
3	27 of Scorpio	3	0 of Cancer
4	9 of Sagittarius	4	13 of Cancer
5	22 of Sagittarius	5	25 of Cancer
6	5 of Capricorn	6	8 of Leo
7	20 of Capricorn	7	20 of Leo
8	8 of Aquarius	8	2 of Virgo
9	29 of Aquarius	9	14 of Virgo
10	23 of Pisces	10	26 of Virgo
11	17 of Aries	11	8 of Libra

JANUARY 21

A.M.		P.M.	
12 Midnight	24 of Libra	12 Noon	16 of Taurus
1 o'clock	6 of Scorpio	1 o'clock	5 of Gemini

2	18 of Scorpio	2	21 of Gemini
3	0 of Sagittarius	3	4 of Cancer
4	13 of Sagittarius	4	18 of Cancer
5	26 of Sagittarius	5	0 of Leo
6	10 of Capricorn	6	12 of Leo
7	26 of Capricorn	7	24 of Leo
8	15 of Aquarius	8	6 of Virgo
9	6 of Pisces	9	18 of Virgo
10	1 of Aries	10	0 of Libra
11	25 of Aries	11	12 of Libra

JANUARY 26

A.M.		P.M.	
12 Midnight	28 of Libra	**12 Noon**	23 of Taurus
1 o'clock	10 of Scorpio	**1 o'clock**	10 of Gemini
2	22 of Scorpio	2	25 of Gemini
3	4 of Sagittarius	3	9 of Cancer
4	17 of Sagittarius	4	21 of Cancer
5	0 of Capricorn	5	4 of Leo
6	15 of Capricorn	6	16 of Leo
7	2 of Aquarius	7	28 of Leo
8	21 of Aquarius	8	10 of Virgo
9	14 of Pisces	9	22 of Virgo
10	9 of Aries	10	4 of Libra
11	2 of Taurus	11	16 of Libra

JANUARY 31

A.M.		P.M.	
12 Midnight	2 of Scorpio	**12 Noon**	29 of Taurus
1 o'clock	14 of Scorpio	**1 o'clock**	15 of Gemini
2	26 of Scorpio	2	0 of Cancer
3	9 of Sagittarius	3	13 of Cancer
4	21 of Sagittarius	4	26 of Cancer
5	5 of Capricorn	5	8 of Leo
6	20 of Capricorn	6	20 of Leo
7	8 of Aquarius	7	2 of Virgo

8	29 of Aquarius	8	14 of Virgo
9	22 of Pisces	9	26 of Virgo
10	17 of Aries	10	8 of Libra
11	10 of Taurus	11	20 of Libra

FEBRUARY 5

A.M.		P.M.	
12 Midnight	6 of Scorpio	12 Noon	5 of Gemini
1 o'clock	18 of Scorpio	1 o'clock	20 of Gemini
2	0 of Sagittarius	2	4 of Cancer
3	12 of Sagittarius	3	17 of Cancer
4	26 of Sagittarius	4	29 of Cancer
5	9 of Capricorn	5	11 of Leo
6	25 of Capricorn	6	23 of Leo
7	14 of Aquarius	7	6 of Virgo
8	6 of Pisces	8	17 of Virgo
9	0 of Aries	9	0 of Libra
10	24 of Aries	10	12 of Libra
11	16 of Taurus	11	24 of Libra

FEBRUARY 10

A.M.		P.M.	
12 Midnight	10 of Scorpio	12 Noon	10 of Gemini
1 o'clock	22 of Scorpio	1 o'clock	25 of Gemini
2	4 of Sagittarius	2	9 of Cancer
3	17 of Sagittarius	3	21 of Cancer
4	0 of Capricorn	4	3 of Leo
5	15 of Capricorn	5	16 of Leo
6	1 of Aquarius	6	28 of Leo
7	21 of Aquarius	7	10 of Virgo
8	14 of Pisces	8	22 of Virgo
9	8 of Aries	9	4 of Libra
10	2 of Taurus	10	16 of Libra
11	22 of Taurus	11	28 of Libra

FEBRUARY 15

A.M.		P.M.	
12 Midnight	14 of Scorpio	**12 Noon**	15 of Gemini
1 o'clock	26 of Scorpio	**1 o'clock**	0 of Cancer
2	8 of Sagittarius	**2**	13 of Cancer
3	21 of Sagittarius	**3**	25 of Cancer
4	5 of Capricorn	**4**	7 of Leo
5	20 of Capricorn	**5**	19 of Leo
6	8 of Aquarius	**6**	2 of Virgo
7	28 of Aquarius	**7**	14 of Virgo
8	22 of Pisces	**8**	26 of Virgo
9	16 of Aries	**9**	8 of Libra
10	9 of Taurus	**10**	20 of Libra
11	29 of Taurus	**11**	2 of Scorpio

FEBRUARY 20

A.M.		P.M.	
12 Midnight	18 of Scorpio	**12 Noon**	20 of Gemini
1 o'clock	0 of Sagittarius	**1 o'clock**	4 of Cancer
2	12 of Sagittarius	**2**	17 of Cancer
3	25 of Sagittarius	**3**	29 of Cancer
4	9 of Capricorn	**4**	11 of Leo
5	25 of Capricorn	**5**	23 of Leo
6	14 of Aquarius	**6**	5 of Virgo
7	5 of Pisces	**7**	17 of Virgo
8	0 of Aries	**8**	0 of Libra
9	24 of Aries	**9**	12 of Libra
10	16 of Taurus	**10**	24 of Libra
11	4 of Gemini	**11**	6 of Scorpio

FEBRUARY 25

A.M.		P.M.	
12 Midnight	22 of Scorpio	**12 Noon**	25 of Gemini
1 o'clock	4 of Sagittarius	**1 o'clock**	8 of Cancer

2	17 of Sagittarius	2	21 of Cancer
3	0 of Capricorn	3	3 of Leo
4	14 of Capricorn	4	15 of Leo
5	1 of Aquarius	5	27 of Leo
6	21 of Aquarius	6	9 of Virgo
7	14 of Pisces	7	22 of Virgo
8	8 of Aries	8	4 of Libra
9	1 of Taurus	9	16 of Libra
10	22 of Taurus	10	28 of Libra
11	10 of Gemini	11	10 of Scorpio

MARCH 2

A.M.		P.M.	
12 Midnight	27 of Scorpio	12 Noon	0 of Cancer
1 o'clock	9 of Sagittarius	1 o'clock	14 of Cancer
2	22 of Sagittarius	2	26 of Cancer
3	5 of Capricorn	3	8 of Leo
4	21 of Capricorn	4	20 of Leo
5	8 of Aquarius	5	2 of Virgo
6	29 of Aquarius	6	14 of Virgo
7	23 of Pisces	7	26 of Virgo
8	17 of Aries	8	9 of Libra
9	10 of Taurus	9	21 of Libra
10	0 of Gemini	10	3 of Scorpio
11	16 of Gemini	11	15 of Scorpio

MARCH 7

A.M.		P.M.	
12 Midnight	0 of Sagittarius	12 Noon	4 of Cancer
1 o'clock	12 of Sagittarius	1 o'clock	17 of Cancer
2	25 of Sagittarius	2	29 of Cancer
3	9 of Capricorn	3	11 of Leo
4	25 of Capricorn	4	23 of Leo
5	14 of Aquarius	5	5 of Virgo
6	5 of Pisces	6	17 of Virgo
7	0 of Aries	7	0 of Libra

8	24 of Aries	8	12 of Libra
9	16 of Taurus	9	24 of Libra
10	4 of Gemini	10	6 of Scorpio
11	20 of Gemini	11	18 of Scorpio

MARCH 12

A.M.		P.M.	
12 Midnight	4 of Sagittarius	12 Noon	8 of Cancer
1 o'clock	16 of Sagittarius	1 o'clock	21 of Cancer
2	0 of Capricorn	2	3 of Leo
3	14 of Capricorn	3	15 of Leo
4	1 of Aquarius	4	27 of Leo
5	20 of Aquarius	5	9 of Virgo
6	13 of Pisces	6	21 of Virgo
7	8 of Aries	7	4 of Libra
8	1 of Taurus	8	16 of Libra
9	22 of Taurus	9	28 of Libra
10	10 of Gemini	10	11 of Scorpio
11	25 of Gemini	11	22 of Scorpio

MARCH 17

A.M.		P.M.	
12 Midnight	8 of Sagittarius	12 Noon	13 of Cancer
1 o'clock	21 of Sagittarius	1 o'clock	25 of Cancer
2	4 of Capricorn	2	7 of Leo
3	19 of Capricorn	3	19 of Leo
4	7 of Aquarius	4	1 of Virgo
5	28 of Aquarius	5	13 of Virgo
6	21 of Pisces	6	25 of Virgo
7	16 of Aries	7	8 of Libra
8	8 of Taurus	8	20 of Libra
9	28 of Taurus	9	2 of Scorpio
10	15 of Gemini	10	14 of Scorpio
11	29 of Gemini	11	26 of Scorpio

MARCH 22

A.M.		P.M.	
12 Midnight	12 of Sagittarius	12 Noon	17 of Cancer
1 o'clock	25 of Sagittarius	1 o'clock	29 of Cancer
2	7 of Capricorn	2	11 of Leo
3	25 of Capricorn	3	23 of Leo
4	13 of Aquarius	4	5 of Virgo
5	5 of Pisces	5	17 of Virgo
6	29 of Pisces	6	29 of Virgo
7	24 of Aries	7	12 of Libra
8	15 of Taurus	8	24 of Libra
9	4 of Gemini	9	6 of Scorpio
10	20 of Gemini	10	18 of Scorpio
11	4 of Cancer	11	0 of Sagittarius

MARCH 27

A.M.		P.M.	
12 Midnight	16 of Sagittarius	12 Noon	21 of Cancer
1 o'clock	29 of Sagittarius	1 o'clock	3 of Leo
2	14 of Capricorn	2	15 of Leo
3	0 of Aquarius	3	27 of Leo
4	20 of Aquarius	4	9 of Virgo
5	13 of Pisces	5	21 of Virgo
6	7 of Aries	6	3 of Libra
7	1 of Taurus	7	15 of Libra
8	21 of Taurus	8	27 of Libra
9	9 of Gemini	9	10 of Scorpio
10	24 of Gemini	10	22 of Scorpio
11	8 of Cancer	11	4 of Sagittarius

APRIL 1

A.M.		P.M.	
12 Midnight	21 of Sagittarius	12 Noon	25 of Cancer
1 o'clock	4 of Capricorn	1 o'clock	7 of Leo

2	19 of Capricorn	2	19 of Leo
3	7 of Aquarius	3	1 of Virgo
4	27 of Aquarius	4	13 of Virgo
5	21 of Pisces	5	25 of Virgo
6	15 of Aries	6	7 of Libra
7	8 of Taurus	7	19 of Libra
8	28 of Taurus	8	2 of Scorpio
9	14 of Gemini	9	14 of Scorpio
10	29 of Gemini	10	26 of Scorpio
11	12 of Cancer	11	8 of Sagittarius

APRIL 6

A.M.		P.M.	
12 Midnight	25 of Sagittarius	12 Noon	29 of Cancer
1 o'clock	9 of Capricorn	1 o'clock	11 of Leo
2	25 of Capricorn	2	23 of Leo
3	13 of Aquarius	3	5 of Virgo
4	5 of Pisces	4	17 of Virgo
5	29 of Pisces	5	29 of Virgo
6	23 of Aries	6	11 of Libra
7	15 of Taurus	7	24 of Libra
8	4 of Gemini	8	6 of Scorpio
9	20 of Gemini	9	18 of Scorpio
10	3 of Cancer	10	0 of Sagittarius
11	16 of Cancer	11	12 of Sagittarius

APRIL 11

A.M.		P.M.	
12 Midnight	29 of Sagittarius	12 Noon	3 of Leo
1 o'clock	14 of Capricorn	1 o'clock	15 of Leo
2	0 of Aquarius	2	27 of Leo
3	20 of Aquarius	3	9 of Virgo
4	13 of Pisces	4	21 of Virgo
5	7 of Aries	5	3 of Libra
6	1 of Taurus	6	15 of Libra
7	21 of Taurus	7	27 of Libra

8	9 of Gemini	8	10 of Scorpio
9	24 of Gemini	9	22 of Scorpio
10	8 of Cancer	10	4 of Sagittarius
11	21 of Cancer	11	16 of Sagittarius

APRIL 16

A.M.		P.M.	
12 Midnight	4 of Capricorn	12 Noon	7 of Leo
1 o'clock	19 of Capricorn	1 o'clock	19 of Leo
2	6 of Aquarius	2	1 of Virgo
3	27 of Aquarius	3	13 of Virgo
4	20 of Pisces	4	25 of Virgo
5	15 of Aries	5	7 of Libra
6	8 of Taurus	6	19 of Libra
7	27 of Taurus	7	1 of Scorpio
8	14 of Gemini	8	14 of Scorpio
9	29 of Gemini	9	25 of Scorpio
10	12 of Cancer	10	8 of Sagittarius
11	25 of Cancer	11	20 of Sagittarius

APRIL 21

A.M.		P.M.	
12 Midnight	9 of Capricorn	12 Noon	11 of Leo
1 o'clock	24 of Capricorn	1 o'clock	23 of Leo
2	13 of Aquarius	2	5 of Virgo
3	4 of Pisces	3	17 of Virgo
4	29 of Pisces	4	29 of Virgo
5	23 of Aries	5	11 of Libra
6	15 of Taurus	6	23 of Libra
7	3 of Gemini	7	5 of Scorpio
8	19 of Gemini	8	17 of Scorpio
9	3 of Cancer	9	29 of Scorpio
10	16 of Cancer	10	12 of Sagittarius
11	29 of Cancer	11	25 of Sagittarius

APRIL 26

A.M.		P.M.	
12 Midnight	14 of Capricorn	12 Noon	15 of Leo
1 o'clock	0 of Aquarius	1 o'clock	27 of Leo
2	20 of Aquarius	2	9 of Virgo
3	12 of Pisces	3	21 of Virgo
4	7 of Aries	4	3 of Libra
5	0 of Taurus	5	15 of Libra
6	21 of Taurus	6	27 of Libra
7	9 of Gemini	7	9 of Scorpio
8	24 of Gemini	8	21 of Scorpio
9	8 of Cancer	9	3 of Sagittarius
10	20 of Cancer	10	16 of Sagittarius
11	3 of Leo	11	29 of Sagittarius

MAY 1

A.M.		P.M.	
12 Midnight	19 of Capricorn	12 Noon	18 of Leo
1 o'clock	6 of Aquarius	1 o'clock	1 of Virgo
2	27 of Aquarius	2	13 of Virgo
3	20 of Pisces	3	25 of Virgo
4	15 of Aries	4	7 of Libra
5	7 of Taurus	5	19 of Libra
6	27 of Taurus	6	1 of Scorpio
7	14 of Gemini	7	13 of Scorpio
8	29 of Gemini	8	25 of Scorpio
9	12 of Cancer	9	7 of Sagittarius
10	24 of Cancer	10	20 of Sagittarius
11	6 of Leo	11	4 of Capricorn

MAY 6

A.M.		P.M.	
12 Midnight	24 of Capricorn	12 Noon	22 of Leo
1 o'clock	12 of Aquarius	1 o'clock	4 of Virgo

2	4 of Pisces	2	17 of Virgo
3	28 of Pisces	3	29 of Virgo
4	22 of Aries	4	11 of Libra
5	14 of Taurus	5	23 of Libra
6	3 of Gemini	6	5 of Scorpio
7	19 of Gemini	7	17 of Scorpio
8	3 of Cancer	8	29 of Scorpio
9	16 of Cancer	9	11 of Sagittarius
10	28 of Cancer	10	24 of Sagittarius
11	10 of Leo	11	8 of Capricorn

MAY 11

A.M.		P.M.	
12 Midnight	0 of Aquarius	12 Noon	26 of Leo
1 o'clock	19 of Aquarius	1 o'clock	8 of Virgo
2	12 of Pisces	2	21 of Virgo
3	6 of Aries	3	3 of Libra
4	0 of Taurus	4	15 of Libra
5	21 of Taurus	5	27 of Libra
6	9 of Gemini	6	9 of Scorpio
7	24 of Gemini	7	21 of Scorpio
8	8 of Cancer	8	3 of Sagittarius
9	20 of Cancer	9	16 of Sagittarius
10	2 of Leo	10	29 of Sagittarius
11	14 of Leo	11	13 of Capricorn

MAY 16

A.M.		P.M.	
12 Midnight	6 of Aquarius	12 Noon	0 of Virgo
1 o'clock	27 of Aquarius	1 o'clock	13 of Virgo
2	20 of Pisces	2	25 of Virgo
3	15 of Aries	3	7 of Libra
4	7 of Taurus	4	19 of Libra
5	27 of Taurus	5	1 of Scorpio
6	14 of Gemini	6	13 of Scorpio
7	29 of Gemini	7	25 of Scorpio

8	12 of Cancer	8	7 of Sagittarius
9	24 of Cancer	9	20 of Sagittarius
10	6 of Leo	10	4 of Capricorn
11	18 of Leo	11	18 of Capricorn

MAY 21

A.M.		P.M.	
12 Midnight	12 of Aquarius	12 Noon	4 of Virgo
1 o'clock	4 of Pisces	1 o'clock	16 of Virgo
2	28 of Pisces	2	29 of Virgo
3	22 of Aries	3	11 of Libra
4	14 of Taurus	4	23 of Libra
5	3 of Gemini	5	5 of Scorpio
6	19 of Gemini	6	17 of Scorpio
7	3 of Cancer	7	29 of Scorpio
8	16 of Cancer	8	11 of Sagittarius
9	28 of Cancer	9	24 of Sagittarius
10	10 of Leo	10	8 of Capricorn
11	22 of Leo	11	24 of Capricorn

MAY 26

A.M.		P.M.	
12 Midnight	19 of Aquarius	12 Noon	8 of Virgo
1 o'clock	11 of Pisces	1 o'clock	20 of Virgo
2	6 of Aries	2	3 of Libra
3	0 of Taurus	3	15 of Libra
4	20 of Taurus	4	27 of Libra
5	8 of Gemini	5	9 of Scorpio
6	24 of Gemini	6	21 of Scorpio
7	7 of Cancer	7	3 of Sagittarius
8	20 of Cancer	8	16 of Sagittarius
9	2 of Leo	9	29 of Sagittarius
10	14 of Leo	10	13 of Capricorn
11	26 of Leo	11	0 of Aquarius

MAY 31

A.M.		P.M.	
12 Midnight	26 of Aquarius	12 Noon	12 of Virgo
1 o'clock	20 of Pisces	1 o'clock	25 of Virgo
2	14 of Aries	2	7 of Libra
3	7 of Taurus	3	19 of Libra
4	27 of Taurus	4	1 of Scorpio
5	14 of Gemini	5	13 of Scorpio
6	28 of Gemini	6	25 of Scorpio
7	12 of Cancer	7	7 of Sagittarius
8	24 of Cancer	8	20 of Sagittarius
9	6 of Leo	9	3 of Capricorn
10	18 of Leo	10	18 of Capricorn
11	0 of Virgo	11	6 of Aquarius

JUNE 5

A.M.		P.M.	
12 Midnight	4 of Pisces	12 Noon	16 of Virgo
1 o'clock	28 of Pisces	1 o'clock	29 of Virgo
2	22 of Aries	2	11 of Libra
3	14 of Taurus	3	23 of Libra
4	3 of Gemini	4	5 of Scorpio
5	19 of Gemini	5	17 of Scorpio
6	3 of Cancer	6	29 of Scorpio
7	16 of Cancer	7	11 of Sagittarius
8	28 of Cancer	8	24 of Sagittarius
9	10 of Leo	9	8 of Capricorn
10	22 of Leo	10	24 of Capricorn
11	4 of Virgo	11	12 of Aquarius

JUNE 10

A.M.		P.M.	
12 Midnight	11 of Pisces	12 Noon	20 of Virgo
1 o'clock	5 of Aries	1 o'clock	2 of Libra

2	29 of Aries	2	14 of Libra
3	20 of Taurus	3	27 of Libra
4	8 of Gemini	4	9 of Scorpio
5	23 of Gemini	5	21 of Scorpio
6	7 of Cancer	6	3 of Sagittarius
7	20 of Cancer	7	15 of Sagittarius
8	2 of Leo	8	28 of Sagittarius
9	14 of Leo	9	13 of Capricorn
10	26 of Leo	10	29 of Capricorn
11	8 of Virgo	11	18 of Aquarius

JUNE 15

A.M.		P.M.	
12 Midnight	19 of Pisces	12 Noon	24 of Virgo
1 o'clock	14 of Aries	1 o'clock	7 of Libra
2	7 of Taurus	2	19 of Libra
3	26 of Taurus	3	1 of Scorpio
4	13 of Gemini	4	13 of Scorpio
5	28 of Gemini	5	25 of Scorpio
6	11 of Cancer	6	7 of Sagittarius
7	24 of Cancer	7	19 of Sagittarius
8	6 of Leo	8	3 of Capricorn
9	18 of Leo	9	18 of Capricorn
10	0 of Virgo	10	5 of Aquarius
11	12 of Virgo	11	26 of Aquarius

JUNE 20

A.M.		P.M.	
12 Midnight	27 of Pisces	12 Noon	24 of Virgo
1 o'clock	22 of Aries	1 o'clock	7 of Libra
2	13 of Taurus	2	23 of Libra
3	3 of Gemini	3	5 of Scorpio
4	18 of Gemini	4	17 of Scorpio
5	3 of Cancer	5	29 of Scorpio
6	16 of Cancer	6	11 of Sagittarius
7	28 of Cancer	7	24 of Sagittarius

8	10 of Leo	8	8 of Capricorn
9	22 of Leo	9	23 of Capricorn
10	4 of Virgo	10	12 of Aquarius
11	16 of Virgo	11	3 of Pisces

JUNE 25

A.M.		P.M.	
12 Midnight	5 of Aries	12 Noon	2 of Libra
1 o'clock	29 of Aries	1 o'clock	14 of Libra
2	20 of Taurus	2	27 of Libra
3	8 of Gemini	3	9 of Scorpio
4	23 of Gemini	4	21 of Scorpio
5	7 of Cancer	5	3 of Sagittarius
6	20 of Cancer	6	15 of Sagittarius
7	2 of Leo	7	28 of Sagittarius
8	14 of Leo	8	13 of Capricorn
9	26 of Leo	9	29 of Capricorn
10	8 of Virgo	10	18 of Aquarius
11	20 of Virgo	11	10 of Pisces

JUNE 30

A.M.		P.M.	
12 Midnight	13 of Aries	12 Noon	6 of Libra
1 o'clock	6 of Taurus	1 o'clock	18 of Libra
2	26 of Taurus	2	1 of Scorpio
3	13 of Gemini	3	13 of Scorpio
4	28 of Gemini	4	25 of Scorpio
5	11 of Cancer	5	7 of Sagittarius
6	24 of Cancer	6	19 of Sagittarius
7	6 of Leo	7	3 of Capricorn
8	18 of Leo	8	18 of Capricorn
9	0 of Virgo	9	5 of Aquarius
10	12 of Virgo	10	25 of Aquarius
11	24 of Virgo	11	19 of Pisces

JULY 5

A.M.		P.M.	
12 Midnight	21 of Aries	12 Noon	10 of Libra
1 o'clock	13 of Taurus	1 o'clock	22 of Libra
2	2 of Gemini	2	5 of Scorpio
3	18 of Gemini	3	17 of Scorpio
4	2 of Cancer	4	29 of Scorpio
5	15 of Cancer	5	11 of Sagittarius
6	28 of Cancer	6	24 of Sagittarius
7	10 of Leo	7	8 of Capricorn
8	22 of Leo	8	23 of Capricorn
9	4 of Virgo	9	11 of Aquarius
10	16 of Virgo	10	3 of Pisces
11	28 of Virgo	11	27 of Pisces

JULY 10

A.M.		P.M.	
12 Midnight	29 of Aries	12 Noon	14 of Libra
1 o'clock	20 of Taurus	1 o'clock	27 of Libra
2	8 of Gemini	2	9 of Scorpio
3	23 of Gemini	3	21 of Scorpio
4	7 of Cancer	4	3 of Sagittarius
5	20 of Cancer	5	15 of Sagittarius
6	2 of Leo	6	28 of Sagittarius
7	14 of Leo	7	13 of Capricorn
8	26 of Leo	8	29 of Capricorn
9	8 of Virgo	9	18 of Aquarius
10	20 of Virgo	10	11 of Pisces
11	2 of Libra	11	5 of Aries

JULY 15

A.M.		P.M.	
12 Midnight	6 of Taurus	12 Noon	18 of Libra
1 o'clock	26 of Taurus	1 o'clock	0 of Scorpio

2	13 of Gemini	2	12 of Scorpio
3	28 of Gemini	3	24 of Scorpio
4	11 of Cancer	4	7 of Sagittarius
5	23 of Cancer	5	19 of Sagittarius
6	6 of Leo	6	3 of Capricorn
7	18 of Leo	7	17 of Capricorn
8	0 of Virgo	8	5 of Aquarius
9	12 of Virgo	9	25 of Aquarius
10	24 of Virgo	10	18 of Pisces
11	6 of Libra	11	13 of Aries

JULY 20

A.M.		P.M.	
12 Midnight	13 of Taurus	12 Noon	22 of Libra
1 o'clock	2 of Gemini	1 o'clock	4 of Scorpio
2	18 of Gemini	2	16 of Scorpio
3	2 of Cancer	3	28 of Scorpio
4	15 of Cancer	4	11 of Sagittarius
5	28 of Cancer	5	23 of Sagittarius
6	10 of Leo	6	7 of Capricorn
7	22 of Leo	7	23 of Capricorn
8	4 of Virgo	8	11 of Aquarius
9	16 of Virgo	9	3 of Pisces
10	28 of Virgo	10	26 of Pisces
11	10 of Libra	11	21 of Aries

JULY 25

A.M.		P.M.	
12 Midnight	20 of Taurus	12 Noon	26 of Libra
1 o'clock	8 of Gemini	1 o'clock	8 of Scorpio
2	23 of Gemini	2	20 of Scorpio
3	7 of Cancer	3	2 of Sagittarius
4	19 of Cancer	4	15 of Sagittarius
5	2 of Leo	5	28 of Sagittarius
6	14 of Leo	6	12 of Capricorn
7	26 of Leo	7	29 of Capricorn

8	8 of Virgo	**8**	18 of Aquarius
9	20 of Virgo	**9**	10 of Pisces
10	2 of Libra	**10**	5 of Aries
11	14 of Libra	**11**	29 of Aries

JULY 30

A.M.		P.M.	
12 Midnight	26 of Taurus	**12 Noon**	0 of Scorpio
1 o'clock	13 of Gemini	**1 o'clock**	12 of Scorpio
2	27 of Gemini	**2**	24 of Scorpio
3	11 of Cancer	**3**	6 of Sagittarius
4	23 of Cancer	**4**	19 of Sagittarius
5	5 of Leo	**5**	2 of Capricorn
6	17 of Leo	**6**	17 of Capricorn
7	29 of Leo	**7**	4 of Aquarius
8	11 of Virgo	**8**	24 of Aquarius
9	24 of Virgo	**9**	18 of Pisces
10	6 of Libra	**10**	12 of Aries
11	18 of Libra	**11**	6 of Taurus

AUGUST 4

A.M.		P.M.	
12 Midnight	2 of Gemini	**12 Noon**	4 of Scorpio
1 o'clock	18 of Gemini	**1 o'clock**	16 of Scorpio
2	2 of Cancer	**2**	28 of Scorpio
3	15 of Cancer	**3**	10 of Sagittarius
4	27 of Cancer	**4**	23 of Sagittarius
5	9 of Leo	**5**	7 of Capricorn
6	21 of Leo	**6**	22 of Capricorn
7	3 of Virgo	**7**	11 of Aquarius
8	16 of Virgo	**8**	2 of Pisces
9	28 of Virgo	**9**	26 of Pisces
10	10 of Libra	**10**	20 of Aries
11	22 of Libra	**11**	12 of Taurus

AUGUST 9

A.M.		P.M.	
12 Midnight	7 of Gemini	12 Noon	8 of Scorpio
1 o'clock	23 of Gemini	1 o'clock	20 of Scorpio
2	6 of Cancer	2	2 of Sagittarius
3	19 of Cancer	3	15 of Sagittarius
4	1 of Leo	4	28 of Sagittarius
5	13 of Leo	5	12 of Capricorn
6	25 of Leo	6	28 of Capricorn
7	7 of Virgo	7	17 of Aquarius
8	20 of Virgo	8	10 of Pisces
9	2 of Libra	9	4 of Aries
10	14 of Libra	10	28 of Aries
11	26 of Libra	11	19 of Taurus

AUGUST 14

A.M.		P.M.	
12 Midnight	13 of Gemini	12 Noon	12 of Scorpio
1 o'clock	27 of Gemini	1 o'clock	24 of Scorpio
2	11 of Cancer	2	6 of Sagittarius
3	23 of Cancer	3	19 of Sagittarius
4	5 of Leo	4	2 of Capricorn
5	17 of Leo	5	17 of Capricorn
6	29 of Leo	6	4 of Aquarius
7	11 of Virgo	7	24 of Aquarius
8	24 of Virgo	8	18 of Pisces
9	6 of Libra	9	12 of Aries
10	18 of Libra	10	6 of Taurus
11	0 of Scorpio	11	26 of Taurus

AUGUST 19

A.M.		P.M.	
12 Midnight	18 of Gemini	12 Noon	16 of Scorpio
1 o'clock	2 of Cancer	1 o'clock	28 of Scorpio

2	15 of Cancer	2	10 of Sagittarius
3	27 of Cancer	3	23 of Sagittarius
4	9 of Leo	4	7 of Capricorn
5	21 of Leo	5	22 of Capricorn
6	3 of Virgo	6	10 of Aquarius
7	15 of Virgo	7	2 of Pisces
8	28 of Virgo	8	26 of Pisces
9	10 of Libra	9	20 of Aries
10	22 of Libra	10	12 of Taurus
11	4 of Scorpio	11	1 of Gemini

AUGUST 24

A.M.		P.M.	
12 Midnight	22 of Gemini	12 Noon	20 of Scorpio
1 o'clock	6 of Cancer	1 o'clock	2 of Sagittarius
2	19 of Cancer	2	14 of Sagittarius
3	1 of Leo	3	27 of Sagittarius
4	13 of Leo	4	12 of Capricorn
5	25 of Leo	5	28 of Capricorn
6	7 of Virgo	6	17 of Aquarius
7	19 of Virgo	7	9 of Pisces
8	2 of Libra	8	4 of Aries
9	14 of Libra	9	28 of Aries
10	26 of Libra	10	19 of Taurus
11	8 of Scorpio	11	7 of Gemini

AUGUST 29

A.M.		P.M.	
12 Midnight	27 of Gemini	12 Noon	24 of Scorpio
1 o'clock	11 of Cancer	1 o'clock	6 of Sagittarius
2	23 of Cancer	2	19 of Sagittarius
3	5 of Leo	3	2 of Capricorn
4	17 of Leo	4	17 of Capricorn
5	29 of Leo	5	4 of Aquarius
6	11 of Virgo	6	24 of Aquarius
7	23 of Virgo	7	17 of Pisces

8	6 of Libra	**8**	12 of Aries
9	18 of Libra	**9**	5 of Taurus
10	0 of Scorpio	**10**	25 of Taurus
11	12 of Scorpio	**11**	12 of Gemini

SEPTEMBER 3

A.M.		P.M.	
12 Midnight	2 of Cancer	**12 Noon**	28 of Scorpio
1 o'clock	14 of Cancer	**1 o'clock**	10 of Sagittarius
2	27 of Cancer	**2**	23 of Sagittarius
3	9 of Leo	**3**	7 of Capricorn
4	21 of Leo	**4**	22 of Capricorn
5	3 of Virgo	**5**	10 of Aquarius
6	15 of Virgo	**6**	1 of Pisces
7	27 of Virgo	**7**	25 of Pisces
8	10 of Libra	**8**	20 of Aries
9	22 of Libra	**9**	12 of Taurus
10	4 of Scorpio	**10**	1 of Gemini
11	16 of Scorpio	**11**	17 of Gemini

SEPTEMBER 8

A.M.		P.M.	
12 Midnight	6 of Cancer	**12 Noon**	2 of Sagittarius
1 o'clock	19 of Cancer	**1 o'clock**	14 of Sagittarius
2	1 of Leo	**2**	27 of Sagittarius
3	13 of Leo	**3**	12 of Capricorn
4	25 of Leo	**4**	28 of Capricorn
5	7 of Virgo	**5**	17 of Aquarius
6	19 of Virgo	**6**	9 of Pisces
7	1 of Libra	**7**	4 of Aries
8	14 of Libra	**8**	27 of Aries
9	26 of Libra	**9**	19 of Taurus
10	8 of Scorpio	**10**	7 of Gemini
11	20 of Scorpio	**11**	22 of Gemini

SEPTEMBER 13

A.M.		P.M.	
12 Midnight	10 of Cancer	12 Noon	6 of Sagittarius
1 o'clock	23 of Cancer	1 o'clock	18 of Sagittarius
2	5 of Leo	2	2 of Capricorn
3	17 of Leo	3	17 of Capricorn
4	29 of Leo	4	4 of Aquarius
5	11 of Virgo	5	24 of Aquarius
6	23 of Virgo	6	17 of Pisces
7	6 of Libra	7	12 of Aries
8	18 of Libra	8	5 of Taurus
9	0 of Scorpio	9	25 of Taurus
10	12 of Scorpio	10	12 of Gemini
11	24 of Scorpio	11	27 of Gemini

SEPTEMBER 18

A.M.		P.M.	
12 Midnight	14 of Cancer	12 Noon	10 of Sagittarius
1 o'clock	27 of Cancer	1 o'clock	23 of Sagittarius
2	9 of Leo	2	7 of Capricorn
3	21 of Leo	3	22 of Capricorn
4	3 of Virgo	4	10 of Aquarius
5	15 of Virgo	5	1 of Pisces
6	27 of Virgo	6	25 of Pisces
7	10 of Libra	7	20 of Aries
8	22 of Libra	8	12 of Taurus
9	4 of Scorpio	9	1 of Gemini
10	16 of Scorpio	10	17 of Gemini
11	28 of Scorpio	11	2 of Cancer

SEPTEMBER 23

A.M.		P.M.	
12 Midnight	18 of Cancer	12 Noon	14 of Sagittarius
1 o'clock	1 of Leo	1 o'clock	27 of Sagittarius

2	13 of Leo	**2**	11 of Capricorn
3	25 of Leo	**3**	27 of Capricorn
4	7 of Virgo	**4**	17 of Aquarius
5	19 of Virgo	**5**	9 of Pisces
6	1 of Libra	**6**	3 of Aries
7	13 of Libra	**7**	27 of Aries
8	26 of Libra	**8**	18 of Taurus
9	8 of Scorpio	**9**	6 of Gemini
10	20 of Scorpio	**10**	22 of Gemini
11	2 of Sagittarius	**11**	6 of Cancer

SEPTEMBER 28

A.M.		P.M.	
12 Midnight	22 of Cancer	**12 Noon**	18 of Sagittarius
1 o'clock	4 of Leo	**1 o'clock**	2 of Capricorn
2	17 of Leo	**2**	16 of Capricorn
3	29 of Leo	**3**	3 of Aquarius
4	11 of Virgo	**4**	23 of Aquarius
5	23 of Virgo	**5**	17 of Pisces
6	5 of Libra	**6**	11 of Aries
7	18 of Libra	**7**	5 of Taurus
8	0 of Scorpio	**8**	25 of Taurus
9	12 of Scorpio	**9**	12 of Gemini
10	24 of Scorpio	**10**	27 of Gemini
11	6 of Sagittarius	**11**	10 of Cancer

OCTOBER 3

A.M.		P.M.	
12 Midnight	27 of Cancer	**12 Noon**	23 of Sagittarius
1 o'clock	9 of Leo	**1 o'clock**	6 of Capricorn
2	21 of Leo	**2**	22 of Capricorn
3	3 of Virgo	**3**	10 of Aquarius
4	15 of Virgo	**4**	1 of Pisces
5	27 of Virgo	**5**	25 of Pisces
6	9 of Libra	**6**	19 of Aries
7	21 of Libra	**7**	12 of Taurus

8	4 of Scorpio	8	1 of Gemini
9	16 of Scorpio	9	17 of Gemini
10	28 of Scorpio	10	1 of Cancer
11	10 of Sagittarius	11	14 of Cancer

OCTOBER 8

A.M.		P.M.	
12 Midnight	1 of Leo	12 Noon	27 of Sagittarius
1 o'clock	13 of Leo	1 o'clock	11 of Capricorn
2	25 of Leo	2	27 of Capricorn
3	7 of Virgo	3	16 of Aquarius
4	19 of Virgo	4	8 of Pisces
5	1 of Libra	5	3 of Aries
6	13 of Libra	6	27 of Aries
7	25 of Libra	7	18 of Taurus
8	7 of Scorpio	8	6 of Gemini
9	19 of Scorpio	9	22 of Gemini
10	1 of Sagittarius	10	6 of Cancer
11	14 of Sagittarius	11	18 of Cancer

OCTOBER 13

A.M.		P.M.	
12 Midnight	5 of Leo	12 Noon	2 of Capricorn
1 o'clock	17 of Leo	1 o'clock	16 of Capricorn
2	29 of Leo	2	3 of Aquarius
3	11 of Virgo	3	23 of Aquarius
4	23 of Virgo	4	16 of Pisces
5	5 of Libra	5	11 of Aries
6	17 of Libra	6	4 of Taurus
7	29 of Libra	7	24 of Taurus
8	11 of Scorpio	8	12 of Gemini
9	23 of Scorpio	9	26 of Gemini
10	6 of Sagittarius	10	10 of Cancer
11	18 of Sagittarius	11	22 of Cancer

OCTOBER 18

A.M.			P.M.		
12 Midnight	9 of Leo		12 Noon	6 of Capricorn	
1 o'clock	21 of Leo		1 o'clock	21 of Capricorn	
2	3 of Virgo		2	9 of Aquarius	
3	15 of Virgo		3	1 of Pisces	
4	27 of Virgo		4	25 of Pisces	
5	9 of Libra		5	19 of Aries	
6	21 of Libra		6	11 of Taurus	
7	3 of Scorpio		7	0 of Gemini	
8	15 of Scorpio		8	17 of Gemini	
9	27 of Scorpio		9	1 of Cancer	
10	10 of Sagittarius		10	14 of Cancer	
11	22 of Sagittarius		11	27 of Cancer	

OCTOBER 23

A.M.			P.M.		
12 Midnight	13 of Leo		12 Noon	11 of Capricorn	
1 o'clock	25 of Leo		1 o'clock	27 of Capricorn	
2	7 of Virgo		2	16 of Aquarius	
3	19 of Virgo		3	8 of Pisces	
4	1 of Libra		4	3 of Aries	
5	13 of Libra		5	27 of Aries	
6	25 of Libra		6	18 of Taurus	
7	7 of Scorpio		7	6 of Gemini	
8	19 of Scorpio		8	22 of Gemini	
9	1 of Sagittarius		9	6 of Cancer	
10	14 of Sagittarius		10	18 of Cancer	
11	27 of Sagittarius		11	1 of Leo	

OCTOBER 28

A.M.			P.M.		
12 Midnight	16 of Leo		12 Noon	16 of Capricorn	
1 o'clock	28 of Leo		1 o'clock	3 of Aquarius	

2	11 of Virgo	2	23 of Aquarius
3	23 of Virgo	3	16 of Pisces
4	5 of Libra	4	10 of Aries
5	17 of Libra	5	4 of Taurus
6	29 of Libra	6	24 of Taurus
7	11 of Scorpio	7	11 of Gemini
8	23 of Scorpio	8	26 of Gemini
9	5 of Sagittarius	9	10 of Cancer
10	18 of Sagittarius	10	22 of Cancer
11	1 of Capricorn	11	4 of Leo

NOVEMBER 2

A.M.		P.M.	
12 Midnight	20 of Leo	12 Noon	21 of Capricorn
1 o'clock	2 of Virgo	1 o'clock	9 of Aquarius
2	15 of Virgo	2	0 of Pisces
3	27 of Virgo	3	24 of Pisces
4	9 of Libra	4	19 of Aries
5	21 of Libra	5	11 of Taurus
6	3 of Scorpio	6	0 of Gemini
7	15 of Scorpio	7	16 of Gemini
8	27 of Scorpio	8	1 of Cancer
9	9 of Sagittarius	9	14 of Cancer
10	22 of Sagittarius	10	26 of Cancer
11	6 of Capricorn	11	8 of Leo

NOVEMBER 7

A.M.		P.M.	
12 Midnight	24 of Leo	12 Noon	27 of Capricorn
1 o'clock	6 of Virgo	1 o'clock	16 of Aquarius
2	19 of Virgo	2	8 of Pisces
3	1 of Libra	3	2 of Aries
4	13 of Libra	4	26 of Aries
5	25 of Libra	5	18 of Taurus
6	7 of Scorpio	6	6 of Gemini
7	19 of Scorpio	7	21 of Gemini

8	1 of Sagittarius	8	5 of Cancer
9	14 of Sagittarius	9	18 of Cancer
10	27 of Sagittarius	10	0 of Leo
11	11 of Capricorn	11	12 of Leo

NOVEMBER 12

A.M.		P.M.	
12 Midnight	28 of Leo	12 Noon	3 of Aquarius
1 o'clock	10 of Virgo	1 o'clock	22 of Aquarius
2	22 of Virgo	2	15 of Pisces
3	5 of Libra	3	10 of Aries
4	17 of Libra	4	3 of Taurus
5	29 of Libra	5	24 of Taurus
6	11 of Scorpio	6	11 of Gemini
7	23 of Scorpio	7	26 of Gemini
8	5 of Sagittarius	8	10 of Cancer
9	18 of Sagittarius	9	22 of Cancer
10	1 of Capricorn	10	4 of Leo
11	16 of Capricorn	11	16 of Leo

NOVEMBER 17

A.M.		P.M.	
12 Midnight	2 of Virgo	12 Noon	9 of Aquarius
1 o'clock	14 of Virgo	1 o'clock	0 of Pisces
2	27 of Virgo	2	24 of Pisces
3	9 of Libra	3	18 of Aries
4	21 of Libra	4	11 of Taurus
5	3 of Scorpio	5	0 of Gemini
6	15 of Scorpio	6	16 of Gemini
7	27 of Scorpio	7	1 of Cancer
8	9 of Sagittarius	8	14 of Cancer
9	22 of Sagittarius	9	26 of Cancer
10	6 of Capricorn	10	8 of Leo
11	21 of Capricorn	11	20 of Leo

NOVEMBER 22

A.M.		P.M.	
12 Midnight	6 of Virgo	12 Noon	15 of Aquarius
1 o'clock	18 of Virgo	1 o'clock	8 of Pisces
2	1 of Libra	2	1 of Aries
3	13 of Libra	3	26 of Aries
4	25 of Libra	4	17 of Taurus
5	7 of Scorpio	5	6 of Gemini
6	19 of Scorpio	6	21 of Gemini
7	1 of Sagittarius	7	5 of Cancer
8	13 of Sagittarius	8	18 of Cancer
9	26 of Sagittarius	9	0 of Leo
10	11 of Capricorn	10	12 of Leo
11	27 of Capricorn	11	24 of Leo

NOVEMBER 27

A.M.		P.M.	
12 Midnight	10 of Virgo	12 Noon	22 of Aquarius
1 o'clock	22 of Virgo	1 o'clock	15 of Pisces
2	4 of Libra	2	9 of Aries
3	17 of Libra	3	3 of Taurus
4	29 of Libra	4	23 of Taurus
5	11 of Scorpio	5	11 of Gemini
6	23 of Scorpio	6	26 of Gemini
7	5 of Sagittarius	7	9 of Cancer
8	17 of Sagittarius	8	22 of Cancer
9	1 of Capricorn	9	4 of Leo
10	15 of Capricorn	10	16 of Leo
11	2 of Aquarius	11	28 of Leo

DECEMBER 2

A.M.		P.M.	
12 Midnight	14 of Virgo	12 Noon	29 of Aquarius
1 o'clock	26 of Virgo	1 o'clock	23 of Pisces

2	9 of Libra	2	17 of Aries
3	21 of Libra	3	10 of Taurus
4	3 of Scorpio	4	0 of Gemini
5	15 of Scorpio	5	16 of Gemini
6	27 of Scorpio	6	0 of Cancer
7	9 of Sagittarius	7	14 of Cancer
8	22 of Sagittarius	8	26 of Cancer
9	5 of Capricorn	9	8 of Leo
10	21 of Capricorn	10	20 of Leo
11	9 of Aquarius	11	2 of Virgo

DECEMBER 7

A.M.		P.M.	
12 Midnight	18 of Virgo	12 Noon	7 of Pisces
1 o'clock	0 of Libra	1 o'clock	1 of Aries
2	13 of Libra	2	25 of Aries
3	25 of Libra	3	17 of Taurus
4	7 of Scorpio	4	5 of Gemini
5	19 of Scorpio	5	21 of Gemini
6	1 of Sagittarius	6	5 of Cancer
7	13 of Sagittarius	7	18 of Cancer
8	26 of Sagittarius	8	0 of Leo
9	10 of Capricorn	9	12 of Leo
10	27 of Capricorn	10	24 of Leo
11	15 of Aquarius	11	6 of Virgo

DECEMBER 12

A.M.		P.M.	
12 Midnight	22 of Virgo	12 Noon	15 of Pisces
1 o'clock	4 of Libra	1 o'clock	9 of Aries
2	17 of Libra	2	3 of Taurus
3	29 of Libra	3	23 of Taurus
4	11 of Scorpio	4	11 of Gemini
5	23 of Scorpio	5	26 of Gemini
6	5 of Sagittarius	6	9 of Cancer
7	17 of Sagittarius	7	22 of Cancer

8	1 of Capricorn	**8**	4 of Leo
9	15 of Capricorn	**9**	16 of Leo
10	2 of Aquarius	**10**	28 of Leo
11	22 of Aquarius	**11**	10 of Virgo

DECEMBER 17

A.M.		**P.M.**	
12 Midnight	26 of Virgo	**12 Noon**	23 of Pisces
1 o'clock	8 of Libra	**1 o'clock**	17 of Aries
2	21 of Libra	**2**	10 of Taurus
3	3 of Scorpio	**3**	29 of Taurus
4	15 of Scorpio	**4**	16 of Gemini
5	27 of Scorpio	**5**	0 of Cancer
6	9 of Sagittarius	**6**	13 of Cancer
7	22 of Sagittarius	**7**	26 of Cancer
8	5 of Capricorn	**8**	8 of Leo
9	20 of Capricorn	**9**	20 of Leo
10	8 of Aquarius	**10**	2 of Virgo
11	29 of Aquarius	**11**	14 of Virgo

DECEMBER 22

A.M.		**P.M.**	
12 Midnight	0 of Libra	**12 Noon**	1 of Aries
1 o'clock	12 of Libra	**1 o'clock**	25 of Aries
2	25 of Libra	**2**	17 of Taurus
3	7 of Scorpio	**3**	5 of Gemini
4	19 of Scorpio	**4**	21 of Gemini
5	1 of Sagittarius	**5**	5 of Cancer
6	13 of Sagittarius	**6**	18 of Cancer
7	26 of Sagittarius	**7**	0 of Leo
8	10 of Capricorn	**8**	12 of Leo
9	26 of Capricorn	**9**	24 of Leo
10	15 of Aquarius	**10**	6 of Virgo
11	7 of Pisces	**11**	18 of Virgo

DECEMBER 27

A.M.			P.M.		
12 Midnight	4 of Libra		12 Noon	9 of Aries	
1 o'clock	16 of Libra		1 o'clock	3 of Taurus	
2	29 of Libra		2	23 of Taurus	
3	11 of Scorpio		3	11 of Gemini	
4	23 of Scorpio		4	26 of Gemini	
5	5 of Sagittarius		5	9 of Cancer	
6	17 of Sagittarius		6	22 of Cancer	
7	0 of Capricorn		7	4 of Leo	
8	15 of Capricorn		8	16 of Leo	
9	2 of Aquarius		9	28 of Leo	
10	22 of Aquarius		10	10 of Virgo	
11	14 of Pisces		11	22 of Virgo	

4

MERCURY
and Your Mind

How does your mind work? Is your intelligence above average? Do you have a remarkable memory? Do you speak and write with ease? Have you a memorable singing voice? The planet you should consult is Mercury. And it is important for every adult who must either use his mind to solve the problems of daily life or to withstand the rigors of a mentally demanding profession to understand the position of Mercury in his particular horoscope.

In ancient Greek mythology, Mercury was the messenger of the gods, the patron of thought and its source, the human mind. Always represented as the slender, winged youth, Mercury had special rulership over young people; when Mercury is prominent in a horoscope, that person has a youthful quality that he retains no matter how old he grows. In Roman times, Mercury became the god of merchants and thieves and was thought to make his subjects glib, quick-witted, adept at bargaining and clever with their hands, qualities also associated in present-day astrology with the planet Mercury.

Mercury, like its namesake, the metallic element quicksilver, is both chameleon-like and volatile. Just as quicksilver takes on the color of the background or object on which it is placed, just as Mercury in a thermometer rises and falls with every temperature change, so Mercury in the human horoscope is the most responsive to its sign position and to the other planets aspecting it.

Mercury rules the mind, the memory, the powers of speech, the nerves, arms, hands and fingers. When prominent in the horoscope, it gives a restless, nervous, high-strung disposition and a very active mind. You need more rest and fresh air than the average person. However, you are more inclined to prefer city life to life in the country.

The last chapter explained how the senses, ruled by the Moon, provide food for the mind. In this chapter, you will see how different minds, represented by different Mercurys, deal with this food—each in his own special way. Lots of people knew about time and space before Einstein, but it was he who evolved the theory of relativity. Abstracting and theorizing from the particular is as much the business of the mind as memory and all the ordinary thought processes necessary for conducting the business of ordinary daily life.

When well aspected, Mercury promises an excellent mind. These people are logical and able to memorize quickly and accurately. When presented with a problem, they immediately begin to observe, to analyze and to deduce. They have the ability to express themselves cogently in speech and writing, and may even go in for public speaking or literature. When concerned with the mechanics of writing instead of the creative part, these people make efficient secretaries and superior typists; their handwriting is legible. Others with favorable Mercury aspects make superior critics, lawyers, scientists, writers, inventors or journalists. A Mercury also rules the voice, a favorable sign and good aspects to Mercury are essential for those who want to sing or act.

A badly aspected Mercury, on the other hand, often causes speech impediments, faulty memory and slow thinking. These people lack the ability to communicate in speech or writing. They do not read easily or efficiently. They probably were indifferent students when they were in school, and later in life they were not able to pick up new subjects on their own. Sometimes, however, these people are perfectly intelligent and well able to speak and write, but they are unpleasantly shrewd and sharp and don't submit to mental discipline or make the most of the abilities they have. They are often unprincipled, argumentative, mean and sly, and whether from thoughtlessness or malice, they are apt to tell tales out of school and even outright lies.

In some cases, they are actually very clever, but tricky and deceitful. Swindlers and forgers are likely to have afflicted Mercurys.

If your father, husband or the other men in your life are highly intelligent, Mercury is quite likely to be in good aspect to the Sun. This is also good for being a clever trader or bargainer and can be a great commercial asset, quickening and sharpening the mind. Mercury does not move far enough from the Sun to form seriously adverse aspects to it.

There is no better promise of a sound intelligent, youthful mother and brainy wife or sweetheart than Mercury in good aspect to the Moon. When Moon-Mercury aspects are adverse, the Mother is apt to be a scold, the wife a nag or else so garrulous that you want to run away. This is not a good influence for your own mind, there being a faulty link between it and your senses. You are inclined to be forgetful, inattentive and loose-tongued.

Mercury in good aspect to Venus gives loving thoughts, beauty of expression and an appreciation of line in art. You approach art with your intellect, and if Mercury is in one of the air signs, especially Libra, you can be a good critic. This is also a good aspect for an artist who specializes in drawings or engravings.

Those of you who have Mercury in good aspect to Mars no doubt find that your mind works smoothly and forcefully and that you are able to convince others of your ideas skillfully. Mercury in bad aspect to Mars makes you argumentative, but a shrewd antagonist in a debate. You tend to be sarcastic and can devastate your opponent with the turn of a phrase.

Mercury in good aspect to Jupiter gives basic good judgment and truthfulness as well as the ability to say the right thing at the right time. Mercury in bad aspect to Jupiter, on the other hand, gives misfortune through bad judgment and tends to make one boast and brag. These people often state things in such a way as to create an erroneous impression, or when they cannot be evasive, they simply lie.

Mercury's favorable aspects to Saturn are the best of all for profound thought. The tendency is to think conservatively and not to accept propositions without having them proven first. Without Saturn aspects to Mercury, one is sometimes gullible. Saturn is such a favorable influence on Mercury that even its bad aspects are in some ways beneficial, insuring the same depth of thought and healthy skepticism as the good aspects, but having the disadvantage of mental depression or pessimism and sometimes causing a speech impediment.

Good Mercury-Uranus aspects make one witty and amusing and often give great originality and inventiveness. You have ideas in advance of your times, and love to meet new people and try out new ideas. Mercury adversely aspecting Uranus gives erratic thought processes and unconventional ideas. Either you stutter when you speak or you are arbitrary and abrupt.

When Mercury favorably aspects Neptune, you may love either to read or write poetry and have a voice that is mellifluous and pleasing. When you express yourself in speech or writing, you choose your words with extraordinary charm and grace. Mercury in adverse aspect to Neptune describes the person whose every word and thought are calculated to deceive. He weaves a spell and creates illusions to make palatable the most dishonest schemes. This is the aspect par excellence of the cad, the confidence man and other tricksters.

You must, of course, figure out for yourself which aspects of Mercury apply to you. But the following describes quite accurately the manner in which your mind works. Consult the descriptions given below to find out in which of the twelve signs of the Zodiac your Mercury is placed and exactly what this means to you.

If your date is mentioned twice, your Mercury is at the end of one sign or the beginning of another. The characteristics of either or both may apply to you.

MERCURY IN ARIES

There is no better position of Mercury for mental strength and brilliance. You are also very original and love new ideas and intellectual adventures. You aren't, however, capable of concentrating on a new idea for very long, but require the constant stimulation of something novel to keep your interest from flagging.

You are witty and amusing, always able to come up with a clever answer and quick repartee. You are capable of directing others because of your originality and ability to think on your feet. You use your mind to control your followers and persuade them to carry out your most daring plans.

You are, however, very impatient of opposition and want your own way immediately. If others do not accept your rules, you do not want to play the game. You can be willful and headstrong. You feel it is your prerogative to dictate the terms, and you do make a very capable executive. If you have other Aries planets, you were surely born to lead. This is also a good position for scientific genius, literature, and conducting an orchestra, army or any other form of leadership.

If afflicted, you may be prone to have bad headaches or even epileptic fits.

March 30, 1890	through	April 14, 1890
March 22, 1891		April 6, 1891
March 13, 1892		March 31, 1892
April 19, 1892		May 15, 1892
March 5, 1893		May 12, 1893
April 16, 1894		May 5, 1894
April 11, 1895		April 27, 1895
April 3, 1896		April 18, 1896
March 26, 1897		April 10, 1897
March 18, 1898		April 2, 1898
March 10, 1899		May 15, 1899
March 3, 1900		March 29, 1900
April 17, 1900		May 10, 1900
April 15, 1901		May 3, 1901
April 9, 1902		April 25, 1902
April 1, 1903		April 16, 1903
March 23, 1904		April 7, 1904
March 15, 1905		April 1, 1905
April 28, 1905		May 15, 1905
March 7, 1906		May 14, 1906
March 3, 1907		March 13, 1907
March 18, 1907		May 8, 1907
April 12, 1908		April 29, 1908
April 5, 1909		April 21, 1909
March 29, 1910		April 12, 1910
March 20, 1911		April 5, 1911
March 11, 1912		May 16, 1912
March 4, 1913		April 7, 1913
April 13, 1913		May 11, 1913
April 16, 1914		May 4, 1914

April 10, 1915	April 26, 1915
April 2, 1916	April 17, 1916
March 25, 1917	April 8, 1917
March 16, 1918	April 2, 1918
March 9, 1919	May 15, 1919
March 2, 1920	March 19, 1920
April 17, 1920	May 8, 1920
April 13, 1921	April 30, 1921
April 7, 1922	April 22, 1922
March 30, 1923	April 14, 1923
March 21, 1924	April 5, 1924
March 13, 1925	April 1, 1925
April 15, 1925	May 16, 1925
March 5, 1926	May 13, 1926
April 17, 1927	May 6, 1927
April 10, 1928	April 27, 1928
April 3, 1929	April 18, 1929
March 26, 1930	April 10, 1930
March 18, 1931	April 3, 1931
March 9, 1932	May 15, 1932
March 3, 1933	March 25, 1933
April 17, 1933	May 10, 1933
April 14, 1934	May 2, 1934
April 8, 1935	April 24, 1935
March 30, 1936	April 14, 1936
March 22, 1937	April 6, 1937
March 14, 1938	April 1, 1938
April 23, 1938	May 16, 1938
March 7, 1939	May 14, 1939
March 4, 1940	March 7, 1940
April 16, 1940	May 6, 1940
April 12, 1941	April 28, 1941
April 5, 1942	April 20, 1942
March 28, 1943	April 11, 1943
March 19, 1944	April 3, 1944
March 11, 1945	May 16, 1945
March 4, 1946	April 1, 1946
April 16, 1946	May 11, 1946
April 15, 1947	May 3, 1947
April 8, 1948	April 24, 1948
April 1, 1949	April 16, 1949

March 24, 1950	April 8, 1950
March 16, 1951	April 1, 1951
May 1, 1951	May 14, 1951
March 7, 1952	May 14, 1952

Famous people with Mercury in Aries

Carol Burnett	Arturo Toscanini
Gregory Peck	Hayley Mills
Shirley MacLaine	Warren Beatty
Albert Einstein	Elizabeth II
Charlie Chaplin	Ann-Margret
Nicolaus Copernicus	Virgil Grissom
Edward Steichen	William Shakespeare
Pat Nixon	Vincent Van Gogh

Adolf Hitler

MERCURY IN TAURUS

Mentally, you are very patient and practical. You are a true conservative, for you tend to adhere to the tenets of your upbringing, to resist all outside influences and to accept only the tried and true. For you there is no test like the test of time.

You stick to your opinions very stubbornly. Once you have decided on an idea or course of action, you are almost never persuaded to change your mind.

While you may have a very fine intellect, you probably learn more from actual experience than from what you read or learned in school. While you are mentally very constructive, you place a high value on having the necessary experience before you attempt a project. Slowly, steadily, surely, you build a solid structure indeed, flattening all opposition as inevitably as a steam roller, nor are you distracted by side issues from your purpose once you have begun.

You have sound ideas in the field of financial management. You tend to have a grasp of money and banking and can be trusted to follow the most conservative policies when handling your own or other people's funds.

You may also be very knowledgeable about collecting art objects, jewelry and other beautiful personal possessions.

Well aspected, this position of Mercury also tends to give a memorable voice. Many of the most successful popular singers have their Mercurys in Taurus.

April 14, 1890	through	April 30, 1890
April 6, 1891		June 13, 1891
March 31, 1892		April 19, 1892
May 15, 1892		June 6, 1892
May 12, 1893		May 29, 1893
May 6, 1894		May 20, 1894
April 28, 1895		May 11, 1895
April 18, 1896		May 3, 1896
April 10, 1897		April 29, 1897
May 22, 1897		June 13, 1897
April 2, 1898		June 10, 1898
May 16, 1899		June 3, 1899
May 10, 1900		May 26, 1900
May 3, 1901		May 17, 1901
April 25, 1902		May 9, 1902
April 16, 1903		May 2, 1903
April 7, 1904		June 13, 1904
April 1, 1905		April 28, 1905
May 15, 1905		June 8, 1905
May 14, 1906		May 31, 1906
May 8, 1907		May 23, 1907
April 29, 1908		May 13, 1908
April 21, 1909		May 5, 1909
April 12, 1910		April 30, 1910
June 1, 1910		June 11, 1910
April 5, 1911		June 12, 1911
May 16, 1912		June 4, 1912
May 12, 1913		May 27, 1913
May 4, 1914		May 19, 1914
April 26, 1915		May 10, 1915
April 17, 1916		May 2, 1916
April 8, 1917		June 14, 1917
April 2, 1918		June 9, 1918
May 15, 1919		June 2, 1919
May 8, 1920		May 23, 1920

May 1, 1921	May 15, 1921
April 22, 1922	May 6, 1922
April 14, 1923	April 30, 1923
April 5, 1924	June 12, 1924
April 1, 1925	April 15, 1925
May 16, 1925	June 6, 1925
May 13, 1926	May 29, 1926
May 6, 1927	May 20, 1927
April 27, 1928	May 11, 1928
April 18, 1929	May 3, 1929
April 10, 1930	April 30, 1930
May 17, 1930	June 14, 1930
April 3, 1931	June 10, 1931
May 15, 1932	June 2, 1932
May 10, 1933	May 25, 1933
May 2, 1934	May 16, 1934
April 24, 1935	May 8, 1935
April 14, 1936	April 30, 1936
April 6, 1937	June 13, 1937
April 1, 1938	April 23, 1938
May 16, 1938	June 7, 1938
May 14, 1939	May 30, 1939
May 6, 1940	May 21, 1940
April 28, 1941	May 12, 1941
April 20, 1942	May 4, 1942
April 11, 1943	April 30, 1943
May 26, 1943	June 13, 1943
April 3, 1944	June 11, 1944
May 16, 1945	June 4, 1945
May 11, 1946	May 26, 1946
May 4, 1947	May 18, 1947
April 24, 1948	May 8, 1948
April 16, 1949	May 1, 1949
April 8, 1950	June 14, 1950
April 1, 1951	May 1, 1951
May 14, 1951	June 9, 1951
May 14, 1952	June 14, 1952

Famous people with Mercury in Taurus

Margot Fonteyn	Joe Namath
Jean-Paul Sartre	J. Robert Oppenheimer

Henry Fonda	Otto Klemperer
Barbra Streisand	Perry Como
Richard Wagner	Bing Crosby
John F. Kennedy	Willem de Kooning
Eddie Arnold	Willie Mays
Hubert Humphrey	Henry Luce
J. William Fulbright	Nikolai Lenin

Edmund Wilson

MERCURY IN GEMINI

As Mercury, the planet of mind, rules the mental sign of Gemini, it is a very strong position for intellectual prowess. You are probably good at mathematics and languages. In some cases, your mind is rather like a calculating machine.

You are very logical, but when you are in an argument, you tend to leave out a basic premise and in that way to come to conclusions that are false. It takes a clever opponent to realize this, however, because the average person will be convinced by your rational remarks.

Nevertheless, you are quick thinkers, and the fact that you love logic makes you excellent teachers, writers, newspapermen, public speakers and lawyers. Where Mercury refers to manual rather than mental dexterity, you may be a good seamstress, secretary or carpenter, or you may excel in some other field where it is important to be clever with your hands. Where Mercury refers to the voice, you may be an excellent singer or actor.

You have a great variety of interests. Your mind flits from one idea to another, and any suggestion starts you out in a new direction. You don't concentrate on any one idea for long.

You have a marked tendency to live too much on an intellectual plane, the mind being stressed above all else. When Mercury is well aspected, few stronger minds exist. When Mercury is afflicted, mental strain can cause nervous breakdowns, and you should try not to worry and overwork.

April 30, 1890	through	July 7, 1890
June 13, 1891		June 30, 1891
June 6, 1892		June 20, 1892

May 29, 1893	June 11, 1893
May 20, 1894	June 3, 1894
May 12, 1895	May 28, 1895
May 3, 1896	July 11, 1896
April 29, 1897	May 21, 1897
June 13, 1897	July 4, 1897
June 10, 1898	June 26, 1898
June 3, 1899	June 17, 1899
May 26, 1900	June 9, 1900
May 17, 1901	June 1, 1901
May 9, 1902	May 29, 1902
June 26, 1902	July 13, 1902
May 2, 1903	July 10, 1903
June 14, 1904	July 1, 1904
June 8, 1905	June 23, 1905
May 31, 1906	June 14, 1906
May 23, 1907	June 6, 1907
May 13, 1908	May 29, 1908
May 5, 1909	July 12, 1909
April 30, 1910	June 1, 1910
June 11, 1910	July 6, 1910
June 12, 1911	June 28, 1911
June 5, 1912	June 19, 1912
May 27, 1913	June 10, 1913
May 19, 1914	June 2, 1914
May 10, 1915	May 29, 1915
May 2, 1916	July 10, 1916
June 14, 1917	July 3, 1917
June 9, 1918	June 24, 1918
June 2, 1919	June 16, 1919
May 23, 1920	June 6, 1920
May 15, 1921	May 30, 1921
May 7, 1922	May 31, 1922
May 10, 1922	July 13, 1922
May 1, 1923	July 8, 1923
June 12, 1924	June 29, 1924
June 6, 1925	June 20, 1925
May 29, 1926	June 12, 1926
May 20, 1927	June 4, 1927
May 11, 1928	May 28, 1928
May 3, 1929	July 11, 1929

May 1, 1930	May 17, 1930
June 14, 1930	July 4, 1930
June 11, 1931	June 26, 1931
June 2, 1932	June 16, 1932
May 25, 1933	June 8, 1933
May 16, 1934	June 1, 1934
May 8, 1935	May 29, 1935
June 20, 1935	July 13, 1935
April 30, 1936	July 8, 1936
June 13, 1937	June 30, 1937
June 7, 1938	June 22, 1938
May 30, 1939	June 13, 1939
May 21, 1940	June 4, 1940
May 12, 1941	May 29, 1941
May 4, 1942	July 12, 1942
April 30, 1943	May 26, 1943
June 13, 1943	July 6, 1943
June 11, 1944	June 26, 1944
June 4, 1945	June 18, 1945
May 26, 1946	June 9, 1946
May 18, 1947	June 2, 1947
May 9, 1948	May 28, 1948
June 28, 1948	July 11, 1948
May 1, 1949	July 9, 1949
June 14, 1950	July 2, 1950
June 9, 1951	June 23, 1951
June 14, 1952	June 30, 1952

Famous people with Mercury in Gemini

Audrey Hepburn	Harry Truman
Françoise Sagan	Robert McNamara
Steve Lawrence	Bob Hope
Bobby Darin	James A. McDivitt
James Arness	Paul McCartney
Dean Martin	Laurence Rockefeller
William Styron	John Wayne

Julie Nixon Eisenhower

MERCURY IN CANCER

You are not original like Mercury in Aries, stable like Mercury in Taurus or logical like a Gemini Mercury, but you have a kind of sixth sense and your intuition is unbeatable. You can be sure of something without exactly knowing how you know.

You may, however, be somewhat passive mentally. Only when someone argues with you do you resent it. An appeal to the senses and not logic influences you.

If your Mercury is badly aspected, your memory may be poor, but if it is well aspected, few better memories exist, especially for names, dates and historical events. You love to refer to the past, and your answer to a present-day problem is to quote a precedent from antiquity rather than dealing with the circumstances at hand. This may be an asset for the kind of lawyer whose case rests primarily on research rather than requiring reasoning powers and more aggressive traits of mind. It is also good for scholars, historians and antique dealers. Some of the most knowledgeable collectors come under this influence owing to a deep appreciation of artifacts and relics of the past.

You are very sensitive to other people and to your surroundings. Yet, while you are kind and very sympathetic, you cannot tolerate being with uncongenial people. You are, however, very tolerant of other people's ideas.

Unless there are strengthening aspects to Mercury, this is not a good position for mental vigor, the mind being inactive and overly impressionable.

July 8, 1890	through	July 22, 1890
June 30, 1891		July 14, 1891
June 20, 1892		July 5, 1892
June 12, 1893		June 28, 1893
June 4, 1894		June 26, 1894
July 18, 1894		August 11, 1894
May 29, 1895		August 5, 1895
July 11, 1896		July 27, 1896
July 4, 1897		July 18, 1897

June 26, 1898	July 10, 1898
June 17, 1899	July 2, 1899
June 9, 1900	June 27, 1900
June 1, 1901	August 9, 1901
May 29, 1902	June 25, 1902
July 13, 1902	August 2, 1902
July 10, 1903	July 25, 1903
July 1, 1904	July 15, 1904
June 23, 1905	July 7, 1905
June 14, 1906	June 30, 1906
June 6, 1907	June 27, 1907
June 26, 1907	August 12, 1907
May 29, 1908	August 6, 1908
July 13, 1909	July 29, 1909
July 6, 1910	July 21, 1910
June 28, 1911	July 12, 1911
June 19, 1912	July 4, 1912
June 10, 1913	June 27, 1913
June 3, 1914	August 10, 1914
May 29, 1915	August 4, 1915
July 10, 1916	July 25, 1916
July 3, 1917	July 17, 1917
June 24, 1918	July 9, 1918
June 16, 1919	July 1, 1919
June 6, 1920	June 26, 1920
August 2, 1920	August 10, 1920
May 30, 1921	August 7, 1921
May 31, 1922	June 10, 1922
July 13, 1922	July 31, 1922
July 8, 1923	July 22, 1923
June 29, 1924	July 13, 1924
June 20, 1925	July 5, 1925
June 12, 1926	June 28, 1926
June 4, 1927	June 28, 1927
July 13, 1927	August 11, 1927
May 28, 1928	August 4, 1928
July 11, 1929	July 27, 1929
July 4, 1930	July 18, 1930
June 26, 1931	July 10, 1931
June 16, 1932	July 2, 1932
June 8, 1933	June 26, 1933

June 1, 1934	August 9, 1934
May 29, 1935	June 20, 1935
July 13, 1935	August 1, 1935
July 8, 1936	July 23, 1936
June 30, 1937	July 14, 1937
June 22, 1938	July 6, 1938
June 13, 1939	June 30, 1939
June 4, 1940	June 26, 1940
July 20, 1940	August 11, 1940
May 29, 1941	August 5, 1941
July 12, 1942	July 28, 1942
July 6, 1943	July 29, 1943
June 26, 1944	July 11, 1944
June 18, 1945	July 3, 1945
June 9, 1946	June 27, 1946
June 2, 1947	August 10, 1947
May 28, 1948	June 28, 1948
July 11, 1948	August 2, 1948
July 9, 1949	July 24, 1949
July 2, 1950	July 16, 1950
June 23, 1951	July 8, 1951
June 30, 1952	September 7, 1952

Famous people with Mercury in Cancer

Prince Philip	Van Cliburn
Leslie Caron	Paul Anka
Nelson Rockefeller	Mary McCarthy
Igor Stravinsky	Luci Baines Johnson Nugent
Thomas Mann	David Rockefeller

MERCURY IN LEO

This is an excellent position for Mercury. Mercury rules the mind; Leo, the heart—and the combination is unbeatable. It gives you the human touch as well as a sound, impressive intellect. Your mind works in a manner that would be sympathetic and emotionally satisfying to the majority of people.

Despite your fine mind, you would never be an intellectual in an ivory tower. You love people too much. You are more inclined to be a leader in the affairs of the world, deserving of your followers' affection, loyalty and respect. You are indeed well fitted to command.

You may, however, be angry when you don't get your own way. You are a born leader and you consider others' obedience your just due. You vindicate yourself with a flourish, and are noble and forgiving once the opposition has been put in its place.

You may tend to be proud and even a bit boastful. You are often ostentatious and like to impress others with your accomplishments. You do not conceive your plans on a small scale but in the grand manner. You are a natural showman with an instinct for spectacular display.

This is a good position for having not only a popular singing voice but also the personal charisma to go with it. Your public speeches, acting or writing can win you others' admiration and love. And if you do not actually perform, your ability to plan and direct popular entertainments can make you very successful indeed.

July 22, 1890	through	August 7, 1890
July 14, 1891		July 31, 1891
July 5, 1892		July 25, 1892
August 30, 1892		September 9, 1892
June 28, 1893		September 5, 1893
June 27, 1894		July 17, 1894
August 11, 1894		August 28, 1894
August 5, 1895		August 20, 1895
July 27, 1896		August 11, 1896
July 18, 1897		August 3, 1897
July 10, 1898		July 28, 1898
July 2, 1899		July 26, 1899
August 14, 1899		September 9, 1899
June 27, 1900		September 2, 1900
August 10, 1901		August 25, 1901
August 2, 1902		August 17, 1902
July 25, 1903		August 9, 1903
July 15, 1904		August 1, 1904
July 7, 1905		July 27, 1905
June 30, 1906		September 7, 1906
June 27, 1907		July 26, 1907
August 12, 1907		August 30, 1907
August 6, 1908		August 21, 1908

July 29, 1909	August 13, 1909
July 21, 1910	August 5, 1910
July 12, 1911	July 30, 1911
July 4, 1912	July 26, 1912
August 21, 1912	September 10, 1912
June 27, 1913	September 4, 1913
August 11, 1914	August 27, 1914
August 4, 1915	August 18, 1915
July 25, 1916	August 9, 1916
July 17, 1917	August 2, 1917
July 8, 1918	July 27, 1918
July 1, 1919	September 8, 1919
June 26, 1920	August 2, 1920
August 10, 1920	August 31, 1920
August 8, 1921	August 23, 1921
July 31, 1922	August 15, 1922
July 22, 1923	August 7, 1923
July 13, 1924	July 30, 1924
July 5, 1925	July 26, 1925
August 27, 1925	September 10, 1925
June 28, 1926	September 5, 1926
June 28, 1927	July 13, 1927
August 11, 1927	August 28, 1927
August 4, 1928	August 19, 1928
July 27, 1929	August 11, 1929
July 18, 1930	August 3, 1930
July 10, 1931	July 28, 1931
July 2, 1932	July 27, 1932
August 10, 1932	September 8, 1932
May 26, 1933	September 1, 1933
August 9, 1934	August 24, 1934
August 1, 1935	August 16, 1935
July 23, 1936	August 7, 1936
July 14, 1937	July 31, 1937
July 6, 1938	July 26, 1938
September 2, 1938	September 10, 1938
June 30, 1939	September 6, 1939
June 26, 1940	July 20, 1940
August 11, 1940	August 29, 1940
August 5, 1941	August 20, 1941
July 28, 1942	August 12, 1942

July 20, 1943	August 5, 1943
July 11, 1944	July 28, 1944
July 3, 1945	July 26, 1945
August 17, 1945	September 10, 1945
June 27, 1946	September 3, 1946
August 10, 1947	August 26, 1947
August 2, 1948	August 17, 1948
July 24, 1949	August 9, 1949
July 16, 1950	August 1, 1950
July 8, 1951	July 27, 1951
September 7, 1952	September 7, 1952

Famous people with Mercury in Leo

Jacqueline Kennedy Onassis	Benito Mussolini
Ernest Hemingway	Louis Armstrong (Sachmo)
Napoleon Bonaparte	Fidel Castro
Ringo Starr	Marc Chagall
Jimmy Dean	Casey Stengel
Eddie Fisher	Anne-Marie of Greece
Tex Thornton	Peter Duchin
Merv Griffin	Paul Tillich

MERCURY IN VIRGO

This is a strong position for Mercury, but it is primarily an intellectual one. Your approach is that of pure reason, so much so that you often forget to take human failings into consideration. Most of you are therefore better at solving abstract problems than those involving flesh-and-blood people, and you must always guard against expecting reality to conform to your theories about life. Some of you, however, understand human feelings with your mind but not with your emotions so that you can handle others in a practical but somewhat impersonal way.

Your detachment from emotional considerations can make you an excellent scientist. The same quality is also good for doctors or nurses as it makes them thorough, efficient and careful though not inclined to give their patients a lot of sympathy. This position is good for dieticians as well.

Despite its intellectual prowess, Mercury in Virgo can be a sign of practicality and a down-to-earth quality. Some of these people make the kind of farmers who use and understand the most up-to-date agricultural methods. They can also make excellent secretaries or succeed in other fields where it is necessary to be well organized or clever with their hands.

You may also be a good lawyer although you are not as adept at argument as Mercury in Gemini. Your attention to detail may, in fact, make you a bit tedious in speech and writing.

You learn so easily, you often forget what you have learned in short order. But you have a fine mind and could make an excellent writer, critic and language student, and can do well in any field where being analytical is an asset. You tend, however, to be very critical, and you have little tolerance for slow-witted people.

August 7, 1890	through	August 27, 1890
July 31, 1891		October 7, 1891
July 25, 1892		August 29, 1892
September 10, 1892		September 29, 1892
September 5, 1893		September 21, 1893
August 28, 1894		September 13, 1894
August 20, 1895		September 6, 1895
August 11, 1896		August 29, 1896
August 3, 1897		August 25, 1897
September 22, 1897		October 10, 1897
July 28, 1898		October 4, 1898
July 26, 1899		August 14, 1899
September 9, 1899		September 26, 1899
September 2, 1900		September 18, 1900
August 25, 1901		September 10, 1901
August 17, 1902		September 3, 1902
August 9, 1903		August 28, 1903
August 1, 1904		August 28, 1904
September 7, 1904		October 8, 1904
July 27, 1905		October 1, 1905
September 7, 1906		September 23, 1906
August 31, 1907		September 15, 1907
August 21, 1908		September 7, 1908
August 13, 1909		August 31, 1909
August 5, 1910		August 26, 1910

September 28, 1910   October 11, 1910
July 30, 1911   October 6, 1911
July 26, 1912   August 20, 1912
September 10, 1912   September 27, 1912
September 4, 1913   September 20, 1913
August 27, 1914   September 12, 1914
August 19, 1915   September 5, 1915
August 9, 1916   August 28, 1916
August 2, 1917   August 26, 1917
September 14, 1917   October 9, 1917
July 24, 1918   October 2, 1918
September 8, 1919   September 25, 1919
August 31, 1920   September 16, 1920
August 23, 1921   September 8, 1921
August 15, 1922   September 1, 1922
August 7, 1923   August 27, 1923
October 4, 1923   October 11, 1923
July 30, 1924   October 6, 1924
July 26, 1925   August 26, 1925
September 10, 1925   September 29, 1925
September 5, 1926   September 21, 1926
August 28, 1927   September 13, 1927
August 19, 1928   September 5, 1928
August 11, 1929   August 29, 1929
August 3, 1930   August 26, 1930
September 19, 1930   October 10, 1930
July 28, 1931   October 4, 1931
July 27, 1932   August 9, 1932
September 9, 1932   September 25, 1932
September 2, 1933   September 17, 1933
August 24, 1934   September 10, 1934
August 16, 1935   September 3, 1935
August 7, 1936   August 27, 1936
July 31, 1937   October 8, 1937
July 26, 1938   September 2, 1938
September 10, 1938   September 30, 1938
September 6, 1939   September 22, 1939
August 29, 1940   September 14, 1940
August 20, 1941   September 6, 1941
August 12, 1942   August 31, 1942
August 5, 1943   August 26, 1943

September 25, 1943   October 11, 1943
July 28, 1944   October 4, 1944
July 26, 1945   August 17, 1945
September 10, 1945   September 27, 1945
September 3, 1946   September 19, 1946
August 26, 1947   September 11, 1947
August 17, 1948   September 3, 1948
August 9, 1949   August 28, 1949
August 1, 1950   August 27, 1950
September 10, 1950   October 9, 1950
July 27, 1951   October 2, 1951
September 7, 1952   September 23, 1952

Famous people with Mercury in Virgo

Lyndon B. Johnson   Dag Hammarskjold
Princess Margaret Rose   Douglas Dillon
Vladimir Horowitz   Lucille Ball
William Faulkner   Dr. Ralph Bunche
Anne Bancroft   James Baldwin
Percy B. Shelley   Alan Jay Lerner
Leo Tolstoi   Ben Hogan
Leonard Bernstein   Geraldine Chaplin
Truman Capote   Princess Anne
Pope Paul VI   Romy Schneider
Greta Garbo   Mike Douglas
Eero Saarinen

MERCURY IN LIBRA

Primarily, you are concerned with deciding what is just and right. But your mind is in so delicate a balance that you find it difficult to commit yourself to a course of action. You weigh each consideration carefully, then find that it is hard to choose. When after very thorough, accurate study you finally come to a conclusion, you may change your mind abruptly without anything to explain the change.

Sometimes, though, in a flash, you know the answer to a problem, but then you try to reason logically and are led astray. It is best for you to learn to follow your intuition. You can achieve a lot that way.

Intellectually, you are very ambitious, but you often shrink back from doing the hard work necessary for success. If you are not careful, you may know a little bit about a lot of things and not a great deal about any one.

When the rest of the horoscope indicates forcefulness, Mercury in Libra adds to it a precision of judgment that is hard to beat. Usually, these people have capable, sensitive minds which can be successful in so many different fields that it is hard to judge without taking into consideration the whole horoscope. When the position is well aspected, there is much real wisdom; badly aspected, a superficial, frivolous mind.

August 27, 1890	through	November 1, 1890
October 7, 1891		October 25, 1891
September 29, 1892		October 16, 1892
September 21, 1893		October 9, 1893
September 13, 1894		October 2, 1894
September 6, 1895		September 27, 1895
October 27, 1895		November 11, 1895
August 29, 1896		November 5, 1896
August 25, 1897		September 21, 1897
October 10, 1897		October 29, 1897
October 4, 1898		October 21, 1898
September 26, 1899		October 14, 1899
September 18, 1900		October 7, 1900
September 11, 1901		September 30, 1901
September 3, 1902		September 28, 1902
September 15, 1902		November 10, 1902
August 29, 1903		November 3, 1903
August 28, 1904		September 7, 1904
October 8, 1904		October 26, 1904
October 1, 1905		October 19, 1905
September 23, 1906		October 11, 1906
September 16, 1907		October 4, 1907
September 7, 1908		September 28, 1908
November 1, 1908		November 11, 1908
August 31, 1909		November 7, 1909
August 27, 1910		September 28, 1910
October 12, 1910		October 31, 1910
October 6, 1911		October 23, 1911

September 28, 1912	October 16, 1912
September 20, 1913	October 8, 1913
September 12, 1914	October 1, 1914
September 5, 1915	September 28, 1915
October 20, 1915	November 11, 1915
August 28, 1916	November 4, 1916
August 26, 1917	September 14, 1917
October 9, 1917	October 27, 1917
October 2, 1918	October 20, 1918
September 25, 1919	October 13, 1919
September 16, 1920	October 5, 1920
September 8, 1921	September 29, 1921
September 1, 1922	October 1, 1922
October 4, 1922	November 8, 1922
August 27, 1923	October 4, 1923
October 11, 1923	November 1, 1923
October 6, 1924	October 24, 1924
September 29, 1925	October 16, 1925
September 21, 1926	October 9, 1926
September 13, 1927	October 3, 1927
September 5, 1928	September 27, 1928
October 24, 1928	November 11, 1928
August 30, 1929	November 5, 1929
August 26, 1930	September 19, 1930
October 10, 1930	October 29, 1930
October 4, 1931	October 21, 1931
September 25, 1932	October 13, 1932
September 17, 1933	October 6, 1933
September 10, 1934	September 30, 1934
September 3, 1935	September 28, 1935
October 12, 1935	November 9, 1935
August 27, 1936	November 2, 1936
October 8, 1937	October 25, 1937
September 30, 1938	October 18, 1938
September 22, 1939	October 10, 1939
September 14, 1940	October 3, 1940
September 6, 1941	September 28, 1941
October 29, 1941	November 11, 1941
August 31, 1942	November 6, 1942
August 27, 1943	September 25, 1943
October 11, 1943	October 30, 1943

October 4, 1944	October 22, 1944
September 27, 1945	October 14, 1945
September 19, 1946	October 7, 1946
September 11, 1947	October 1, 1947
September 3, 1948	September 27, 1948
October 16, 1948	November 9, 1948
August 28, 1949	November 3, 1949
August 27, 1950	September 10, 1950
October 9, 1950	October 27, 1950
October 2, 1951	October 19, 1951
September 23, 1952	October 11, 1952

Famous people with Mercury in Libra

Dwight David Eisenhower	Queen Elizabeth I
Henry Ford II	Savonarola
David McCallum	Arnold Palmer
Paul Kruger	Al Capp
Margaret Chase Smith	C. P. Snow

MERCURY IN SCORPIO

You have a shrewd, sharp powerful mind and remarkably clear foresight and vision. You cannot be deceived, perhaps because you are often so devious yourself that you are swift to sense another's motives. You are intensely critical and subject those with whom you come in contact to a pitiless examination.

Indeed, you make a dangerous opponent. Once you have entered into a fight, you have neither scruples in your own actions nor pity for your opponent. You are both vicious and vengeful. You will do anything no matter how unfair and underhanded in an effort to defeat and humiliate an adversary.

You are equally ruthless with your remarks. You think quickly and are never at a loss for words. In fact, when the occasion arises, you can wield words like a lethal weapon. Your ability to insinuate is diabolical. You instinctively sense another's most vulnerable points and know how to destroy him utterly.

The higher types use this ability in worthy ways and are generally very high-principled. The lower types can be arrogant and intolerant. They look down upon anyone who differs with them.

You know how to dissimulate and can deceive others for long periods. You are both secretive and good at ferreting out others' secrets. You therefore make excellent detectives, police investigators and spies, or else avid detective-story readers.

When the mind is possessed of all the higher qualities of Mercury in Scorpio, it can be brilliant, penetrating and determined, able to fight for a noble cause, engage in medical research or investigate the mysteries of the universe and human life.

November 1, 1890	through	November 20, 1890
October 25, 1891		November 12, 1891
October 16, 1892		November 5, 1892
October 9, 1893		October 30, 1893
November 29, 1893		December 12, 1893
October 2, 1894		December 8, 1894
September 27, 1895		October 27, 1895
November 11, 1895		December 2, 1895
November 5, 1896		November 23, 1896
October 29, 1897		November 16, 1897
October 21, 1898		November 9, 1898
October 14, 1899		November 3, 1899
October 7, 1900		October 30, 1900
November 19, 1900		December 12, 1900
October 1, 1901		December 6, 1901
September 28, 1902		October 15, 1902
November 10, 1902		November 29, 1902
November 4, 1903		November 22, 1903
October 26, 1904		November 14, 1904
October 19, 1905		November 7, 1905
October 11, 1906		November 1, 1906
December 6, 1906		December 12, 1906
October 4, 1907		December 10, 1907
September 28, 1908		November 1, 1908
November 11, 1908		December 3, 1908
November 7, 1909		November 26, 1909
October 31, 1910		November 19, 1910
October 24, 1911		November 11, 1911
October 16, 1912		November 4, 1912

October 8, 1913	October 30, 1913
November 23, 1913	December 13, 1913
October 2, 1914	December 7, 1914
September 28, 1915	October 20, 1915
November 11, 1915	December 1, 1915
November 4, 1916	November 22, 1916
October 27, 1917	November 15, 1917
October 29, 1918	November 8, 1918
October 13, 1919	November 2, 1919
October 5, 1920	October 30, 1920
November 10, 1920	December 10, 1920
September 29, 1921	December 4, 1921
October 1, 1922	October 4, 1922
November 8, 1922	November 27, 1922
November 1, 1923	November 20, 1923
October 24, 1924	November 12, 1924
October 16, 1925	November 5, 1925
October 9, 1926	October 31, 1926
November 27, 1926	December 13, 1926
October 3, 1927	December 9, 1927
September 27, 1928	October 24, 1928
November 11, 1928	December 1, 1928
November 5, 1929	November 24, 1929
October 29, 1930	November 16, 1930
October 21, 1931	November 9, 1931
October 13, 1932	November 2, 1932
October 6, 1933	October 30, 1933
November 15, 1933	December 11, 1933
September 30, 1934	December 5, 1934
September 28, 1935	October 12, 1935
November 9, 1935	November 28, 1935
November 2, 1936	November 20, 1936
October 25, 1937	November 13, 1937
October 18, 1938	November 6, 1938
October 10, 1939	November 1, 1939
December 2, 1939	December 13, 1939
October 3, 1940	December 9, 1940
September 28, 1941	October 29, 1941
November 11, 1941	December 2, 1941
November 6, 1942	November 25, 1942
October 30, 1943	November 18, 1943

October 22, 1944   November 10, 1944
October 14, 1945   November 3, 1945
October 7, 1946   October 30, 1946
November 20, 1946   December 12, 1946
October 1, 1947   December 7, 1947
September 27, 1948   October 16, 1948
November 9, 1948   November 29, 1948
November 3, 1949   November 22, 1949
October 27, 1950   November 14, 1950
October 19, 1951   November 7, 1951
October 11, 1952   November 1, 1952

Famous people with Mercury in Scorpio

Ed Sullivan   Felix Frankfurter
Walt Disney   Johnny Carson
Pablo Picasso   Billy Graham
Winston Churchill   Jonas Salk
Robert Louis Stevenson   Prince Charles
Mark Twain   John Lindsay
Oscar Wilde   Pope John XXIII
Martin Luther   John F. Kennedy, Jr.
Helen Hayes   Juan Peron
Le Corbusier   Leon Trotsky
                Mohandas K. Gandhi

MERCURY IN SAGITTARIUS

Your mind is swift and brilliant, but unless Mercury is remarkably well aspected, you do not have the ability to concentrate deeply for long periods of time. Reason and memory are not your strong points. Your ideas tend to be disconnected; you lack mental poise and balance. But Jupiter's influence on this sign tends to improve the judgment. You rarely go wrong following your hunches. Indeed, your intuition is hard to beat.

At heart you are very honest and would never mislead anyone knowingly. You are forthright, direct and guileless. You like to tell the truth. So much so that you tend to say exactly what comes into your mind without pausing to think it over or to consider its effect on other people, and you are surprised when others react and you have to take the consequences. If you should lie, you would do so impulsively. You would not be able to deceive others for any length of time.

You do not deliberately hurt people with your remarks like Mercury in Scorpio. When you do hurt them, you are sorry about it later, but you just don't stop to think. You often interrupt yourself or others in order to relate a thought the very moment it occurs to you.

You may find that it is difficult for you to weigh one idea against another and come up with a result. If you like to write you would be better at short stories than something of novel length. Your style is breezy. Your letters tend to be like telegrams.

November 20, 1890	through	December 9, 1890
November 13, 1891		December 3, 1891
January 3, 1892		January 13, 1892
November 5, 1892		January 10, 1893
October 30, 1893		November 29, 1893
December 12, 1893		January 4, 1894
December 8, 1894		December 28, 1894
December 2, 1895		December 21, 1895
November 24, 1896		December 13, 1896
November 16, 1897		December 6, 1897
November 9, 1898		November 30, 1898
December 22, 1898		January 13, 1899
November 3, 1899		January 8, 1900
October 30, 1900		November 18, 1900
December 12, 1900		January 2, 1901
December 6, 1901		December 26, 1901
November 29, 1902		December 18, 1902
November 22, 1903		December 11, 1903
November 14, 1904		December 4, 1904
November 7, 1905		December 1, 1905
December 9, 1905		January 12, 1906
November 1, 1906		December 6, 1906
December 12, 1906		January 6, 1907
December 10, 1907		December 30, 1907
December 3, 1908		December 22, 1908
November 26, 1909		December 15, 1909
November 19, 1910		December 8, 1910

November 11, 1911	December 2, 1911
December 27, 1911	January 14, 1912
November 4, 1912	January 9, 1913
October 30, 1913	November 23, 1913
December 13, 1913	January 3, 1914
December 7, 1914	December 27, 1914
December 1, 1915	December 20, 1915
November 22, 1916	December 11, 1916
November 15, 1917	December 5, 1917
November 8, 1918	December 1, 1918
December 15, 1918	January 13, 1919
November 2, 1919	January 7, 1920
October 30, 1920	November 10, 1920
December 10, 1920	December 31, 1920
December 4, 1921	December 23, 1921
November 27, 1922	December 16, 1922
November 20, 1923	December 9, 1923
November 12, 1924	December 2, 1924
December 31, 1924	January 13, 1925
November 5, 1925	January 10, 1926
October 31, 1926	November 27, 1926
December 13, 1926	January 4, 1927
December 9, 1927	December 29, 1927
December 1, 1928	December 20, 1928
November 24, 1929	December 13, 1929
November 16, 1930	December 6, 1930
November 9, 1931	December 1, 1931
December 20, 1931	January 14, 1932
November 2, 1932	January 8, 1933
October 30, 1933	November 15, 1933
December 11, 1933	January 1, 1934
December 5, 1934	December 25, 1934
November 29, 1935	December 18, 1935
November 20, 1936	December 9, 1936
November 13, 1937	December 3, 1937
January 6, 1938	January 12, 1938
November 6, 1938	January 11, 1939
November 1, 1939	December 2, 1939
December 13, 1939	January 6, 1940
December 9, 1940	December 29, 1940
December 2, 1941	December 21, 1941

November 25, 1942	December 14, 1942
November 18, 1943	December 7, 1943
November 10, 1944	December 1, 1944
December 23, 1944	January 13, 1945
November 3, 1945	January 9, 1946
October 30, 1946	November 20, 1946
December 12, 1946	January 2, 1947
December 7, 1947	December 26, 1947
November 29, 1948	December 18, 1948
November 22, 1949	December 11, 1949
November 14, 1950	December 4, 1950
November 7, 1951	December 1, 1951
December 12, 1951	January 12, 1952
November 1, 1952	December 31, 1952

Famous people with Mercury in Sagittarius

Lady Bird Johnson	Chiang Kai-Shek
Joan Sutherland	Andy Williams
Rudyard Kipling	J. Paul Getty
Marie Antoinette	Sammy Davis, Jr.
Sir Isaac Newton	J. D. Salinger
Joan of Arc	Rock Hudson
Robert F. Kennedy	Charles de Gaulle
Petula Clark	Jule Styne
Patty Duke	Caroline Kennedy
Frank Sinatra	John Osborne
Willy Brandt	Eugene Ionesco

MERCURY IN CAPRICORN

You have a profound mind—very steady, serious and sincere. You are capable of meditating deeply for long periods of time. Although you are very thorough when it comes to detail, you never lose sight of the whole. Because you are so responsible and wise, you may inspire others to look up to you. For this reason, when you are young, you may seem older than you really are.

In any event, you must guard against appearing to hand down dictums when you express yourself. Your outlook is moral; your manner, dignified. Unless Mercury is softened by some aspect of Jupiter or Venus, this position might detract from your popularity and give you a somewhat narrow and pedantic point of view.

Your memory is excellent. Like the elephant, you never forget. If someone offends you once, he never gets a second chance, particularly if you feel that he was laughing at you. Sometimes you take yourself so seriously that you may be annoyed by what you consider the frivolity of other people. You don't mind being alone and are quite capable of amusing yourself.

You are very suspicious and you examine facts with the utmost care. You are a firm believer in cause and effect. You should try, however, to be more optimistic and cheerful because you have a pronounced tendency to be pessimistic, fearful or depressed.

You would make an excellent statesman, since you can be very diplomatic. However, in a position of responsibility, you may also tend to be authoritarian. You should make an effort to be more tolerant. You are always so sure of being right that you may not listen to the other side of the question. You are not critical so much as disapproving when others don't agree with you.

January 1, 1890	through	January 4, 1890
December 9, 1890		January 2, 1891
January 7, 1891		February 13, 1891
December 3, 1891		January 3, 1892
January 13, 1892		February 7, 1892
January 10, 1893		January 30, 1893
January 4, 1894		January 23, 1894
December 28, 1894		January 16, 1895
December 21, 1895		January 8, 1896
December 13, 1896		January 1, 1897
January 24, 1897		February 14, 1897
December 6, 1897		February 10, 1898
December 1, 1898		December 21, 1898
January 31, 1899		February 4, 1899
January 8, 1900		January 29, 1900
January 2, 1901		January 20, 1901
December 26, 1901		January 13, 1902
December 18, 1902		January 6, 1903
December 11, 1903		January 2, 1904

January 13, 1904	February 15, 1904
December 4, 1904	February 8, 1905
December 2, 1905	December 9, 1905
January 12, 1906	February 2, 1906
January 6, 1907	January 25, 1907
December 30, 1907	January 18, 1908
December 22, 1908	January 10, 1909
December 15, 1909	January 3, 1910
January 30, 1910	February 15, 1910
December 8, 1910	February 12, 1911
December 2, 1911	December 27, 1911
January 14, 1912	February 6, 1912
January 9, 1913	January 29, 1913
January 3, 1914	January 22, 1914
December 27, 1914	January 14, 1915
December 20, 1915	January 7, 1916
December 12, 1916	January 1, 1917
January 17, 1917	February 14, 1917
December 5, 1917	February 10, 1918
December 1, 1918	December 15, 1918
January 13, 1919	February 3, 1919
January 7, 1920	January 27, 1920
December 31, 1920	January 18, 1921
December 24, 1921	January 11, 1922
December 16, 1922	January 4, 1923
February 6, 1923	February 13, 1923
December 9, 1923	February 13, 1924
December 2, 1924	December 31, 1924
January 14, 1925	February 6, 1925
January 11, 1926	January 31, 1926
January 4, 1927	January 23, 1927
December 29, 1927	January 16, 1928
December 20, 1928	January 8, 1929
December 13, 1929	January 2, 1930
January 22, 1930	February 15, 1930
December 6, 1930	February 11, 1931
December 1, 1931	December 19, 1931
January 14, 1932	February 4, 1932
January 8, 1933	January 27, 1933
January 1, 1934	January 20, 1934
December 25, 1934	January 12, 1935

December 18, 1935	January 5, 1936
December 10, 1936	January 1, 1937
January 9, 1937	February 13, 1937
December 3, 1937	January 6, 1938
January 12, 1938	February 8, 1938
January 12, 1939	February 1, 1939
January 6, 1940	January 25, 1940
December 29, 1940	January 16, 1941
December 21, 1941	January 9, 1942
December 14, 1942	January 3, 1943
January 27, 1943	February 15, 1943
December 7, 1943	February 12, 1944
December 1, 1944	December 23, 1944
January 13, 1945	February 5, 1945
January 9, 1946	January 29, 1946
January 2, 1947	January 21, 1947
December 26, 1947	January 13, 1948
December 18, 1948	January 6, 1949
December 11, 1949	January 1, 1950
January 15, 1950	February 14, 1950
December 4, 1950	February 9, 1951
December 1, 1951	December 12, 1951
January 13, 1952	February 3, 1952

Famous people with Mercury in Capricorn

Cary Grant	Joan Baez
Lewis Carroll	Barry Goldwater
Edgar Allan Poe	Henri Matisse
Lord Byron	Jack Nicklaus
Louis Pasteur	Shelley Berman
Douglas MacArthur	Pablo Casals
Danny Kaye	Margaret Chase Smith
Everett Dirksen	Richard Nixon
Ronald Reagan	W. C. Fields

MERCURY IN AQUARIUS

You are a true humanitarian and an excellent judge of human nature. Your interest in other people is often unselfish and impersonal. You love to analyze character—everyone from the most casual acquaintance to those near and dear. You are even interested in total strangers and may like to watch them in public places or eavesdrop on the next table in a restaurant.

You may also be interested in astrology because of the psychological insights it gives you. You have a fine mind, with the ability to concentrate. You are logical and analytical, resourceful and ingenious, and you have a driving passion for the truth.

In an argument, you are a formidable adversary, able to see both sides of a question, sophisticated in your approach. You frequently enter into debates on controversial subjects as an opportunity to exercise your wits. You do just that, but would never go to extremes.

You are an excellent student. Your powers of observation are tremendous and you have vision. You intuitively know what people are and how they will behave, and you can predict the outcome of actions and situations with astonishing accuracy. You understand so much, in fact, that it is a shame that, in most cases, you lack an artistic imagination. No matter how exalted your idea, it tends to sound ordinary or trite when you express it.

January 4, 1890	through	March 12, 1890
January 2, 1891		January 6, 1891
February 13, 1891		March 5, 1891
February 7, 1892		February 26, 1892
January 31, 1893		February 17, 1893
January 23, 1894		February 9, 1894
January 16, 1895		February 2, 1895
March 4, 1895		March 17, 1895
January 8, 1896		March 15, 1896
January 1, 1897		January 24, 1897
February 14, 1897		March 9, 1897
February 10, 1898		March 2, 1898
February 4, 1899		February 22, 1899
January 29, 1900		February 14, 1900
January 21, 1901		February 7, 1901
January 13, 1902		February 1, 1902
February 17, 1902		March 18, 1902
January 6, 1903		March 14, 1903
January 2, 1904		January 13, 1904

February 15, 1904	March 7, 1904
February 9, 1905	February 27, 1905
February 2, 1906	February 19, 1906
January 25, 1907	February 12, 1907
January 18, 1908	February 4, 1908
January 10, 1909	March 17, 1909
January 3, 1910	January 30, 1910
February 15, 1910	March 11, 1910
February 12, 1911	March 4, 1911
February 6, 1912	February 24, 1912
January 29, 1913	February 16, 1913
January 22, 1914	February 8, 1914
February 23, 1915	March 19, 1915
January 14, 1915	February 2, 1915
January 7, 1916	March 14, 1916
January 1, 1917	January 17, 1917
February 14, 1917	March 8, 1917
February 10, 1918	February 28, 1918
February 3, 1919	February 21, 1919
January 27, 1920	February 13, 1920
January 18, 1921	February 5, 1921
January 11, 1922	February 1, 1922
February 8, 1922	March 17, 1922
January 4, 1923	February 6, 1923
February 13, 1923	March 12, 1923
February 13, 1924	March 4, 1924
February 7, 1925	February 25, 1925
January 31, 1926	February 17, 1926
January 23, 1927	February 9, 1927
January 16, 1928	February 3, 1928
February 29, 1928	March 17, 1928
January 8, 1929	March 15, 1929
January 2, 1930	January 22, 1930
February 15, 1930	March 9, 1930
February 11, 1931	March 2, 1931
February 4, 1932	February 22, 1932
January 27, 1933	February 13, 1933
January 20, 1934	February 6, 1934
January 12, 1935	February 1, 1935
February 14, 1935	March 18, 1935
January 5, 1936	March 12, 1936

January 1, 1937	January 9, 1937
February 13, 1937	March 6, 1937
February 8, 1938	February 26, 1938
February 1, 1939	February 19, 1939
January 25, 1940	February 11, 1940
January 16, 1941	February 3, 1941
March 7, 1941	March 16, 1941
January 9, 1942	March 16, 1942
January 3, 1943	January 27, 1943
February 15, 1943	March 10, 1943
February 12, 1944	March 2, 1944
February 5, 1945	February 23, 1945
January 29, 1946	February 15, 1946
January 21, 1947	February 7, 1947
January 14, 1948	February 1, 1948
February 19, 1948	March 18, 1948
January 6, 1949	March 14, 1949
January 1, 1950	January 14, 1950
February 14, 1950	March 7, 1950
February 9, 1951	February 28, 1951
February 3, 1952	February 20, 1952

Famous people with Mercury in Aquarius

John Steinbeck	Edward Albee
Jackie Gleason	Aleksei N. Kosygin
Frédéric Chopin	John L. Lewis
Thomas Edison	Samuel Barber
Luther Burbank	Carson McCullers
George Washington	Artur Rubinstein
Rex Harrison	Cassius Clay
Adlai Stevenson	Mia Farrow
Dr. Martin Luther King, Jr.	Pope Pius XII
Carol Channing	Virginia Woolf
Franklin Delano Roosevelt	Gertrude Stein

MERCURY IN PISCES

Your memory is excellent; your ability to concentrate unsurpassed. Your mind is not essentially objective or scientific, but you are amazingly psychic. It is as though you had access to a mystical fund of information. You make statements for which you have no apparent source or proof, but more often than not you turn out to be right. Usually, though, you can't explain how you knew. When Mercury is very afflicted, you can be prey to the strangest delusions and fantasies. When Mercury is well aspected, your creative imagination can be extraordinary.

Your mind may puzzle the average person. You like to reason abstractly, but when put to the test, you tend to act in accordance with your intuition and common sense. For this reason, in many cases, your actions may appear to belie your ideals.

Sometimes your mind seems at a standstill, but when you are apparently doing nothing, you are at your most creative. Your subconscious is at work. People who judge their accomplishments by the number of actual hours they put in can't understand the importance of this period of mental gestation.

People with this kind of horoscope are extremely sensitive to their environment and the people around them, and if these make them feel uncomfortable, they are inclined not to talk. On the other hand, in more congenial company, they tend to go to the other extreme and say too much. Their speech, while fluent, is sometimes careless, and they tell tales out of school without realizing how much harm it will cause.

Yet at heart, you are a true romantic, subtle and artistic, not virile and strong. Your mind is delicate—so sensitive and receptive to outer influences that you are subject to nervous breakdowns after long periods of stress.

March 12, 1890	through	March 30, 1890
March 5, 1891		March 22, 1891
February 26, 1892		March 12, 1892
February 17, 1893		March 5, 1893
February 9, 1894		April 16, 1894
February 2, 1895		March 3, 1895
March 17, 1895		April 11, 1895
March 15, 1896		April 3, 1896
March 9, 1897		March 26, 1897
March 2, 1898		March 18, 1898
February 22, 1899		March 10, 1899

February 14, 1900	March 3, 1900
March 29, 1900	April 16, 1900
February 7, 1901	April 15, 1901
February 1, 1902	February 17, 1902
March 18, 1902	April 9, 1902
March 14, 1903	April 1, 1903
March 7, 1904	March 23, 1904
February 27, 1905	March 15, 1905
February 19, 1906	March 7, 1906
February 12, 1907	March 3, 1907
March 13, 1907	April 18, 1907
February 4, 1908	April 12, 1908
March 17, 1909	April 5, 1909
March 11, 1910	March 29, 1910
March 4, 1911	March 20, 1911
February 25, 1912	March 11, 1912
February 16, 1913	March 4, 1913
April 7, 1913	April 13, 1913
February 8, 1914	April 16, 1914
February 2, 1915	February 23, 1915
March 19, 1915	April 10, 1915
March 14, 1916	April 2, 1916
March 8, 1917	March 25, 1917
March 1, 1918	March 16, 1918
February 21, 1919	March 9, 1919
February 13, 1920	March 2, 1920
March 19, 1920	April 17, 1920
February 5, 1921	April 13, 1921
February 1, 1922	February 8, 1922
March 18, 1922	April 7, 1922
March 13, 1923	March 30, 1923
March 4, 1924	March 21, 1924
February 25, 1925	March 13, 1925
February 17, 1926	March 5, 1926
February 10, 1927	April 17, 1927
February 3, 1928	February 28, 1928
March 17, 1928	April 10, 1928
March 15, 1929	April 3, 1929
March 9, 1930	March 26, 1930
March 2, 1931	March 18, 1931
February 22, 1932	March 9, 1932

February 13, 1933	March 3, 1933
March 25, 1933	April 17, 1933
February 6, 1934	April 14, 1934
February 1, 1935	February 14, 1935
March 18, 1935	April 8, 1935
March 13, 1936	March 30, 1936
March 6, 1937	March 22, 1937
February 26, 1938	March 14, 1938
February 19, 1939	March 7, 1939
February 11, 1940	March 4, 1940
March 7, 1940	April 16, 1940
February 3, 1941	March 6, 1941
March 16, 1941	April 12, 1941
March 16, 1942	April 4, 1942
March 10, 1943	March 28, 1943
March 2, 1944	March 19, 1944
February 23, 1945	March 11, 1945
February 15, 1946	March 4, 1946
April 1, 1946	April 16, 1946
February 7, 1947	April 15, 1947
February 1, 1948	February 19, 1948
March 18, 1948	April 8, 1948
March 14, 1949	April 1, 1949
March 7, 1950	March 24, 1950
February 28, 1951	March 16, 1951
February 20, 1952	March 7, 1952

Famous people with Mercury in Pisces

Adelina Patti	Gordon Cooper
Leontyne Price	Nathan Pusey
Victor Hugo	Charlotte Ford Niarchos
Abraham Lincoln	Sidney Poitier
Eugene McCarthy	Prince Edward
Earl Warren	Prince Andrew
W. E. B. DuBois	Robert Frost
Arthur Goldberg	Tricia Nixon

5

VENUS
and Your Kind of Love

Are you lovable? Do other people like to do favors for you? Are you the most popular person in your circle of friends? Do you get along well with the opposite sex? The planet you should consult is Venus. And it is important for every adult who is interested in his love life, his social adjustment and the pleasures and luxuries of life to know about the position of Venus in his particular horoscope.

In ancient Greek mythology, Venus, the goddess of love, was the most beautiful of the goddesses on Mount Olympus. Her symbol is a circle above a cross, the circle meaning eternity, the cross, earth, and both together symbolizing the triumph of ideal love over earthly considerations. In its truest form, Venus symbolizes a love that lasts for all eternity.

Ideal love, however, is the exception with the astrological Venus. It does exist, but more often Venus gives the gifts of beauty and ease. People with Venus in their horoscopes are among society's darlings. Indolent and pleasure-seeking, they have a somewhat superficial attitude toward life. They are so fortunate, in fact, that they do not have the discipline to meet the sterner challenges. They can become lotus-eaters, tasting the sweets rather than the realities. They are always, however, pleasant and agreeable and delightful company.

Venus rules love and beauty. It is essentially feminine like the Moon. Like Jupiter, it is a benefic and its gift of happiness is often enjoyed as an end in itself. Marriage is a circumstance of Venus. The inclination is to marry young for physical attraction and to regret it later when passion diminishes and the union is not compatible by more lasting standards.

A well-aspected Venus often endows a person with true beauty. The Venus type is usually lovable and gets along well with people generally. If such a person is not actually beautiful, he will most certainly be attractive, dressing tastefully and always being well groomed. He will inevitably have a great appeal for the opposite sex, and much good fortune as a result.

Gifts of flowers, jewels and other luxuries, a favorable social position with lots of invitations, entertainments and other pleasures are the type of benefits to expect of a well-aspected Venus. Venus rules artistic ability whether you actually design, sculpt, paint or visit museums and study art history. Or it may mean that you expend your talents on beautifying your home or collecting objects of art. This often extends as well to an interest in the other arts of music and poetry.

A badly aspected Venus, on the other hand, often portends a disappointing love life, the sort of person who is always in love with someone who does not reciprocate or else is himself the sort of person who never truly loves. The women tend to overexpress themselves when it comes to their appearance, and are usually found in outlandish getups, too many eyelashes, heavy perfume and a vulgar display of costume jewelry. Poor taste in artistic matters is also often the case. Badly aspected, Venus can produce dissolute characters—lazy, extravagant, degenerate and immoral. They are also liable to take the line of least resistance and to become involved with undesirable companions who lead to their undoing and eventual disrepute.

Venus in good aspect to Mercury gives good taste in all artistic matters and a pleasant, soft-spoken manner.

Venus in good aspect to Mars may give a sense of form in art, especially in sculpture and architecture. It gives a passionate, forceful expression of the sex instinct and lots of sex appeal. Venus in bad aspect to Mars may give an equal amount of sex interest, but the passions are rough and unruly and are apt to bring on disgrace.

Venus in good aspect to Jupiter represents the union of the smaller and greater fortunes and gives a love with dignity, opulence and position. These people are among the social elite and may be found attending parties, museums, theaters and concerts. Venus in bad aspect to Jupiter gives undesirable conditions, and the people attracted into your social life do not add to your position.

When Venus favorably aspects Saturn, you are discreet in love and morally correct and faithful. Venus in bad aspect to Saturn gives an unrefined sensuality, a coarse or even repulsive love-nature and a liking for crude humor. These people are at the same time immoral and cold, and selfish in any romantic relationship.

Venus in good aspect to Uranus gives magnetic attractiveness and sex appeal. These people are very romantic and more often than not fall in love at first sight. Venus in bad aspect to Uranus gives unconventional romances. You attract or are attracted to odd, strange, eccentric characters who behave in the most erratic, unpredictable fashion.

Venus in good aspect to Neptune gives the most idyllic, inspiring, idealistic love relationship imaginable. Venus afflicted by Neptune causes you to have weird, disappointing, disillusioning experiences of love, to be treated in the most inexplicable fashion, to be loved one moment and rejected for no apparent reason the next. It is a weird influence and is often disgraceful in ways that defy definition.

Venus in good aspect to the Sun guarantees that a woman's husband and father will be doting, and may make a man very successful with the ladies.

Venus in good aspect to the Moon gives you a loving, beautiful mother and makes the other women in your life romantic and agreeable. Venus in bad aspect to the Moon makes the women with whom you come in contact unsympathetic and unlovable and indicates a mother who withheld her affection, was unfeeling and unkind.

All the above is very general. You must figure out for yourself which aspects apply to you. But the following describes quite accurately truths about your love-nature. Venus changes radically in the different signs, so pay special attention to the description that applies to your birth-date to find the sign position of your Venus and exactly what this means to you.

If your date is mentioned twice, your Venus is at the end of one sign or the beginning of another. The characteristics of either or both may apply to you.

VENUS IN ARIES

Venus in Aries is brilliant and exciting rather than soothing, domestic or calm. You tend to attract others because of your dash and spirit, but while you please and stimulate, you never satisfy.

You love by sight. How someone looks is very important to you; yet in the final analysis, you choose more with your head than with your heart. The mental qualities of your loved one influence your choice to a large extent.

You are impulsive emotionally and you go after the object of your affection with a single-minded drive. Your method is contradictory; you are passionate and aggressive one minute, cold and disinterested the next. You also stand ready to repel the advances of others once you have staked out a claim. However, you tend to be more interested in conquest than in settling down.

You may even appear fickle, but that is because you are searching for an ideal love you can never find. You dream of love, but are never content with the imperfect reality.

Venus is not its most typical in Aries. But it is better for the person who is dedicated to achievement not to be distracted by Venus's more typical pleasures, comforts and social leanings. It is therefore an excellent position of Venus for a scientist or man of affairs.

March 14, 1890	through	April 7, 1890
April 27, 1891		May 22, 1891
February 13, 1892		March 9, 1892
March 29, 1893		April 22, 1893
May 6, 1894		June 3, 1894
February 27, 1895		March 23, 1895
April 12, 1896		May 6, 1896
February 2, 1897		March 4, 1897
March 13, 1898		April 7, 1898
April 26, 1899		May 21, 1899
February 13, 1900		March 10, 1900
March 29, 1901		April 22, 1901

May 7, 1902	June 3, 1902
February 27, 1903	March 24, 1903
April 12, 1904	May 7, 1904
February 2, 1905	March 5, 1905
May 9, 1905	May 28, 1905
March 14, 1906	April 7, 1906
April 27, 1907	May 22, 1907
February 13, 1908	March 10, 1908
March 29, 1909	April 22, 1909
May 6, 1910	June 3, 1910
February 27, 1911	March 23, 1911
April 12, 1912	May 6, 1912
February 2, 1913	March 6, 1913
May 1, 1913	May 31, 1913
March 13, 1914	April 6, 1914
April 26, 1915	May 21, 1915
February 13, 1916	March 9, 1916
March 28, 1917	April 21, 1917
May 6, 1918	June 2, 1918
February 26, 1919	March 23, 1919
April 11, 1920	May 6, 1920
February 2, 1921	March 7, 1921
April 25, 1921	June 1, 1921
March 13, 1922	April 6, 1922
April 26, 1923	May 21, 1923
February 12, 1924	March 9, 1924
March 27, 1925	April 21, 1925
May 6, 1926	June 2, 1926
February 26, 1927	March 22, 1927
April 11, 1928	May 5, 1928
February 2, 1929	March 8, 1929
April 19, 1929	June 3, 1929
March 12, 1930	April 5, 1930
April 25, 1931	May 20, 1931
February 12, 1932	March 8, 1932
March 27, 1933	April 20, 1933
May 6, 1934	June 2, 1934
February 25, 1935	March 22, 1935
April 10, 1936	May 5, 1936
February 2, 1937	March 9, 1937
April 13, 1937	June 3, 1937

March 12, 1938	April 5, 1938
April 25, 1939	May 20, 1939
February 12, 1940	March 8, 1940
March 26, 1941	April 19, 1941
May 5, 1942	June 1, 1942
February 25, 1943	March 21, 1943
April 10, 1944	May 4, 1944
February 2, 1945	March 11, 1945
April 7, 1945	June 4, 1945
March 11, 1946	April 4, 1946
April 24, 1947	May 19, 1947
February 11, 1948	March 7, 1948
March 26, 1949	April 19, 1949
May 5, 1950	June 1, 1950
February 24, 1951	March 21, 1951
April 9, 1952	May 4, 1952

Famous people with Venus in Aries

Audrey Hepburn	Perry Como
Henry Fonda	Bing Crosby
Elizabeth Taylor	Willem de Kooning
Abraham Lincoln	Charlotte Ford Niarchos
John Lennon	Julie Christie
Gordon Cooper	Mia Farrow
J. Robert Oppenheimer	Rudolf Nureyev
Henry Luce	Willie Mays
Robert Frost	Laurence Rockefeller

Edward M. Kennedy

VENUS IN TAURUS

Physical attraction is very important to you. Platonic love does not exist for those with a Taurus Venus. You possess a wonderful understanding of nature, and are natural and direct in any love relationship. Your instincts are so pure that you have no sense of shame. It takes very serious afflictions of Venus to make you abnormal or perverse.

Although you probably were late developing physically, you always would have attracted admirers of the opposite sex. You don't however, fall in love until the right person arrives. You know immediately when this happens, and unless Venus has bad aspects, you love for life. You are basically very conventional in this respect.

Once you have found your love, you are not only very tenacious but you are also tremendously affectionate and demonstrative. You like gifts, sweet messages and flowers—all the accoutrements of love.

Your disposition is kindly and cheerful and you are usually very popular as a result. You can always afford comfort and the luxuries of life, and you are domestically inclined.

Venus in the sign she rules gives a plethora of Venus character-istics, featuring pleasures and a very sympathetic nature. It also gives a sense of form in art. If these people are not actually artists, their appreciation of art is great and they may be art collectors.

April 7, 1890	through	May 1, 1890
May 22, 1891		June 16, 1891
March 9, 1892		April 5, 1892
April 22, 1893		May 16, 1893
June 3, 1894		June 29, 1894
March 23, 1895		April 17, 1895
May 6, 1896		May 31, 1896
March 4, 1897		July 7, 1897
April 7, 1898		May 1, 1898
May 21, 1899		June 15, 1899
March 10, 1900		April 5, 1900
April 22, 1901		May 17, 1901
June 3, 1902		June 30, 1902
March 24, 1903		April 18, 1903
May 7, 1904		May 31, 1904
March 6, 1905		May 9, 1905
May 28, 1905		July 8, 1905
April 7, 1906		May 1, 1906
May 22, 1907		June 16, 1907
March 10, 1908		April 5, 1908
April 22, 1909		May 16, 1909
June 3, 1910		June 29, 1910
March 23, 1911		April 17, 1911
May 6, 1912		May 31, 1912
March 6, 1913		May 1, 1913
May 31, 1913		July 8, 1913
April 6, 1914		May 1, 1914

May 21, 1915	June 15, 1915
March 9, 1916	April 5, 1916
April 21, 1917	May 15, 1917
June 2, 1918	June 29, 1918
March 23, 1919	April 17, 1919
May 6, 1920	May 30, 1920
March 7, 1921	April 25, 1921
June 1, 1921	July 8, 1921
April 6, 1922	April 30, 1922
May 21, 1923	June 15, 1923
March 9, 1924	April 4, 1924
April 21, 1925	May 15, 1925
June 2, 1926	June 28, 1926
March 22, 1927	April 16, 1927
May 5, 1928	May 30, 1928
March 8, 1929	April 19, 1929
June 3, 1929	July 7, 1929
April 5, 1930	April 30, 1930
May 20, 1931	June 14, 1931
March 8, 1932	April 4, 1932
April 20, 1933	May 14, 1933
June 2, 1934	June 28, 1934
March 22, 1935	April 16, 1935
May 5, 1936	May 29, 1936
March 9, 1937	April 13, 1937
June 4, 1937	July 7, 1937
April 5, 1938	April 29, 1938
May 20, 1939	June 14, 1939
March 8, 1940	April 4, 1940
April 19, 1941	May 14, 1941
June 1, 1942	June 27, 1942
March 21, 1943	April 15, 1943
May 4, 1944	May 29, 1944
March 11, 1945	April 7, 1945
June 4, 1945	July 7, 1945
April 4, 1946	April 29, 1946
May 19, 1947	June 13, 1947
March 8, 1948	April 4, 1948
April 19, 1949	May 13, 1949
June 1, 1950	June 27, 1950

March 21, 1951   April 15, 1951
May 4, 1952   May 28, 1952

Famous people with Venus in Taurus

Doris Day	James Arness
Prince Philip	Warren Beatty
Jean-Paul Sartre	Ann-Margret
Charlie Chaplin	James A. McDivitt
Richard Wagner	Otto Klemperer
Richard Chamberlain	Paul McCartney
Bobby Darin	Hayley Mills
Eugene McCarthy	David Rockefeller
John Wayne	Prince Edward

VENUS IN GEMINI

Venus is not at its best in Gemini, for Venus is essentially emotional and earthy and Gemini is airy and rational. The result is that Venus is transferred to the abstract plane and very little of her natural demonstrativeness and warmth remain. People with this position of Venus rarely like to be touched or fondled, and in some cases, when they express their devotion, it is of the spirit and mind rather than the body.

Indeed, you tend to have mental and ideal attractions rather than the physical or domestic ones. Your interest in love is easily aroused, but you have a short attention span, and you don't really want concrete attachments. You might enjoy a relationship with someone who caught your fancy, only to be abashed were they to take you seriously.

You are basically intellectual about love. You like to read about it and think about it. While you understand love, you rarely feel it. This is a good position for a scientist who needs to be free of distractions in his intellectual pursuits.

Your admirers always come in pairs or larger numbers, and you have a terrible time deciding which one to choose. Often you don't choose at all but simply enjoy all the popularity and attention. If a man, you would enjoy a harem. If a woman, the feminine equivalent. At times, one might even call you frivolous.

If Venus is afflicted, your feelings can be superficial and shallow. If Venus is well aspected, you can be very faithful and idealistic about love. Since Pluto was in Gemini for those born from 1890 to parts of 1913 and 1914, those with Venus in Gemini were likely to have found a true soul mate among persons born in that era.

May 1, 1890	through	May 26, 1890
June 16, 1891		July 11, 1891
April 5, 1892		May 4, 1892
May 16, 1893		June 10, 1893
June 29, 1894		July 25, 1894
April 17, 1895		May 12, 1895
May 31, 1896		June 24, 1896
July 7, 1897		August 5, 1897
May 1, 1898		May 26, 1898
June 15, 1899		July 10, 1899
April 5, 1900		May 5, 1900
May 17, 1901		June 10, 1901
June 30, 1902		July 25, 1902
April 18, 1903		May 13, 1903
May 31, 1904		June 25, 1904
July 8, 1905		August 6, 1905
May 1, 1906		May 26, 1906
June 16, 1907		July 10, 1907
April 5, 1908		May 5, 1908
May 16, 1909		June 9, 1909
June 29, 1910		July 25, 1910
April 17, 1911		May 12, 1911
May 31, 1912		June 24, 1912
July 8, 1913		August 5, 1913
May 1, 1914		May 25, 1914
June 15, 1915		July 10, 1915
April 5, 1916		May 5, 1916
May 15, 1917		June 9, 1917
June 29, 1918		July 24, 1918
April 17, 1919		May 12, 1919
May 30, 1920		June 24, 1920
July 8, 1921		August 5, 1921
April 30, 1922		May 25, 1922

June 23, 1923	July 9, 1923
April 5, 1924	May 5, 1924
May 15, 1925	June 8, 1925
June 28, 1926	July 24, 1926
April 16, 1927	May 12, 1927
May 30, 1928	June 23, 1928
July 7, 1929	August 4, 1929
April 30, 1930	May 24, 1930
June 14, 1931	July 9, 1931
April 4, 1932	May 6, 1932
July 13, 1932	July 28, 1932
May 14, 1933	June 8, 1933
June 28, 1934	July 23, 1934
April 16, 1935	May 11, 1935
May 29, 1936	June 23, 1936
July 7, 1937	August 4, 1937
April 29, 1938	May 24, 1938
June 14, 1939	July 8, 1939
April 4, 1940	May 6, 1940
July 5, 1940	July 31, 1940
May 14, 1941	June 7, 1941
June 27, 1942	July 22, 1942
April 15, 1943	May 11, 1943
May 29, 1944	June 22, 1944
July 7, 1945	August 4, 1945
April 29, 1946	May 23, 1946
June 13, 1947	July 8, 1947
April 4, 1948	May 7, 1948
June 29, 1948	August 2, 1948
May 13, 1949	June 7, 1949
June 27, 1950	July 22, 1950
April 15, 1951	May 10, 1951
May 28, 1952	June 21, 1952

Famous people with Venus in Gemini

Jacqueline Kennedy Onassis	Mary McCarthy
Leslie Caron	Luci Baines Johnson Nugent
William Shakespeare	Peter Duchin
John F. Kennedy	Yehudi Menuhin
Ringo Starr	Tex Thornton
John Glenn	Benjamin Spock

Van Cliburn   Franz Kafka
Richard Strauss   Edmund Wilson
          Julie Nixon Eisenhower

VENUS IN CANCER

Love is a prime requirement for you. In fact, you need an emotional outlet for your health and general well-being. While you tend to be passive in matters of affection, you are always very emotional. You don't go out looking for love. You wait until it comes to you. When someone pursues you, you accept their attentions gratefully. You find it difficult to resist the advances of another.

However, Cancer is a cardinal sign, and when Venus is strongly aspected, especially by Mars or Uranus, you yourself may be the sexual aggressor. In either case, you are apt to be very demonstrative and emotional.

Your feelings are deep and quiet. You are intensely sentimental and have strong love and family ties. Although you take love very seriously, you are apt to get over disappointments quite quickly.

You are basically good humored and therefore very popular. You like your comforts and always manage to have them. You are lucky in being able to have many small conveniences. You like to eat. You are so fond of food, in fact, you are apt to overindulge.

Since Pluto was in Cancer for those born during parts of 1913 and 1914 through parts of 1938 and 1939, those with Venus in Cancer are likely to have found a true soul-mate among persons born in that era.

May 26, 1890	through	June 20, 1890
July 11, 1891		August 4, 1891
May 4, 1892		September 7, 1892
June 10, 1893		July 4, 1893
July 25, 1894		August 19, 1894
May 12, 1895		June 8, 1895
June 24, 1896		July 19, 1896
August 5, 1897		September 1, 1897
May 26, 1898		June 19, 1898
July 10, 1899		August 4, 1899

May 5, 1900	September 8, 1900
June 10, 1901	July 4, 1901
July 25, 1902	August 19, 1902
May 13, 1903	June 8, 1903
June 25, 1904	July 19, 1904
August 6, 1905	September 1, 1905
May 26, 1906	June 20, 1906
July 11, 1907	August 4, 1907
May 5, 1908	September 8, 1908
June 9, 1909	July 4, 1909
July 25, 1910	August 18, 1910
May 12, 1911	June 8, 1911
June 24, 1912	July 19, 1912
August 5, 1913	September 1, 1913
May 25, 1914	June 19, 1914
July 10, 1915	August 3, 1915
May 5, 1916	September 8, 1916
June 9, 1917	July 3, 1917
July 24, 1918	August 18, 1918
May 12, 1919	June 8, 1919
May 24, 1920	July 18, 1920
August 5, 1921	August 31, 1921
May 25, 1922	June 19, 1922
July 9, 1923	August 3, 1923
May 5, 1924	September 8, 1924
June 8, 1925	July 3, 1925
July 24, 1926	August 17, 1926
May 12, 1927	June 7, 1927
June 23, 1928	July 18, 1928
August 4, 1929	August 31, 1929
May 24, 1930	June 18, 1930
July 9, 1931	August 2, 1931
May 6, 1932	July 13, 1932
July 28, 1932	September 8, 1932
June 8, 1933	July 2, 1933
July 23, 1934	August 17, 1934
May 11, 1935	June 7, 1935
June 23, 1936	July 17, 1936
August 4, 1937	August 30, 1937
May 24, 1938	June 18, 1938
July 8, 1939	August 2, 1939

May 6, 1940	July 5, 1940
July 31, 1940	September 8, 1940
June 7, 1941	July 2, 1941
July 23, 1942	August 16, 1942
May 11, 1943	June 7, 1943
June 22, 1944	July 16, 1944
August 4, 1945	August 30, 1945
May 23, 1946	June 17, 1946
July 8, 1947	August 1, 1947
May 7, 1948	June 29, 1948
August 2, 1948	September 8, 1948
June 7, 1949	July 1, 1949
July 22, 1950	August 16, 1950
May 10, 1951	June 6, 1951
June 21, 1952	July 16, 1952

Famous people with Venus in Cancer

Lyndon B. Johnson	Louis Armstrong
Judy Garland	Bob Hope
Margot Fonteyn	James Baldwin
Napoleon Bonaparte	Casey Stengel
Nelson Rockefeller	Constantine of Greece
Dean Martin	Princess Anne
Harry Truman	William Styron
Leslie Uggams	Hubert Humphrey
Igor Stravinsky	Joe Namath

VENUS IN LEO

This position of Venus can make you very popular. You just naturally attract the warmest feelings on the part of others. They are drawn to you because of your kindliness and heartfelt geniality. Even your worst enemies have nothing to say against you personally. Although some people may not admire you, they have to like you because you're so genuinely big-hearted.

Your will power and magnetism are tied in with the dictates of your heart. You are very magnanimous with the world at large, and your nobility and decency are always apparent. You are a great humanitarian.

In your more intimate relationships with your family and those you love, you can be loyal beyond the call of duty. Where you love, you are generous to a fault with your affections as well as with your material possessions. Leo's fire may or may not make you passionate, but you are always demonstrative and warm.

Whom you love depends on an appeal to your deeper emotions. You like to dominate those you love, and part of your personal magnetism stems from your strong will power. Still, you are capable of great self-sacrifice for a worthy cause or for the happiness and welfare of your loved ones.

June 20, 1890	through	July 15, 1890
August 4, 1891		August 28, 1891
September 7, 1892		October 7, 1892
July 4, 1893		July 29, 1893
August 19, 1894		September 12, 1894
June 8, 1895		July 6, 1895
July 19, 1896		August 12, 1896
September 1, 1897		September 26, 1897
June 19, 1898		July 15, 1898
August 4, 1899		August 28, 1899
September 8, 1900		October 8, 1900
July 4, 1901		July 29, 1901
August 19, 1902		September 13, 1902
June 8, 1903		July 7, 1903
July 19, 1904		August 13, 1904
September 1, 1905		September 26, 1905
June 20, 1906		July 15, 1906
August 4, 1907		August 28, 1907
September 8, 1908		October 8, 1908
July 4, 1909		July 28, 1909
August 19, 1910		September 12, 1910
June 8, 1911		July 7, 1911
July 19, 1912		August 12, 1912
September 1, 1913		September 26, 1913
June 19, 1914		July 15, 1914
August 3, 1915		August 28, 1915
September 8, 1916		October 7, 1916
July 3, 1917		July 28, 1917
August 18, 1918		September 11, 1918

June 8, 1919	July 7, 1919
July 18, 1920	August 11, 1920
August 31, 1921	September 25, 1921
June 19, 1922	July 14, 1922
August 3, 1923	August 27, 1923
September 8, 1924	October 7, 1924
July 3, 1925	July 27, 1925
August 17, 1926	September 11, 1926
June 7, 1927	July 7, 1927
July 18, 1928	August 11, 1928
August 31, 1929	September 25, 1929
June 18, 1930	July 14, 1930
August 2, 1931	August 27, 1931
September 8, 1932	October 6, 1932
July 2, 1933	July 27, 1933
August 17, 1934	September 10, 1934
June 7, 1935	July 7, 1935
July 17, 1936	August 10, 1936
August 30, 1937	September 24, 1937
June 18, 1938	July 13, 1938
August 2, 1939	August 26, 1939
September 8, 1940	October 6, 1940
July 2, 1941	July 26, 1941
August 16, 1942	September 10, 1942
June 7, 1943	July 7, 1943
July 16, 1944	August 10, 1944
August 30, 1945	September 24, 1945
June 17, 1946	July 13, 1946
August 1, 1947	August 26, 1947
September 8, 1948	October 6, 1948
July 1, 1949	July 26, 1949
August 16, 1950	September 9, 1950
June 6, 1951	July 7, 1951
July 16, 1952	August 9, 1952

Famous people with Venus in Leo

William Faulkner	George Bernard Shaw
Françoise Sagan	Leonard Bernstein
Percy B. Shelley	Jimmy Dean
Leo Tolstoi	Eddie Fisher
Arnold Palmer	Alan Jay Lerner

Merv Griffin   Geraldine Chaplin
Greta Garbo   Truman Capote
        Eero Saarinen

VENUS IN VIRGO

Either your affections are diverted into intellectual channels or you tend to be somewhat cerebral in your intimate relations. Some of you can be cold and materialistic when it comes to love; others will dedicate themselves to a worthy cause that enlists their mind more than their emotions.

You tend to be somewhat aloof and solitary. Because you like to keep people at a distance, you have more acquaintances than close friends. You divide your affections among a lot of people. You are considerate but never wholeheartedly in love.

You are very critical of those who offer you their love. You tend to analyze them so thoroughly that you can't help but find fault with them. When you do love, you are still very practical. You don't sweep others off their feet by your ardor and depth of emotion, but you can make your loved one very comfortable indeed. When you fail to find a personal love, you may be a blessing to all humanity instead. Doctors and nurses with Venus in Virgo usually serve their patients conscientiously and with great consideration.

This is also an excellent position for writers, actors, lawyers and public speakers who have the ability to simulate emotions they understand intellectually but do not feel.

July 15, 1890	through	August 10, 1890
August 29, 1891		September 22, 1891
October 7, 1892		November 3, 1892
July 29, 1893		August 22, 1893
September 12, 1894		October 6, 1894
July 6, 1895		August 13, 1895
September 12, 1895		November 6, 1895
August 12, 1896		September 5, 1896
September 26, 1897		October 21, 1897
July 15, 1898		August 10, 1898
August 28, 1899		September 21, 1899

October 8, 1900

July 29, 1901

September 13, 1902

July 7, 1903

September 6, 1903

August 13, 1904

September 26, 1905

July 15, 1906

August 28, 1907

October 8, 1908

July 29, 1909

September 12, 1910

July 7, 1911

August 12, 1912

September 26, 1913

July 15, 1914

August 28, 1915

October 7, 1916

July 28, 1917

September 11, 1918

July 7, 1919

August 11, 1920

September 25, 1921

July 14, 1922

August 27, 1923

October 7, 1924

July 27, 1925

September 11, 1926

July 7, 1927

August 11, 1928

September 25, 1929

July 14, 1930

August 27, 1931

October 6, 1932

July 27, 1933

September 10, 1934

July 7, 1935

August 10, 1936

September 24, 1937

July 13, 1938

August 26, 1939

November 3, 1900

August 23, 1901

October 7, 1902

August 17, 1903

November 8, 1903

September 6, 1904

October 21, 1905

August 10, 1906

September 21, 1907

November 3, 1908

August 22, 1909

October 6, 1910

November 8, 1911

September 5, 1912

October 20, 1913

August 10, 1914

September 21, 1915

November 2, 1916

August 22, 1917

October 6, 1918

November 9, 1919

September 5, 1920

October 20, 1921

August 10, 1922

September 20, 1923

November 2, 1924

August 21, 1925

October 5, 1926

November 9, 1927

September 4, 1928

October 19, 1929

August 9, 1930

September 20, 1931

November 1, 1932

August 21, 1933

October 5, 1934

November 9, 1935

September 4, 1936

October 19, 1937

August 9, 1938

September 19, 1939

October 6, 1940	November 1, 1940
July 26, 1941	August 20, 1941
September 10, 1942	October 4, 1942
July 7, 1943	November 9, 1943
August 10, 1944	September 3, 1944
September 24, 1945	October 18, 1945
July 13, 1946	August 9, 1946
August 26, 1947	September 19, 1947
October 6, 1948	October 31, 1948
July 26, 1949	August 20, 1949
September 9, 1950	October 3, 1950
July 7, 1951	November 9, 1951
August 9, 1952	September 3, 1952

Famous people with Venus in Virgo

Ed Sullivan	Anne Bancroft
Ernest Hemingway	Chiang Kai-Shek
Julie Andrews	Steve Lawrence
Lucille Ball	Eleanor Roosevelt
Fidel Castro	Ben Hogan
Diahann Carroll	Mike Douglas
Douglas Dillon	Margaret Sanger

VENUS IN LIBRA

To you, all love is sacred. You tend to worship the one you love and to place him on a pedestal. You love with the mind and spirit. You are repelled by anything coarse, earthy or crude. Because you are so refined and subtle, you are often misunderstood, especially by common, ordinary people who react by being afraid of you.

While you can be very sincere in your feelings, you are, at the same time, interested in the form in which things are done. Love and courtship are a very important ritual in your eyes.

In Libra, love cannot be chained to material expression, but must be absolutely free. Venus would need to have very severe afflictions for you to marry for money or position, and then you would be utterly miserable. Even when you love truly, you can be offended when your love takes a physical form. You have a horror of anything ordinary and banal, and can resort to perversions, not because you are immoral but because you are so imaginative and refined.

You love harmonious surroundings, and a discordant environment could make you physically ill. Beauty and simplicity are your highest standards. This is a wonderful position for an artist. There is a superb sense of proportion, color and line.

You can be charming and sympathetic, but you avoid intimacy on the part of others and can be coldly aloof if anyone tries to presume. If people lack attractive manners, you don't care how many other virtues they possess. You like to be very exclusive socially.

Ballet is one of your favorite art forms, and you may also love to dance.

August 10, 1890	through	September 6, 1890
September 22, 1891		October 16, 1891
November 3, 1892		November 28, 1892
August 22, 1893		September 16, 1893
October 6, 1894		October 30, 1894
August 13, 1895		September 12, 1895
November 6, 1895		December 8, 1895
September 5, 1896		September 30, 1896
October 21, 1897		November 14, 1897
August 10, 1898		September 6, 1898
September 21, 1899		October 15, 1899
November 3, 1900		November 28, 1900
August 23, 1901		September 17, 1901
October 7, 1902		October 31, 1902
August 17, 1903		September 6, 1903
November 8, 1903		December 9, 1903
September 5, 1904		September 30, 1904
October 21, 1905		November 14, 1905
August 10, 1906		September 7, 1906
September 21, 1907		October 16, 1907
November 3, 1908		November 28, 1908
August 22, 1909		September 16, 1909
October 6, 1910		October 30, 1910
November 8, 1911		December 9, 1911
September 5, 1912		September 29, 1912
October 21, 1913		November 14, 1913
August 10, 1914		September 7, 1914

September 21, 1915
November 2, 1916
August 22, 1917
October 6, 1918
November 9, 1919
September 5, 1920
October 20, 1921
August 10, 1922
September 20, 1923
November 2, 1924
August 21, 1925
October 5, 1926
November 9, 1927
September 4, 1928
October 19, 1929
August 9, 1930
September 20, 1931
November 1, 1932
August 21, 1933
October 5, 1934
November 9, 1935
September 4, 1936
October 19, 1937
August 9, 1938
September 19, 1939
November 1, 1940
August 20, 1941
October 4, 1942
November 9, 1943
September 3, 1944
October 18, 1945
August 9, 1946
September 19, 1947
November 1, 1948
August 20, 1949
October 3, 1950
November 9, 1951
September 3, 1952

October 15, 1915
November 27, 1916
September 16, 1917
October 30, 1918
December 8, 1919
September 29, 1920
November 13, 1921
September 7, 1922
October 14, 1923
November 27, 1924
September 15, 1925
October 29, 1926
December 8, 1927
September 29, 1928
November 13, 1929
September 6, 1930
October 14, 1931
November 26, 1932
September 15, 1933
October 29, 1934
December 8, 1935
September 28, 1936
November 12, 1937
September 6, 1938
October 13, 1939
November 26, 1940
September 14, 1941
October 28, 1942
December 8, 1943
September 27, 1944
November 12, 1945
September 6, 1946
October 13, 1947
November 25, 1948
September 14, 1949
October 27, 1950
December 7, 1951
September 27, 1952

Famous people with Venus in Libra

Princess Margaret Rose	Martin Luther
Henry Ford II	Petula Clark
Pablo Picasso	Anne-Marie of Greece
Oscar Wilde	Prince Charles

VENUS IN SCORPIO

You love intensely and in a physical sense, and you are so willful that you tend to go to extremes. If someone doesn't return your love, you dislike them completely; even if they do return it, your love life is bound to be stormy. You expect the object of your affection to surrender to you completely and abjectly to do your will. Few people are willing to put up with this once the initial fascination passes.

You are very straightforward, but you may be so determined and direct that you frighten the person with whom you are in love. You must try to be more tactful and reserved.

You are passionate, possessive and jealous, and you must guard against excesses of feeling. Love may give rise to jealousy in the initial stages, but soon jealousy is all-consuming and your desire for revenge is implacable.

Many people, however, find you magnetically attractive. But you can be sensual and earthy, and no matter how much you give expression to your animal desires, you are never really satisfied. Common types with Venus in Scorpio dissipate relentlessly and are frequently degenerates or drunks. Most of you overdo when it comes to sex.

Sometimes the strength of your passions can be diminished by a Libra or Sagittarius Sun or Mercury. In other cases, because of your environment and training, you may repress your instincts and experience frustration and discontent as a result. But this position can have its constructive side as well. If you would only learn to control and direct your terrific emotional drive, you could accomplish wonders.

September 6, 1890	through	October 7, 1890
October 16, 1891		November 9, 1891
November 28, 1892		December 22, 1892
September 16, 1893		October 11, 1893
October 30, 1894		November 23, 1894
December 8, 1895		January 4, 1896
September 30, 1896		October 24, 1896
November 14, 1897		December 8, 1897
September 6, 1898		October 7, 1898
October 15, 1899		November 8, 1899
November 28, 1900		December 23, 1900
September 17, 1901		October 12, 1901
October 31, 1902		November 24, 1902
December 9, 1903		January 4, 1904
September 30, 1904		October 24, 1904
November 14, 1905		December 8, 1905
September 7, 1906		October 9, 1906
December 15, 1906		December 25, 1906
October 16, 1907		November 9, 1907
November 28, 1908		December 22, 1908
September 16, 1909		October 12, 1909
October 30, 1910		November 23, 1910
December 9, 1911		January 4, 1912
September 29, 1912		October 24, 1912
November 14, 1913		December 8, 1913
September 7, 1914		October 9, 1914
December 5, 1914		December 30, 1914
October 15, 1915		November 8, 1915
November 27, 1916		December 22, 1916
September 16, 1917		October 11, 1917
October 30, 1918		November 23, 1918
December 8, 1919		January 4, 1920
September 29, 1920		October 23, 1920
November 13, 1921		December 7, 1921
September 7, 1922		October 10, 1922
November 28, 1922		January 2, 1923
October 14, 1923		November 7, 1923
November 27, 1924		December 21, 1924
September 15, 1925		October 11, 1925
October 29, 1926		November 22, 1926
December 8, 1927		January 3, 1928

September 29, 1928	October 23, 1928
November 13, 1929	December 7, 1929
September 6, 1930	October 11, 1930
November 22, 1930	January 3, 1931
October 14, 1931	November 7, 1931
November 26, 1932	December 21, 1932
September 15, 1933	October 10, 1933
October 29, 1934	November 21, 1934
December 8, 1935	January 3, 1936
September 28, 1936	October 22, 1936
November 12, 1937	December 6, 1937
September 6, 1938	October 13, 1938
November 15, 1938	January 4, 1939
October 13, 1939	November 6, 1939
November 26, 1940	December 20, 1940
September 14, 1941	October 10, 1941
October 28, 1942	November 21, 1942
December 8, 1943	January 2, 1944
September 28, 1944	October 22, 1944
November 12, 1945	December 5, 1945
September 6, 1946	October 16, 1946
November 8, 1946	January 5, 1947
October 13, 1947	November 6, 1947
November 25, 1948	December 19, 1948
September 14, 1949	October 10, 1949
October 27, 1950	November 20, 1950
December 7, 1951	January 2, 1952
September 27, 1952	October 21, 1952

Famous people with Venus in Scorpio

Joan Sutherland	Mohandas K. Gandhi
Mary Martin	J. Paul Getty
Marie Antoinette	Billy Graham
Patty Duke	Robert Vaughn
David McCallum	Sophia Loren
Andy Williams	Vladimir Horowitz
Connie Francis	Al Capp

VENUS IN SAGITTARIUS

Your love is like a shooting star, brilliant but impermanent. You lack warmth and the power to sustain emotion. You often attract someone who has ordinary passions, only to disappoint them by failing to respond. You may therefore seem to be cold or fickle. In reality, your attention span in romance is fleeting and ephemeral.

Part of your apparent fickleness is due to your intrinsic nature. Because you are high-spirited and refined, you demand these qualities in the object of your affections. If you find a lack of idealism or pride, you immediately lose interest. The slightest indelicacy or flaw will put you off forever. As most human beings have some defects, it is almost impossible for you to find satisfaction.

This is not true in friendship where you display the highest type of loyalty and affection. A certain detachment from physical considerations is typical of this position of Venus. You separate physical love from the ideal. You could never love anyone gross or earthy.

In love, you must be absolutely free. To you, a conventional romance would be banal. If someone tried to tie you down, you would be bored and take the nearest avenue of escape. Only the most subtle and intense ploys will attract you. But your usual disillusionment and resulting inconstancy account for the fact that many of you with Venus so placed remain bachelors, faithful to no one but your ideal.

The women are delicate and equally elusive. They have no more desire than do the men to sacrifice themselves for love.

October 7, 1890	through	February 5, 1891
November 9, 1891		December 3, 1891
December 22, 1892		January 15, 1893
October 11, 1893		November 6, 1893
November 23, 1894		December 17, 1894
January 4, 1896		January 29, 1896
October 24, 1896		November 17, 1896
December 8, 1897		January 1, 1898
October 7, 1898		February 5, 1899
November 8, 1899		December 2, 1899

December 23, 1900	January 16, 1901
October 12, 1901	November 7, 1901
November 24, 1902	December 17, 1902
January 4, 1904	January 30, 1904
October 25, 1904	November 18, 1904
December 8, 1905	January 1, 1906
October 9, 1906	December 15, 1906
December 25, 1906	February 6, 1907
November 9, 1907	December 3, 1907
December 22, 1908	January 15, 1909
October 12, 1909	November 7, 1909
November 23, 1910	December 17, 1910
January 4, 1912	January 29, 1912
October 24, 1912	November 17, 1912
December 8, 1913	December 31, 1913
October 9, 1914	December 5, 1914
December 30, 1914	February 6, 1915
November 8, 1915	December 2, 1915
December 22, 1916	January 15, 1917
October 11, 1917	November 6, 1917
November 23, 1918	December 16, 1918
January 4, 1920	January 29, 1920
October 23, 1920	November 17, 1920
December 7, 1921	December 21, 1921
October 10, 1922	November 28, 1922
January 2, 1923	February 6, 1923
November 7, 1923	December 1, 1923
December 21, 1924	January 14, 1925
October 11, 1925	November 6, 1925
November 22, 1926	December 16, 1926
January 3, 1928	January 28, 1928
October 23, 1928	November 16, 1928
December 7, 1929	December 30, 1929
October 11, 1930	November 22, 1930
January 3, 1931	February 6, 1931
November 7, 1931	December 1, 1931
December 21, 1932	January 14, 1933
October 10, 1933	November 6, 1933
November 21, 1934	December 15, 1934
January 3, 1936	January 28, 1936
October 22, 1936	November 16, 1936

December 6, 1937	December 30, 1937
October 13, 1938	November 15, 1938
January 4, 1939	February 6, 1939
November 6, 1939	November 30, 1939
December 20, 1940	January 13, 1941
October 10, 1941	November 6, 1941
November 21, 1942	December 15, 1942
January 2, 1944	January 27, 1944
October 22, 1944	November 16, 1944
December 5, 1945	December 29, 1945
October 16, 1946	November 8, 1946
January 5, 1947	February 5, 1947
November 6, 1947	November 30, 1947
December 19, 1948	January 13, 1949
October 10, 1949	November 5, 1949
November 20, 1950	December 14, 1950
January 2, 1952	January 27, 1952
October 21, 1952	November 15, 1952

Famous people with Venus in Sagittarius

Dwight David Eisenhower	Margaret Chase Smith
James Thurber	Joan Baez
Cary Grant	Jane Fonda
Winston Churchill	Charles de Gaulle
Robert Louis Stevenson	Jule Styne
Lewis Carroll	Jonas Salk
Rudyard Kipling	Pablo Casals
Mark Twain	Romy Schneider
Douglas MacArthur	Joe DiMaggio
Johnny Carson	John Osborne

VENUS IN CAPRICORN

You may develop an interest in the opposite sex later than the average person, but you form strong permanent attachments when you do. Sometimes an interest in sex is submerged completely when other interests concern you so much more.

When it comes to animal pleasures, you can be lustful and earthy, yet at the same time detached and cold. People with Venus in Capricorn may spend a lot in their quest for a good time, but they can be very small-minded about it, expecting the other person to comply with their wishes completely. They can be selfish, expecting much more of other people than they themselves are willing to give.

You can be jealous and touchy and very particular about other people's attitudes toward you. Because you are afraid of being refused, you are inclined to be very suspicious, and you expect the other person to make the first move. Once you are sure of being wanted, you then feel confident enough to commit yourself. But you need every encouragement before you can relax and love.

You want to possess your loved one completely and to have him respond by being even more enthusiastic than you are. As long as intimacy lasts, you are perfectly content and act decently. You are, however, very proud, and should you feel rejected, instead of being warm and demonstrative, you can become antagonistic and cold.

Happily settled, you are faithful and domestic. You prefer staying at home to a lot of social life and parties. Usually your artistic instincts are not very developed, but this can be modified according to the degree in which Venus is found. Ordinarily, moral beauty appeals to you more than the physical kind.

January 1, 1890	through	January 25, 1890
February 5, 1891		March 6, 1891
December 3, 1891		December 27, 1891
January 15, 1893		February 8, 1893
November 6, 1893		December 4, 1893
December 17, 1894		January 10, 1895
January 29, 1896		February 23, 1896
November 17, 1896		December 12, 1896
January 1, 1898		January 24, 1898
February 5, 1899		March 5, 1899
December 2, 1899		December 26, 1899
January 16, 1901		February 9, 1901
November 7, 1901		December 5, 1901
December 18, 1902		January 10, 1903
January 30, 1904		February 23, 1904
November 18, 1904		December 13, 1904
January 1, 1906		January 25, 1906
February 6, 1907		March 6, 1907

December 3, 1907	December 27, 1907
January 15, 1909	February 8, 1909
November 7, 1909	December 5, 1909
December 17, 1910	January 10, 1911
January 29, 1912	February 23, 1912
November 17, 1912	December 12, 1912
December 31, 1913	January 24, 1914
February 6, 1915	March 6, 1915
December 2, 1915	December 26, 1915
January 15, 1917	February 8, 1917
November 6, 1917	December 5, 1917
December 16, 1918	January 9, 1919
January 29, 1920	February 22, 1920
November 17, 1920	December 12, 1920
December 21, 1921	January 24, 1922
February 6, 1923	March 5, 1923
December 1, 1923	December 26, 1923
January 14, 1925	February 7, 1925
November 6, 1925	December 5, 1925
December 16, 1926	January 9, 1927
January 28, 1928	February 22, 1928
November 17, 1928	December 11, 1928
December 30, 1929	January 23, 1930
February 6, 1931	March 5, 1931
December 1, 1931	December 25, 1931
January 14, 1933	February 7, 1933
November 6, 1933	December 5, 1933
December 15, 1934	January 8, 1935
January 28, 1936	February 21, 1936
November 16, 1936	December 11, 1936
December 30, 1937	January 23, 1938
February 6, 1939	March 5, 1939
November 30, 1939	December 25, 1939
January 13, 1941	February 6, 1941
November 6, 1941	December 5, 1941
December 15, 1942	January 8, 1943
January 27, 1944	February 21, 1944
November 16, 1944	December 10, 1944
December 29, 1945	January 22, 1946
February 6, 1947	March 4, 1947
November 30, 1947	December 24, 1947

January 13, 1949   February 6, 1949
November 5, 1949   December 5, 1949
December 14, 1950   January 7, 1951
January 27, 1952   February 20, 1952
November 15, 1952   December 10, 1952

Famous people with Venus in Capricorn

Frank Sinatra   Prince Andrew
Joan of Arc   John F. Kennedy, Jr.
Robert F. Kennedy   Rock Hudson
Richard Burton   Aleksei Kosygin
J. D. Salinger   Artur Rubinstein
              Caroline Kennedy

VENUS IN AQUARIUS

You are not likely to settle down easily with only one person. You love all humanity and are prone to become interested in a whole series of people. You try first one, then another in an effort to find the ideal; but you have such a fine understanding of human nature that you cannot be deceived by those who do not live up to your high standards.

When Venus is well aspected, your love is very idealistic. Your mate may be jealous, however, because you have so many friends of the opposite sex, but his fears are without foundation. Your friends are just that, and you encourage them because of all the human interest those associations bring. When Venus is afflicted, on the other hand, there is a tendency to have love affairs with all and sundry, and to be somewhat callous about marriage bonds.

There is little that is passionate or earthy about an Aquarian Venus. You are too human for animal instincts to be uppermost. Sometimes, Venus's more personal expression is idealized and transformed into a love for all mankind, and you feel obliged to perform a mission for the benefit of the world.

If an artist, you capture your subjects' essence because your grasp of human nature is so great. Of all the arts, music is probably your favorite and the one in which you express yourself best. If you do not prefer classical music, the popular variety will appeal to your sense of sound and rhythm instead.

People with Venus in Aquarius make excellent parents. You do not spoil your children but treat them fairly and help them to develop their best traits. You undeniably love your nearest and dearest, but your personal and family ties never prevent you from doing the right thing.

January 25, 1890	through	February 18, 1890
March 6, 1891		April 1, 1891
December 27, 1891		January 20, 1892
February 8, 1893		March 4, 1893
December 4, 1893		January 8, 1894
February 12, 1894		April 2, 1894
January 10, 1895		February 3, 1895
February 23, 1896		March 18, 1896
December 12, 1896		January 6, 1897
January 24, 1898		February 17, 1898
March 5, 1899		April 1, 1899
December 26, 1899		January 19, 1900
February 9, 1901		March 5, 1901
December 5, 1901		January 11, 1902
February 6, 1902		April 4, 1902
January 10, 1903		February 3, 1903
February 23, 1904		March 19, 1904
December 13, 1904		January 7, 1905
January 25, 1906		February 18, 1906
March 6, 1907		April 1, 1907
December 27, 1907		January 20, 1908
February 8, 1909		March 4, 1909
December 5, 1909		January 15, 1910
January 29, 1910		April 5, 1910
January 10, 1911		February 3, 1911
February 23, 1912		March 18, 1912
December 12, 1912		January 6, 1913
January 24, 1914		February 17, 1914
March 6, 1915		April 1, 1915
December 26, 1915		January 19, 1916
February 8, 1917		March 4, 1917
December 5, 1917		April 5, 1918
January 9, 1919		February 2, 1919

February 22, 1920

December 12, 1920

January 24, 1922

March 5, 1923

December 26, 1923

February 7, 1925

December 5, 1925

January 9, 1927

February 22, 1928

December 11, 1928

January 23, 1930

March 5, 1931

December 25, 1931

February 7, 1933

December 5, 1933

January 8, 1935

February 21, 1936

December 11, 1936

January 23, 1938

March 5, 1939

December 25, 1939

February 6, 1941

December 5, 1941

January 8, 1943

February 21, 1944

December 10, 1944

January 22, 1946

March 5, 1947

December 24, 1947

February 6, 1949

December 6, 1949

January 7, 1951

February 20, 1952

December 10, 1952

March 18, 1920

January 6, 1921

February 17, 1922

March 31, 1923

January 19, 1924

March 3, 1925

April 5, 1926

February 2, 1927

March 17, 1928

January 6, 1929

February 16, 1930

March 31, 1931

January 18, 1932

March 3, 1933

April 6, 1934

February 1, 1935

March 17, 1936

January 5, 1937

February 16, 1938

March 31, 1939

January 18, 1940

March 2, 1941

April 6, 1942

February 1, 1943

March 16, 1944

January 5, 1945

February 15, 1946

March 30, 1947

January 17, 1948

March 2, 1949

April 5, 1950

January 31, 1951

March 16, 1952

December 31, 1952

Famous people with Venus in Aquarius

Lady Bird Johnson

John Steinbeck

Lord Byron

Frédéric Chopin

Dick Van Dyke

Arturo Toscanini

Henri Matisse

Rita Tushingham

Walter M. Schirra

Franklin Delano Roosevelt

Earl Warren   Edward Albee
Sammy Davis, Jr.   Samuel Barber
Virgil Grissom   Carson McCullers
              Cassius Clay

VENUS IN PISCES

Venus is at her finest in the loving, emotional, idealistic sign of Pisces. You are soft and tender in love and have an unequalled capacity for dedication and self-sacrifice. You are very considerate of others and intuitively know how best to please them. But you do the nice things so quietly and with so little pretense that people all too often fail to appreciate you.

In the same way, you love so wholeheartedly and ask so little for yourself in return, that those you love tend not to value you as highly as you deserve. You think only of giving pleasure to your loved ones; that is very often where your own true pleasure lies. You long for an ideal union where you give yourself completely. You are truly devoted once you have given your love.

On the other hand, you are not especially particular about the kind of person you give your heart to. You may even feel there is greater nobility in loving someone inferior who depends on you and sorely needs your love.

In fact, your tendency is not to use your head at all, but rather to depend on intuition where your affections are concerned. Your love is pure; you are charming, romantic and poetic, and there is great delicacy in your love's expression. You may be emotional, you are never earthy or crude.

This is a wonderful position for an artist, giving heroic grandeur in the subjects portrayed and sometimes, owing to Neptune's influence in this sign, a certain perversity. It is also excellent for all dramatic expression in writing and acting; in the case of a singer, it may greatly enhance the purity and sweetness of the voice.

February 18, 1890 through March 14, 1890
April 1, 1891   April 27, 1891
January 20, 1892   February 13, 1892

March 4, 1893	March 29, 1893
January 8, 1894	February 12, 1894
April 2, 1894	May 6, 1894
February 3, 1895	February 27, 1895
March 18, 1896	April 12, 1896
January 6, 1897	February 2, 1897
February 17, 1898	March 13, 1898
April 1, 1899	April 26, 1899
January 19, 1900	February 13, 1900
March 5, 1901	March 29, 1901
January 11, 1902	February 6, 1902
April 4, 1902	May 6, 1902
February 3, 1903	February 27, 1903
March 19, 1904	April 12, 1904
January 7, 1905	February 2, 1905
February 18, 1906	March 14, 1906
April 1, 1907	April 27, 1907
January 20, 1908	February 13, 1908
March 4, 1909	March 28, 1909
January 15, 1910	January 29, 1910
April 5, 1910	May 6, 1910
February 3, 1911	February 27, 1911
March 18, 1912	April 12, 1912
January 6, 1913	February 2, 1913
February 17, 1914	March 13, 1914
April 1, 1915	April 26, 1915
January 19, 1916	February 13, 1916
March 4, 1917	March 28, 1917
April 5, 1918	May 6, 1918
February 2, 1919	February 26, 1919
March 18, 1920	April 11, 1920
January 6, 1921	February 2, 1921
February 17, 1922	March 13, 1922
March 31, 1923	April 26, 1923
January 19, 1924	February 12, 1924
March 3, 1925	March 27, 1925
April 5, 1926	May 6, 1926
February 2, 1927	February 26, 1927
March 17, 1928	April 11, 1928
January 6, 1929	February 2, 1929
February 16, 1930	March 12, 1930

March 31, 1931	April 25, 1931
January 18, 1932	February 12, 1932
March 3, 1933	March 27, 1933
April 6, 1934	May 6, 1934
February 1, 1935	February 25, 1935
March 17, 1936	April 10, 1936
January 5, 1937	February 2, 1937
February 16, 1938	March 12, 1938
March 31, 1939	April 25, 1939
January 18, 1940	February 12, 1940
March 2, 1941	March 26, 1941
April 6, 1942	May 5, 1942
February 1, 1943	February 25, 1943
March 16, 1944	April 10, 1944
January 5, 1945	February 2, 1945
February 15, 1946	March 11, 1946
March 30, 1947	April 24, 1947
January 17, 1948	February 11, 1948
March 2, 1949	March 26, 1949
April 5, 1950	May 5, 1950
January 31, 1951	February 24, 1951
March 16, 1952	April 9, 1952

Famous people with Venus in Pisces

Leontyne Price	Carol Burnett
Barbra Streisand	Tricia Nixon
Shirley MacLaine	Arthur Goldberg
Edgar Allan Poe	Adlai Stevenson
Victor Hugo	Dr. Martin Luther King, Jr.
George Washington	Carol Channing
Edward M. Kennedy	Thomas Schippers
Sandra Dee	George Harrison
Danny Kaye	Lynda Bird Johnson Robb
Richard Nixon	Ronald Reagan
Elizabeth II	Sidney Poitier

Vincent Van Gogh

6

Your Forcefulness and
MARS

Are you strong and energetic? Do you usually manage to get your own way? Have you the power of endurance in sports? Do you often find yourself getting into accidents or fights?

For the answers to all these questions, you must consult the planet Mars, and it is important for every adult who wants to impress his ideas and actions on the world around him to understand the position of Mars in his own particular horoscope.

In Roman times, Mars was the god of War. His priests danced in armor and carried shields throughout the city in March, his sacred month. The symbol of Mars is a circle and arrow: the circle symbolizes the eternal; the arrow symbolizes earthly energy and outgoing physical force.

Mars is a fiery planet. Its color is reddish, and when it is near the earth, there is violence abroad in the land. All sorts of murders, rapes, holdups, accidents and fires are most likely under such an influence. This is also true when Mars is close to the Sun or retrograde.

Mars rules the head and face, also the muscular system in general, and more specifically, the sex organs, particularly the male ones, since Mars also represents masculine physical love. When Mars is afflicted in the horoscope, it results in fevers, burns and wounds or cuts. It can also cause trouble to the teeth, headaches or jaundice. In general, Mars when afflicted causes injury to the part of the body ruled by the sign Mars is in. This can apply to medical operations as well. For instance, if Mars is in Leo and afflicted, there is the possibility of heart surgery; if afflicted in Scorpio, prostate operations or hysterectomies; if in Capricorn, a knee injury, and so on.

Mars is, above all, the planet of physical force. This can be used constructively or destructively, depending on the aspects. In either case the Mars person is busy and active and likes to feel that he is winning a contest and pushing obstacles aside in his fight for practical accomplishment. Without Mars, no one would be able to make use of the capacities and qualities given by the other planets. Mars turns idea into action, gives purpose, physical expression. Mars is, in other words, the planet that gets things done.

Well aspected, Mars promises much vigor and force of character. These people are energetic and brave. They are, above all, courageous because when they enter into a fight, they are more than likely to win. They do not knuckle under to other people. Their role is to dominate and conquer. They make excellent military men and are in their element during times of war. In a man, a well-aspected Mars makes you successful with the ladies. In either sex, it gives practical will power and the ability to put your plans across. You are both vital and ambitious. People with a well-aspected Mars have excellent coordination and are likely to be successful athletes or at least good at sports. These people are outgoing, generous and at the same time prudent. They stop short of going too far and know exactly when they have gone far enough.

A badly aspected Mars, on the other hand, makes one violent and contentious. Such a person can't stay away from a fight or resist entering into a quarrel. He is either an unregenerate bully or he himself is the victim of another's aggression. He is usually so pugnacious and antagonistic, however, that more often than not he loses the fight he has provoked. He brings out "the beast" in other people. He not only brings disaster on himself in other ways, he is also inclined to be careless and foolhardy. He takes unnecessary chances and is, consequently, accident prone. Mars badly aspected gives a lot of excess energy which these people inevitably expend by getting into some kind of trouble. This can also be a sign of physical weakness. Such people haven't the endurance to win at sports. Their practical will power is wanting. They never seem to accomplish what they set out to do.

The various aspects of Mars are indicative of the manner in which you act concretely. Mars in good aspect to Mercury makes you fluent in speech or writing, able to express yourself smoothly and harmoniously on an intellectual plane. Mars in bad aspect to Mercury, however, makes you sarcastic and argumentative. You often find that your ideas and actions are in conflict.

Mars in good aspect to Venus gives a lot of sex appeal, and relations with the opposite sex tend to work out to your satisfaction and best advantage. Mars in bad aspect to Venus, on the other hand, makes your sex relationships either unconventional or inharmonious. You do not easily find accord with those who attract you or those whom you attract.

Mars in good aspect to Jupiter is an excellent sign of fortunate monetary circumstances and money that comes in regularly and with ease. This enables you to spend freely and still remain solvent. When Mars afflicts Jupiter, either you tend to be extravagant, or you are always overextended financially. Your generosity, which is often unwise, knows no bounds.

Mars in good aspect to Saturn is the indication par excellence of the capable executive. You just naturally run things—you are an expert at putting your plans across and accomplishing what you set out to do. There is no worse sign of a terrible temper than Mars adversely aspecting Saturn. Or it can mean that all your affairs tend to be stalemated. You meet with obstructions and insurmountable obstacles, or else you see projects you have devoted a great deal of time to fail because you weren't able to put your plans across.

Mars in good aspect to Uranus denotes great harmony between inner will and a capacity for external action. This is often a sign of genius in your particular field. You act dynamically and with flair and imagination. Mars in bad aspect to Uranus, on the other hand, gives erratic spur-of-the-moment behavior. There may be signs of genius, but the expression is inharmonious and at odds with the world at large. Or it can merely make you very eccentric and incapable of making a sustained effort, as well as inclined to periodic explosions of temper.

With Mars in good aspect to Neptune, you are able to charm people into doing what you want them to do. Mars in adverse aspect to Neptune is a weird influence felt by those whose lives are touched by scandal and who overindulge in liquor or use narcotics. Under this influence, you are sure to experience unreasonable conditions in many forms.

When the Sun is in good aspect to Mars, your father and the other men in your life are vigorous and strong. Women with this aspect nearly always give birth to sons. When Mars afflicts the Sun, the men in your life are antagonistic and domineering if you are a woman. If a man, other men in positions of authority are not well disposed and may actively fight to spoil your plans.

When Mars is in good aspect to your Moon, your mother was forceful and determined, and your women friends energetic and positive. With Moon in bad aspect to Mars, on the other hand, you would have resented a bossy, quarrelsome mother. If you are a man, the women in your life would be so aggressive they would literally chase you down.

If your Mars is not favorably aspected now, do not despair. Many Mars afflictions describe external conditions you can learn to handle or personal problems you can overcome by practice and self-discipline.

All the above is very general. You must figure out for yourself which aspects apply to you. But the following describes quite accurately the way in which you act concretely; so consult the description connected with your birthdate to find out where in the twelve signs of the Zodiac your Mars is placed and exactly what this means for you.

If your date is mentioned twice, your Mars is at the end of one sign or the beginning of the next, and the characteristics of either or both may apply to you.

MARS IN ARIES

Mars in Aries gives brilliance, forcefulness and courage in action. Mars is very strong in its own sign, enabling you to do what you set out to do. Whether your desires are foolish or noble, you fulfill them with a dynamic purpose that is hard to beat.

You have all the determination and practical ability to succeed in life. Whether your energy is mental or physical or both, you have an indomitable will to win. For you to fail, Mars must have some very strong afflictions. And even if afflicted, your powers are formidable. When well aspected, they are hard to beat.

This is an excellent influence for a man of action, whether his fields are politics or business. In art, writing and music, your works will be popular. You could be successful at spreading propaganda or planning advertising campaigns. You know exactly how to go about making an idea popular in the world at large.

If your Mars refers to sports, you are championship material. You have all the will power, strength and co-ordination of a real winner.

You will have real sex appeal for people born from March 21 to April 20 and from September 23 to October 23, as well as for some of the people born between June 21 and July 23, and between December 22 and January 20.

January 26, 1891	through	March 8, 1891
December 27, 1892		February 11, 1893
June 23, 1894		August 19, 1894
October 13, 1894		December 31, 1894
May 21, 1896		July 1, 1896
April 28, 1898		June 7, 1898
April 7, 1900		May 17, 1900
March 18, 1902		April 27, 1902
February 26, 1904		April 6, 1904
February 4, 1906		March 17, 1906
January 10, 1908		February 22, 1908
July 21, 1909		September 26, 1909
November 20, 1909		January 22, 1910
June 2, 1911		July 15, 1911
May 7, 1913		June 16, 1913
April 16, 1915		May 25, 1915
March 26, 1917		May 4, 1917
March 6, 1919		April 14, 1919
February 12, 1921		March 24, 1921
January 21, 1923		March 3, 1923
December 19, 1924		February 5, 1925
June 14, 1926		August 1, 1926
May 16, 1928		June 26, 1928

April 24, 1930	June 2, 1930
April 3, 1932	May 12, 1932
March 14, 1934	April 22, 1934
February 21, 1936	April 1, 1936
January 30, 1938	March 12, 1938
January 3, 1940	February 16, 1940
July 1, 1941	January 11, 1942
May 27, 1943	July 7, 1943
May 2, 1945	June 11, 1945
April 11, 1947	May 20, 1947
March 21, 1949	April 29, 1949
March 1, 1951	April 10, 1951

Famous people with Mars in Aries

James Thurber	Paul Anka
Charles Dickens	Jack Nicklaus
Frédéric Chopin	Perry Como
Douglas Dillon	Emile Zola
Oliver Cromwell	Emanuel Swedenborg
Charles Baudelaire	Richard Strauss

Joe Namath

MARS IN TAURUS

Mars in Taurus gives the capacity for a slow, steady climb to success. In fire signs such as Aries, Mars has more quick vitality and dash, but there is no better sign than Taurus to give to your actions that brand of dogged determination that succeeds over the long pull.

Steadiness and sincerity are your outstanding traits. You meet obstacles with quiet courage. You are patient. You persevere tirelessly and, more often than not, perseverence wins. Whether you are a general in the army, a politician or a banker, you can be relied on to execute your plans firmly and conservatively.

When Mars is seriously afflicted, you can sometimes seem cruel or unfeeling because you fail to see another's point of view. You must also guard against pouring too much of your energy into relationships with the opposite sex. Mars in Taurus often gives great pleasure and prowess in sex.

In art or literature, you express yourself in a more earthy, voluptuous fashion than the brilliant Aries Mars. Well aspected, there is no better sign for muscular co-ordination and grace in gymnastics and ballet. Where voice is the manner of expression, Mars in Taurus adds to its power and pleasing qualities.

You will have special sex appeal for people born from April 20 to May 21 and from October 23 to November 22, as well as for some of the people born between July 23 and August 23 and between January 20 and February 19.

March 8, 1891	through	April 19, 1891
February 11, 1893		March 28, 1893
August 19, 1894		October 13, 1894
December 31, 1894		March 1, 1895
July 1, 1896		August 15, 1896
June 7, 1898		July 18, 1898
May 17, 1900		June 27, 1900
April 27, 1902		June 7, 1902
April 6, 1904		May 17, 1904
March 17, 1906		April 28, 1906
February 22, 1908		April 6, 1908
January 22, 1910		March 14, 1910
July 15, 1911		September 5, 1911
November 29, 1911		January 30, 1912
June 16, 1913		July 29, 1913
May 15, 1915		July 5, 1915
May 4, 1917		June 14, 1917
April 14, 1919		May 26, 1919
March 25, 1921		May 5, 1921
March 3, 1923		April 15, 1923
February 5, 1925		March 23, 1925
August 1, 1926		February 21, 1927
June 26, 1928		August 8, 1928
June 2, 1930		July 14, 1930
May 12, 1932		June 22, 1932
April 22, 1934		June 2, 1934
April 1, 1936		May 13, 1936
March 12, 1938		April 23, 1938
February 16, 1940		April 1, 1940
January 11, 1942		March 7, 1942

July 7, 1943	August 23, 1943
June 11, 1945	July 23, 1945
May 20, 1947	June 30, 1947
April 29, 1949	June 9, 1949
April 10, 1951	May 21, 1951

Famous people with Mars in Taurus

Joan Sutherland	Joseph Stalin
Leontyne Price	Lucille Ball
Margot Fonteyn	Walter M. Schirra
Shirley MacLaine	J. Robert Oppenheimer
Charlie Chaplin	Otto Klemperer
Sir Isaac Newton	John L. Lewis
Douglas MacArthur	Samuel Barber
John F. Kennedy	Bing Crosby
Earl Warren	Willem de Kooning
David Rockefeller	Rudolf Nureyev
Carol Burnett	Tex Thornton
Pope Pius XII	Sidney Poitier
Adolf Hitler	Leon Trotsky

Arthur Ashe

MARS IN GEMINI

In the airy sign of Gemini, Mars expresses himself on the mental plane. You are not as likely to engage in action in the practical or physical worlds. Your energy is intellectual. Your accomplishments are likely to be in terms of brain instead of brawn.

It may be difficult for you to assert yourself with any efficacy. You are high-strung and easily excited. You tend to vacillate rather than being forceful and persistent in mental as well as practical concerns. You hesitate and hold back when you should be pressing forward, like Hamlet "sicklied o'er with the pale cast of thought."

Gemini is ruled by Mercury, and when it is associated with Mars, Gemini often gives expression through the voice; well aspected, it can give power through its exercise. Both Franklin Delano Roosevelt and Martin Luther King, Jr. possessed the ability to inspire others to follow their actions by virtue of speech rather than physical force.

Mars in this position does not give much stamina in athletics. Mentally, though, you can accomplish wonders, but you must learn to put enough power into your projects to bring them to a successful conclusion. In art, literature and music, your expression is refined and intellectual.

You have special sex appeal for those born between May 21 and June 21 and between November 22 and December 22, and for some of the people born between August 23 and September 23 and between February 19 and March 21.

April 19, 1891	through	June 3, 1891
March 28, 1893		May 13, 1893
March 1, 1895		April 21, 1895
August 15, 1896		March 21, 1897
July 18, 1898		September 2, 1898
June 27, 1900		August 9, 1900
June 7, 1902		July 20, 1902
May 17, 1904		June 30, 1904
April 28, 1906		June 11, 1906
April 6, 1908		May 22, 1908
March 14, 1910		May 1, 1910
September 5, 1911		November 29, 1911
January 30, 1912		April 5, 1912
July 29, 1913		September 15, 1913
July 6, 1915		August 19, 1915
June 14, 1917		July 27, 1917
May 26, 1919		July 8, 1919
May 5, 1921		June 18, 1921
April 15, 1923		May 30, 1923
March 23, 1925		May 9, 1925
February 21, 1927		April 16, 1927
August 8, 1928		October 2, 1928
December 19, 1928		March 10, 1929
July 14, 1930		August 28, 1930
June 22, 1932		August 4, 1932
June 2, 1934		July 15, 1934
May 13, 1936		June 25, 1936
April 23, 1938		June 6, 1938
April 1, 1940		May 17, 1940
March 7, 1942		April 25, 1942

August 23, 1943	March 28, 1944
July 23, 1945	September 7, 1945
June 30, 1947	August 13, 1947
June 9, 1949	July 22, 1949
May 21, 1951	July 3, 1951

Famous people with Mars in Gemini

Princess Margaret Rose	Eddie Fisher
Phyllis Diller	Van Cliburn
Prince Philip	Dr. Martin Luther King, Jr.
Ernest Hemingway	Gordon Cooper
Barbra Streisand	Marc Chagall
Bobby Darin	Franklin Delano Roosevelt
Dean Martin	Lynda Bird Johnson Robb
Virginia Woolf	Rita Tushingham
Benito Mussolini	Luci Baines Johnson Nugent

MARS IN CANCER

Mars in Cancer indicates subtlety and an emotional approach to action. An active water sign, Cancer makes the planet of action powerful as the waves of the ocean that eat away the rocks. And so it is by your actions that you with Mars so placed wear away and dissolve opposition.

With ordinary people, this position indicates a quiet, peaceful nature and a tendency to express themselves in domestic matters, the family and the home. Cancer being the Moon's sign, it is especially good for a mother who is able to handle her children wisely without making an issue of discipline.

Mars in Cancer is an especially wonderful influence, however, if you are creative. Whether you act, paint, write or are musical, it gives a wonderful breadth of comprehension not only of your special field but also of its relationship to the whole of life and the rest of human endeavor. You work not for yourself or for any particular person or country but for the universal good.

You have sympathy and understanding for all humanity. Your knowledge of history, of mankind's struggles and triumphs, is truly remarkable. You have many interests, but they are all related. You must guard, however, against dissipation when your work is through.

You have special sex appeal for people born from June 21 to July 23 and from December 22 to January 20, and for some of the people born between March 21 and April 20 and between September 23 and October 23.

June 3, 1891	through	July 19, 1891
May 13, 1893		June 29, 1893
April 21, 1895		June 10, 1895
March 21, 1897		May 18, 1897
September 2, 1898		October 30, 1898
January 15, 1899		April 15, 1899
August 9, 1900		September 26, 1900
July 20, 1902		September 4, 1902
June 30, 1904		August 14, 1904
June 11, 1906		July 27, 1906
May 22, 1908		July 7, 1908
May 1, 1910		June 18, 1910
April 5, 1912		May 28, 1912
September 15, 1913		May 1, 1914
August 19, 1915		October 7, 1915
July 27, 1917		September 12, 1917
July 8, 1919		August 22, 1919
June 18, 1921		August 3, 1921
May 30, 1923		July 15, 1923
May 9, 1925		June 26, 1925
April 16, 1927		June 6, 1927
October 2, 1928		December 19, 1928
March 10, 1929		May 12, 1929
August 28, 1930		October 20, 1930
February 16, 1931		March 29, 1931
August 4, 1932		September 20, 1932
July 15, 1934		August 30, 1934
June 25, 1936		August 10, 1936
June 6, 1938		July 22, 1938
May 17, 1940		July 3, 1940
April 26, 1942		June 13, 1942
March 28, 1944		May 22, 1944
September 7, 1945		November 11, 1945
December 26, 1945		April 22, 1946
August 13, 1947		September 30, 1947

July 22, 1949   September 6, 1949
July 3, 1951   August 18, 1951

Famous people with Mars in Cancer

Audrey Hepburn	Marie Antoinette
Mary Martin	Hayley Mills
Henry Ford II	John Glenn
Pablo Picasso	Dr. Ralph Bunche
William Shakespeare	John W. Young
Lord Byron	Laurence Rockefeller
Nicolaus Copernicus	Margaret Sanger
William Styron	Pope John XXIII
Arturo Toscanini	Edmund Wilson
John F. Kennedy, Jr.	Willy Brandt

Tricia Nixon

MARS IN LEO

This is an even better sign for Mars than Aries. You are enterprising and courageous. You tend to do what you set out to do somewhat like Mars in Aries, but with more perspective and without the one-track mind of the Aries Mars.

Mars in Leo indicates a very full and noble expression of the emotions and a terrific amount of actual force and drive. You are not only ardent in your affections, but you also express yourself in an open, confident manner and with a certain warmth and heart.

You are a proud and genial leader, noble in your actions and the execution of your plans. You can lead because others love and admire you. Both your equals and your followers look up to you and are inspired by the example you set.

You do things with a flourish and in the grand manner. Your ambitions are the highest. All your ideas are splendid and grandiose. You are a great showman; your productions are truly magnificent. Mars in Leo is good for being successful in the world of entertainment.

When you speak or write, you are eloquent and persuasive. Your appeal is from the heart and so is the response that you inspire.

You have special sex appeal for those born between July 23 and

August 23 and between January 20 and February 19, as well as for some of the people born from April 20 to May 21 and from October 23 to November 22.

July 19, 1891	through	September 4, 1891
June 29, 1893		August 16, 1893
June 10, 1895		July 28, 1895
May 18, 1897		July 8, 1897
October 30, 1898		January 15, 1899
April 15, 1899		June 15, 1899
September 26, 1900		November 23, 1900
March 1, 1901		May 10, 1901
September 4, 1902		October 23, 1902
August 14, 1904		October 1, 1904
July 27, 1906		September 12, 1906
July 7, 1908		August 23, 1908
June 18, 1910		August 5, 1910
May 28, 1912		July 16, 1912
May 1, 1914		June 25, 1914
October 7, 1915		May 28, 1916
September 12, 1917		November 2, 1917
August 22, 1919		October 9, 1919
August 3, 1921		September 19, 1921
July 15, 1923		August 31, 1923
June 26, 1925		August 12, 1925
June 6, 1927		July 24, 1927
May 12, 1929		July 4, 1929
October 20, 1930		February 16, 1931
March 29, 1931		June 10, 1931
September 20, 1932		November 13, 1932
August 30, 1934		October 17, 1934
August 10, 1936		September 26, 1936
July 22, 1938		September 7, 1938
July 3, 1940		August 19, 1940
June 13, 1942		August 1, 1942
May 22, 1944		July 11, 1944
November 11, 1945		December 26, 1945
April 22, 1946		June 20, 1946
September 30, 1947		December 1, 1947
February 12, 1948		May 18, 1948

September 6, 1949   October 26, 1949
August 18, 1951   October 4, 1951

Famous people with Mars in Leo

Frank Sinatra	Edward H. White 2nd
Gregory Peck	James A. McDivitt
Ed Sullivan	Casey Stengel
Jackie Gleason	Mary McCarthy
Andy Williams	Willie Mays
Harry Truman	Yehudi Menuhin
Eugene McCarthy	Mike Douglas
Igor Stravinsky	Merv Griffin
Helen Hayes	Le Corbusier

MARS IN VIRGO

Mars is very efficient in Virgo, but the actions of persons who have this position in their horoscope are cool and impersonal. No matter what you decide to do, you do it with a certain detachment. Despite the fact that you are deeply involved in a problem, you are able to go about solving it as if it scarcely had anything to do with you at all.

You do not have the warmth and enthusiasm of the Mars Leo, but once you have decided on a course of action, you can be very determined. You have a strong will, but unless Mars has modifying aspects, you may appear to other people to be cold-blooded. You do not seem to be distracted by the passions of ordinary mortals, but you can be staunch in your dedication to a cause.

Because your emotions are not involved in your actions, you may be very good at acting. Whereas real emotion would be very embarrassing, you can be quite professional in simulating emotions you do not necessarily feel. This is an excellent position for a military man who must calculate every move without being distracted by emotional considerations.

You are proud and ambitious as well as outstandingly able. You may, however, not be as popular as people who are less reserved.

For the best success, you should try to present your ideas in a more imaginative fashion.

You have special sex appeal for those born between August 23 and September 23 and from February 19 to March 21, as well as for some born between May 21 and June 21 and from November 22 to December 22.

September 4, 1891	through	October 21, 1891
August 16, 1893		October 2, 1893
July 28, 1895		September 13, 1895
July 8, 1897		August 25, 1897
June 15, 1899		August 5, 1899
November 23, 1900		March 1, 1901
May 11, 1901		July 13, 1901
October 23, 1902		December 19, 1902
April 19, 1903		May 30, 1903
October 1, 1904		November 20, 1904
September 12, 1906		October 29, 1906
August 24, 1908		October 9, 1908
August 5, 1910		September 21, 1910
July 16, 1912		September 2, 1912
June 25, 1914		August 14, 1914
May 28, 1916		July 22, 1916
November 2, 1917		January 11, 1918
February 25, 1918		June 23, 1918
October 9, 1919		November 30, 1919
September 19, 1921		November 6, 1921
August 31, 1923		October 17, 1923
August 12, 1925		September 28, 1925
July 25, 1927		September 10, 1927
July 4, 1929		August 21, 1929
June 10, 1931		August 1, 1931
November 13, 1932		July 6, 1933
October 17, 1934		December 11, 1934
September 26, 1936		November 14, 1936
September 7, 1938		October 24, 1938
August 19, 1940		October 5, 1940
August 1, 1942		September 17, 1942
July 11, 1944		August 28, 1944
June 20, 1946		August 9, 1946
December 1, 1947		February 12, 1948

May 18, 1948	July 16, 1948
October 26, 1949	December 25, 1949
March 28, 1950	June 11, 1950
October 4, 1951	November 23, 1951

Famous people with Mars in Virgo

Bob Hope	Robert McNamara
Jacqueline Kennedy Onassis	Fidel Castro
Lyndon B. Johnson	Ben Hogan
Leslie Caron	Robert Vaughn
Chiang Kai-Shek	Geraldine Chaplin
Napoleon Bonaparte	Romy Schneider
Joan of Arc	Eddie Arnold
Benjamin Spock	Alexander the Great
Eero Saarinen	Julie Nixon Eisenhower

MARS IN LIBRA

Your sense of justice is frequently outraged. You like fair play above all, and as life is so often arbitrary and fate capricious, you may find yourself protesting its inequities loudly and clearly. You are willing to fight to the bitter end for what you consider fair.

You act as prudently as a judge and with careful consideration. You stop and take aim before you fire and therefore avoid wasted motion. Because of this, the impact of your actions is doubly strong. You do just enough—never too much—and in this way conserve your energies and powers of endurance.

You are always forceful, never violent. You are disciplined and have a great deal of self-control. You act with true prudence. Your means are admirably well suited to your ends.

Mars in Libra can be good for expressing yourself in artistic or literary fields. It gives balanced judgment and the ability to weigh the pros and cons before you act.

If Mars is afflicted, you may experience strife in partnership or marriage. If it is well aspected, you are able to express yourself in conjunction with others and are unlikely to go to extremes.

You have special sex appeal for people born between March 21

and April 20 and from September 23 to October 23, and for some
of the people born from June 21 to July 23 and from December 22
to January 20.

October 21, 1891	through	December 7, 1891
October 2, 1893		November 17, 1893
September 14, 1895		October 29, 1895
August 25, 1897		October 9, 1897
August 5, 1899		September 20, 1899
July 13, 1901		August 31, 1901
December 19, 1902		April 19, 1903
May 30, 1903		August 6, 1903
November 20, 1904		January 13, 1905
October 29, 1906		December 17, 1906
October 10, 1908		November 25, 1908
September 21, 1910		November 6, 1910
September 2, 1912		October 17, 1912
August 14, 1914		September 29, 1914
July 22, 1916		September 8, 1916
January 11, 1918		February 25, 1918
June 23, 1918		August 16, 1918
November 30, 1919		January 31, 1920
April 23, 1920		July 10, 1920
November 6, 1921		December 26, 1921
October 17, 1923		December 3, 1923
September 28, 1925		November 13, 1925
September 10, 1927		October 25, 1927
August 21, 1929		October 6, 1929
August 1, 1931		September 17, 1931
July 6, 1933		August 25, 1933
December 11, 1934		July 29, 1935
November 14, 1936		January 5, 1937
October 25, 1938		December 11, 1938
October 5, 1940		November 20, 1940
September 17, 1942		November 1, 1942
August 28, 1944		October 13, 1944
August 9, 1946		September 24, 1946
July 16, 1948		September 3, 1948
December 26, 1949		March 28, 1950
June 11, 1950		August 10, 1950
November 23, 1951		January 19, 1952

Famous people with Mars in Libra

William Faulkner	Abraham Lincoln
Françoise Sagan	Richard Burton
Winston Churchill	John Lennon
Percy B. Shelley	Johnny Carson
Edgar Allan Poe	Arnold Palmer
George Bernard Shaw	Paul Tillich
Martin Luther	Pope Paul VI

John Lindsay

MARS IN SCORPIO

You are ruthless and merciless in action. You do not give way to anyone. Your determination is fixed. Your force is deadly. Nor are you inclined to be adaptable. You do not change as the situation changes; your methods remain the same. There are no holds barred when it comes to your getting your own way. You sting like the scorpion, or, when you reflect the nobler aspects of this sign, like the giant eagle, you swoop down on your prey.

This is a powerful position for a man of action. It indicates energy and shrewdness but carries with it the tendency to be cruel. When opposed, Mars in Scorpio can resort to violence. You can be implacable in getting your revenge.

In writers, the imagination is bloodthirsty and they may depict murderous characters and outrageous crimes. In ordinary people, this position may indicate a liking for horror movies or scary television shows.

Mars in Scorpio can also be expressed in terms of science or medicine. When it is well aspected, you can be an able surgeon or scientist who probes the secrets of the universe. Or if less subtlety is shown, you may excel as a butcher or mortician.

The position indicates strong passions and a tremendous sex drive.

You have special sex appeal for people born from October 23 to November 23 and from April 20 to May 21, and for some born from July 23 to August 23 and from January 20 to February 19.

January 1, 1890	through	February 28, 1890
June 17, 1890		July 21, 1890
December 8, 1891		January 24, 1892
November 17, 1893		December 31, 1893
October 29, 1895		December 11, 1895
October 9, 1897		November 21, 1897
September 21, 1899		November 2, 1899
August 31, 1901		October 14, 1901
August 6, 1903		September 22, 1903
January 13, 1905		August 21, 1905
December 17, 1906		February 5, 1907
November 25, 1908		January 9, 1909
November 6, 1910		December 20, 1910
October 17, 1912		November 30, 1912
September 29, 1914		November 11, 1914
September 8, 1916		October 21, 1916
August 16, 1918		September 30, 1918
January 31, 1920		April 23, 1920
July 10, 1920		September 4, 1920
December 26, 1921		February 18, 1922
December 3, 1923		January 19, 1924
November 13, 1925		December 27, 1925
October 25, 1927		December 8, 1927
October 6, 1929		November 18, 1929
September 17, 1931		October 30, 1931
August 26, 1933		October 9, 1933
July 29, 1935		September 16, 1935
January 5, 1937		March 12, 1937
May 14, 1937		August 8, 1937
December 11, 1938		January 29, 1939
November 20, 1940		January 4, 1941
November 1, 1942		December 15, 1942
October 13, 1944		November 25, 1944
September 24, 1946		November 6, 1946
September 3, 1948		October 16, 1948
August 10, 1950		September 25, 1950
January 19, 1952		August 27, 1952

Famous people with Mars in Scorpio

Jean-Paul Sartre	Rock Hudson
Henry Fonda	Eleanor Roosevelt

Robert Louis Stevenson   Alan Jay Lerner
George Washington   Jonas Salk
Robert F. Kennedy   Pablo Casals
Leonard Bernstein   Princess Anne
David McCallum   Artur Rubinstein
Sammy Davis, Jr.   Caroline Kennedy
Eugene Ionesco   Mohandas K. Gandhi
J. William Fulbright   Dag Hammarskjold

MARS IN SAGITTARIUS

You may be dashing and exciting, but you lack the power of endurance, the ability to continue with any given action for long. You start something, then become distracted and put it down. What you do quickly, you do well, but you are not capable of persisting in anything for long.

Your method is swift as the flight of an arrow, but it takes heavy artillery to win a war. You must try to make a sustained effort. Your acts are as disconnected as that of the archer who has to stop after every shot to reload his bow.

In speech or writing, you may be brilliant and quick-witted, but you tend to choose a variety of subjects unrelated to one another. If a writer, you should not attempt long novels, but would do better with short stories. If a speaker, you can be very amusing and cogent, but you should make a special effort to correlate your remarks.

Because of Jupiter's influence, Mars in this sign gives a certain geniality to the actions. You are also straightforward and direct, even ingenuous in your approach. You would never stoop to doing anything devious or underhanded. When Mars is afflicted, however, there may be a lack of energy.

You have sex appeal for people born from November 22 to December 22 and from May 21 to June 21, and for some born from February 19 to March 21 and from August 23 to September 23.

March 1, 1890	through	June 17, 1890
July 21, 1890		September 23, 1890
January 24, 1892		March 13, 1892
December 31, 1893		February 13, 1894

December 11, 1895	January 22, 1896
November 21, 1897	January 1, 1898
November 3, 1899	December 13, 1899
October 14, 1901	November 23, 1901
September 22, 1903	November 2, 1903
August 21, 1905	October 7, 1905
February 5, 1907	April 1, 1907
January 9, 1909	February 23, 1909
December 20, 1910	January 31, 1911
November 30, 1912	January 10, 1913
November 11, 1914	December 21, 1914
October 21, 1916	December 1, 1916
October 1, 1918	November 11, 1918
September 4, 1920	October 18, 1920
February 18, 1922	September 13, 1922
January 19, 1924	March 6, 1924
December 27, 1925	February 8, 1926
December 8, 1927	January 18, 1928
November 18, 1929	December 29, 1929
October 30, 1931	December 9, 1931
October 9, 1933	November 19, 1933
September 16, 1935	October 28, 1935
March 13, 1937	May 14, 1937
August 8, 1937	September 30, 1937
January 29, 1939	March 21, 1939
January 4, 1941	February 17, 1941
December 15, 1942	January 27, 1943
November 25, 1944	January 5, 1945
November 6, 1946	December 17, 1946
October 16, 1948	November 26, 1948
September 25, 1950	November 5, 1950
August 27, 1952	October 11, 1952

Famous people with Mars in Sagittarius

Lady Bird Johnson	Felix Frankfurter
Judy Garland	Richard Nixon
Julie Andrews	Warren Beatty
Lewis Carroll	Joan Baez
Rudyard Kipling	Billy Graham
Mark Twain	Barry Goldwater
Oscar Wilde	Shelley Berman

Patty Duke   Cassius Clay
Everett Dirksen   Brenda Lee
Joe DiMaggio   Prince Charles
John Osborne   Margaret Chase Smith
              Greta Garbo

MARS IN CAPRICORN

In Capricorn, Mars is very powerful. If you have this position in your horoscope, you display much dynamic force in action. You have all the vaulting ambition of the leaping goat and the vigor and tenacity to succeed. In whatever field you find yourself, whether it be politics, business or science, you have the energy and will power to reach the top.

You make a very capable executive or leader. You are stern and you command obedience. You have the personal magnetism to inspire others to follow after you.

You don't beat around the bush, but are direct and very persistent. You hammer away at your chosen project. You have the ability to put your plans across. This is an even stronger position than Mars in Aries for getting your own way, and Mars has to be very afflicted indeed for you to weaken or fail.

You have such a strong will, in fact, that it takes a very brave person to oppose you, and you override those who do.

Mars in Capricorn is an excellent position for victory for a military man, determination in an inventor, mastery of technique in an artist and forcefulness in an actor. In athletics, this position gives great strength and endurance. If Mars is well aspected, you should be a champion.

You have special sex appeal for people born from December 22 to January 20 and from June 21 to July 23, as well as for some born between September 23 and October 23 and from March 21 to April 20.

September 23, 1890 through   November 6, 1890
March 13, 1892   May 6, 1892
February 13, 1894   March 28, 1894
January 22, 1896   March 3, 1896

January 1, 1898	February 10, 1898
December 13, 1899	January 21, 1900
November 23, 1901	January 1, 1902
November 3, 1903	December 12, 1903
October 7, 1905	November 17, 1905
April 1, 1907	October 13, 1907
February 23, 1909	April 9, 1909
January 31, 1911	March 13, 1911
January 10, 1913	February 19, 1913
December 21, 1914	January 29, 1915
December 1, 1916	January 9, 1917
November 11, 1918	December 20, 1918
October 18, 1920	November 27, 1920
September 13, 1922	October 30, 1922
March 6, 1924	April 24, 1924
February 8, 1926	March 22, 1926
January 18, 1928	February 27, 1928
December 29, 1929	February 6, 1930
December 9, 1931	January 17, 1932
November 19, 1933	December 27, 1933
October 28, 1935	December 6, 1935
September 30, 1937	November 11, 1937
March 21, 1939	May 24, 1939
July 21, 1939	September 23, 1939
February 17, 1941	April 2, 1941
January 26, 1943	March 8, 1943
January 5, 1945	February 14, 1945
December 17, 1946	January 25, 1947
November 26, 1948	January 4, 1949
November 6, 1950	December 15, 1950
October 11, 1952	November 21, 1952

Famous people with Mars in Capricorn

Doris Day	Danny Kaye
Dwight D. Eisenhower	Rex Harrison
Walt Disney	Henri Matisse
Albert Einstein	Nathan Pusey
Leo Tolstoi	John Wayne
Thomas Edison	C. P. Snow
Louis Pasteur	Thomas Mann

MARS IN AQUARIUS

Like Gemini and Libra, also air signs, your field of action tends to be intellectual, but Aquarius adds moral strength. You are forthright, liberty-loving and candid. Like King Solomon, your every act is remarkably wise.

Since Aquarius is ruled by Uranus, you can direct your energies into the field of music. You can also be an excellent writer, since your understanding of your fellow man is thorough and complete. You always take the factor of human nature into consideration before you act. You should therefore also go into the fields of politics or diplomacy, or you could excel in psychiatry or social work.

If badly aspected, this position could give nervous, high-strung, agitated behavior, but the afflictions have to be very severe for that to happen and are the exception rather than the rule.

Your methods are free, even a bit careless on occasion. Your force tends to be mental rather than practical, and your techniques are better suited to conceiving ideas rather than executing them. In other words, you are better at planning the battle beforehand than at leading in the troops. In fields like literature and the arts, your manner of expression is comprehensive and broad.

You have special sex appeal for people born between January 20 and February 19 and from July 23 to August 23, as well as for some born between April 20 and May 21 and from October 23 to November 22.

November 6, 1890	through	December 16, 1890
May 6, 1892		November 9, 1892
March 28, 1894		May 9, 1894
March 3, 1896		April 11, 1896
February 10, 1898		March 20, 1898
January 21, 1900		February 28, 1900
January 1, 1902		February 8, 1902
December 12, 1903		January 19, 1904
November 17, 1905		December 27, 1905
October 13, 1907		November 28, 1907
April 9, 1909		May 25, 1909

March 13, 1911	April 23, 1911
February 19, 1913	March 29, 1913
January 30, 1915	March 9, 1915
January 9, 1917	February 16, 1917
December 20, 1918	January 27, 1919
November 27, 1920	January 5, 1921
October 30, 1922	December 11, 1922
April 24, 1924	June 24, 1924
August 24, 1924	October 19, 1924
March 22, 1926	May 3, 1926
February 27, 1928	April 7, 1928
February 6, 1930	March 16, 1930
January 17, 1932	February 24, 1932
December 27, 1933	February 3, 1934
December 6, 1935	January 14, 1936
November 11, 1937	December 21, 1937
May 24, 1939	July 21, 1939
September 23, 1939	November 19, 1939
April 2, 1941	May 15, 1941
March 8, 1943	April 17, 1943
February 14, 1945	March 24, 1945
January 25, 1947	March 4, 1947
January 4, 1949	February 11, 1949
December 15, 1950	January 22, 1951
November 21, 1952	December 30, 1952

Famous people with Mars in Aquarius

Cary Grant	Pat Nixon
Victor Hugo	J. D. Salinger
Richard Wagner	Thomas Schippers
Luther Burbank	Virgil Grissom
Edward M. Kennedy	Edward Albee
Elizabeth II	Charles de Gaulle
Arthur Goldberg	Charlotte Ford Niarchos
Adlai Stevenson	Julie Christie
Edward Steichen	Truman Capote

W. E. B. DuBois

MARS IN PISCES

This is as close as you can come to a passive position for Mars. Mars is fiery and dynamic; Pisces, watery, psychic and compliant; so there is ordinarily some lack of vigor and difficulty in putting your plans across. There are of course exceptions, and in those cases where Mars is extraordinarily well aspected, more strength and determination can result. Some of the more masterful people with Mars in Pisces can also be explained by the fact that Mars progressed into the dynamic sign of Aries in their maturity.

However, although some very successful people have had Mars in Pisces, the position is weak, and in general they accomplish their aims owing to the action of their other planets or because they represent other people's emotions, not their own. This position is a factor in an actor's or politician's ability to inspire empathy in his audience or the masses he seeks to control.

Most of you tend not to change the environment in which you are placed to any remarkable extent. On the contrary, it changes you. In most cases, you are a follower rather than a leader. You are receptive to every impression. You do not forcefully go out and bend others to your will. In writers, however, this gives intuition and the ability to express themselves with subtlety and imagination.

You have special sex appeal for people born from February 19 to March 21 and from August 23 to September 23, and for some born from May 21 to June 21 and from November 22 to December 22.

December 16, 1890	through	January 25, 1891
November 9, 1892		December 27, 1892
May 9, 1894		June 23, 1894
April 11, 1896		May 21, 1896
March 21, 1898		April 28, 1898
February 28, 1900		April 7, 1900
February 8, 1902		March 18, 1902
January 9, 1904		February 26, 1904
December 27, 1905		February 4, 1906
November 28, 1907		January 10, 1908
May 25, 1909		July 21, 1909

September 26, 1909	November 20, 1909
April 23, 1911	June 2, 1911
March 30, 1913	May 7, 1913
March 9, 1915	April 16, 1915
February 16, 1917	March 26, 1917
January 27, 1919	March 6, 1919
January 5, 1921	February 12, 1921
December 11, 1922	January 21, 1923
June 24, 1924	August 24, 1924
October 19, 1924	December 19, 1924
May 3, 1926	June 14, 1926
April 7, 1928	May 16, 1928
March 16, 1930	April 24, 1930
February 24, 1932	April 3, 1932
February 3, 1934	March 14, 1934
January 14, 1936	February 21, 1936
December 21, 1937	January 30, 1938
November 19, 1939	January 3, 1940
May 15, 1941	July 1, 1941
April 17, 1943	May 27, 1943
March 24, 1945	May 2, 1945
March 4, 1947	April 11, 1947
February 11, 1949	March 21, 1949
January 22, 1951	March 1, 1951
December 31, 1952	

Famous people with Mars in Pisces

John Steinbeck	Vincent Van Gogh
Elizabeth Taylor	James Baldwin
J. Paul Getty	Aleksei N. Kosygin
Leslie Uggams	Jule Styne
Carol Channing	Carson McCullers
Al Capp	Henry Luce
Hubert Humphrey	Prince Edward

Gertrude Stein

7
JUPITER
and Your Luck

Are you a good provider? Are you generous or just downright extravagant? Do you have a genial manner? Is respect for law and order one of the fundamental precepts of your life?

Jupiter is an influence in all such behavior. It is important for every adult who wants to know where his best luck and most fortunate career opportunities lie to understand the position of Jupiter in his particular horoscope.

In Roman times, the god Jupiter was considered the guardian of law, the defender of truth and the protector of justice and virtue. He was identified with Zeus, the father of the gods on the ancient Greeks' mythical Mount Olympus. In astrology, Jupiter is called "the greater Fortune," and his favorable aspects are very benefic indeed.

Jupiter is a clear, bright planet and goes through every sign of the Zodiac in slightly less than twelve years. He is a hot, moist, masculine, convivial planet and showers many blessings on those who are born strongly under his rays.

The parts of the body governed by Jupiter are the liver, veins, blood and the entrails, and an afflicted Jupiter can result in trouble in any or all these parts. Physically, you can often recognize someone born strongly under Jupiter by their ruddy complexion and sanguine attributes.

Jupiter is primarily the planet of material good fortune and philosophical wisdom. Where his influence is powerful, he can be relied on to rescue you at the last minute and to give you the break or boost you need in the most impossible situations. Jupiter gives you the strength to endure adversity and the philosophy to realize that through your trials you have gained real wisdom and valuable experience. Jupiter is very protective; his only difficulties come from not making the most of the opportunities that come his way.

Well aspected, Jupiter promises much good fortune. His blessings come easily and without much effort on your part. A person under the influence of Jupiter is either born wealthy or is destined to become affluent later on. Or else he is peaceful and optimistic and is contented with what he has. People with well-aspected Jupiters are generous and genial. They are hospitable and like to have a good time. They also have a deep respect for law and order and have moral instincts. For such people, conscience is a reliable guide. Their religious sense is well developed and true. They are truthful, affable, good and wise. The only real danger in a well-aspected Jupiter is that you can be so lucky in a material sense that you neglect Jupiter's spiritual benefits. These can be of even greater value and may lead to an interest in law, philosophy and religion, and harmony with friends in foreign lands.

Badly aspected, Jupiter can make you boastful and extravagant. You can be careless about your possessions and always in debt or borrowing money from your friends. You are lazy and luxury loving, and apt to indulge your slightest whim. Such a person is not sufficiently reserved and quite typically will act like a boon companion to someone he scarcely knows. He has little respect for law or for moral values, and he is either a religious bigot or too shallow to develop an interest either in religion or a philosophy of life.

If your ideas are always well considered and apt to bring you honors, praise and rewards, if you speak and write easily and fluently, chances are that Jupiter is in good aspect to your Mercury. If your ideas are never well thought out but are too ambitious and overshoot the mark, if you speak and write pretentiously, no doubt your Jupiter is in bad aspect to Mercury.

If you can afford the comforts and luxuries of life, if you are charitable to those less fortunate than yourself, if you tend to fall in love with someone in a good position, chances are that Jupiter favorably aspects your Venus. Jupiter in adverse aspect to Venus often makes you feel at a disadvantage socially. This can also give you a garish taste in clothes and ornaments, or you may be overzealous in religious matters.

With Jupiter in good aspect to Mars, your money comes in faster than it is spent. Such a position is an excellent influence for good business judgment and wise actions generally, and indicates good co-ordination in sports. With Jupiter in adverse aspect to Mars, you are profligate with money and spend more than you have or can earn. This aspect is also found in the horoscope of those who suffer religious persecution. It is adverse for energy and co-ordination in sports.

There is no better aspect for inherited wealth or sound financial prospects than Jupiter in good aspect to Saturn. Jupiter unfavorably aspecting Saturn puts a damper on your enthusiasms and is not good for you financially. If you are rich, you are stingy. If poor, you need caution and thrift and often have a hard time accumulating money.

If you have good earning power and it is tied up with the newest, most up-to-date methods, the latest inventions or advanced ideas, then chances are your Jupiter favorably aspects Uranus. If you always seem to spend on crackpot schemes, if your money does not come in steadily but in fits and starts, then Jupiter unfavorably aspects Uranus.

Jupiter in good aspect to Neptune is called the "millionaire" aspect and can make you wealthy at some time in your life. Although you may be born poor, you can obtain great riches. There may be love of pomp and ceremony in religion, and you may aspire to be a prince of the church or an honorable participant of lesser rank. Jupiter in adverse aspect to Neptune tends to financial excess and unsuccessful or dishonest schemes. With this aspect, you should never invest in risky propositions.

With Jupiter in good aspect to the Sun, your father would have been of greatest benefit to you. In a woman's chart, this aspect increases her good fortune through the men in her life. When this aspect is in a man's chart, he is favored by those in positions of authority. Jupiter in bad aspect to the Sun would have made your father something of a spendthrift who would have failed to put his finances on a sound basis. For women, this aspect gives men who promise her more than they deliver. For men, his superiors will be arrogant and unreliable.

There is no better aspect for a benevolent mother, and much good fortune and moral decency through her training, than Moon favorably aspected by Jupiter. For a man, the women in his life will be fortunate and of irreproachable moral character. For a woman, the other women in your life will benefit you. Moon in adverse aspect to Jupiter, on the other hand, would have given you a profligate, impractical mother. If a man, the other women in your life will run you into debt and expect too much of you. If a woman, other women will try to impress you with their extravagances and grand airs.

If your Jupiter is badly aspected, don't be discouraged. A badly aspected Jupiter is never all bad, but brings lessons that are for your own eventual good, blessings in disguise as it were.

The following passages describe the sign position of your Jupiter and will often indicate the areas in which your best luck lies. The discussion can also give you a clue to your most profitable occupation, although of course the entire horoscope must be taken into consideration for an accurate determination.

JUPITER IN ARIES

Your best luck comes from your original ideas and executive ability. You are, in fact, a natural leader, and will do well in any field where you can rise to a position of authority or top command. You have the confidence and ability to run the show. You are capable of administering a large organization or business empire if Jupiter is well aspected, or at least of being in a position of authority at whatever level of achievement you have attained. You women can be the directors of clubs and other social organizations if you don't actively enter the business world, and you will run your homes like generals.

You dislike routine and being under another's authority. If this is necessary when you are starting out, you should be careful not to appear so confident as to arouse jealousy on the part of your superiors.

However, you have your own plans and somehow manage to put them into effect in such a way as to be in an independent position. Your ideas are so original, that you can be thought to be impractical at first, but you are capable of convincing influential people of your point of view.

This position of Jupiter promises much success and material good fortune. Politics and the military may be lucky for you as well as any field in which fire or machinery are involved. There are, however, no limits to the number of fields in which you can make your mark. You are idealistic and generous, and you have the pioneering instinct. Others just naturally follow you because your enthusiasm is so contagious.

Your views on religion are not passive, and you probably regard the church as a man-made political institution rather than a spiritual one.

Your best opportunities come to you between March 21 and April 20, between July 23 and August 23, and between November 22 and December 22. People born at these times tend to see the value of your ideas and to help advance your career. They are also likely to be of benefit to you financially.

March 16, 1892	through	March 25, 1893
February 29, 1904		August 8, 1904
August 31, 1904		March 7, 1905
February 12, 1916		June 25, 1916
October 26, 1916		February 12, 1917
June 6, 1927		September 10, 1927
January 22, 1928		June 3, 1928
May 11, 1939		October 29, 1939
December 20, 1939		May 16, 1940
April 21, 1951		April 28, 1952

Famous people with Jupiter in Aries

Gregory Peck	Helen Keller
Jackie Gleason	Fidel Castro
George Bernard Shaw	Edward Albee
Frédéric Chopin	Jack Nicklaus
J. Paul Getty	Bing Crosby
Robert McNamara	Willem de Kooning

Dr. Ralph Bunche	Yehudi Menuhin
J. Robert Oppenheimer	Vladimir Horowitz
Eugene McCarthy	

JUPITER IN TAURUS

You can be successful in banking or any field where money management is involved. But no matter what your profession, you have a conservative, sound approach to handling your own funds. You can also do well in any field connected with building or real estate. You may construct roads, skyscrapers, housing developments, shopping centers or hotels. Agriculture, mining, or ranching could also be fortunate for you, or you could benefit from these through a marriage partner.

This position of Jupiter often gives a pleasing or memorable voice. As you can see in the list that follows, many popular singers and actors have Jupiter in Taurus. You may also profit through artistic talent. Not only do the artists among you have considerable ability, but they are also fortunate in being recognized and reaping the rewards of financial success.

Even though you may not actually be an artist, you love beauty in every form. You are particularly attached to your personal possessions and may be very proud of them for their aesthetic as well as their financial value. Jewelry, paintings and other objects and adornments—any or all of these may be very important to you. You are generally very domestic and so devoted to your home and family that you are seldom away from them. Unless there are other contrary aspects in your horoscope, you would travel as little as possible; but if you were to take a pleasure trip, you would enjoy visiting museums and other centers of art.

You are very definite in your ideas and opinions. Usually success comes to you because you are so constructive in a positive way. You do not take unnecessary chances, but build slowly and carefully for solid, sound results. However, when afflicted, Jupiter in Taurus can make you extravagant to a fault.

Your religious beliefs are down to earth and practical, but you are also devout, warmhearted and sincere. You must be careful, however, not to be so impressed with the forms of religion that you overlook their meaning. Keats's creed, "Beauty is truth, truth, beauty," may be your own.

Your best opportunities come to you between April 20 and May 21, August 23 and September 23, December 22 and January 20. Even apparently unimportant developments at these times may give you that break you've waited for. People born at these times contribute to your success and are fortunate for you in a financial sense.

March 25, 1893	through	August 20, 1893
October 19, 1893		April 2, 1894
August 8, 1904		August 31, 1904
March 7, 1905		July 20, 1905
December 4, 1905		March 9, 1906
June 25, 1916		October 26, 1916
February 12, 1917		June 29, 1917
June 3, 1928		June 12, 1929
May 16, 1940		May 26, 1941
April 28, 1952		December 31, 1952

Famous people born with Jupiter in Taurus

Audrey Hepburn	J. William Fulbright
Jean-Paul Sartre	Ann-Margret
Henry Fonda	Dr. Martin Luther King, Jr.
Pablo Picasso	James A. McDivitt
John F. Kennedy	Henri Matisse
Ringo Starr	Franklin Delano Roosevelt
John Lennon	Charlotte Ford Niarchos
Jimmy Dean	Constantine of Greece
Dean Martin	Jule Styne
Eddie Fisher	Carson McCullers
Joan Baez	Julie Christie
Pope John XXIII	Nikolai Lenin
Virginia Woolf	Mohandas K. Gandhi

JUPITER IN GEMINI

Luck and success come to you through intellectual pursuits. You would not be inclined to do manual work unless you happen to be particularly clever and skillful with your hands.

Patience is not your strong point. You are not very persistent, and you do not like routine work. You are, however, a true diplomat and adept at manipulating situations and people without antagonizing anyone.

A profession may appeal to you more than any of the business fields; if a woman, you might benefit from one of the professional fields through a husband.

The luckiest fields for you are writing, teaching, science, banking, stockbroking, diplomacy, the law, the lecture platform, the stage, or any business having to do with transportation by air. You may also benefit through composing music, playing an instrument or singing, or through art that depends on ideas. This is a favorable position of Jupiter for success as an executive secretary.

You have such a variety of interests that you may be involved in several projects at the same time. This can be lucky for you. You should, however, guard against becoming concerned with so many different things at the same time that you dissipate your energies. In business, you should investigate carefully any propositions that are presented to you because you tend to attract those who are not strictly aboveboard.

You may be less generous than those with Jupiter in the other signs, or you can be generous to a fault. This will depend on the aspects. However, you are usually sympathetic, kind, and have great humanitarian instincts.

You approach religion with your mind and reason and are also interested in its cultural by-products. This does not preclude your having some unorthodox or unusual beliefs.

Your best opportunities come to you between May 21 and June 21, September 23 and October 23, January 20 and February 19. People born at these times tend to be of benefit to you professionally and to further your financial interests.

August 20, 1893 through	October 19, 1893
April 2, 1894	August 19, 1894
January 1, 1895	April 10, 1895
July 20, 1905	December 4, 1905
March 9, 1906	July 30, 1906
June 29, 1917	July 12, 1918
June 12, 1929	June 26, 1930
May 26, 1941	June 10, 1942

Famous people with Jupiter in Gemini

Jacqueline Kennedy Onassis	Thomas Edison
Phyllis Diller	Sandra Dee
Henry Ford II	Paul Anka
Barbra Streisand	Thomas Schippers
Charles Dickens	Arnold Palmer
Lord Byron	Rita Tushingham
Igor Stravinsky	Eddie Arnold
C. P. Snow	John Osborne
Dag Hammarskjold	Greta Garbo

JUPITER IN CANCER

This is one of the luckiest positions of Jupiter, and you will enjoy life and all its pleasures to the full. You have a wonderful disposition and, unless Jupiter is very afflicted, you are always optimistic and in a good humor. You are generous and kindly, and it is through your extreme good nature that your good fortune often comes.

With Jupiter in Cancer, you may want to devote your whole life to having a good time. If you have a more serious purpose or goal in mind, you must guard against too much merrymaking when your work is through. No matter how dedicated you may be, the hedonistic tendencies are there, but a good many successful people have managed to accomplish wonders despite them. You are in any event inclined to commit excesses and can be very extravagant at times.

You are intuitive and have a vivid imagination. You enjoy travel, especially by water and in the most luxurious fashion. You delight in entertaining people in your home and are a wonderful host or hostess. You love to eat and are interested in everything to do with food and drink. If you yourself cook, and you frequently do, you would use the richest ingredients. For this reason, you may need to watch your weight and to control your appetite.

You women are fortunate to be able to provide for yourselves if you are not well taken care of by your husbands or fathers, as is usually the case. Despite the fact that you are very generous, you are still able to increase the money you receive.

Both sexes have a deep sense of inner security that comes of having had great confidence and comfort from a demonstrative, provident mother. You are accustomed to a good home and all its comforts. You women make excellent housewives and mothers.

You enjoy great popularity and may benefit financially through it. You may even go into politics or marry a politician. You or your life-partner may be especially fortunate in all business enterprises having to do with liquids, with the public and its demands, or with nursing and the home.

People born between February 19 and March 21, between June 21 and July 21 and between October 21 and November 21 are lucky for you financially. Excellent opportunities come to you at these times of the year.

August 19, 1894	through	January 1, 1895
April 10, 1895		September 4, 1895
February 29, 1896		April 18, 1896
July 30, 1906		August 18, 1907
July 12, 1918		August 2, 1919
June 26, 1930		July 17, 1931
June 10, 1942		June 30, 1943

Famous people born with Jupiter in Cancer

Leonard Bernstein	Leslie Caron
Margot Fonteyn	Billy Graham
George Harrison	Princess Margaret Rose
Willie Mays	J. D. Salinger
Harry Truman	James Thurber
Andy Williams	John W. Young
Jay Gould	Oliver Cromwell
Mark Twain	William Shakespeare
Margaret Sanger	John Wayne

Edmund Wilson   Felix Frankfurter
Benito Mussolini   Joe Namath

JUPITER IN LEO

Like those with Jupiter in Aries, your best luck comes to you through being in an executive capacity. You must be in a position of authority or you will never realize your true potential. Whether in government, finance, business or the army, you are a natural leader. If you were to take a job that placed you in an inferior capacity, you would be resentful and very unhappy. Aside from that, your superiors would be jealous of you. This is a wonderful position of Jupiter for grandeur and success. You experience this in a material sense, however, and are not inclined to be particularly religious, although the pomp and ceremony connected with the church might appeal to your well-developed sense of the dramatic.

You are lucky through an expansive, generous, warmhearted disposition and are a splendid showman in all you undertake. Your sense of drama is, in fact, superb. You are well suited for the theater, motion pictures, public life, or any field that can be enhanced by a genius for public relations and effective advertising.

You may profit greatly from your popularity and the devotion and admiration of other people. Unless Jupiter is very afflicted, you have great public appeal. You think big. You do things on a large scale and in the grand manner. Your manner is confident and expansive, and you are capable of inspiring real hero-worship.

You are proud and very ambitious. Your inner urge is to reach the top. You aspire to achieve the best in everything, and you sincerely believe that everything you have is the best. You love power and you wield it masterfully.

You are particularly fond of entertainments of every sort and make a wonderful host or hostess. You may also benefit through having a way with young people and children, either as a teacher or as a devoted and indulgent parent.

Your best opportunities tend to come to you between March 21 and April 20, between July 23 and August 23, and between November 22 and December 22. You can expect the greatest good fortune from projects started at these times. People born at these times are especially lucky for you.

September 4, 1895 through	February 29, 1896
April 18, 1896	September 28, 1896
August 18, 1907	September 12, 1908
August 2, 1919	August 26, 1920
July 17, 1931	August 10, 1932
June 30, 1943	July 25, 1944

Famous people with Jupiter in Leo

Anne Bancroft	Arthur Ashe
Rex Harrison	Elizabeth Taylor
Lyndon B. Johnson	Edward M. Kennedy
Nelson Rockefeller	Eleanor Roosevelt
Alexander the Great	J. P. Morgan
Brigham Young	Luther Burbank
Richard Wagner	Algernon C. Swinburne
	Juan Peron

JUPITER IN VIRGO

Your best luck comes to you through being practical and down to earth. You have sound business judgment because you are analytical and discriminating and know the true value both of ideas and material things. In all financial matters, you are sober and discreet, and while you do not ordinarily yearn to build empires, you manage your own money carefully. You are a wise buyer, whatever your circumstances. You acquire the necessary and avoid waste.

Despite intellectual overtones, Virgo is primarily an earth sign, and Jupiter in Virgo is too material for you to be particularly religious. You do not tend to be especially generous or jovial. You are instead matter of fact and realistic, and your good fortune lies in being able to understand the practical matters that you need to deal with from day to day. You gain, furthermore, from method and attention to detail. You are the person who benefits by inventing time and motion studies and bringing the maximum efficiency to production-line techniques.

While you are as intellectual as Jupiter in Gemini, you have more common sense. You do not lose by the extravagances of Jupiter in Cancer, nor are you carried away by the sometimes foolish enthusiasms of Jupiter in Leo.

Not only do you profit by making your intellect useful, but you also gain both benefit and satisfaction from applying your mind to purely intellectual pursuits. Your powers of analysis, mind for detail, and systematic approach can make you an excellent scientist. This is also a good position for teachers and writers or for a laboratory technician, doctor or nurse. It is good for the earthy occupations such as mining and farming and for building, construction and real estate. You can also be excellent secretaries and CPA's.

Your best chances come to you between December 20 and January 20, between April 20 and May 21 and between August 23 and September 23, although at the time they may not seem as important as they later turn out to be. People born at these times may be of benefit to you and help you to achieve worldly success.

September 28, 1896	through	October 27, 1897
September 12, 1908		October 11, 1909
August 26, 1920		September 25, 1921
August 11, 1932		September 9, 1933
July 25, 1944		August 24, 1945

Famous people with Jupiter in Virgo

Carol Channing	Petula Clark
John Glenn	Prince Philip
Albrecht Dürer	Paul Kruger
Sir Humphry Davy	Victor Hugo
Ralph Waldo Emerson	Sir Thomas More
Guy de Maupassant	Petrarch
Al Capp	Douglas Dillon
Robert Frost	Pope Paul VI

JUPITER IN LIBRA

Your best luck would tend to come to you through your artistic talent or your deep sense of justice. You also profit from the exercise of abstract reason. Your ability to weigh the pros and cons is note-worthy, and if Jupiter is well aspected, the resulting decisions are re-markably wise.

Jupiter in Libra indicates a sincere and profound religious sense. You are very just and gentle, seeing spiritual values as they really are rather than being misled by material or superficial ones. If there is aggressiveness or drive as in the cases of Joan of Arc or Martin Luther, it is owing to the action of planets other than your Jupiter.

This position of Jupiter often makes you a blessing to your as-sociates, and conversely you benefit through association with others. If you were to go into business, you would be well advised to take a partner. Otherwise, it would be more fortunate for you to work for a large firm rather than being strictly on your own.

You would prefer a profession rather than another kind of job no matter how well you would do in it. Even when your financial judg-ment is astute, you would have more success handling other people's money than your own.

Unless there are powerful indications to the contrary in the rest of the horoscope, marriage is very fortunate for you, and your spouse can turn out to be a blessing in your life. Often your best luck comes after you have selected a mate. You adjust easily to marriage because you are normally peaceful, companionable and very considerate.

You can be successful as a diplomat, judge, lawyer, banker, broker, engineer, architect, electrician, artist, mathematician or worker in the field of transportation by air.

Your best opportunities tend to come to you from January 20 to February 19, from May 21 to June 21, and from September 23 to October 23. People born at these times are likely to be lucky for you in financial matters and to help further your career.

October 27, 1897	through	November 27, 1898
October 11, 1909		November 11, 1910
September 25, 1921		October 26, 1922
September 9, 1933		October 10, 1934
August 25, 1945		September 25, 1946

Famous people with Jupiter in Libra

Judy Garland	Tricia Nixon
Ernest Hemingway	Joan of Arc
Shirley MacLaine	Van Cliburn
Winston Churchill	Arthur Goldberg
Percy B. Shelley	Marc Chagall
Robert Louis Stevenson	Samuel Barber
Marie Antoinette	Carol Burnett
Martin Luther	John Lindsay
George Washington	Margaret Chase Smith
Laurence Rockefeller	Caroline Kennedy
Paul Tillich	Thomas Mann
Henry Luce	Gertrude Stein

Eero Saarinen

JUPITER IN SCORPIO

The sex instinct is your driving force. You feel that your powers are god-given, so that your faith in God and therefore in yourself is strong. You have the greatest respect for the creative forces in nature.

Often, your good luck comes through having great attraction for the opposite sex, and unless Jupiter is very afflicted, you are almost certain to win the one who appeals to you most. You are so sure of yourself where sex is concerned that other people just naturally respond to you.

You will do well in any field where both self-confidence and dedication are important. For this reason, you make excellent doctors, diagnosticians, surgeons and nurses, and assistants or researchers in every branch of medicine. You excel in science where shrewdness and the ability to detect nature's secrets are required.

You do well, in fact, in very demanding jobs and those requiring cunning and secrecy. Spies with Jupiter in Scorpio are able, deadly and astute. It is a good position for detectives and policemen. They are able to ferret out secrets others would prefer to conceal. However, if in a professional capacity someone were to confide in you, you could be utterly relied upon never to betray his confidence.

Luck also comes to you in war, and you are very likely to be crowned with glory after combat. Your wily strategies and innate shrewdness make you a formidable opponent indeed. This is an excellent position of Jupiter for generals whose conquests extend from the battlefield to the boudoir.

You can be clever at finance or so dedicated to a job serving humanity in some altruistic way that you are totally unconcerned about monetary rewards. In either case, you should be comfortable financially. You are either very materialistic or a great idealist where your job or profession is concerned. You may also excel as actors, musicians, engineers, chemists, dentists, morticians, masseuses and mechanics.

Your best opportunities come to you from February 19 to March 21, June 21 to July 23, October 23 to November 22, and you should be careful to take advantage of them. People born at these times may help you financially or further your career.

November 27, 1898	through	December 25, 1899
November 11, 1910		December 11, 1911
October 26, 1922		November 24, 1923
October 10, 1934		November 8, 1935
September 25, 1946		October 23, 1947

Famous people with Jupiter in Scorpio

Julie Andrews	Richard Chamberlain
Françoise Sagan	Patty Duke
Chiang Kai-Shek	James Arness
Leo Tolstoi	Lucille Ball
Napoleon Bonaparte	Walter M. Schirra
Louis Pasteur	Luci Baines Johnson Nugent
Steve Lawrence	Sophia Loren
Elvis Presley	Benjamin Disraeli
Le Corbusier	Richard Strauss

JUPITER IN SAGITTARIUS

This is the best sign for financial success. Either you would have inherited a great deal of money or you yourself would have the ability to earn money easily. You women are usually well provided for by either your fathers or husbands, but if not, you could easily build and administer a business of your own; in case of the death of your provider, you could take over and run his affairs successfully. Both sexes make natural financiers.

You are destined to be wealthy and a power in your world. You should never try to economize. It goes against your nature. You can afford to spend more freely than others. It brings you luck.

You are at your best when you think big. People of wealth and position just naturally trust you. In a menial position, you would never realize your true destiny.

You have good ideas when it comes to making or managing money. Or you may, on the other hand, benefit through an interest in the law, philosophy, religion or diplomacy. You will, in fact, do well in any field where intellectual sharpness and precision are valuable.

Often, you are fortunate because your intuition warns you of danger or alerts you to make an advantageous move. You have a sure knowledge of where your best luck lies. You also have a kind of sixth sense. You know what people are going to do before they do it. You also know when someone is lying because you have a sure instinct for the truth.

You like to live well and are generous, convivial and optimistic. You love to give parties and are such an entertaining, jovial host that your guests inevitably have a good time. You are likely to receive honors, and even your enemies can't help but have a good opinion of you.

Your best chances tend to come to you from March 21 to April 20, from July 23 to August 23 and from November 22 to December 22. People born at these times may be lucky for you financially and bring out the jovial side of your nature.

December 26, 1899 through	January 19, 1901
December 10, 1911	January 2, 1913
November 24, 1923	December 17, 1924
November 8, 1935	December 2, 1936
October 23, 1947	November 15, 1948

Famous people with Jupiter in Sagittarius

Lady Bird Johnson	Julie Nixon Eisenhower
Doris Day	Shelley Berman
Bobby Darin	Ben Hogan
Louis Armstrong (Sachmo)	Mary McCarthy
Adlai Stevenson	Pablo Casals
James Baldwin	Prince Charles
Prince Andrew	Truman Capote
Julia Child	Helen Hayes

Eugene Ionesco

JUPITER IN CAPRICORN

Your best luck comes to you through your industry and ambition. While you will do well in almost any career you choose to follow, you are particularly fortunate in occupations that have to do with the earth, such as geology, mining, farming, real estate, contracting and construction.

You can also do well in wholesaling and merchandizing. You are a careful planner and are steady and conscientious when it comes to performing your daily duties. In routine matters, you are completely reliable and you pay close attention to detail.

You are naturally adept in business matters, and are more likely to benefit through some form of commerce, although success in one of the professions is not ruled out.

When it comes to money, you are very reluctant to spend when it is a matter of pennies, but big purchases don't faze you in the least. There is less generosity and geniality than with Jupiter in Sagittarius, and you are less optimistic. But your driving ambition can lead to accomplishments of the highest order.

Afflicted, Jupiter in Capricorn can result in the most degenerate behavior. Sexual perversity can be the case or there can be a coarse or crude attitude toward sensual pleasures.

In religion, you may not subscribe to conventional dogmas, but you take your beliefs very seriously. After careful consideration, you formulate your own opinions about religious and philosophical matters. You know how to put the spiritual into terms people can understand.

You may also benefit through your leadership ability. Whether in politics, business or entertainment, your desire to excel and your willingness to put in as much hard work as it takes, can result in your reaching a pinnacle of success. Your empires are built through industry rather than the luck or brilliance of Jupiter in other signs.

Your best opportunities tend to come to you from April 20 to May 21, August 23 to September 23 and December 22 to January 20. People born at these times of the year tend to be of benefit to you financially and to further your ambitions.

January 1, 1890	through	February 22, 1890
January 19, 1901		February 6, 1902
January 2, 1913		January 21, 1914
December 17, 1924		January 5, 1926
December 2, 1936		December 19, 1937
November 15, 1948		April 12, 1949
June 27, 1949		November 30, 1949

Famous people with Jupiter in Capricorn

Mary Martin	Danny Kaye
Walt Disney	Richard Nixon
Charlie Chaplin	Warren Beatty
Rudyard Kipling	Sammy Davis, Jr.
Oscar Wilde	Rock Hudson
Robert F. Kennedy	Perry Como
Richard Burton	Peter Duchin
Dick Van Dyke	Artur Rubinstein
Johnny Carson	Tex Thornton
Merv Griffin	William Styron
Mike Douglas	Adolf Hitler
Pat Nixon	Willy Brandt

JUPITER IN AQUARIUS

Your good fortune tends to come to you through pleasurable relationships with your friends. With a well-aspected Jupiter, such friends are loyal and sincere, and you thoroughly enjoy many good times with them. Often, however, you are of benefit to them financially, and through other favors more than they are to you. But you don't mind because you enjoy their company so much.

This position of Jupiter gives you great political know-how, and you have much luck through being able to handle people and situations so expertly. You instinctively know your way around in organizations, and it is never long after you have joined that you become an officer or a moving force. You are, however, better able to obtain benefits for your friends than for yourself, because generally you tend to be luckier for others than they are for you. Perhaps this is because you think in terms of the good of the whole group rather than your own personal advantage.

You have strong intuitions and original ideas, and you like to cultivate your mind. You do not value money for its own sake, but for what it can do to satisfy the material needs of others. You are a humanitarian first and foremost. Purely commercial ventures bore you.

You do not tend to be particularly religious, and the religious views you do have are unusual or unconventional. You would never place religious dogmas or strictures above the good of the human beings involved.

You make excellent scientists, doctors, lawyers, architects, inventors, bankers, ambassadors and statesmen. You would do well as teachers, speakers, scientists, labor leaders and psychologists. You may also be fortunate in the many fields of entertainment, and particularly in music.

You are likely to be active in charitable or social work, and you can excel in jobs connected with transportation by air. Often, also, your best opportunities lie in government or other big organizations, or where it is an advantage to be popular with the masses.

You should make the most of any chances coming to you between January 20 and February 19, between May 21 and June 21 and between September 23 and October 23. People born at these times tend to encourage and sympathize with you and to help you advance professionally.

February 23, 1890	through	March 7, 1891
February 6, 1902		February 20, 1903
January 21, 1914		February 3, 1915
January 5, 1926		January 18, 1927

December 19, 1937   May 14, 1938
July 29, 1938   December 29, 1938
April 12, 1949   June 27, 1949
November 30, 1949   April 15, 1950
September 14, 1950   December 1, 1950

Famous people with Jupiter in Aquarius

Joan Sutherland	Elizabeth II
Dwight David Eisenhower	Jane Fonda
John Steinbeck	Virgil Grissom
Ed Sullivan	Charles de Gaulle
Albert Einstein	Jonas Salk
Lewis Carroll	Rudolf Nureyev
Connie Francis	Romy Schneider
Joe DiMaggio	Arturo Toscanini

JUPITER IN PISCES

There is great sympathy between Jupiter and Pisces, and sooner or later you may expect to be very fortunate. You are both kind and generous in your relationships with other people, and although at times they may not appreciate you fully, you benefit spiritually through the good you do.

You like and do best in fields where you have to associate with others, where there is emotion and human interest, and where others' response to you and yours to them is important. You love the dramatic, whether it is a classical tragedy or simply the drama of everyday life. Mere intellectual work does not appeal to you.

You are very co-operative and get along well with associates. Your good fortune can come through your being well liked and popular. In government or other forms of public life, your wisdom and high ideals can prove a source of inspiration to your admirers.

You could do research in social fields or any other work for the benefit of humanity. You can be good secretaries, teachers, clergymen, public speakers and playwrights. If you write fiction, you love the strange and supernatural. You probably love to dance, and if you are not a professional actor or actress, you may enjoy taking part in amateur theatricals. This position of Jupiter also produces scientists whose grasp of the theoretical transcends the average experimenter's capacity for detail.

You may benefit greatly through travel, especially when it is across water. Either you meet people who are sympathetic or helpful, or you gain a broader viewpoint through new experiences. You are also lucky through occupations that have to do with oil, chemicals, the sea or liquids in general.

You may be interested in a Western version of Eastern philosophy or religion, and whatever your belief or creed, you are deeply religious. You love your fellow man and practice the Golden Rule, and are almost psychic when it comes to sensing others' needs and feelings.

Your best opportunities come to you between February 19 and March 21, June 21 and July 23, October 23 and November 22. People born at these times tend to sympathize with you and help you financially or give you spiritual guidance.

March 7, 1891	through	March 16, 1892
February 20, 1903		February 29, 1904
February 3, 1915		February 11, 1916
January 18, 1927		June 6, 1927
September 10, 1927		January 22, 1928
May 14, 1938		July 29, 1938
December 29, 1938		May 11, 1939
October 29, 1939		December 20, 1939
April 15, 1950		September 14, 1950
December 1, 1950		April 21, 1951

Famous people with Jupiter in Pisces

Leontyne Price	Earl Warren
Frank Sinatra	Bob Hope
Cary Grant	Gordon Cooper
Edgar Allan Poe	Aleksei N. Kosygin
Sir Isaac Newton	John L. Lewis
Abraham Lincoln	Casey Stengel
Douglas MacArthur	Princess Anne
David Rockefeller	Sidney Poitier
Benjamin Spock	Johann W. von Goethe
Edward Steichen	Leon Trotsky
W. E. B. DuBois	Joseph Stalin

8
SATURN
and Your Responsibilities

Are you pessimistic and prone to depression? Do you accept burdens and responsibilities willingly? Do you work harder than other people? Is your path in life rocky through no fault of your own?

Saturn influences all such behavior and situations. It is important for every adult who has encountered more than his share of obstacles to understand the position of Saturn in his particular horoscope.

In ancient Greek mythology, Saturn or Cronos was the god of agriculture. Warned that he would be destroyed by his own children, he devoured the infants as soon as they were born, all except Zeus who was hidden by his mother and who later overthrew his father and claimed his throne. Saturn became the old man, Father Time, cynical and bitter, envious of the young. In astrology, Saturn refers to older people, all that clogs and impedes, everything that has been decayed or destroyed by the passage of time.

When Saturn affects the disposition, it inclines to a gloomy, depressed state of mind. These people are often solitary souls, partly because they repel others by their attitude, partly because it is their natural tendency to want to be alone.

Saturn is the planet of restrictions, hardships and delays. It acts to deter advancement, to hold you back from realizing your dreams.

This often comes through inherited burdens and other circumstances beyond your control. It is usually felt through people, situations or conditions that in some way disappoint and hinder you. Waste of time or resources that cannot be helped, lack of opportunity through no fault of your own, loss and other impediments that prevent you from making the progress that could normally be expected from the effort spent—all these are in the province of Saturn. Colds and dental troubles are the most common of Saturn's health defects.

As overcoming obstacles often builds character, some people born strongly under Saturn develop sterling traits. Others are discouraged by their bad luck and simply stop trying. Saturn elevated in a horoscope, however, can give great worldly power. When the devil took Jesus up to a mountain top and promised him all the kingdoms of the earth if he would fall down and worship him, he was showing him the circumstances of an elevated Saturn.

If Saturn is the ruler of your ascendant, you tend to be industrious and conscientious, but you are apt to do things the hard way. Not everything that Saturn promises, however, is fraught with difficulties. A well-aspected Saturn is a fine asset indeed. Well aspected, Saturn makes you a born conservative, cautious and discreet. You are serious, trustworthy and very dependable. You are strictly moral and can always be relied upon to do the right thing. Hardships have only polished and developed your character. You are extremely disciplined and self-controlled. You are thrifty without being parsimonious. "Waste not, want not" may be part of your creed.

Saturn badly aspected, on the other hand, indicates handicaps, disappointments and delays. Bad luck has made you overly cautious, and because you have been discouraged by it, you often fail to take advantage of the opportunities at hand. In the same way, your manner is too solemn and depressed to attract good fortune as does the Jupiterian. You don't appeal to others when you whine and complain. You are stingy, even miserly when it comes to money, either because you have a hard time earning it or because you are naturally mean. In either case, your instinct is to hoard and save. Often the person with an afflicted Saturn counts poor health among his disadvantages.

Saturn in good aspect to Mercury gives a deep mind with excellent powers of concentration and the ability to write and speak on weighty subjects. When Saturn is in an unfavorable aspect to Mercury in your horoscope, you always see the dark side of things and tend to be fearful and negative in your thinking.

If your Saturn is in good aspect to Venus, you will always be faithful to the love of your life, although you may not be especially demonstrative, lighthearted or romantic unless of course there are other aspects to Venus. Saturn in adverse aspect to Venus makes you cold and indifferent to other people's feelings or promiscuous in relationships with the opposite sex. If you should be faithful, as is sometimes the case, you would be too disagreeable in love matters for it to be appreciated.

Saturn in good aspect to Mars gives you the power to control and direct other people. It is the aspect par excellence of leadership ability. Saturn in adverse aspect to Mars makes you stubborn and dictatorial and makes it difficult for you to dominate either people or events.

With Saturn favorably aspecting Jupiter, you are blessed in financial matters. Sound investments yield generous results. If Jupiter is in bad aspect to Saturn, you may invest so conservatively that your investments do not keep up with the inflationary trend of the economy and your capital diminishes.

If Saturn favorably aspects Uranus, you are incredibly well organized. Before you tackle any problem, you sort it out logically into its component parts and spare yourself unnecessary work and confusion. Saturn in bad aspect to Uranus means a disorganized, haphazard approach to the tasks that confront you, resulting in a lot of superfluous effort and disorder.

Saturn in good aspect to Neptune gives a universal understanding and a sense of the unity of all living things. Unfavorable Saturn-Neptune aspects give adverse conditions that are both confusing and grim, a very eccentric character, or one that is morally corrupt.

If Saturn is in good aspect to your Sun, your father was conservative and morally sound and a constructive influence in your life. If Saturn is in adverse aspect to the Sun, your father would have been poor or else harsh and domineering. He would not have helped you get a good start in life but would instead have added to your burdens. If a woman, the men in your life tend not to be of benefit to you.

With Saturn favorably aspecting your Moon, your mother would have been sensible and stable, would have imbued in you the highest moral standards, and would have given you help and sound advice. With men, the women in your life would add to your reputation and be faithful and conservative. If Saturn afflicts your Moon, your mother was pessimistic and stern or gave you very little assistance in practical matters. Instead of taking care of you, you would have had to look after her. If a man, you are likely to come in contact with disagreeable, selfish women.

All the above is very general, but in the descriptions that follow, you will be able to find out in exactly which sign your Saturn can be found. Saturn is slow and heavy and changes with the different signs less than the faster, more impressionable planets.

SATURN IN ARIES

Saturn in Aries places severe limitations on the success you can achieve in life. Although success can come to you through some activity that appeals to the public at large, it is not yours for the asking and is usually arrived at after much turmoil and pain. Often it is denied altogether as if fate decreed that you would be harried by every conceivable obstacle and prevented from realizing your promise to the full. While many famous and successful people have this position of Saturn, most of them have experienced disappointed ambitions in some way or loss of popularity or both.

Sometimes, your afflictions come instead through chronic poor health, although you may heroically try to conduct a normal life despite it. Or there is some external affliction that prevents you from reaching your goal. You should, however, never be defeatist but should remember that it is the experiences in life that are valuable rather than the outcome, which is so often decided by forces beyond your control.

You are, however, apt to be prominent either within your own circle or in the world at large. You are sure of yourself and quite ambitious, although you have a tendency to be strict and somewhat solitary. In some cases, you may be a hermit or recluse at heart. You may also be inclined to be rather grumpy on social occasions and have a hard time fitting in. You may have more acquaintances than close friends.

Saturn in Aries often represents an affliction to the sight or hearing, severe headaches or trouble with the teeth.

March 19, 1908	through	May 16, 1910
December 15, 1910		January 19, 1911
April 25, 1937		October 17, 1937
January 14, 1938		July 5, 1939
September 22, 1939		March 20, 1940

Famous people with Saturn in Aries

Robert Louis Stevenson	Joseph Stalin
Guy de Maupassant	Charles Baudelaire
George Washington	Herbert Spencer
Mary Baker Eddy	Douglas Dillon
Cecil B. de Mille	Ethel Barrymore
Peter Duchin	Samuel Barber
Albert Einstein	Nelson Rockefeller
Barry Goldwater	Lyndon B. Johnson
Rudolf Nureyev	Al Capp
Helen Keller	Leon Trotsky

W. C. Fields

SATURN IN TAURUS

You tend to be stubborn, determined and very stable. You are usually moral and have a fine sense of responsibility. You are able to overcome whatever difficulties come your way, but your path in life is not ordinarily strewn with insurmountable obstacles.

You have firm convictions and will fight to preserve them. You have the will and the ability to persevere and win over any opposition. You may not do this overnight. However, yours is no flash-in-the-pan brilliance but a patient, plodding dedication to a cause.

This is an excellent position for victory for a military man. As you can see in the list of famous names at the end of this description, Ulysses S. Grant, Joan of Arc and Alexander the Great all had Saturn in Taurus. The firm will and driving determination to win are an asset not only in war but may lead to a triumphant career in other fields. In fact, you can achieve success in any vocation where patience and perseverance are required.

This is not a particularly fortunate position financially unless there are other powerful indications in the rest of the horoscope. You usually do not make money easily, and to compensate for this, you tend to save the money you do get and are not particularly generous.

The most vulnerable part of your body is your throat and such diseases as goiter, tonsilitis and cancer can result. This position of Saturn may tend to somewhat dull the senses of taste and touch.

May 17, 1910	through	December 14, 1910
January 20, 1911		July 6, 1912
November 30, 1912		March 26, 1913
July 6, 1939		September 22, 1939
March 20, 1940		May 8, 1942

Famous people with Saturn in Taurus

Joan of Arc	Cecil Rhodes
Mary McCarthy	Laurence Rockefeller
Pope John XXIII	Igor Stravinsky
Louis Pasteur	Ulysses S. Grant
Percy B. Shelley	Stanford White
Joan Baez	Danny Kaye
Lady Bird Johnson	Alexander the Great
Ronald Reagan	Richard Nixon
Eero Saarinen	Vincent Van Gogh
Felix Frankfurter	Pat Nixon
Virginia Woolf	

SATURN IN GEMINI

Because Mercury rules Gemini, Saturn is well placed therein. As Saturn is considered the best influence on Mercury, this can be an altogether felicitous combination of worldly wisdom and youthful intellect. It can result in a person capable of the suave sophistication of a venerable diplomat cloaked by a kind of school boy naiveté.

Saturn so placed serves to steady the mind and at the same time quicken it and make it more versatile. There can be great success in intellectual endeavors. At the same time, these people commonly experience sorrow in childhood or through relatives, or they have difficulty in getting an education. At some time in their life, they could even be forced to live in exile. When Saturn is badly aspected, there is a tendency to be sardonic or sarcastic and bitter.

The patience and thought essential to great literary efforts is implicit in those whose Saturn is well aspected. The understanding is comprehensive and profound, and at the same time highly intellectual.

With a well-aspected Saturn, you may have a flair for finance, although you may not always be clever with figures or simple arithmetic. This can also give musical ability for conducting, composing or singing. In art, there is a formidable mastery of line with the very great; with ordinary people, a natural ability to draw. Should Uranus also be prominent, the writer or artist can achieve brilliant satirical effects.

Saturn in Gemini tends to have an adverse effect on the chest and lungs. Badly aspected, there is danger in transportation by air.

July 7, 1912	through	November 30, 1912
March 26, 1913		August 24, 1914
December 7, 1914		May 11, 1915
May 8, 1942		June 20, 1944

Famous people with Saturn in Gemini

Tex Thornton	Margaret Sanger
Cassius Clay	Otto Klemperer
Sigmund Freud	Albrecht Dürer
Ben Hogan	Dante Alighieri
Oscar Wilde	Franz Kafka
Eugene Ionesco	Willy Brandt

SATURN IN CANCER

This is not a particularly favorable position of Saturn, as it results in laxity and laziness and a tendency to overindulge in food, drink, sex and other sensual pleasures. This does not rule out outstanding accomplishments in the professions, or the artistic or business worlds, but these people are ordinarily dissolute and intemperate when their work is through.

The stomach is the most vulnerable part of the body as well as the breast in the case of a woman. Obesity, ulcers, cancer and other obstructions or wasting diseases involving digestion are probable, especially if Saturn is afflicted.

Often the home and mother prove a source of sorrow. Either you lose your mother at a very early age, or she would have had troubles she shared with you or burdens she thrust upon you. Sometimes, instead, she would have been overly strict and a harsh disciplinarian. In any event, complexes later on in life would stem from your early association with your mother.

In some cases, your childhood home would have failed to provide you with even the most meager comforts. In others, Saturn in Cancer could refer to adversity in the home of your declining years or a downfall of some kind at the end of your career. If you have experienced none of these disadvantages, your Saturn is indeed very well aspected.

August 24, 1914	through	December 7, 1914
May 11, 1915		October 17, 1916
December 7, 1916		June 24, 1917
June 20, 1944		August 2, 1946

Famous people with Saturn in Cancer

David Rockefeller	Dean Martin
Eugene McCarthy	Marc Chagall
Paul Tillich	Mia Farrow
Honoré de Balzac	John F. Kennedy
Jackie Gleason	William Shakespeare
Napoleon Bonaparte	Michelangelo

Tricia Nixon

SATURN IN LEO

There is little harmony between the slow, heavy, depressing Saturn and the noble, expansive Leo. This may give you more than your share of heartaches and disappointments. Saturn in Leo gives many frustrations and restricts your emotional responses in some way.

You are inclined to be rather cold and analytical. Although you may have friends, they are usually of your own choosing. You are not particularly susceptible to the friendly advances of other people. You tend to be suspicious that compliments are merely another form of flattery, nor do you like others to openly display their affection for you.

You are often a very able diplomat, however, since you calculate every move. This can be an asset in public life or entertainment. You know exactly what to do to be popular, but Saturn in Leo may make you less warm and human than you might otherwise be. You are, however, so subtle and astute that others may not easily suspect the true extent of your inner reserve.

When badly aspected, Saturn in this position can cause a tragic downfall. It is unfavorable for heads of governments or military leaders. With ordinary people, it not only causes them to experience sorrows, but it also makes them heartless about inflicting unhappiness on other people.

This aspect can give heart trouble or restrict the flow of blood in the arteries.

February 25, 1890	through	June 27, 1890
October 17, 1916		December 7, 1916
June 24, 1917		August 12, 1919
August 2, 1946		September 18, 1948
April 2, 1949		May 29, 1949

Famous people with Saturn in Leo

Margot Fonteyn	Patty Duke
Phyllis Diller	J. D. Salinger

Henry Ford II	Billy Graham
Chiang Kai-Shek	Alan Jay Lerner
Charlie Chaplin	Luci Baines Johnson Nugent
Leo Tolstoi	Theodore Roosevelt
Leonard Bernstein	Eddie Arnold
Caesar Borgia	Le Corbusier
Adolf Hitler	Julie Nixon Eisenhower

SATURN IN VIRGO

There is much harmony between Saturn and Virgo, and the effect on the mind is admirable. As in the case of Saturn in Gemini, we find that Mercury's rulership of the sign in which Saturn is found again has the effect of combining the wisdom of age with the mental vigor of youth. Only Saturn in Virgo is more earthy and more practical.

When well aspected, this position gives the ability to understand intellectually very weighty matters. It also produces the power to analyze, criticize, and organize. When coupled with other configurations that promise leadership ability, this adds mental strength and stability.

The position gives the ability to reason in both a practical and theoretical way. The result is true wisdom and a strong sense of morality as well. Whether in politics or literature, profound thought and practical judgment result from a well-aspected Saturn in Virgo. Badly aspected, there may be some unnecessary niggling over details or petty tyrannies.

There may be a bent for agriculture, and you can be possessed of a green thumb when it comes to growing things. Your farming techniques are the most effective because your approach is based on up-to-date scholarship as well as on sound instincts.

You tend to be something of a lone wolf. You are capable of keeping your own counsel and are refreshed and nourished by your moments of solitude.

January 1, 1890	through	February 25, 1890
June 27, 1890		December 26, 1891
January 23, 1892		August 29, 1892
August 12, 1919		October 7, 1921

September 18, 1948   April 2, 1949
May 29, 1949   November 20, 1950
March 7, 1951   August 13, 1951

Famous people with Saturn in Virgo

Prince Philip	Casey Stengel
John Glenn	Prince Charles
Earl Warren	Princess Anne
Carol Channing	Artur Rubinstein
Charles de Gaulle	Victor Hugo
George Sand	Ralph Waldo Emerson

Dwight D. Eisenhower

SATURN IN LIBRA

This is a truly excellent position of Saturn. You have extraordinarily good judgment and, unless Saturn is very afflicted, you are quite capable of looking out for your own interests. You are tactful in your dealings with other people and make an astute politician as well as a just administrator. At your best, you are philosophical and wise.

You can benefit through partnership with an older person, or you may even marry someone older or more serious than yourself. You are a devoted spouse unless Saturn is very afflicted, and you need marriage for its stabilizing influence. If Saturn is afflicted, you will experience sorrow in marriage or suffering through divorce.

You may be a mystic in religion, and you are truly religious in the deepest sense. Your sense of justice is highly developed. You have a deep-seated desire to be fair. Politicians with Saturn so placed are just, clever and astute.

This is a favorable influence for artistic endeavors, indicating a masterful technique and terseness of expression. There is not one superfluous detail or line to detract from the austere purity of the composition.

When Saturn is well aspected, you save a great deal of time traveling by air. When it is afflicted, there may be either danger or discomfort in air transport.

Except when Saturn rules your financial dealings, you are less stern and egotistical than is usual with Saturn and much more altruistic.

This position may indicate some trouble with the back or obstructions affecting the kidneys.

December 27, 1891 through	January 22, 1892
August 29, 1892	November 6, 1894
October 7, 1921	December 19, 1923
April 6, 1924	September 13, 1924
November 20, 1950	March 7, 1951
August 13, 1951	December 31, 1952

Famous people with Saturn in Libra

James Arness	Walter M. Schirra
James Baldwin	Benjamin Disraeli
Judy Garland	Oliver Cromwell
Henri Toulouse-Lautrec	Joseph Smith
J. M. W. Turner	Sir William Hamilton
J. Paul Getty	Emanuel Swedenborg
Jay Gould	Petrarch
John Lindsay	Richard Strauss

SATURN IN SCORPIO

Saturn lends subtlety and ambition to the most passionate of all the zodiacal signs. You are shrewd and astute, and you use your innate worldly wisdom to gain the material power you usually desire. Your ego is strong, and you are well able to advance yourself in the course of your lifetime.

You are a forceful character, but you conceal your strength under a pleasant, agreeable exterior. Not only do you control and direct your own passions, but you also dominate other people. However, in private life, you tend to be rather selfish and absolute.

If Saturn is badly aspected, you are in danger of losing your reputation and becoming unpopular through scandalmongering and character assassination.

This position is disadvantageous for health when you are young, but once that danger point is past, you have a good chance of living to a ripe old age. There are exceptions. Bobby Kennedy's assassination can be attributed astrologically to an evil aspect of his Saturn in Scorpio. As Scorpio is the sign of death, there can be sorrow through the deaths of others as well as the possibility of a premature demise. Health difficulties promised by this position of Saturn tend to affect you through the generative organs.

You may derive much benefit from joining secret societies or mystical groups. You are naturally very secretive and are inclined to be interested in the occult.

November 6, 1894	through	February 6, 1897
April 9, 1897		October 27, 1897
December 19, 1923		April 6, 1924
September 13, 1924		December 2, 1926

Famous people with Saturn in Scorpio

Doris Day	Johnny Carson
William Faulkner	Everett Dirksen
James Thurber	Elizabeth II
Robert F. Kennedy	Sammy Davis, Jr.
Richard Burton	Rock Hudson
Dick Van Dyke	Virgil Grissom
Truman Capote	Shelley Berman
William Styron	Arturo Toscanini
Pope Paul VI	Mike Douglas
Johann W. von Goethe	Merv Griffin
Juan Peron	

SATURN IN SAGITTARIUS

This position of Saturn does not tend to easy success. However, success is not denied. Instead it is delayed, and you may suffer some early setbacks or put in many years and more than your share of disappointments before you have accomplished what you set out to do.

Perhaps it is this kind of adversity that teaches you the philosophy and wisdom that make your contributions so valuable later on, and gives you your understanding of human nature and compassion for others. You are an idealist, but you have vision and can show true dedication to a cause.

If Saturn is well aspected, this is a wonderful position for ministers and lawyers, philosophers, writers, scientists, statesmen and those answering any calling requiring a knowledge of foreign affairs. Travel and occupations connected with it may be sobering experiences, but they give you a broader point of view.

There is a high incidence of deaths for political reasons among public figures with this position of Saturn. Lincoln, Gandhi and Martin Luther King, Jr. all died at the hands of assassins at a time when they were espousing controversial issues and defending their ideals. Their Saturn in Sagittarius, however, was to a great extent responsible for their integrity and prominence in public life.

You are naturally thrifty, and while you are generous with others, you do not spend profligately on yourself.

February 7, 1897	through	April 9, 1897
October 27, 1897		January 21, 1900
July 18, 1900		October 16, 1900
December 2, 1926		March 15, 1929
March 5, 1929		November 29, 1929

Famous people with Saturn in Sagittarius

Thomas Huxley	Nikolai Lenin
Abraham Lincoln	Mohandas K. Gandhi
Booth Tarkington	P. T. Barnum
Peter Ilyich Tchaikovsky	Horace Greeley
Emile Zola	Thomas Hardy
Fidel Castro	Edward Albee
Dr. Martin Luther King, Jr.	Gordon Cooper
Arthur Goldberg	Henri Matisse
Henry Luce	Sidney Poitier
W. E. B. DuBois	Margaret Chase Smith

Caroline Kennedy

SATURN IN CAPRICORN

Saturn in his own sign emphasizes some of the planet's less-desirable traits. You may have to contend with more than your share of obstacles and hardships, and you are definitely not prepared to endure them with equanimity.

Indeed, you are very determined. You want your own way, and if someone denies it to you, you are apt to become enraged. In fact, from the time you were small, you have been furious when anyone opposed you. Sometimes you are downright dictatorial. You do not have the finesse of Saturn in Libra or Sagittarius, and your methods can appear rough or harsh in comparison.

Saturn's better qualities are also emphasized, however, by his placement in his own sign. There is much worldly ambition and know-how. You try not to be in a position of dependence on anyone, and you have a tendency to do everything yourself, the hard way. In some cases, this is your lot through force of circumstances. In others, the reason you have such a difficult time is that you tend not to listen to those who would spare you unnecessary troubles. In either case, you learn by experience and when you have finished, you can stand very solidly on your own two feet.

You may have been a timid child, but as an adult, you are authoritarian and a power in your world. This position indicates a certain selfishness, and loneliness is sometimes the result. However, if there are aspects to ameliorate this position of Saturn, you may have many sterling qualities and be well liked.

This position can give rheumatism in the joints, especially the knees.

January 21, 1900	through	July 18, 1900
October 17, 1900		January 19, 1903
March 15, 1929		May 4, 1929
November 29, 1929		February 23, 1932
August 13, 1932		November 19, 1932

Famous people with Saturn in Capricorn

John Steinbeck	Charles Dickens
William E. Gladstone	Walt Disney
Anne Bancroft	Ed Sullivan
Adlai Stevenson	Thomas Schippers
Princess Margaret Rose	Edward M. Kennedy
Bertrand Russell	Willie Mays

John Osborne

SATURN IN AQUARIUS

Well aspected, Saturn in Aquarius can give a great deal of influence and prosperity, especially in government and other large organizations. You are well known among a wide circle of friends and acquaintances, whatever your walk of life. If you were to become a public figure of importance, you would have great appeal for the masses.

You can be recognized in the fields of music, either popular or classic, or, like Bob Hope, you can be an eminent humorist. You can also excel in literature or science, and there are no limits to the heights you can attain in politics.

You are more democratic than your friends with Saturn in Capricorn, but nevertheless you like to run things and have your own way. You are, however, more subtle about getting it.

Aquarius's influence on Saturn makes you less self-centered than is usual and more understanding of the human condition. You realize your own true importance in proportion to the rest of the world, and while you can be autocratic, you are not bound up in your own ego.

You are a humanitarian, first and foremost, and have true insight into human nature and believe in the brotherhood of man. This position often gives real wisdom in maturity.

Saturn in Aquarius can cause accidents to the lower leg or ankles, cancer of the lymph glands or strokes under afflictions to Saturn.

January 19, 1903	through	April 12, 1905
August 16, 1905		January 8, 1906
February 23, 1932		August 13, 1932
November 19, 1932		February 14, 1935

Famous people with Saturn in Aquarius

Lord Byron	Louis XIV
William Blake	Dr. Ralph Bunche
Van Cliburn	Bing Crosby
Willem de Kooning	Cary Grant
Bob Hope	Vladimir Horowitz
Aleksei Kosygin	J. Robert Oppenheimer
Winston Churchill	Elvis Presley
Jule Styne	Benjamin Spock
Gertrude Stein	Robert Frost
C. P. Snow	J. William Fulbright
Greta Garbo	Thomas Mann

SATURN IN PISCES

This is a good position for gathering wisdom for the soul's eternal enlightenment, but Pisces is the sign of sorrows, and a planet as restricting as Saturn therein is not fortunate in a material sense. Afflicted, it is an indication of worldly misfortune; well aspected, the harshness of Saturn is lessened and the egocentricity reduced.

Unless Saturn is very well aspected, there is disappointment over the position you may have to occupy in life. At some time, your popularity may suffer, and if you are in an enviable position, you can be attacked by both inferiors and equals. If in an inferior position, you may suffer at some time through the animosity of superiors. Saturn in Pisces can cause others to try to detract from your good reputation, and you can suffer on this account.

Well aspected, Saturn in Pisces can give a vivid imagination as well as great vision. This is a real asset for the creative scientist. With writers, poets or performers, there is a certain whimsical quality that adds charm.

You may be fascinated by any writings, or teachings that are tinged with mysticism. If Saturn is well aspected, you may derive great solace from your chosen religion or from the study of astrology.

You are not inclined to be as self-centered and materialistic as is usual with Saturn, and life may demand from you more than the usual amount of self-sacrifice. If Saturn is well aspected, however, you have learned to accept the conditions of your life philosophically.

You are especially susceptible to ailments caused by impurities in the fluids of your system, and the most vulnerable parts of your body are your feet.

April 13, 1905	through	August 16, 1905
January 8, 1906		March 19, 1908
February 14, 1935		April 24, 1937
October 17, 1937		January 14, 1938

Famous people with Saturn in Pisces

George Eliot	John Ruskin
Sir Isaac Newton	Thomas Edison
Julie Andrews	Warren Beatty
Henry Fonda	Jane Fonda
Sandy Koufax	Rex Harrison
Nathan Pusey	Steve Lawrence
Françoise Sagan	Carl Sandburg
Diahann Carroll	Jean-Paul Sartre
Pope Pius XII	John Wayne

Dag Hammarskjold

9
URANUS
and Your Inner Will

Are you magnetically attractive to other people? Have you a compelling determination and indomitable inner will? Do you like to take part in revolutionary causes? Have you a kind of genius for whatever it is you do? Are you interested in new inventions or original new ideas?

For the clues to this behavior, you should consult the planet Uranus. It is important for everyone who wants to foresee events and dominate his environment to understand the position of Uranus in his particular horoscope.

In ancient Greek mythology, Uranus was the god of heaven whose son, Saturn, dethroned and mutilated him. The Greeks never worshiped him in historical times, but he served his purpose as the origin of the gods. The Planet Uranus apparently was not known to the ancients, but was discovered by the English astronomer, Sir William Herschel, in 1781. It is only since then, in comparatively modern times, that astrologers have had a chance to observe the effects of this planet on members of the human race.

Uranus is the planet of the unusual or unexpected. In its highest form, it can give rise to genius; more commonly, it is the indication of erratic behavior or eccentricity. The Uranian is a "character." He is both unique and original. He gives you the feeling that there is no other person like him on this earth, nor will there be again, nor has there been before.

One of the surest signs of the Uranian is his love of mechanical gadgets or other inventions and sound. At best, he is musical. More commonly, he is noisy. He can't stand a moment of silence. Wherever he goes, he turns on the radio, the television set or the record player, often all at once.

Having a Uranian around activates everything. He is the person who runs the whole show. When he is around, everything and everyone starts moving. He is usually active and finds things to do, both for others and for himself.

While the Uranian believes firmly in the brotherhood of man, he can, at the same time, be somewhat autocratic. He may plan projects and conceive inventions for the good of the masses. But he is never numbered among the latter. He is too outstanding, too individual.

Where Uranus affects your destiny, there are many ups and downs. Plans you make can fall through at the last minute. Good breaks can come just as precipitously. Uranus inclines us to be self-reliant and independent. His adverse effects always remove some person or condition from your life. It is futile to cling to the past under Uranus afflictions. Whether you like it or not, you will be thrust forceably into new situations or new environments, probably for your own ultimate good. Uranus blessings, on the other hand, are always sudden and unexpected, and you have to take advantage of them promptly or they are over in the twinkling of an eye. Whether for good or for ill, Uranus indicates that we are not to cling to people or conditions but to be free, independent, and ready to go unafraid where life takes us.

Finance is a field in which Uranians abound. They are not in it so much for the money, like the Jupiterian, but because it is a challenging game. Uranians are frequently inventors; they have a compulsion to improve man's lot. They can also be scientists or musicians. They love to be *au courant*. Uranians are not only up to date, but they are also ahead of their times.

Uranians are no respecters of time-honored customs. They see with the eye of the eternal and often are considered odd when they flaunt man-made conventions. While they are brilliant and original, they are not always easy to live with. They love independence too much. The best way to stay married to a Uranian is to let him pursue his own interests and to have interests of your own to pursue.

In matters of health, Uranus has rulership over the nervous system and causes diseases that are hard to cure or diagnose.

Sufficiently well aspected, Uranus makes you able and original in your chosen field. It also indicates integrity and an inner purpose that is hard to defeat. It gives a strongly magnetic character and an almost magical inner will. You are resourceful and inventive. You want to achieve in a practical manner, and you have the ability to predict the shape of things to come. Astrologers, hypnotists and psychics often have Uranus well aspected in their horoscopes.

Badly aspected, Uranus can produce eccentricity akin to madness, revolutionaries who plot to overthrow the government or misfits who make a fetish of unconventionality. They are undisciplined and have no respect for authority. Their urge to create has been thwarted and they turn to being destructive instead. They are erratic and inconsistent and can't persist in any policy for long. They think only of themselves and have no respect for others' rights. In human relationships, they can be cruel and sadistic. They also tend to be reckless and accident-prone. If a badly aspected Uranus does not refer to defects of character, it can instead portend great misfortunes in a worldly sense.

Uranus in good aspect to Mercury indicates an excellent sense of humor. You are quick-witted and entertaining. You express yourself in both speech and writing with verve. Uranus in bad aspect to Mercury gives a brain that works in fits and starts. When you express yourself, you are disorganized, arbitrary and abrupt.

Uranus in good aspect to Venus gives style in dress and imagination in art. If you are an artist, your works have a life of their own. Uranus in adverse aspect to Venus, on the other hand, may give a taste for loud colors and garish patterns both in personal dress and in the arts.

With Uranus in good aspect to Mars, you execute your plans with originality and flair. You have a strong will and terrific inner drive. If you are imprudent in your actions, if you are reckless and accident-prone, or if you dislike restraint so much you could resort to violence, then your Uranus no doubt afflicts your Mars.

Uranus in favorable aspect to Jupiter usually promises either material good fortune or luck with speculations. It can also mean inspiration through travel and advanced ideas. Uranus afflicting Jupiter often causes you to lose through risky speculations. You do not have a steady income or else your business judgment is unreliable.

With Uranus favorably aspecting Saturn, you have self-control and behave in an orderly fashion. You make your plans well in advance. Once you have decided on a course of action, you stick to it, even though it takes you many years to do what you set out to do. Uranus in adverse aspect to Saturn is not favorable for self-control, but gives an unruly disposition, or else it may impair the health in some way.

Good Uranus-Neptune aspects can give a sense of the theoretical in science or mathematics. If part of a larger configuration, it can promise genius in creative work. When Uranus is in bad aspect to Neptune, genius can also result but there is a more common tendency to sexual perversion.

With Uranus in good aspect to the Sun, your father would have been original and inventive, an inspiration to you. If a woman, the men in your life would be dashing, romantic and extraordinary in some way. With Uranus in adverse aspect to the Sun, your father would have been unreliable and eccentric, so unpredictable that you would never have known where you stood with him. If a woman, you would have a hard time getting along with the men in your life, since they would be so erratic, unconventional and generally difficult.

If Uranus is in good aspect to your Moon, you would have had a brilliant, well-organized mother who would have run her household perfectly, and she may also have been very musical. If a man, the women in your life would be original, daring and very unusual in some way. If Uranus is in bad aspect to the Moon, the mother would have been arbitrary and eccentric and would have disciplined you in the most unpredictable fashion. If a man, the women in your life would be willful and unstable and would in no way contribute either to your reputation or your career.

URANUS IN LIBRA

Uranus in Libra gives an inner longing for partnerships and other attachments. When these refer to the opposite sex, they may or may not be conventional, but they are always romantic. Well aspected, there is much inspiration through marriage or other relationships. When afflicted, many upsets with partners, marital and otherwise, occur.

There is also a deep-seated urge to be an instrument of justice, but sometimes your sense of what is fair will be outraged by unpredictable events. Well aspected, it gives a firm religious orientation, as far as decency and brotherly love are concerned.

In art, literature or acting, there is a certain lovable whimsy. Everything is made more entertaining and unusual. Marc Chagall's enchanting figures floating in the air of his pictorial dreams, Victor Hugo's imaginative caricatures of the hunchback, Charlie Chaplin's unforgettable tramp are all examples of how Uranus in Libra in the horoscopes of geniuses will act. Uranus may sometimes be a disturbing influence in the peaceful sign of Libra, even in ordinary people; but when it is well aspected, it gives the ability to express oneself freely and memorably.

January 1, 1890   through   December 9, 1890
April 5, 1891   September 26, 1891

Famous people with Uranus in Libra

Dwight D. Eisenhower	Charles de Gaulle
Paul Tillich	Victor Hugo
Chiang Kai-Shek	Albrecht Dürer
Charlie Chaplin	George Sand
Marc Chagall	Le Corbusier

URANUS IN SCORPIO

In this combination, we find the will power most often linked with the sex instinct. At its strongest, you can be magnetically attractive in a physical sense. There is a certain combination of passion and subtle fascination that make you indeed a force to reckon with.

In its highest form, there is a drive to achievement in science or the arts. In medicine, surgery or research, the will to understand and control the forces of nature is penetrating. In literature, there is the passion for life of a Hemingway, the keen observations of a Dickens. In sculpture, there is the strength, perversity and finesse of a Michelangelo. In music, the passion and brilliance of a Chopin, the power and sensuality of Wagner; and in finance, the astuteness and ability to accumulate wealth of a J. Paul Getty.

There is a long list of powerful people with this position of Uranus. In ordinary people, this position may give shrewdness and a drive for sensual pleasures, or else absolute dedication to a high purpose or worthy cause.

December 10, 1890 through	April 4, 1891
September 26, 1891	December 1, 1897
July 4, 1898	September 10, 1898

Famous people with Uranus in Scorpio

Pope Paul VI	Juan Peron
Everett Dirksen	Michelangelo
William Faulkner	Frédéric Chopin
Ernest Hemingway	Richard Wagner
Nicolaus Copernicus	Charles Dickens
Sir Isaac Newton	Alfred Lord Tennyson

Immanuel Kant

URANUS IN SAGITTARIUS

Where Jupiter is well placed and well aspected in the horoscope, this can be a very fortunate position of Uranus, the inner drive being for some measure of material success. In more developed persons, there is also a philosophical acceptance of life and its vicissitudes. The temperament is exceedingly volatile and high spirited and the conversation is often witty, amusing and gay.

With Uranus well aspected, these people have both courage and nobility. They are willing to accept life unflinchingly, not blaming their difficulties on their antecedents and sparing their children as much as it is in their power to spare.

They have will power and determination and a sure sense of the direction in which they want to go. They accomplish their aims with true finesse and have a great capacity for enjoyment. Their conviviality is contagious, their example an inspiration to all.

Uranus in Sagittarius badly aspected can cause a variety of troubles, some of them attributable to exterior circumstances, some of them to a sporadic, inconsistent will.

December 2, 1897   through   July 3, 1898
September 11, 1898   December 20, 1904

Famous people with Uranus in Sagittarius

Arthur Goldberg   Benjamin Spock
Ralph Bunche   Bing Crosby
Margaret Chase Smith   Willem de Kooning
Henry Luce   Walt Disney
Vladimir Horowitz   Bob Hope
Aleksei Kosygin   William Shakespeare
Martin Luther   Queen Victoria
George Orwell   Helen Hayes

URANUS IN CAPRICORN

This position gives a dynamic, driving inner will with the power to eliminate all opposition. At its best, it is an indomitable, disciplined force; at worst, it is tyrannical and pigheaded.

Your deepest urge is for supremacy, and you are willing to fight to achieve it. You back up your urge with great determination and practicality. You are forceful and hard working. All of these attributes combine to make you very powerful indeed. This position produces politicians who want to run the whole show and be the ultimate authority on everything, a kind of governmental father figure.

Where Uranus is afflicted, there can be personal problems and fatalistic conditions that stagger the will. Since in this generation Neptune afflicts Uranus (this was true of Uranus in Sagittarius as well), there can either be a tendency to alcoholism or unpleasant close association with alcoholics. It can also indicate perversions and masochistic or sadistic inclinations depending on its position in the particular horoscope.

Generally, though, this is a very strong and vigorous position and produces people of firm character and powerful will. Sometimes when talented, there is the devastating satirical wit of an Al Capp or the comic style of a Lucille Ball.

December 20, 1904   through   January 30, 1912
September 4, 1912   November 11, 1912

Famous people with Uranus in Capricorn

Lucille Ball	Douglas Dillon
Al Capp	John Wayne
Laurence Rockefeller	Samuel Barber
Henry Fonda	Hubert Humphrey
Barry Goldwater	Leo Tolstoi
Rex Harrison	Mary Baker Eddy
Lyndon B. Johnson	Ulysses S. Grant
C. P. Snow	Eero Saarinen
Dag Hammarskjold	J. William Fulbright

URANUS IN AQUARIUS

In Aquarius, Uranus is in his own sign. The planet of genius in sign of brotherhood and advanced thought can produce an idealist who is out to improve mankind's lot. This results in a great love of freedom and equality, but the nature is peace loving and unassuming as well. The egocentricity of Uranus in Capricorn is softened and the inner will directed for the good of others and the need and appreciation of associates and friends.

This is an excellent position for a public figure because the inner urge impels toward great popularity. Unless, however, there are strength-producing indications in the rest of the horoscope, such a person may be agreeable enough but somewhat ineffectual in putting his plans across. In the case of Joan of Arc, Uranus indicated the liberty-loving inspiration and the will to liberate her nation, but the strength shown in the rest of Joan's horoscope made her a force to reckon with.

Ordinarily, people with Uranus in Aquarius express their inner drives on a somewhat more intellectual but nevertheless popular plane. Examples are the genius for finance of a David Rockefeller, Henry Ford II or a Tex Thornton, and the popular evangelistic zeal of a Billy Graham. It is also a marvelous influence for a sense of humor. There is the far-out, wry humor of a Phyllis Diller, the classic folk humor of a Mark Twain or the whimsy of a Danny Kaye. As Aquarius is also the sign of music, it is a wonderful influence for singers and composers as well.

January 30, 1912	through	September 4, 1912
November 12, 1912		March 31, 1919
August 16, 1919		January 22, 1920

Famous people with Uranus in Aquarius

David Rockefeller	Leonard Bernstein
Dean Martin	Perry Como
Joe DiMaggio	Phyllis Diller
Tex Thornton	Henry Ford II

Mary McCarthy	Jackie Gleason
Eddie Arnold	Billy Graham
Lady Bird Johnson	Ben Hogan
John F. Kennedy	Danny Kaye
Richard Nixon	Alan Jay Lerner
Eugene Ionesco	Johann W. von Goethe
Julia Child	Pat Nixon

URANUS IN PISCES

As Uranus is a planet associated with will power and Pisces is a very psychic sign, this is an excellent combination for an inner drive that is receptive as well as outgoing. These people are not out so much to dominate others. Instead they seek to intuit their wants and their feelings. While other planets might give a person with Uranus in Pisces domineering instincts, it will not be due to the action of the planet in the sign.

In Pisces, the aggressiveness of Uranus is softened and refined. This gives a good deal of sensitivity and finesse. It is also an excellent position for a student of astrology or anyone else interested in the science of the stars.

It is very good for understanding and expressing human emotions in an appealing fashion by a writer like Truman Capote or actors like Sidney Poitier or Richard Burton. Or since Pisces is the sign ruling the feet and is also associated with dancing, we find in Margot Fonteyn the talent for superb expression in the field of ballet. Johnny Carson, Merv Griffin and Mike Douglas all have this position of Uranus, which enables them to express themselves by drawing others out.

In ordinary people, the will is somewhat passive unless there are other intensifying indications in the rest of the horoscope.

March 31, 1919	through	August 16, 1919
January 22, 1920		March 31, 1927
November 4, 1927		January 12, 1928

Famous people with Uranus in Pisces

Sidney Poitier	J. P. Morgan
Truman Capote	James Arness
William Styron	Richard Burton
Mike Douglas	Carol Channing
Merv Griffin	Gordon Cooper
Johnny Carson	Sammy Davis, Jr.
John Lindsay	Elizabeth II
James Baldwin	Margot Fonteyn
Judy Garland	John Glenn
Robert F. Kennedy	Adelina Patti

Emile Zola

URANUS IN ARIES

Uranus in Aries gives the will to dominate and lead. There is great fire and independence of spirit. These people have an inner urge for supremacy and they brook no opposition. The temper can be explosive when they are thwarted. They consider that people who have differed with them have committed a positive affront and they deal with them accordingly.

With these people, their will and their head are as one. They often have a fixed idea that is compatible with their inner drive, and if Uranus is in a strong position in their horoscope, they will concentrate all their forces on realizing their ambitions and convincing the world of their idea.

Nevertheless, their will, while equally strong, is not as consistent as Uranus in Capricorn or Taurus, since they become bored with a particular project for no apparent reason and expend all their forces to realize some entirely different goal. Although it may in its turn occupy them for a time, they can drop this too just as suddenly.

For this reason, while there is a certain enterprising spirit and true courage, it is hard for these people to build consistently. Where the rest of the horoscope shows constructive force, however, this tendency can be mitigated to some extent.

March 31, 1927   through   November 4, 1927
January 13, 1928   June 6, 1934
October 10, 1934   March 27, 1935

Famous people with Uranus in Aries

Thomas Edison   Anne Bancroft
Robert Louis Stevenson   Fidel Castro
Carol Burnett   Petula Clark
Edward M. Kennedy   Eddie Fisher
Leslie Caron   Jacqueline Kennedy Onassis
Audrey Hepburn   Edward Albee
Dr. Martin Luther King, Jr.   Luther Burbank
John Osborne

URANUS IN TAURUS

Uranus in Taurus is a position par excellence for remarkable will power and determination. The inner drive is expressed in the most positive ways. The desire is to build, but whether this desire is to further some high ideal or achieve a more material goal depends on the rest of the horoscope.

This position can, in some cases, give a magnetic and distinctive quality to the voice and can for this reason be an asset for those who sing or act. When afflicted, it can result in some irritation of the throat or sympathetically the heart or generative organs.

In Taurus, Uranus gives a prodigious amount of energy. The will to do is monumental. This can account for Guy de Maupassant's extensive works, George Bernard Shaw's considerable list of plays and Napoleon's urge to build empires. Sigmund Freud's labors to implement his theories of psychoanalysis are also typical of the giants this position of Uranus can produce.

In ordinary people, this position gives great firmness, diligence and patience and a dogged determination to be constructive, whatever their field.

June 6, 1934   through   October 9, 1934
March 27, 1935   August 7, 1941
October 5, 1941   May 14, 1942

Famous people with Uranus in Taurus

Diahann Carroll	Sigmund Freud
Julie Christie	Sandy Koufax
Van Cliburn	Steve Lawrence
Bobby Darin	John Lennon
Jane Fonda	Napoleon Bonaparte
George Bernard Shaw	Guy de Maupassant
Woodrow Wilson	Dante Alighieri
Julie Andrews	Joan Baez
Oscar Wilde	Warren Beatty
Connie Francis	Cecil Rhodes

URANUS IN GEMINI

It is through ideas rather than actions that you express your inner drive. You are gentle and intellectual when it comes to persuading others to do your will, and your strongest urges express themselves through the spoken and written word rather than through actual physical force in the majority of cases.

There are, of course, exceptions like Cassius Clay, but even he exerts his will by the deft, rapid movements of his fists which are ruled by the sign of Gemini. Mercury's sign, Gemini, can also have to do with the voice, and its magnetism in singers and actors or orators like William Jennings Bryan is evident. In art, the expression can be linear and highly intellectualized, as in the case of Toulouse-Lautrec.

Unless Uranus is well placed in your horoscope, however, you may be somewhat ineffectual at getting your own way, but when it is well placed and well aspected, you may express yourself successfully as a writer, teacher, lawyer, scientist, musician, secretary or in any other occupation where being clever with your mind, voice or fingers is important.

Afflicted, Uranus in Gemini can cause accidents in air travel.

August 8, 1941	through	October 5, 1941
May 14, 1942		August 29, 1948
November 12, 1948		June 9, 1949

Famous people with Uranus in Gemini

Sir Thomas More
Maurice Maeterlinck
W. B. Yeats
William Jennings Bryan
Theodore Roosevelt
J. M. W. Turner
Patty Duke
Hayley Mills
Leslie Uggams
Paul McCartney
William Randolph Hearst
Tricia Nixon
George Harrison
Cassius Clay
Geraldine Chaplin
Brenda Lee
Lynda Bird Johnson Robb
Luci Baines Johnson Nugent
Anne-Marie of Denmark
Mia Farrow
Prince Charles
Aristide Maillol
Henri Toulouse-Lautrec
Julie Nixon Eisenhower

URANUS IN CANCER

Your deepest inner urges tend to be passive, not active. You obey the dictates of your subconscious. You are sensitive and receptive rather than positive and strong-willed. In negative types, there is a very placid disposition. Chameleon-like, they take on the colors of their environment. Other types can be highly developed on a psychic plane.

With Uranus in Cancer, the will power is not particularly aggressive unless the Sun is in Taurus, Leo, Scorpio, or Aquarius. Even when the Uranus traits of magnetism and will are fully developed as in the case of Gandhi, his leadership took the form of passive and spiritual resistance rather than an openly declared war.

In ordinary people, there is the will to express themselves as gourmets, cooks, or collectors of antiques. The men as well as the women have an urge to be homemakers and to mother the young, or else themselves desire to be mothered and enjoy all the comforts of home.

Many of you would like to be popular and you can be. In politics, literature or advertising, you have the common touch. In business, you sense public demand, especially when you deal in commodities for the home.

When Uranus is well aspected, the artistic or musical sensibilities tend to be exquisite. When badly aspected, such people can have explosive temperaments, disrupting their environments willfully and arbitrarily, and they are often trials to their mothers and in their own homes as well.

August 30, 1948   through   November 11, 1948
June 10, 1949   December 31, 1952

Famous people with Uranus in Cancer

Rudyard Kipling   Elizabeth I
Lord Byron   Princess Anne
Savonarola   Henry Ford
Mohandas K. Gandhi   André Gide
Bertrand Russell   Henri Matisse
Marie Curie   Arturo Toscanini
Nikolai Lenin   W. E. B. DuBois

10

NEPTUNE

Your Charm and Your Ideals

Are you fond of peace and quiet? Do you try to live up to your loftiest ideals? Do you create the impression of being absent-minded and otherworldly? Are other people responsive to your charm?

Neptune influences all such behavior. It is important for every adult who has encountered strange, incomprehensible influences in his public or private life to understand the position of that mysterious planet in his horoscope.

In ancient Rome, Neptune was the god of the sea. Astrologically, the planet Neptune has rulership over the ocean, oil and other liquids, although Neptune has entered into astrological lore comparatively recently. The existence of Neptune, a new planet, was first predicted in 1846 by the mathematical calculations of the French astronomer Urbain Jean Joseph Leverrier. That same year, Johann Gottfried Galle, a German astronomer, discovered Neptune within 1 degree of the position Leverrier had described. Astrologers have observed its effect on human destiny ever since.

Neptunians are never run-of-the-mill types but unique individuals with characteristics that are different and distinct from more ordinary mortals. They are outstanding always, and often somewhat strange.

The higher types understand life's meaning in an ideal or spiritual sense. The lower types tend not to enjoy normal, sensual pleasures. They have a longing for the distortion of alcohol and drugs, anything to erase the boundaries between the fantastic and the real. Both types, however, have a desire for a higher perfection not attainable in this finite sphere.

Sometimes this materializes as a subtle perversity. Either the Neptunian prefers to do things backward or upside down or any way other than the normal. These people love to masquerade, to appear to be something they are not, to reverse the relationships between what they are and what they now pretend to be. Often this tendency is found in crooks who advance their bogus schemes as real, for an afflicted Neptune is a prime example of fraud, trickery and deceit.

Neptune is also a strong influence in cases of sexual perversions. The Neptunian is always the feminine partner or the masochist in contrast to the Uranian, who is aggressive, masculine and sadistic.

One of Neptune's most outstanding gifts is a formidable charm. Sometimes, it is superficial and only a sugar-coated facade to cloak the insincere. In other cases, it is the outer and visible expression of a true inner grace, and it shows itself in the kindest consideration for others' feelings and reactions, and is almost supernatural in its depth of understanding.

Indeed, the supernatural is always Neptune's province. The highly organized nervous system, which can if afflicted be prey to such a variety of subtle disorders, is at the same time intensely psychic. Clairvoyants and people who are more or less intuitive and sensitive to others and to their environments are influenced strongly by the planet Neptune. Visionaries, prophets, and other seers whose knowledge of the future is gained by being able to erase the boundaries between reality and the dream are also Neptunians.

Genius is the province of Neptune as well as Uranus, but the Neptunian is the subtle, visionary, receptive type whereas the Uranian is the disruptive, dynamic, forceful side of genius. The Neptunian is the idealist who sees beyond the limitations of material form. The Uranian is the advanced thinker whose theories help improve the conditions of the world.

In a physical sense, the Neptunian is high-strung and sensitive. He cannot withstand long, continuous strains as can other people, and too much pressure over an extended period can result in a nervous breakdown. Heart palpitations, cancer and a variety of diseases that are hard to diagnose can be traced to Neptune's afflictions.

If Neptune is the ruler of your Ascendant and is well aspected, you are charming, emotional and very sensitive. Badly aspected, you are either fraudulently charming or likely to be easily deceived and apt to experience the strangest, most inexplicable conditions in your life.

With Neptune well aspected, you are gentle, unassuming and visionary. You have a great awareness of spiritual values. You like to preserve an illusion of graciousness and charm. You require solitude and silence to nurture your psychic forces. Your sense of rhythm is well developed. You are in tune with the shimmering, changing colors and motion of the sea. Debussy and the Impressionists were typical Neptunians.

A badly aspected Neptune, on the other hand, may make you nervous and easily upset. If your environment is not congenial, you don't go out and try to change it but tend to retreat into a dream world where everything is well and happy. These people are basically irresponsible. They may resort to alcohol or drugs to preserve their illusions. They may, on the other hand, trick others into bogus schemes that promise something for nothing and involve losing everything, or they may be the victims of this kind of salesmanship themselves. They can also tend to hypochondria and are subject to complaints where imagination and worry cause serious psychical complications. They can be morally corrupt and subject their bodies to various abuses as a result.

It takes approximately fourteen years for Neptune to pass through a single sign. And so it is true that the sign your Neptune is in applies to your entire generation. Its position determines what you and your contemporaries will do to make history. It tells you the characteristics you have in common with others of your age group. It shows what your generation will contribute after it has taken over the task of running the world. Often, the people with the slower moving, heavier planets such as Uranus, Neptune and Pluto very prominently in their horoscopes are the leaders of the important movements that determine the history of the world.

Neptune in good aspect to Mercury gives a soft-spoken, charming manner of expression. Even poorly educated people with this aspect have a talent for speaking and writing with extraordinary grace. Neptune in adverse aspect to Mercury gives the ability to mislead through speech or writing. These people are not to be trusted because of perverse, distorted minds.

Neptune in good aspect to Venus gives a love ideal beyond your wildest dreams. You place your love on a pedestal and love truly in a spiritual sense. With Neptune in bad aspect to Venus, you are undervalued by your loved one and not as appreciated as you deserve.

When Neptune favorably aspects Mars, you tend to act in accordance with your highest ideals and handle other people with great consideration and finesse. With Neptune afflicting Mars, you are subject to the strangest, most unreasonable conditions imaginable and experience malefic events that are both unforeseen and unavoidable and where the only antidote is spiritual strength.

Neptune favorably aspecting Jupiter gives either great material good fortune or spiritual illumination and peace. If you see visions the world considers false and illusory, like Joan of Arc, if you are the victim of religious persecution or if, on the other hand, you are the instrument by which others experience such torment, no doubt your Neptune is in unfavorable aspect to your Jupiter.

With Neptune in good aspect to Saturn, you are imaginative and at the same time conservative, all of your most fantastic notions being subject to the influence of sound common sense. If Neptune is in unfavorable aspect to your Saturn, you can alternate from moods of complete depression to the illusions of an alcoholic stupor or drug addiction.

Neptune in good aspect to Uranus makes you both inventive and creative. You may be a musician with a sense both of sound and rhythm or an artist equally adept at both color and line. With Neptune in unfavorable aspect to Uranus, you can have to cope with a series of unreasonable exterior conditions most of your life, or else if the defect is in your character instead, you may be confused and irresponsible or the exponent of outlandish, crackpot ideas.

Neptune in good aspect to the Sun means that your father would have been charming, idealistic and somewhat whimsical. If a woman, men tend to put you on a pedestal and have the highest regard for you. Neptune adversely aspecting the Sun may have given you a father whose example to you encouraged low principles, or he may have been incontinent with alcohol or addicted to drugs. If a woman, the men in your life would be degenerate and irresponsible. They could also be downright dishonest and inclined to tempt you to be immoral.

If Neptune is in good aspect to your Moon, your mother would have been socially charming and morally upright. She would have inspired the highest ideals in you. If a man, the women in your life would be gracious and captivating and would bring all your best instincts to the fore. With Neptune in adverse aspect to your Moon, your mother would have been a demoralizing influence in your life and highly irresponsible. If a man, women would be deceptive and dishonest in their relationships with you.

NEPTUNE IN GEMINI

Neptune in Gemini can give mental fantasies and confusion, or it can add the superlative qualities of genius to the mind. This is because Neptune, the planet of illusions, can either cast his mysterious veil over the intellectual qualities of Gemini or else can lend his universality and inspiration to that most versatile of signs.

This generation was charmed by all that cultivates the mind. To them, an education was of prime importance and they idealized the benefits it would give. Some of their ideas were a bit hazy and impractical, but they had high ideals and under their guidance, almost universal education began to be a reality. Their own educations, on the other hand, were a source of inspiration to them. As higher education was not common, those so endowed formed an intellectual elite. They were especially fond of reading and were undeterred by the voluminous tomes of their era.

Under their influence, reading material would have altered drastically. Men like Henry Luce created a magazine empire that spread a Gemini phenomenon like the news in an interesting and, for the times, unusual form. For the people of this generation there was a special charm associated with the various news media.

Flight became a reality during Neptune's passage through the air sign of Gemini, and its miracle was a source of fascination to those with this position of Neptune. Some of these people had a fear of flying; others followed up the pioneers in the field to help establish factories and airlines to facilitate the miracle of man's ascent into the air. Many World War I pilots had this position of Neptune.

Cars also flourished as a mode of transportation, and it was owing to the efforts of this generation that they became a commonplace for their descendants. Short trips took on a new charm for these people, who were generally somewhat restless and interested in variety.

Silent movies were advanced by those with Neptune in Gemini. Such stars as Charlie Chaplin displayed a Neptunian whimsy and muteness in the early films.

A great many women with Neptune so placed grew up to be flappers, not so surprising a style when you consider the faint perversity of Neptune and the slender, young-boyish shape so reminiscent of Mercury's sign, Gemini.

As large families were the rule in this generation, many of these people had a great deal to do with their relatives, especially their brothers and sisters. With Neptune well aspected, they would have idealized and derived great enjoyment from these relationships; badly aspected, weird and unreasonable behavior would have characterized their experiences with relatives. These remarks can apply also to their contacts with their near neighbors.

Singers with the position of Neptune would have had fascinating, memorable voices as would the early entertainers and newscasters on radio, and their influence would have spread by this early form of mass media. In lawyers, this position of Neptune gives finesse in argument. It is also a good influence for charm of expression and vivid imagination among writers.

An interest in mediums and other spiritualists is also characteristic of this generation, as well as unorthodox religious and political interests. Communist ideology would have confused many fuzzy thinkers in this generation and in some cases would have resulted in betrayal of their country, since Neptune in Gemini presents many a deception in an intellectual guise.

As the United States Ascendant is in Gemini, people with Neptune therein could have a great influence on the people of this country, either through Communist infiltration of many of our institutions, especially the schools (in bad aspect to the fifth house in the Declaration of Independence chart) or through well-loved figures like Eisenhower who charmed the whole nation. (Neptune in conjunction with the United States Ascendant.)

January 1, 1890   through   July 19, 1901
December 25, 1901   May 21, 1902

Famous people with Neptune in Gemini

Dwight D. Eisenhower   Casey Stengel
Charles de Gaulle   Everett Dirksen
Margaret Chase Smith   J. Paul Getty
Pope Paul VI   Ernest Hemingway
Henry Luce   William Shakespeare
Charlie Chaplin   George Washington
Arthur Goldberg   William Faulkner
Edmund Wilson   Juan Peron
Adolf Hitler   Helen Hayes

NEPTUNE IN CANCER

Neptune in Cancer is a better position for being receptive and psychic than for being dynamic and positive. At best, Neptune is a planet that well aspected can give high ideals related to the things ruled by the sign in which it is found. At worst, it can cause deception and utter confusion in this connection.

Primarily, Cancer is the Moon's sign, and its negative compliance can make those with Neptune therein more placid and variable than in the other signs. There is a love of luxury and comfort, and the tendency is to dissipate rather than build. Of course, Cancer is a cardinal sign, and in the more active types, Neptune, like the moonlit sea, charms while it wears away the cliffs by its corrosive action.

As Cancer is the sign of motherhood, we can expect mothers with Neptune so placed to be charming and easy, but there is a tendency to be overindulgent. Unless there are aspects in the rest of the horoscope to show sterner qualities, we cannot expect such women to discipline children sufficiently or to strengthen their characters by rigorous early training. The permissive philosophy of a Dr. Spock who influenced a whole generation of mothers and other educators of his era is typical.

At the same time, motherhood in this generation underwent some vital changes in many cases. While these women revered their own mothers who had had large families, they themselves in many cases limited the size of their own families so as to be able to give more advantages to the children they had. More women worked outside the home, and where Neptune was afflicted, were very discontented with their maternal duties. To the woman with a well-aspected Neptune in Cancer, however, homemaking was a sacred art and she would have provided her family with every comfort and endowed her home with special charm

In the decorations of the home itself, the more active type would like everything up to date. Every electric appliance that would contribute to the housewife's ease would have been considered a necessity, and many in this generation would have profited by supplying a variety of household aids to a public eager to use them.

At the same time, this generation would have taken a great interest in antiques. With Neptune well aspected, they would have embellished their homes with the furniture and art objects of other eras, or else reproductions of these.

Cancer rules the stomach and digestion, and Neptune's influence on the sign would have given rise to many rich and fancy food products. Grocery stores would in fact have been expanded and specialized and the supermarket would become a commonplace for this generation, which would also have produced a great many gourmet cooks of both sexes, especially where Jupiter was also in Cancer.

Well aspected, Neptune in Cancer can give a knack for taking the public pulse and knowing both how to create and to satisfy popular demands. Many of those who manufacture, sell or advertise popular products are favored by this position of Neptune. Or they may delight in the role of satisfied consumers.

In politics, this gives an appeal based largely on sentimentality, and there is a certain nostalgia in the outlook. Great loyalty to party and past tradition or an appeal to the emotions, on whichever side they may be, is typical, as is a certain personal conceit when Neptune is afflicted.

In entertainers, Neptune in Cancer can insure true popularity. Phyllis Diller with her jokes about motherhood and homemaking certainly shows the Cancer influence. Walt Disney with his entertainment for the whole family is another. As you can see, there is a very long list of singers, actors, and comedians who have received great public adulation with this position of Neptune.

July 19, 1901	through	December 25, 1901
May 21, 1902		September 23, 1914
December 15, 1914		July 19, 1915

Famous people with Neptune in Cancer

Danny Kaye	Mary McCarthy
David Rockefeller	John Wayne
Aleksei N. Kosygin	Dr. Benjamin Spock
Lucille Ball	Joan of Arc
Tex Thornton	Samuel Barber
Al Capp	Perry Como
Laurence Rockefeller	Bing Crosby
Nelson Rockefeller	Willem de Kooning
Douglas Dillon	Phyllis Diller
Walt Disney	Henry Fonda
Bob Hope	Rex Harrison
Richard Nixon	Lady Bird Johnson
Hubert Humphrey	Lyndon B. Johnson
George Orwell	J. Robert Oppenheimer
Eugene Ionesco	Eero Saarinen
Pat Nixon	Dag Hammarskjold
Dr. Ralph Bunche	Julia Child

NEPTUNE IN LEO

Neptune in Leo indicates noble aspirations coupled with the ability to turn dreams into reality. Those of you with Neptune prominent in your horoscopes can in fact spearhead a movement to revolutionize your world and see that your high ideals are made into practical standards for humanity at large.

Many of the young soldiers who fought for American independence had Neptune in Leo as did many leaders of the French Revolution. In our own time, many civil rights leaders and militants for black power have this highly incendiary position of Neptune. It was also in the horoscopes of many of the younger men who fought for their country's freedom in World War II. In the Cuban crisis, both John F. Kennedy and Fidel Castro had Neptune in Leo, so that both the American President and the Communist leader were dedicated, each to his own cause.

It is well to remember that in our time as in the French and American Revolutions, many of the participants representing the establishment as well as the revolting factions had Neptune in Leo, so that each in his own way demonstrated a certain fanatic zeal.

This position of Neptune tends to produce leaders who can arouse the masses, that is, heroes who have an emotional appeal. Neptune's mystique inspires hero worship. These men have the most loyal and devoted followers, but the emotional climate in which passions are kindled for the cause can also give rise to the kind of fanatic hatred that resulted in two assassinations in the Kennedy family within five years.

As Leo is the sign of leadership, the leaders of man's conquest of space, like John Glenn and Virgil Grissom, have this position of Neptune.

Leo is the sign of schools and children and consequently the confusing and often hazy Neptune therein would sometimes have an adverse effect on education. Some of these children were the first to receive so-called progressive education, and the theories of those with Neptune in Gemini were practiced on this generation with detrimental results. Where Neptune was badly aspected, the lack of discipline and direction in their early schooling had adverse repercussions not only in their own lives but also in those of their children who were brought up by undisciplined, often self-centered adults.

As Leo is the sign of drama, there are outstanding actors and playwrights as well as other literary figures who write to entertain with Neptune in Leo. Where it is well aspected, it is also good for musicians, composers or singers with a flair, and the almost fanatic cult of worship that enshrined Judy Garland in her own lifetime can be traced to the position of Neptune in her particular horoscope. With all entertainers, in fact, it gives great popularity and formidable charm. It is excellent for those connected with musical comedy as well.

It is not surprising to an astrologer that Neptune in Leo, the sign of the heart, is found in the horoscope of Dr. Christiaan Barnard, whose daring and ability achieved the triumph of the first heart transplant in human history. Doctors pioneering in this field can have an added advantage if their Neptune in Leo is in their horoscopes, since Neptune gives a highly organized complexity in Leo, which represents the heart.

Neptune was in Leo in the 20's when stockmarket speculation reached a fever pitch and became a popular form of gambling rather than serious investment. Those with Neptune so placed may be fascinated by the romance and excitement of Wall Street, and although other aspects in their horoscopes may make them turn their interest to the more solid, less glamorous aspects of the market, they will still be charmed by the idea of fantastic growth in their investments. Where Neptune is well aspected, many of them will realize their ambitions in this respect.

Badly aspected, Neptune in Leo gives an indolence and a love of luxury, an inclination to be weak and cowardly or else to be self-centered and a bully. Well aspected, it produces imperious, daring, fiery, masterful, often radical people who will go to great lengths to further their ideals.

September 23, 1914 through	December 14, 1914
July 19, 1915	September 21, 1928
February 19, 1929	July 24, 1929

Famous people with Neptune in Leo

Dean Martin	Fidel Castro
Sidney Poitier	Gordon Cooper
Truman Capote	John Glenn
William Styron	Virgil Grissom
Mike Douglas	Jimmy Dean
Johnny Carson	Elizabeth II

Merv Griffin
John Lindsay
James Baldwin
Leonard Bernstein
Richard Burton
Carol Channing
Alan Jay Lerner
Edward Albee

Margot Fonteyn
Judy Garland
Jackie Gleason
Doris Day
Billy Graham
Sammy Davis, Jr.
John F. Kennedy
Robert F. Kennedy

Dr. Christiaan Barnard

NEPTUNE IN VIRGO

While Neptune is a very spiritual planet, Virgo is a material sign and the combination of the two gives an almost psychic understanding of situations and people and a prophetic knowledge of the outcome of events. If Neptune is well aspected, you do not have to see something with your own eyes to perceive what is going on; you are able to see it in your mind's eye at will.

As Virgo is an earth sign, a well-aspected Neptune therein gives a green thumb. These people have a talent for nurturing growing things and can be attuned to all of nature. Where Virgo refers, as it often does, to city life, you tend to romanticize all the features of urban living and to be very happy when surrounded by cosmopolitan benefits.

Well aspected, Neptune in Virgo gives a practical ability to command colossal organizational projects. These people, at their finest, are able to conceive the plans for tremendous building complexes and shopping centers. They are constructive either in the sense of being master architects and planners, or they may participate actively in the actual building process. On the other hand, they may live in such projects which for them would have a special charm.

When Neptune is afflicted, odd concepts connected with work prevail. The attitude that everybody should be taken care of if they don't choose to work is typical. This does not refer to those who are disabled or unable to contribute to their own support for valid reasons; it refers to those who although able-bodied and capable, simply do not choose to work. In some cases, even when they do hold down jobs, they are lazy and simply pass their time physically at the place of employment without taking an interest or trying to do a good job. At heart, such people feel the world owes them a living, and they are out to collect it with the least possible inconvenience to themselves. Certain policies on the part of the government and labor unions will make laxity and indolence more prevalent than in the past when this generation is running matters.

Well aspected, Neptune in Virgo causes just the opposite behavior. These people romanticize their work and are tremendously capable. They are conscientious and as careful of details as those with an afflicted Neptune are careless. More often, their goal is, however, more practical than idealistic. When Neptune is well aspected, these people are constructively critical and their powers of discrimination are considerable; where Neptune is badly aspected, they tend by their criticism to tear things down.

In Virgo, Neptune affects education as it did in Gemini. The difference is that in Gemini, hazy concepts or romantic attitudes were evident in regard to purely intellectual theories; whereas in Virgo, it affects the practical aspects of learning such as reading, writing, spelling, grammar and arithmetic. This gives rise to fanciful theories about the teaching of these subjects with the result that many in this generation are inadequately schooled in the barest fundamentals an educated person would have taken for granted several generations ago. Neptune in Virgo gives us the concept of universal education, regardless of the intrinsic inability of some people to learn.

People of this generation also tend to romanticize scientific research and to scoff at spiritual values for which there is no apparent physical proof. This is, nevertheless, a good influence for scientists, since it gives them keen analytical powers and an understanding of material things.

This is a good position for writers, making them perceptive and able to express themselves with a special charm. Their report on reality tends to be precise and true to life. It is also a powerfully constructive influence for musicians and artists.

September 21, 1928	through	February 19, 1929
July 24, 1929		October 3, 1942
April 19, 1943		August 2, 1943

Famous people with Neptune in Virgo

Carol Burnett	Napoleon Bonaparte
Diahann Carroll	Anne Bancroft
Edward M. Kennedy	Warren Beatty
Ann-Margret	Leslie Caron
Julie Christie	Petula Clark
Van Cliburn	Bobby Darin
Eydie Gorme	Jane Fonda
Dr. Martin Luther King, Jr.	Jacqueline Kennedy Onassis
Steve Lawrence	Sandy Koufax
Julie Andrews	John Lennon
Joan Baez	Paul McCartney
John Osborne	David McCallum
Arthur Ashe	Joe Namath

NEPTUNE IN LIBRA

Those of you with Neptune in Libra should be well aware that Neptune is a planet of aspiration and high ideals. Put into practice, your concepts of peace and equality could change the world. However, this does not give you much force, and you tend to use forms of passive resistance such as sit-ins, marches and other demonstrations to further your aims.

It is not surprising to an astrologer that you have been called the "love generation." Libra is the sign of Venus, the planet of love, and the idea of universal love is most natural to those of you with Neptune so placed. However, Neptune is also the planet of hazy concepts and illusions, and many of you may discover that your ideal of love can vanish like a mirage. You must learn that to love truly often demands sacrifice, and that to sustain love, one must have a mature acceptance of responsibility.

You have an inborn sense of justice, but Neptune clouds the issue and you may learn that your absolute ideal of what is right and just is hard to put into practice in the world as it is. You must make sure that the confused and impractical among you do not overrule the better judgment of those whose vision is clear.

Libra is the sign of marriage, and those with Neptune therein can expect to revolutionize that institution. Marriage as we know it today will be a thing of the past when your age group dictates public conventions. Old customs will come under scrutiny and will be discarded and changed.

Neptune in Libra has a profound effect on art and literature. Many of the great names of the Italian Renaissance had this position of Neptune. It gives a sense of balance and proportion in sculpture and painting as well as in architecture. Many of the nineteenth-century poets were born under this influence. And like them, many of you will express yourselves in speech and writing with unusual charm, beauty and grace. When Neptune is afflicted, however, you may expect many exaggerations and strange abuses in literature and art.

You will be very concerned with a refinement of manners. The outer forms that express behavior will fascinate you, and while you will reject the standards of the past in many instances, you will borrow from compatible sources and transform them into rituals of your own.

In a lighter vein, you will also express yourselves in the dance. Discothèques have come into being for those of your generation, but you will break with the immediate past and soon evolve your own dance patterns.

Those with Neptune in Libra are true children of the space age. Your scientific discoveries will be phenomenal, and you will participate in explorations that will colonize other planets. You will take to space with the same spirit that Columbus took to the sea.

October 3, 1942   through   April 18, 1943
August 3, 1943   December 30, 1947

Famous people with Neptune in Libra

Percy B. Shelley	Brenda Lee
Lord Byron	Lynda Bird Johnson Robb
Savonarola	Mia Farrow
Patty Duke	Luci Baines Johnson Nugent
Hayley Mills	Anne-Marie of Greece
George Harrison	Prince Charles
Cassius Clay	Princess Anne
Geraldine Chaplin	Tricia Nixon
Julie Nixon Eisenhower	

11
PLUTO
and Your Group Involvement

Are you interested in the wonders of modern science? Have you seen your life reverse its course and go in the opposite direction? Do you like to destroy old theories to make way for the new? Do you belong to a group whose aim is to counter the actions of some other organization? Are you interested in archaeology?

For clues to this behavior, you should consult the planet Pluto. It is important for every adult who wants to understand his role in the mass movements of his generation to know about the position of this most recently discovered of all the planets in his particular horoscope.

In ancient Greek mythology, Pluto was the god of the underworld. The planet Pluto was discovered in 1930 by Clyde U. Tombaugh, working on reckonings made in 1914 by Percival Lowell of the Lowell Observatory in Flagstaff, Arizona. Originally called planet X, it was named Pluto by a little English girl whose suggestion for its new name was the first to arrive. And it is indeed a coincidence that, in astrology, the planet Pluto has been considered, like its ancient namesake, to be connected with death and rebirth. Pluto is the planet of nuclear fission. It is a transformer and annihilator.

Like the sign Scorpio which it rules, the planet Pluto has both constructive and destructive manifestations. And whatever department of life it controls in your particular horoscope, it is like a coin with two sides. The two sides are opposites, but both are part of the same coin. People ruled by Pluto have, for this reason, very contradictory traits of character. They can be positive, strong and forceful, at the same time exhibiting an extreme sensitivity that can result in asthma, skin allergies and a variety of other so-called nervous diseases.

In addition, these people's lives can often take very contradictory paths. For instance, they might work in one direction only to have their work destroyed so that they have to start all over again, usually in a new field. Pluto is, however, like the phoenix that rises from his ashes. If overnight his whole world were to collapse, the Plutonian would awaken the next morning and calmly begin to build it up again. Often people who are exiled from their native land and have to start afresh in another country are born under the strong influence of Pluto.

This applies as well to those who are catalysts of a civilization, who attack and destroy the old order to make way for the new. Often, Pluto splits a group into two opposing factions, the one to counter what the other sets out to do. This is usually done on a grand scale, since Pluto rules mass movements and the mass media and all things that are reproduced or repeated endlessly and automatically. Propaganda and group opinion, especially the subtle, inverted kind that can't be traced to any particular inspiration or source, is also a Pluto phenomenon.

Pluto is the planet of archaeology as well as of the latest and most advanced scientific discovery. It is the planet of crime and its opposite, that is, work for the benefit of all humanity. It is the highest and the lowest. It indicates an extremist in any event, whether an idealistic revolutionary or the supporter of a totalitarian regime. He tends to join with others to further whatever purpose he may espouse. Often this represents gang action, something a person will do in conjunction with others that he wouldn't dare do individually.

Well aspected, Pluto gives you the ability to learn from the past and have insight into the future. It makes you magnetically attractive and strong-willed. Sometimes, it gives a talent for medicine, sometimes for science, or it can mean that you rise to the top as leader of some faction of politics. You either have the will to discover, research or create, or you may have a desire to lead, arbitrate and control. You may be able to tune in on the thoughts of others. You are, more than likely, a dual personality. You gather tremendous strength from reconciling within yourself two extremes. You have great reserves in your subconscious. At the proper moment, the needed information comes to the surface and you have the situation under control. Well aspected, Pluto can be very idealistic and spiritual.

A badly aspected Pluto, on the other hand, brings unrest, conflict and strife. These people are very proud and touchy, jealous of their own rights and at the same time arrogantly ignoring the rights of others. They tend to have irreconcilable traits of character, to be badly adjusted or schizophrenics. They are volcanic in temperament and destructive, or they may be very unfortunate and may vanish from their environment and never be seen again. They can belong to gangs or mobs and perpetrate the most vicious crimes. They can be dictators, fiends or evil geniuses, or else the victims of such types. Badly aspected, Pluto can be very materialistic and cruel.

Pluto is the slowest moving of all the heavier planets. The other planets move within 9 degrees of the Sun's path or the ecliptic, while Pluto moves north and south of the paths of the Sun 17 degrees. Its movement is irregular; the average time for its going through one sign of the Zodiac is twenty-four years. In a larger sense, Pluto while more remote is more powerful. While Uranus and Neptune rule the various characteristics of each generation, Pluto spans the generations to map mass movements in the history of the world. The more recently discovered planets came to light when their effect on human history was actually taking place, and Pluto was discovered at a time when kidnapping, racketeering, the rise of dictators and economic depression all combined to plague the modern world. Both those evils and the practical and spiritual forces that formed to counterbalance them are typical of the activity of Pluto.

Pluto in good aspect to the Sun gives ambition and daring. These people are confident, self-disciplined and self-contained. Their inner resources are tremendous. They are often leaders in a progressive or spiritual cause. With Pluto in unfavorable aspect to the Sun, daring turns into self-seeking and a love of glory. These people are often contentious. They tend to overdo and to overestimate what it is possible for them to do. They run unnecessary risks and are careless of the consequences of their actions. Often, they are very contradictory and are at odds with themselves.

If Pluto favorably aspects the Moon, there is a desire for adventure, courage, even fanatic fervor. This gives a great sensitivity with psychic ability or the experience of prophetic dreams. The sense of touch is usually well developed. It is a good aspect for surgeons and other scientists. Pluto adversely aspecting the Moon gives a lust for sensual pleasures, a foolhardy daring and irresponsible fanaticism. These people are obstinate, tyrannical, revengeful and conceited.

With Pluto in good aspect to Mercury, there is great mental agility and an almost psychic perceptiveness. These people are excellent speakers and natural debaters, quick to sense an opponent's weakness. They are clever with their hands and can be very amusing with their satirical observations and jokes. They make excellent mimics. Pluto in bad aspect to Mercury makes a person quarrelsome and malicious, apt to resort to every kind of underhanded trickery and deceit. At worst, these people can be forgers or blackmailers. Sometimes a badly aspected Pluto indicates nervous breakdowns that result from mental overwork.

Pluto in good aspect to Venus gives great intensity in love and a magnetically attractive personality. These people tend to meet a love they cannot live without and to become completely absorbed by the partner of their romance or marriage, a relationship that is Karmic, i.e., the result of actions and associations in past lives. Sometimes such people are highly idealistic and love all humanity instead. This is also a good aspect for artistic talent. People with Pluto in bad aspect to Venus tend to be coarse, sensual and immoral. This kind of Pluto causes many reverses in the emotions, intrigues, faithlessness and divorce.

When Pluto is in good aspect to Mars, there is a strong mind and iron will. These people tend to be tirelessly active in both a mental and a physical sense. They have great faith in themselves, but the more they accomplish, the more they desire to achieve. They try to break records, and when they reach the top, they try to surpass what they have already done. Pluto in bad aspect to Mars gives a terrible temper and a jealous nature. At worst, there are criminal proclivities. Such people are destructive, brutal and ridden by social disease. They often run the risk of suffering a violent death.

Pluto in good aspect to Jupiter gives pride and dignity, a love of freedom, strong desires. These people have the ability to inspire others. They are religious and philosophical, and fond of ecclesiastical ceremonies. This can be magnificent in a material sense or spiritually illuminating. It can give an interest in the occult or in aeronautics. With Pluto in bad aspect to Jupiter, there is arrogance, bigotry and extravagance. Such people are always discontented and never realize their ambitions or their dreams. They can become adventurers or gamblers, or they may waste their inner resources prodigally.

Pluto in good aspect to Saturn gives great powers of endurance and asceticism in the face of danger, hardship and death. Such people may be silent and stoical. They may also be philosophical and scientific. They are honest, but they have to struggle against enemies who resort to lies and deceit. However, they approach life with an impressive depth of understanding. The bad aspects between Pluto and Saturn indicate harshness, greed and suspicion. These people can betray their friends and be brutal, power-mad and sadistic. When things don't go their way, suicide can result. Criminals, morticians, and executioners often have Pluto afflicting Saturn.

Uranus brings about the sudden and unexpected. Pluto destroys the old to make way for the new, and the combination of the two is explosive. The good aspects give an urge for independence and freedom, spiritual strength and energy, and dauntless courage and will. They also give the ability to transform the materials of the past into startlingly new and original concepts. Adverse Pluto-Uranus aspects give explosive rage, fanatic hatred and great eccentricity. These people are perverted, rude and violent, and cannot bear opposition and delay. They expect others to bend or they will break them. Some of them are mentally unbalanced, destructive or insane. Some may suffer violence or be accident-prone.

Pluto in good aspect to Neptune gives the highest spiritual understanding, a love of the unusual and people out of the ordinary. These people have the ability to see through others at the same time concealing their own faults. This aspect also favors deep-sea diving, the use of submarines and the harnessing of atomic power for constructive and destructive purposes. People with adverse Neptune-Pluto aspects tend to rob, kidnap and assault or be the victims of those who do. This also produces grave illnesses and bodily injuries, loss of position in life or physical falling from high places. These people want to do something new, but cling to the old in such a way that it is impossible, or else they destroy the old without having a replacement. They tend for these reasons to be constantly at war with themselves.

PLUTO IN GEMINI

With Pluto in Gemini well aspected and prominent in the horoscope, you have many facets to your character. You are very quick to take the measure of the people with whom you come into contact, but you are adept at concealing your own weaknesses. You immediately grasp all the elements of any given situation and turn it to your own advantage. Nothing surprises you or catches you unaware. Your most outstanding characteristic is that of being progressive. You are always searching for something better, ever ready to cast aside the obsolete, to discard the past the minute you can improve on it. You are inventive and adventurous, and your spiritual resources are inexhaustible.

These people are often intensely psychic, with very sensitive, highly organized nervous systems. They also have a dual nature, sometimes being self-assured and positive, at other times acting in a negative manner. They are in many cases interested in the occult, astrology, literature, and the intellectual side of detective work.

People with Pluto in Gemini badly aspected and prominent in their horoscopes often choose a variety of vocations. They may try as many as four different fields, only to fail in all of them. A woman with this position of Pluto might be inclined to marry many times. Or this aspect might have other effects on these people and make them sarcastic, skeptical or fond of teasing and tormenting others. They tend to have one standard for themselves and another for the rest of the world. At worst, they indulge in criminal activities which require mental duplicity and agility, like swindling, embezzlement and espionage. At the very least, they may cheat their friends at cards.

Where Pluto applies to the entire generation and its outstanding members, it gives power over the masses in a way hitherto impossible without modern news media. The province of automatic duplication and almost infinite repetition is Pluto's own, and in Gemini is applied to newspapers, radio and television. Walt Disney, who invented the repetitive patterns necessary to create the animated cartoon, is another typical example of a person with Pluto in Gemini.

The public image is a Plutonian phenomenon. Such well-known figures as Eisenhower and de Gaulle have Pluto in Gemini, giving them the power to achieve great popularity. As they also had Neptune in Gemini at the same time, it added the power to charm to Pluto's mass appeal.

Gemini is the sign of mathematics, and the grasp of figures when it comes to multiplying money is found in such Pluto in Gemini types as Laurence Rockefeller, Douglas Dillon and J. Paul Getty. In literature, we have the dry, intellectualized technique of a Mary McCarthy and the style of a William Faulkner or an Ernest Hemingway.

The two people most typical of Pluto in Gemini, however, in their influence on an age were Adolph Hitler and J. Robert Oppenheimer, the one hypnotizing a nation to conquest and mass murder, the other inventing the transforming and annihilating phenomenon of the atom bomb. Oppenheimer's intellectual versatility is truly typical of Pluto in Gemini as was Hitler's diabolically magnetic voice.

In an intellectual sense, Pluto's duality caused different schools of thought with regard to methods of education. Progressive education's advocates and those who ardently opposed it are two typical Pluto in Gemini schools of thought.

Where Gemini refers to brothers and sisters, factions are formed in large families among the various members, and in many cases they are bitterly opposed. This could also be the case with other relatives or neighbors whose grouping occur to counter a group already formed.

Pope Paul VI is in his way another typical Pluto in Gemini figure, with his letter-of-the-law, intellectualized approach to religion, his dictums causing the groups within the church to form pro and con.

It was people with Pluto in Gemini who made air travel a reality by manufacturing planes and founding airlines; their long-term plans of action and ability to duplicate endlessly is typical of Pluto, and resulted in the many and extensive forms of air travel we have now. It was indeed the combination of both Neptune and Pluto in the air sign of Gemini that made possible the miracle associated with flight into space in our own day.

Theirs is indeed a remarkable record. We may criticize them for their failings, but it was Pluto in Gemini's versatile, strong-minded, progressive generation, one which survived two wars, a gangster-ridden prohibition era and a major economic depression, that is responsible for many of the improvements we enjoy today. While they haven't handed down to contemporary youth a perfect world, neither did they inherit one. They made the best of things as they were and valiantly went on from there.

January 1, 1890   through   September 9, 1912
September 29, 1912   July 11, 1913
December 27, 1913   May 27, 1914

Famous people with Pluto in Gemini

Dwight D. Eisenhower	Marc Chagall
Lucille Ball	Chiang Kai-Shek
Al Capp	Charlie Chaplin
Laurence Rockefeller	Everett Dirksen
Arthur Goldberg	Walt Disney
Paul Tillich	William Faulkner
Margaret Sanger	J. Paul Getty
Douglas Dillon	Barry Goldwater
Charles de Gaulle	Cary Grant
Casey Stengel	Rex Harrison
Margaret Chase Smith	Ernest Hemingway
George Orwell	Dag Hammarskjold
Benjamin Spock	Bob Hope
Pope Paul VI	Vladimir Horowitz
Henry Luce	Bing Crosby
Samuel Barber	Lyndon B. Johnson
Otto Klemperer	Aleksei Kosygin
Richard Nixon	Hubert Humphrey
J. Robert Oppenheimer	Adolph Hitler
Dr. Ralph Bunche	Benito Mussolini

PLUTO IN CANCER

Well aspected, Pluto in Cancer gives an active subconscious mind. Such people indulge in dreams and fantasies and have a rich, deep inner life. They have an interest in the many forms a single idea can take, or in the metamorphoses of people and objects. This can take the form of creative acting, and such a person is not limited to portraying a single type, but is very versatile and excels in a wide range of parts.

These people are very determined when it comes to spreading and gaining acceptance for a new idea. They are also good at reproducing objects from the past and at reconstructing archaeological finds as well as treasures of art. They know how to study and understand old traditions in order to develop new standards from them. They can also draw on strong spiritual resources which they in turn pass on to others.

These are people with a phenomenal memory for their personal past. At best, they have a grasp of the totality of human history. Like other people born strongly under Pluto, those with Pluto in Cancer are almost psychic when it comes to intuiting other people's thoughts and feelings. If interested in geology or mining, they are so quick to discover metals or minerals beneath the earth that some of them can be like human divining rods.

With Pluto badly aspected, they can be very lonely with a tendency to become recluses and to alienate their relatives and friends. They can, on the other hand, be intolerant, egotistical and conceited, always trying to impose their will on others. They tend to be highhanded in their methods and at the same time unreliable.

While Neptune in Cancer made people romanticize the joys of motherhood, Pluto in this sign of the home and mother caused the familiar patterns to be transformed and in some cases totally reversed. In this generation, a woman might start out in the feminine role of wife and mother only to give it all up to further a career. So discontented with the traditional, so bored by the trivialities and confinements of a purely domestic life, these women, after contracting for all the responsibilities of marriage, renounce it to seek salvation outside the home. In the cases where their marriages hold together, there is the not uncommon situation of the husband who helps with the housework and mothers the children as much from necessity as from choice.

Coincident with this sociological reversal was a breakdown of the discipline which is normally the function of motherhood. This was the generation that felt they could not communicate traditional values to their young, who in fact failed to teach them many of the civilizing influences other generations succeeded in imparting to the generation that followed. Another characteristic of Pluto in Cancer prominent and afflicted in the horoscope was that the mothers of children not only failed conscientiously to raise their own offspring, but they also expected their parents to assume this burden for them altogether in extreme cases, or by babysitting and housekeeping in others. Indulged by their own parents, they were too spoiled properly to train their young or too indifferent. This is, of course, not true of an entire generation, many of whom have been excellent parents, but rather of the individuals among them with Pluto in Cancer prominent and afflicted in their charts. At the same time that women were avoiding maternal duties, their role as an enticing female was being stressed with special emphasis on the bosom. Sex in general came out in the open and was regarded as a purely animal function devoid of the traditional romance.

Where Pluto's characteristic of endless repetition or reproduction manifests itself in Cancer, there is the manufacture and merchandising of a great variety of popular items for the home. However, for every successful product, there would be several other competing ones that were similar, and the role of competitive advertising, especially on television, is a special province of those with Pluto so placed.

In popular entertainment, we not only have the Plutonian television media, but also the element of competition among the programs on the various networks. A well-aspected Pluto in Cancer is a wonderful influence for actors and comedians, giving them the power to arouse empathy and great sentimental appeal.

Cancer rules food and digestion, and Pluto therein tremendously influences the kind of food consumed by this generation. Frozen and prepared grocery items are a commonplace; fresh foods are gradually becoming obsolete, and mixes have supplanted the traditional home-baked cake. By the time the generation's influence is at its peak, almost everything will be packaged or frozen. However, Pluto in Cancer at the same time counteracts this trend with programs on gourmet cooking on television, fancy cookbooks in all the bookstores, and recipes in the newspapers.

These people would have different attitudes toward the history of their own times, and opposing factions would form among historians who would disagree with one another on what constitutes fair contemporary historical reporting.

While there are in their way many Pluto revolutionaries in this generation as in all the others, this position of Pluto is more passive than Pluto in Gemini or Leo, albeit equally psychic. At worst, there is a certain self-indulgence and self-pity. At best, an intuitive grasp of what is popular as well as what is essential. Pluto in Cancer also represents the beginning rejection of earth as their home by the first astronauts who dared travel in outer space. This new adventure is indeed the most daring of Pluto's achievements.

September 9, 1912	through	September 29, 1912
July 11, 1913		December 27, 1913
May 27, 1914		October 9, 1937
November 15, 1937		August 2, 1938
February 11, 1939		June 12, 1939

Famous people with Pluto in Cancer

David Rockefeller	Alan Jay Lerner
Carol Burnett	Fidel Castro
Diahann Carroll	Carol Channing
Joe DiMaggio	Petula Clark
Tex Thornton	Van Cliburn
Eugene McCarthy	Gordon Cooper
Sidney Poitier	Bobby Darin
Truman Capote	Sammy Davis, Jr.
William Styron	Doris Day
Eddie Arnold	Jimmy Dean
John Lindsay	Phyllis Diller
Edward M. Kennedy	Elizabeth II
James Baldwin	Eddie Fisher

James Arness
Anne Bancroft
Warren Beatty
Leonard Bernstein
Richard Burton
Leslie Caron
Johnny Carson
Bobby Kennedy
Dr. Martin Luther King, Jr.

Jane Fonda
Margot Fonteyn
Henry Ford II
Judy Garland
Jackie Gleason
John Glenn
Billy Graham
Jacqueline Kennedy Onassis
John F. Kennedy

Sandy Koufax

PLUTO IN LEO

Like all the slow-moving planets, Pluto makes its mark on an entire generation who are led by those with Pluto prominent in their charts. Pluto in Leo, well aspected, gives a high-minded, masterful nature with the will to dominate and influence others. The creative urge is very strong whether in the sciences or in the arts. There is a distinct talent for advertising on a grand scale or entertainment in every form, especially acting. There is also a sense of showmanship in politics. Whatever the field, these people exhibit a dynamic energy that is hard to beat.

Badly aspected, Pluto in Leo produces a very maladjusted, difficult character. These people demand their rights vociferously, even while they are infringing on the rights of others. They expect special privileges without commensurate responsibilities. They are touchy, contemptuous of all authority, arrogant, self-centered, selfish and immature.

Pluto in Leo, the sign of leadership, will bring autocratic new leaders to the fore, but will overthrow the few remaining monarchies in the world. Prince Charles will never come to the throne, since by the time this age group is managing the world's affairs, royalty will not only be outmoded, it will also be obsolete.

This is indeed the sign of rebellion and revolution. The instigators of both race and class warfare have an afflicted Pluto in Leo in this generation. As Leo is the sign of schools, Pluto therein causes factions to form in universities the world over to oppose the administration, in fact to take over control. Many of these people were the school dropouts or malcontents who return to make trouble on campus. Or else they can be leaders of various extremist groups, demanding the subservience of the rest of society, violent, tyrannical and domineering. Generally, in fact, it is Pluto in Leo that is responsible for the restlessness and rebellion among the members of this age group.

Pluto in Leo, the sign of pleasures, causes all sorts of abuses and promiscuity in sex. Sex behavior is unconventional by older standards, and those having relations with several persons at once are not at all uncommon in this generation.

Pluto in Leo, the sign of the heart, when afflicted gives incurable heart disease, but when well aspected gives a sturdy, almost superhuman vascular organ. The heart surgeons among their numbers will differ in their opinions of the proper techniques. There will in fact be opposing factions or schools of thought, but many of them will display superlative talents. This generation's playwrights will bring startling new innovations to acting and the theater. The financiers among them will form new theories on speculations and economic trends. This generation's parents and teachers will evolve unusual, sometimes contradictory new concepts about teaching and raising the young.

As man discovers new capacities, he becomes aware of the planetary forces representing them. Thus, the emergence of Pluto coincided with the discovery of atomic energy. The ability to overcome the forces of gravity and air pressure is also Plutonian. This generation's astronauts will go beyond the Moon to discover life on other planets. They will find new uses of atomic power for constructive and destructive purposes.

Man will make startling discoveries about his past as well, and this generation will have a second sense when it comes to archaeology, uncovering evidence of ancient civilizations that had heretofore seemed mere hearsay and myth. They will find that an ancient race evolved much further in a spiritual sense than modern science has progressed in a material way.

Indeed, this position of Pluto has a spiritual as well as a material meaning, and a number of outstanding psychics will emerge to contradict in this materialistic age the thesis that man lives by mechanization alone. The field of parapsychology will advance. Clairaudience, clairvoyance, clair-feeling, in fact clair-sensing in general will be recognized scientific facts.

You with Pluto in Leo will have daring and a sense of adventure. You will destroy the old to make way for the new, tearing down whole cities in order to rebuild them according to modern plans.

Now, while you are still young, you are like wine in the stage of fermentation or a volcano ready to erupt. You will bring to the world revolutionary new changes; you will bridge the gap between the present and the past, and you will accomplish all this with a nobility of purpose and a magnanimity of character that won't be met with again until Pluto once again transits through the sign of Leo.

October 9, 1937   through   November 15, 1937
August 2, 1938   February 11, 1939
June 12, 1939   December 31, 1952

Famous people with Pluto in Leo

Ringo Starr	Leslie Uggams
John Lennon	Ann-Margret
Patty Duke	Paul Anka
Hayley Mills	Jack Nicklaus
Sandra Dee	Charlotte Ford Niarchos
Barbra Streisand	Joe Namath
Connie Francis	Cassius Clay
Paul McCartney	Brenda Lee
Geraldine Chaplin	Mia Farrow
Lynda Bird Johnson Robb	Anne-Marie of Denmark
Luci Baines Johnson Nugent	Prince Charles
Constantine of Greece	Princess Anne
Julie Christie	Arthur Ashe
George Harrison	Tricia Nixon
Joan Baez	Julie Nixon Eisenhower

Appendix

MOON SIGN
Ephemeris

Tables of the Daily Motion of the Moon

In order to use these tables, which enable you to locate the sign your Moon is in, you must be able to identify the symbols for the various signs of the Zodiac. These are as follows:

ARIES ♈	**LEO** ♌	**SAGITTARIUS** ♐
TAURUS ♉	**VIRGO** ♍	**CAPRICORN** ♑
GEMINI ♊	**LIBRA** ♎	**AQUARIUS** ♒
CANCER ♋	**SCORPIO** ♏	**PISCES** ♓

In these tables, you must first locate the year and day of your birth. Where the sign is the same for three days in a row, on the middle day, the Moon is definitely in that sign. For instance, in 1890, the Moon is in Gemini on the 2nd, 3rd and 4th of January. On the 3rd, or middle day, the Moon was definitely in Gemini all day. On the 2nd, it may also have been in the preceding sign of Taurus, while on the 4th, it may also have been in the succeeding sign of Cancer.

If you do not want to make the calculations to be described in this appendix, and you were born on a day when the Moon could be in either of two signs, read the descriptions of the Moon in both signs, and you will immediately know which one refers to you.

In some cases, the same sign is repeated only twice in a row, as on the 10th and 11th of January, 1890. On the 10th, the Moon could be either in Virgo or in the preceding sign of Leo. On the 11th, it could be in either Virgo or the following sign of Libra. So in either case, you could read about the Moon in the two signs involved and decide which applied to you.

Those of you who would like to calculate more exactly can use the following method. The figure noted in the table for a given day and year is calculated for noon at Greenwich, so that if you were born at noon in London on that day, this figure would represent the exact position of your Moon. Thus, if you were born on January 1, 1890, at noon in London, your Moon would be in 19 degrees of Taurus.

When it is noon at Greenwich, it is approximately 7:00 A.M. in New York City, approximately 6:00 A.M. in Chicago, 5:00 A.M. in Denver and approximately 4:00 A.M. in San Francisco. Thus if you were born on January 1, 1890, at 7:00 A.M. in New York City, at 6:00 A.M. in Chicago, at 5:00 A.M. in Denver and at 4:00 A.M. in San Francisco, your Moon would be in 19 degrees of Taurus. The time in a given place when it is noon at Greenwich is called the Noon Mark.*

If you were not born exactly at the time of the Noon Mark, you must make further calculations. For instance, let us say you were born at 1:00 P.M. in New York City on January 9, 1890. The Noon Mark is 7:00 A.M. From 7:00 A.M. to 1:00 P.M. is plus 6 hours. At 7:00 A.M. on January 9, 1890, the Moon is in 24 degrees of Leo. On the following day at 7:00 A.M., the Moon is in 6 degrees of Virgo. Each sign has 30 degrees. From 24 degrees of Leo to 0 degrees of Virgo is 6 degrees plus 6 degrees of Virgo, which equals 12 degrees in 24 hours, or a degree every 2 hours. Thus the 6 hours from 7:00

* Use the following to calculate the Noon Mark for other geographic locations: For places west of Greenwich, subtract from noon 4 minutes of time for every degree of longitude. For instance, Omaha, Nebraska, is 96 degrees west. 96 x 4 is 384. Divide by 60 to find the number of hours and you get 6 hours and 24 minutes. Subtract from noon and the Noon Mark at Omaha is 5:36 A.M. So if you were born on January 1, 1890, at 5:36 A.M., your Moon would be in 19 degrees of Taurus. For places east of Greenwich, add 4 minutes for every degree of longitude to noon.

A.M. to 1:00 P.M. would be 3 degrees. Adding 3 degrees to 24 degrees of Leo, we get 27 degrees of Leo. Hence the Moon would be in Leo at 1:00 P.M. If you were born earlier than the Noon Mark, you would subtract the degrees representing the number of hours before the Noon Mark time.

Suppose, however, that you were born in New York City at 7:00 P.M. on January 9, 1890. This would be 12 hours after the Noon Mark, or 6 degrees. Now 24 degrees of Leo plus 6 degrees equals 0 degrees of Virgo. However, as these tables are not calculated to the minute, where you have 29 degrees of a sign or 0 degrees of the succeeding sign, it would be well to double check your calculations by reading both descriptions.

Where there is an interval between 2 days of more than 12 degrees, you must calculate extra minutes (there are 60 minutes in a degree) for every 2 hours. For instance, if the interval is 13 degrees, calculate 1 degree, 5 minutes for every 2 hours. If 14 degrees, 1 degree 10 minutes. If 15 degrees, 1 degree 15 minutes. A total of 11 degrees is rare as is 16 degrees, but for 11, calculate 55 minutes every 2 hours; for 6 degrees, 1 degree 20 minutes.

Where a sign repeats itself for 2 days in a row, for 24 hours between the two Moon Marks, the Moon is in that sign. For instance, on the 17th and 18th of January, 1890, the Moon is in Sagittarius part of the time. However, from 7:00 A.M. on the 17th to 7:00 A.M. on the 18th in New York City, the Moon is in Sagittarius. But before 7:00 A.M. on the 17th, the Moon may be in the preceding sign of Scorpio. After 7:00 A.M. on the 18th, the Moon may be in the following sign of Capricorn. In both instances, you would have to calculate in order to find out whether the Moon was in Scorpio or Capricorn.

Remember, that the calculations explained here are only approximate,* but they enable you in the majority of cases to know the true sign position of your Moon, which is all that is necessary for the present purposes.

Remember also, if you were born during daylight saving time, begin your calculations by subtracting an hour from your time of birth.

---

* You will not be able to be absolutely exact, as these tables are calculated only to the degree, and not to the minute, and no adjustment is made in the instructions to change local time into local mean time.

JANUARY

	1890	1891	1892	1893	1894	1895	1896	1897	1898	1899	1900	1901	1902
1	19♉	19♏	28♑	26♊	10♏	9♓	19♋	18♐	0♉	29♌	9♑	25♉	8♎
2	1♊	1♎	11♒	11♋	22♍	21♓	3♋	2♑	12♉	11♏	24♑	9♊	20♎
3	13♊	13♎	26♒	26♋	3♌	3♈	17♋	16♑	24♉	24♏	9♒	23♊	2♏
4	25♊	26♎	10♐	10♌	15♌	16♈	2♍	0♒	6♊	6♎	23♒	7♋	14♍
5	7♋	8♏	24♐	24♌	27♌	28♈	16♍	14♒	17♊	19♎	8♐	20♋	25♍
6	19♋	21♍	8♈	7♏	9♑	11♉	0♎	27♒	29♊	2♍	23♐	4♌	7♐
7	1♌	5♐	22♈	20♏	21♑	25♉	15♎	9♓	11♋	16♍	7♈	16♌	19♐
8	12♌	19♐	6♉	2♎	3♒	9♊	29♎	22♓	23♋	0♌	21♈	29♌	1♑
9	24♌	3♑	20♉	14♎	15♒	24♊	12♏	4♈	6♌	14♐	5♉	11♍	14♑
10	6♍	18♑	4♊	26♎	27♒	9♋	26♏	16♈	18♌	29♐	18♉	24♍	26♑
11	19♍	3♒	18♊	8♍	10♐	24♋	9♐	28♈	0♍	14♑	1♊	6♎	9♒
12	1♎	18♒	1♋	20♍	22♐	9♌	23♐	10♉	13♍	0♒	14♊	17♎	22♒
13	14♎	3♓	15♋	2♌	5♈	24♌	6♑	22♉	26♍	15♒	26♊	29♎	5♓
14	27♎	17♓	28♋	14♌	18♈	9♍	19♑	4♊	10♎	0♓	9♋	11♍	18♓
15	10♏	2♈	11♌	26♌	1♉	24♍	1♒	16♊	23♎	14♓	21♋	23♍	2♈
16	24♍	16♈	23♌	8♑	15♉	8♎	13♒	28♊	7♍	29♓	3♌	5♐	15♈
17	8♐	0♉	6♏	21♑	29♉	21♎	26♒	11♋	21♍	12♈	16♌	18♐	29♈
18	23♐	13♉	18♏	4♒	14♊	5♏	8♓	24♋	6♎	26♈	27♌	1♑	13♉
19	8♑	26♉	0♎	17♒	29♊	17♍	19♓	7♌	20♎	8♉	9♍	14♑	27♉
20	23♑	9♊	12♎	0♐	14♋	0♌	1♈	21♌	5♏	21♉	21♍	28♑	12♊
21	8♒	22♊	24♎	13♐	29♋	13♌	13♈	5♍	20♏	3♊	3♎	12♒	26♊
22	23♒	4♋	5♍	21♐	14♌	25♌	25♈	19♍	5♏	15♊	15♎	26♒	11♋
23	8♓	16♋	17♍	11♈	29♌	7♑	7♉	3♎	19♏	27♊	27♎	11♐	26♋
24	23♓	28♋	0♐	25♈	13♍	19♑	19♉	17♎	3♐	9♋	10♍	25♐	10♌
25	7♈	10♌	12♐	9♉	27♍	1♒	2♊	1♍	17♎	21♋	22♍	9♈	24♌
26	20♈	22♌	25♐	23♉	11♎	13♒	15♊	15♍	0♎	3♌	5♐	24♈	7♍
27	3♉	4♍	8♑	7♊	23♎	24♒	29♊	29♍	13♈	14♌	19♐	8♉	20♏
28	16♉	16♍	22♑	21♊	6♏	6♓	13♋	14♎	26♍	26♌	3♑	22♉	3♎
29	28♉	28♍	6♒	6♋	18♏	18♓	27♋	28♎	8♉	8♍	17♑	5♊	16♎
30	10♊	10♎	21♒	20♋	0♐	0♈	12♌	11♏	20♉	21♍	2♒	19♊	28♎
31	22♊	22♎	5♐	4♌	12♐	12♈	26♌	25♑	2♊	3♎	17♒	3♋	10♍

JANUARY

	1903	1904	1905	1906	1907	1908	1909	1910	1911	1912	1913	1914	1915
1	8♒	15♊	17♍	28♐	28♋	6♌	9♉	17♍	19♑	26♉	1♍	7♐	10♋
2	20♒	0♋	1♐	10♈	11♌	21♐	23♉	29♍	1♒	11♊	14♍	19♐	22♋
3	2♓	15♋	14♐	22♈	23♌	6♑	6♊	11♎	14♒	26♊	27♍	1♈	5♌
4	14♓	0♌	28♐	3♉	5♍	21♑	19♊	23♎	27♒	12♋	10♐	12♈	18♌
5	27♓	15♌	11♑	15♉	18♍	6♒	2♋	5♍	10♐	27♋	22♐	24♈	1♍
6	10♈	0♍	24♑	27♉	1♎	21♒	14♋	17♍	23♐	12♌	5♐	6♉	14♏
7	23♈	15♏	7♒	9♊	14♎	6♐	27♋	29♍	6♈	27♌	17♐	19♉	28♏
8	6♉	29♏	19♒	22♊	28♎	20♐	9♌	11♐	20♈	11♏	29♐	1♊	12♎
9	20♉	13♐	1♓	4♋	12♍	4♈	21♌	24♐	4♉	25♏	11♒	14♊	26♎
10	5♊	26♐	13♓	17♋	27♍	18♈	3♍	7♑	18♉	9♎	23♒	27♊	10♏
11	20♊	9♍	25♓	0♌	11♎	1♉	15♍	20♑	3♊	22♎	5♓	11♋	25♏
12	5♋	22♍	7♈	13♌	26♎	14♉	27♍	4♒	17♊	4♍	17♓	25♋	9♐
13	20♋	5♎	19♈	26♌	11♑	26♉	9♎	18♒	2♋	17♍	28♓	9♌	24♐
14	6♌	17♎	1♉	10♍	26♑	8♊	21♎	2♓	17♋	29♍	10♈	23♌	8♑
15	21♌	0♑	13♉	23♍	11♒	20♊	3♏	16♓	2♌	11♐	23♈	8♍	22♑
16	5♍	12♑	25♉	7♎	26♒	2♋	15♏	0♈	16♌	23♐	5♉	22♍	6♒
17	20♍	24♑	8♊	21♎	10♐	14♋	28♏	14♈	0♍	4♑	18♉	6♎	20♒
18	3♎	6♒	21♊	6♍	23♐	26♋	11♐	28♈	14♍	16♑	1♊	20♎	3♓
19	16♎	18♒	5♋	20♍	6♈	8♌	25♐	12♉	27♍	28♑	15♊	5♏	16♓
20	29♎	0♐	19♋	4♐	19♈	20♌	9♑	26♉	9♎	10♒	0♋	18♏	29♐
21	11♏	11♐	3♌	18♐	2♉	1♍	24♑	10♊	22♎	22♒	14♋	2♐	11♈
22	24♏	23♐	18♌	3♑	14♉	13♍	8♒	24♊	4♍	4♐	29♋	16♐	23♈
23	6♐	5♈	2♍	17♑	26♉	26♍	23♒	8♋	15♍	16♐	15♌	29♐	5♉
24	17♐	17♈	17♍	1♒	8♊	8♎	8♐	21♋	27♍	29♐	0♍	12♑	17♉
25	29♐	0♉	1♎	14♒	19♊	20♎	23♐	4♌	9♑	11♈	15♍	25♑	29♉
26	11♑	12♉	16♎	27♒	1♋	3♍	8♈	17♌	21♐	24♈	29♍	8♒	11♊
27	23♑	26♉	0♍	10♓	13♋	17♍	22♈	0♏	3♑	8♉	14♎	21♒	23♊
28	5♒	9♊	14♍	23♓	25♋	0♉	6♉	13♍	15♑	21♉	28♎	3♐	5♋
29	17♒	23♊	27♍	5♈	7♌	14♐	20♉	25♍	28♑	5♊	11♍	15♐	18♋
30	29♒	8♋	11♌	17♈	20♌	29♐	3♊	7♎	10♒	20♊	24♍	27♐	1♌
31	12♓	23♋	24♐	29♈	2♏	14♑	16♊	19♎	23♒	5♋	7♐	9♈	14♌

JANUARY

	1916	1917	1918	1919	1920	1921	1922	1923	1924	1925	1926	1927	1928
1	18♍	23♈	26♌	0♑	9♉	14♎	16♒	20♊	1♍	5♈	6♌	10♉	23♈
2	2♌	6♉	8♏	13♑	23♉	27♎	28♒	3♋	15♍	17♈	18♌	24♉	7♉
3	17♌	18♉	20♏	26♑	8♊	9♍	10♐	17♍	0♌	0♉	0♍	7♑	22♉
4	3♑	1♊	2♎	9♒	23♊	22♍	22♐	1♌	15♌	12♉	12♍	21♑	6♊
5	18♑	13♊	14♎	23♒	8♋	4♌	4♈	14♌	29♌	24♉	24♍	6♒	20♊
6	3♒	25♊	26♎	6♓	23♋	16♌	16♈	29♌	14♑	6♊	6♎	20♒	5♋
7	18♒	7♋	8♏	20♐	8♌	28♌	28♈	13♍	29♑	18♊	18♎	4♐	19♋
8	2♓	19♋	21♏	4♈	22♌	9♑	11♉	27♍	13♒	0♋	1♍	19♐	3♌
9	16♐	1♌	4♐	18♈	6♏	21♑	24♉	11♎	26♒	12♋	14♍	3♈	16♌
10	29♐	13♌	17♐	2♉	20♏	3♒	7♊	25♎	9♓	24♋	28♍	17♈	29♌
11	12♈	25♌	1♑	17♉	2♎	15♒	21♊	9♍	22♓	6♌	12♐	1♉	12♏
12	25♈	7♍	15♑	1♊	15♎	27♒	6♋	23♍	5♈	18♌	27♐	15♉	24♏
13	7♉	19♍	0♒	15♊	27♎	9♓	21♋	7♎	17♈	0♍	11♑	29♉	7♎
14	19♉	1♎	14♒	29♊	9♍	21♓	6♌	21♎	29♈	12♍	26♑	12♊	19♎
15	1♊	13♎	29♒	13♋	21♍	4♈	21♌	4♑	11♉	25♍	12♒	25♊	0♏
16	13♊	26♎	14♐	27♋	3♌	16♈	6♏	18♑	23♉	7♎	27♒	8♋	12♏
17	25♊	9♍	28♐	10♌	15♌	29♈	20♏	1♒	4♊	21♎	12♐	21♋	24♏
18	7♋	22♍	13♈	23♌	26♌	13♉	5♎	14♒	16♊	4♍	26♐	4♌	6♐
19	18♋	6♌	21♈	6♏	8♑	27♉	19♎	26♒	29♊	18♍	10♑	16♌	18♐
20	0♌	20♌	11♉	19♏	21♑	11♊	2♏	8♓	11♋	2♌	24♑	28♌	1♑
21	13♌	5♑	24♉	1♎	3♒	26♊	16♏	20♐	24♋	17♐	7♉	10♏	14♑
22	25♌	20♑	7♊	13♎	16♒	11♋	29♏	3♈	6♌	2♑	20♉	22♏	27♑
23	7♍	5♒	20♐	25♎	28♒	26♋	12♐	14♈	19♌	17♑	3♊	4♎	10♒
24	20♍	20♒	3♋	7♍	11♓	11♌	24♐	26♈	3♍	2♒	15♊	16♎	24♒
25	3♎	5♐	16♋	18♍	24♐	26♌	7♑	8♉	16♏	17♒	27♊	28♎	8♐
26	16♎	20♐	28♋	0♌	8♈	11♏	19♑	20♉	0♎	2♐	9♋	10♍	22♐
27	29♎	5♈	11♌	13♌	21♈	26♏	1♒	2♊	13♎	16♐	21♋	22♍	6♈
28	13♏	19♈	23♌	25♌	5♉	10♎	13♒	15♊	27♎	0♈	3♌	5♐	20♈
29	27♏	2♉	5♏	8♑	19♉	23♎	25♒	28♊	11♏	13♈	15♌	18♐	4♉
30	12♐	15♉	17♏	21♑	3♊	6♏	7♐	11♋	26♏	26♈	27♌	1♑	18♉
31	26♐	28♉	28♏	4♒	18♊	18♍	19♐	25♋	10♐	9♉	9♏	15♑	2♊

JANUARY

	1929	1930	1931	1932	1933	1934	1935	1936	1937	1938	1939	1940	1941
1	25♏	26♑	0♊	15♎	15♐	17♋	20♍	8♈	5♏	7♑	10♌	0♎	25♒
2	8♎	8♒	14♊	29♎	28♐	29♋	4♌	22♈	18♏	19♑	24♌	14♎	8♐
3	20♎	20♒	28♊	14♍	10♈	11♌	18♌	6♉	0♎	1♎	8♊	28♎	20♐
4	3♏	2♐	12♋	28♍	22♈	23♌	3♑	20♉	12♎	13♎	23♊	12♍	2♈
5	15♏	14♐	27♋	12♌	4♉	5♏	18♑	4♊	24♎	25♎	8♋	25♍	14♈
6	26♏	26♐	12♌	26♐	16♉	17♏	3♒	17♊	6♏	8♐	24♋	8♌	26♈
7	8♐	9♈	27♌	10♑	28♉	29♏	18♒	1♋	18♏	21♐	9♌	21♌	7♉
8	20♐	21♈	11♍	23♑	10♊	12♎	3♐	14♋	0♐	4♐	24♌	4♑	19♉
9	2♑	5♉	26♍	6♒	22♊	26♎	17♐	26♋	12♐	17♈	9♍	17♑	1♊
10	14♑	18♉	10♎	19♒	4♋	9♍	1♈	9♌	24♐	1♉	23♍	29♑	14♊
11	26♑	2♊	24♎	2♐	16♋	23♍	15♈	21♌	7♑	15♉	7♎	12♒	27♊
12	8♒	17♊	7♍	14♐	29♋	8♌	29♈	4♍	19♑	29♉	20♎	24♒	10♋
13	21♒	2♋	20♍	26♐	12♌	23♌	12♉	16♍	2♒	14♊	3♏	6♐	23♋
14	3♐	17♋	4♌	8♈	24♌	8♑	25♉	28♍	15♒	29♊	16♏	17♐	7♌
15	16♐	2♌	16♌	20♈	7♏	23♑	8♊	9♎	29♒	14♋	29♏	29♐	21♌
16	29♐	18♌	29♌	2♉	21♏	8♒	20♊	21♎	12♐	29♋	11♐	11♈	4♏
17	12♑	3♍	12♑	14♉	4♎	23♒	2♋	3♏	26♐	14♌	23♐	23♈	19♏
18	26♑	17♍	24♑	26♉	18♎	8♐	15♋	16♏	10♈	28♌	5♑	5♉	3♎
19	10♒	2♎	6♒	8♊	2♍	22♐	26♋	28♏	24♈	12♍	17♑	18♉	17♎
20	24♒	15♎	18♒	21♊	16♍	6♈	8♌	11♐	8♉	26♍	29♑	0♊	1♍
21	8♊	28♎	0♈	4♋	0♐	19♈	20♌	24♐	23♉	9♎	10♈	14♊	15♍
22	23♊	11♍	12♈	17♋	15♐	2♉	2♏	7♑	7♊	22♎	22♎	28♊	29♍
23	8♋	24♍	24♈	1♌	29♐	14♉	14♏	21♑	21♊	4♏	4♏	12♋	13♐
24	23♋	6♌	6♉	15♌	14♑	26♉	26♏	6♒	5♋	16♏	16♐	26♋	27♐
25	7♌	18♌	18♈	29♌	29♑	8♊	8♎	20♒	19♋	28♍	28♈	11♌	11♑
26	22♌	6♑	0♉	14♍	13♒	20♊	20♎	5♐	3♌	10♐	11♈	26♌	24♑
27	6♍	12♑	12♉	28♍	27♒	2♋	2♏	20♐	17♌	22♐	23♌	11♏	7♒
28	20♍	23♑	25♉	12♎	10♐	14♋	15♏	4♈	0♏	4♑	6♉	26♏	20♒
29	3♎	5♒	8♊	26♎	23♐	26♋	28♏	19♈	13♏	16♑	19♉	11♎	3♐
30	16♎	17♒	21♊	10♍	6♈	8♌	12♐	3♉	26♏	28♑	3♊	25♎	15♐
31	29♎	29♒	6♋	24♍	18♈	20♌	26♐	17♉	8♎	10♒	17♊	9♏	28♐

JANUARY

	1942	1943	1944	1945	1946	1947	1948	1949	1950	1951	1952
1	27♊	1♍	22♓	15♌	17♐	22♈	14♏	5♒	7♊	14♎	6♐
2	9♋	15♍	6♈	27♌	0♑	6♉	28♏	17♒	20♊	27♎	20♐
3	22♋	29♍	20♈	9♍	12♑	20♉	12♎	29♒	2♋	12♏	3♈
4	4♌	14♐	4♉	21♍	25♑	5♊	25♎	11♓	15♋	26♏	16♈
5	17♌	29♐	17♉	3♎	7♒	20♊	8♏	23♓	29♋	11♌	29♈
6	29♌	15♑	0♊	15♎	20♒	5♋	21♏	5♈	12♌	26♐	12♉
7	12♍	0♒	13♊	27♎	4♓	20♋	3♐	17♈	26♌	11♑	24♉
8	25♍	15♒	25♊	9♍	17♓	5♌	16♐	29♈	9♍	26♑	6♊
9	9♎	0♓	7♋	21♍	1♈	20♌	28♐	11♉	23♍	11♒	18♊
10	22♎	14♓	20♋	4♐	15♈	5♍	10♑	23♉	7♎	25♒	0♋
11	6♏	28♓	2♌	17♐	29♈	18♍	22♑	6♊	21♎	9♓	12♋
12	21♏	11♈	14♌	0♑	13♉	2♎	4♒	20♊	5♍	22♓	24♋
13	5♐	24♈	25♌	14♑	27♉	15♎	16♒	4♋	19♍	5♈	6♌
14	20♐	7♉	7♍	27♑	12♊	27♎	27♒	18♋	4♐	17♈	18♌
15	5♑	19♉	19♍	11♒	26♊	10♏	9♓	3♌	18♐	0♉	0♍
16	20♑	1♊	1♎	26♒	11♋	22♏	21♓	17♌	2♑	12♉	12♍
17	5♒	13♊	13♎	10♓	25♋	4♐	3♈	2♍	16♑	23♉	24♍
18	19♒	25♊	25♎	25♓	9♌	15♐	16♈	17♍	0♒	5♊	6♎
19	3♓	7♋	8♍	9♈	23♌	27♐	28♈	1♎	13♒	17♊	19♎
20	16♓	19♋	21♍	23♈	6♍	9♑	11♉	16♎	26♒	29♊	2♍
21	29♓	1♌	4♐	7♉	19♍	21♑	25♉	0♏	9♓	11♋	16♍
22	12♈	13♌	18♐	21♉	1♎	3♒	8♊	13♏	21♓	23♋	29♍
23	24♈	25♌	2♑	5♊	14♎	15♒	23♊	27♏	3♈	6♌	14♐
24	6♉	7♍	17♑	19♊	26♎	27♒	8♋	10♐	15♈	18♌	29♐
25	18♉	19♍	2♒	2♋	8♍	10♓	23♋	23♐	27♈	1♏	14♑
26	0♊	1♎	17♒	15♋	20♍	23♓	8♌	6♑	9♉	14♏	29♑
27	12♊	14♎	2♓	28♋	1♐	6♈	23♌	19♑	21♉	27♏	14♒
28	24♊	27♎	17♓	10♌	13♐	19♈	9♏	1♒	3♊	10♎	29♒
29	6♋	10♏	2♈	23♌	25♐	2♉	23♏	13♒	15♊	24♎	14♓
30	18♋	24♍	16♈	5♍	8♑	16♉	8♎	25♒	28♊	8♍	28♓
31	0♌	8♐	0♉	17♍	20♑	0♊	22♎	7♓	11♋	22♍	12♈

FEBRUARY

	1890	1891	1892	1893	1894	1895	1896	1897	1898	1899	1900	1901	1902
1	4♋	4♏	20♐	18♌	24♐	24♈	11♏	8♒	14♊	15♎	2♐	16♋	22♏
2	16♋	17♏	4♈	1♏	6♑	7♉	26♏	22♒	26♊	28♎	17♐	29♋	3♐
3	27♋	0♐	19♈	15♏	18♑	20♉	11♎	4♓	8♋	11♏	2♈	12♌	15♐
4	9♌	13♐	3♉	27♏	0♒	3♊	25♎	17♓	20♋	25♏	17♈	25♌	27♐
5	21♌	27♐	17♉	10♎	12♒	17♊	9♏	29♓	2♌	9♐	1♉	7♏	10♑
6	3♍	11♑	1♊	22♎	24♒	2♋	23♏	12♈	14♌	23♐	15♉	19♍	22♑
7	16♍	26♑	14♊	4♍	7♓	17♋	6♐	24♈	27♌	8♑	28♉	2♎	5♒
8	28♍	11♒	28♊	16♍	19♓	2♌	20♐	5♉	10♏	22♑	11♊	13♎	18♒
9	11♎	26♒	11♋	28♍	2♈	17♌	3♑	17♉	23♏	8♒	24♊	25♎	1♐
10	23♎	11♓	24♋	10♐	15♈	2♍	15♑	29♉	6♎	23♒	6♋	7♍	15♐
11	7♏	26♐	7♌	22♐	28♈	17♍	28♑	11♊	20♎	8♐	18♋	19♍	28♐
12	20♏	11♈	19♌	4♑	11♉	2♎	10♒	24♊	4♏	23♐	0♌	1♐	12♈
13	4♐	26♈	2♍	16♑	25♉	16♎	22♒	6♋	18♏	7♈	12♌	13♐	26♈
14	18♐	10♉	14♍	29♑	9♊	0♏	4♓	19♋	2♐	21♈	24♌	26♐	10♉
15	2♑	23♉	26♍	12♒	24♊	14♏	16♓	2♌	16♐	4♉	6♍	9♑	24♉
16	17♑	6♊	8♎	26♒	8♋	27♏	28♓	16♌	0♑	17♉	18♍	22♑	8♊
17	1♒	19♊	20♎	9♐	23♋	9♐	10♈	0♍	15♑	0♊	0♎	6♒	22♊
18	16♒	1♋	2♍	23♐	8♌	22♐	21♈	14♏	29♑	12♊	12♎	21♒	6♋
19	1♓	13♋	13♍	7♈	22♌	4♑	3♉	28♏	13♒	24♊	24♎	5♐	21♋
20	16♐	25♋	25♍	21♈	7♏	16♑	15♉	13♎	27♒	6♋	6♍	20♐	5♌
21	1♈	7♌	8♐	5♉	21♏	28♑	28♉	27♎	11♐	18♋	18♍	5♈	18♌
22	15♈	19♌	20♐	19♉	5♐	10♒	10♊	12♍	25♐	29♋	1♌	20♈	2♏
23	28♈	1♏	3♑	4♊	18♐	21♒	23♊	26♍	8♈	11♌	14♐	4♉	15♏
24	12♉	13♏	16♑	18♊	1♑	3♓	7♋	10♐	21♈	23♌	27♐	18♉	28♏
25	24♉	25♏	0♒	2♋	14♑	15♓	21♋	24♐	4♉	5♍	11♑	2♊	11♎
26	7♊	7♎	14♒	16♋	26♑	27♓	5♌	8♑	16♐	18♍	25♑	16♊	24♎
27	19♊	19♎	29♒	29♋	8♐	9♈	20♌	21♑	28♉	0♎	10♒	29♊	6♏
28	1♋	1♍	14♓	13♌	20♐	21♈	5♏	5♒	10♊	13♎	25♒	13♋	18♏
29			29♓			20♏							

FEBRUARY

	1903	1904	1905	1906	1907	1908	1909	1910	1911	1912	1913	1914	1915
1	24♐	8♌	7♑	11♉	15♏	29♑	28♊	1♏	6♐	20♋	19♐	20♈	27♌
2	7♈	23♌	20♑	23♉	28♏	14♒	11♎	13♏	20♐	5♌	2♉	2♉	11♏
3	20♈	9♍	3♒	5♊	11♎	29♒	23♏	25♏	3♈	20♌	14♑	14♉	25♏
4	3♉	24♍	15♒	17♊	25♎	14♒	5♏	7♐	17♈	5♏	26♑	26♉	9♎
5	16♉	8♎	27♒	29♊	8♏	29♏	17♏	19♐	0♉	20♏	8♒	9♊	23♎
6	0♊	22♎	9♓	12♋	22♏	13♐	29♏	2♑	14♉	4♎	20♒	22♊	7♍
7	14♊	6♏	21♓	25♋	6♐	26♐	11♍	15♑	28♉	17♎	2♐	5♋	21♍
8	29♊	19♏	3♈	8♌	21♐	10♉	23♍	28♑	13♊	0♏	13♐	19♋	5♐
9	14♋	2♐	15♈	22♌	5♑	23♉	5♎	12♒	27♊	13♏	25♐	3♌	19♐
10	29♋	14♐	27♈	6♍	20♑	5♊	17♎	27♒	11♋	25♏	7♈	17♌	4♑
11	14♌	27♐	9♉	20♍	5♒	17♊	29♎	11♓	26♋	7♐	19♈	2♍	17♑
12	29♌	9♑	21♉	4♎	19♒	29♊	11♏	26♓	10♌	19♐	1♉	17♍	1♒
13	13♍	21♑	3♊	18♎	3♐	11♋	23♏	10♈	24♌	1♑	14♉	2♎	15♒
14	27♍	3♒	16♊	2♏	17♐	23♋	6♐	25♈	8♏	13♑	27♉	16♎	28♒
15	11♎	15♒	29♊	17♏	1♈	5♌	19♐	9♉	21♏	25♑	10♊	1♍	11♓
16	24♎	27♒	13♋	1♐	14♈	17♌	3♑	23♉	4♎	7♒	24♊	15♍	24♓
17	7♏	8♐	27♋	15♐	27♈	28♌	17♑	7♊	17♎	19♒	8♋	29♍	7♈
18	20♏	20♐	11♌	29♐	10♉	10♏	1♒	21♊	29♎	1♐	22♋	13♐	19♈
19	2♐	2♈	26♌	13♑	22♉	23♏	16♒	4♋	11♍	13♐	7♌	26♐	1♉
20	14♐	14♈	11♍	26♑	4♊	5♎	2♓	17♋	23♍	26♐	23♌	9♑	13♉
21	26♐	26♈	26♍	10♒	16♊	17♎	17♓	1♌	5♐	9♈	8♍	22♑	25♉
22	8♑	9♉	11♎	23♒	27♊	0♏	2♈	13♌	17♐	21♈	23♍	5♒	7♊
23	20♑	22♉	26♎	6♐	9♋	13♏	17♈	26♌	29♐	4♉	8♎	17♒	19♊
24	2♒	5♊	10♏	18♐	21♋	26♏	2♉	9♍	11♑	18♉	22♎	29♒	1♋
25	14♒	18♊	24♏	1♈	3♌	10♐	16♉	21♍	23♑	1♊	7♍	11♐	13♋
26	26♒	2♋	8♐	13♈	16♌	24♐	29♉	3♎	6♒	15♊	20♍	23♐	26♋
27	8♓	16♋	21♐	25♈	28♌	8♑	13♊	15♎	19♒	29♊	3♐	5♈	9♌
28	21♓	1♌	4♑	7♉	11♏	22♑	25♊	27♎	2♐	14♋	16♐	17♈	22♌
29		16♌				7♒				29♋			

	1916	1917	1918	1919	1920	1921	1922	1923	1924	1925	1926	1927	1928
1	11♑	10♊	10♎	18♒	2♋	1♐	0♈	9♌	24♐	21♌	21♍	29♑	16♊
2	26♑	22♊	22♎	2♓	17♋	13♐	12♈	24♌	9♑	3♊	3♎	14♒	0♋
3	11♒	4♋	4♍	17♓	1♌	25♐	24♈	8♍	23♑	15♊	15♎	29♒	14♋
4	25♒	16♋	17♍	1♈	16♌	6♑	7♉	23♍	7♒	27♊	27♎	14♓	27♋
5	10♓	28♋	29♍	15♈	0♍	18♑	19♉	7♎	21♒	8♋	10♍	29♓	11♌
6	24♓	10♌	12♎	29♈	14♍	0♒	2♊	22♎	4♓	20♋	23♍	14♈	24♌
7	7♈	22♌	25♎	13♉	27♍	12♒	15♊	6♏	17♓	2♌	6♐	28♈	7♏
8	20♈	4♍	9♏	28♉	10♎	24♒	29♊	20♏	0♈	14♌	20♐	12♉	20♏
9	3♉	16♍	23♏	12♊	23♎	6♓	14♋	4♐	12♈	27♌	5♑	26♉	2♎
10	15♉	28♍	8♒	25♊	5♏	18♓	29♋	17♐	25♈	9♍	19♑	9♊	14♎
11	27♉	10♎	23♒	9♋	17♏	1♈	14♌	1♑	7♉	22♍	4♒	22♊	26♎
12	9♊	22♎	8♓	22♋	29♏	13♈	29♌	14♑	19♉	4♎	20♒	5♋	8♍
13	21♊	5♏	23♓	6♌	11♐	26♈	14♍	27♑	0♊	18♎	5♓	17♋	20♍
14	3♋	18♏	8♈	19♌	23♐	9♉	29♍	10♒	12♊	1♍	20♓	0♌	2♎
15	15♋	1♐	23♈	2♏	5♑	22♉	14♎	22♒	24♊	14♍	5♈	12♌	14♎
16	27♋	15♐	7♉	14♏	17♑	6♊	28♎	4♓	7♋	28♍	19♈	25♌	26♎
17	9♌	29♐	21♉	27♏	29♑	20♊	12♏	17♓	19♋	12♐	3♉	7♍	9♑
18	21♌	13♑	4♊	9♎	12♒	5♋	26♏	29♓	2♌	27♐	16♉	19♍	22♑
19	4♍	28♑	18♊	21♎	24♒	19♋	9♐	10♈	15♌	11♑	29♉	0♎	5♒
20	17♍	13♒	0♋	3♍	8♓	4♌	21♐	22♈	28♌	26♑	12♊	12♎	19♒
21	0♎	28♒	13♋	14♍	21♓	19♌	4♑	4♉	12♍	10♒	24♊	24♎	3♓
22	13♎	13♓	25♋	26♍	4♈	4♍	16♑	16♉	26♍	25♒	6♋	6♍	17♓
23	26♎	28♓	7♌	8♐	18♈	19♍	28♑	28♉	10♎	10♓	18♋	18♍	1♈
24	10♍	13♈	19♌	20♐	2♉	4♎	10♒	10♊	24♎	24♓	0♌	0♐	16♈
25	24♍	27♈	1♏	3♑	16♉	18♎	22♒	23♊	8♍	7♈	12♌	13♐	0♉
26	8♐	10♉	13♏	15♑	0♊	1♏	4♓	6♋	22♍	21♈	24♌	26♐	15♉
27	22♐	24♉	25♏	29♑	14♊	14♏	16♓	19♋	7♐	4♉	6♍	9♑	29♉
28	6♑	7♊	7♎	12♒	28♊	27♏	27♓	3♌	21♐	17♉	18♍	23♑	13♊
29	20♑				12♋				5♑				27♊

FEBRUARY

	1929	1930	1931	1932	1933	1934	1935	1936	1937	1938	1939	1940	1941
1	11♏	11♓	20♋	8♐	0♉	2♏	11♑	0♊	20♎	22♒	1♋	22♏	8♈
2	23♏	23♓	5♌	22♐	12♉	14♏	26♑	14♊	2♏	5♓	16♋	5♌	21♈
3	5♐	6♈	20♌	5♑	24♉	27♏	11♒	27♊	14♏	18♓	2♌	18♐	3♉
4	16♐	18♈	5♍	19♑	6♊	9♐	26♒	10♋	26♏	1♈	17♌	1♑	15♉
5	28♐	1♉	20♍	2♒	18♊	22♐	11♓	23♋	8♐	14♈	2♏	13♑	27♉
6	10♑	14♉	5♎	15♒	0♋	5♑	26♓	5♌	20♐	27♈	17♏	26♑	9♊
7	22♑	27♉	20♎	27♒	12♋	19♑	11♈	18♌	2♑	11♉	2♎	8♒	22♊
8	5♒	11♊	4♏	10♓	25♋	3♒	25♈	0♍	15♑	25♉	16♎	20♒	5♋
9	17♒	25♊	17♏	22♓	8♌	17♒	9♉	12♍	27♑	9♊	29♎	2♓	18♋
10	0♓	10♋	1♐	4♈	20♌	2♓	22♉	24♍	11♒	23♊	13♏	14♓	1♌
11	13♓	25♋	14♐	16♈	4♍	17♓	5♊	6♎	24♒	8♋	25♏	26♓	15♌
12	26♓	10♌	26♐	28♈	17♍	2♈	17♊	18♎	8♓	23♋	8♐	8♈	29♌
13	9♈	26♌	9♑	9♉	1♎	16♈	29♊	29♎	22♓	7♌	23♐	20♈	14♍
14	23♈	11♍	21♑	21♉	15♎	1♉	12♋	11♏	7♈	22♌	6♑	19♈	28♍
15	7♉	26♍	3♒	4♊	29♎	16♉	24♋	24♏	20♈	6♍	14♑	1♉	13♎
16	20♉	10♎	15♒	16♊	13♏	0♊	5♌	6♐	5♉	20♍	26♑	26♉	27♎
17	4♊	24♎	27♒	29♊	27♏	14♊	17♌	19♐	19♉	4♎	7♒	9♊	12♏
18	19♊	7♏	9♓	12♋	11♐	27♊	29♌	2♑	4♎	17♏	19♒	22♊	26♏
19	3♋	20♏	21♓	25♋	25♐	10♋	11♎	15♑	18♎	0♐	1♓	6♋	10♐
20	17♋	2♐	2♈	9♌	9♑	22♋	23♎	29♑	1♏	12♐	13♓	20♋	24♐
21	2♌	15♐	14♈	23♌	24♑	5♌	5♏	14♒	15♏	24♐	25♓	4♌	7♑
22	16♌	27♐	26♈	8♏	8♒	17♌	17♏	28♒	29♏	6♑	8♈	19♌	20♑
23	0♍	8♑	8♉	23♏	21♒	29♌	29♏	14♓	12♐	18♑	20♈	5♏	3♒
24	14♍	20♑	21♉	7♎	5♓	10♍	12♐	29♓	25♐	0♒	3♉	20♏	16♒
25	28♍	2♒	3♊	22♎	18♓	22♍	24♐	14♈	8♑	12♒	16♉	5♎	29♒
26	11♎	14♒	16♊	7♏	1♈	4♎	8♑	29♈	21♑	24♒	29♉	20♎	11♓
27	24♎	26♒	0♋	21♏	14♈	16♎	21♑	13♉	4♒	6♓	12♊	4♏	24♓
28	6♏	8♓	14♋	5♐	26♈	28♎	5♒	27♉	16♏	18♒	26♊	18♍	6♈
29				19♐				11♊				2♐	

FEBRUARY

	1942	1943	1944	1945	1946	1947	1948	1949	1950	1951	1952
1	13♌	23♐	14♉	29♏	3♒	14♊	5♏	19♓	24♋	6♐	25♈
2	26♌	8♑	27♉	11♎	16♒	29♊	18♏	1♈	7♌	21♐	8♉
3	9♏	23♑	10♊	23♎	0♐	13♋	0♐	13♈	21♌	5♑	21♉
4	22♏	8♒	22♊	5♏	14♐	28♋	13♐	25♈	5♏	20♑	3♊
5	6♎	23♒	4♋	17♏	28♐	13♌	25♐	7♉	19♏	4♒	15♊
6	19♎	8♓	17♋	29♏	12♈	28♌	7♑	19♉	4♎	19♒	27♊
7	3♏	22♓	29♋	12♐	26♈	12♏	19♑	1♊	18♎	3♓	9♋
8	17♏	6♈	10♌	24♐	10♉	26♏	1♒	14♊	2♏	17♓	21♋
9	1♐	20♈	22♌	8♑	24♉	10♎	13♒	28♊	16♏	0♈	3♌
10	16♐	3♉	4♏	21♑	8♊	23♎	24♒	12♋	0♐	13♈	15♌
11	0♑	16♉	16♏	5♒	22♊	6♏	6♓	26♋	14♐	25♈	27♌
12	14♑	28♉	28♏	20♒	6♋	18♏	18♓	11♌	28♐	8♉	9♏
13	29♑	10♊	10♎	5♓	20♋	0♐	0♈	26♌	12♑	20♉	21♏
14	13♒	22♊	22♎	20♓	4♌	12♐	13♈	11♏	25♑	2♊	3♎
15	27♒	4♋	4♏	5♈	17♌	24♐	25♈	26♏	9♒	13♊	16♎
16	11♓	16♋	17♏	19♈	1♏	5♑	8♉	11♎	22♒	25♊	29♎
17	24♓	28♋	0♐	4♉	14♏	17♑	20♉	26♎	4♓	7♋	12♏
18	7♈	9♌	13♐	18♉	27♏	29♑	4♊	10♏	17♓	19♋	25♏
19	19♈	21♌	26♐	2♊	9♎	12♒	17♊	24♏	29♓	2♌	9♐
20	2♉	4♏	11♑	16♊	22♎	24♒	1♋	7♐	11♈	14♌	23♐
21	14♉	16♏	25♑	29♊	4♏	7♓	16♋	20♐	23♈	27♌	8♑
22	26♉	28♏	10♒	12♋	16♏	19♓	1♌	3♑	5♉	10♏	22♑
23	8♊	11♎	25♒	24♋	27♏	2♈	16♌	16♑	17♉	23♏	7♒
24	20♊	24♎	10♓	7♌	9♐	16♈	1♏	28♑	29♉	7♎	22♒
25	2♋	7♏	26♓	19♌	21♐	29♈	17♏	10♒	11♊	21♎	7♓
26	14♋	21♏	11♈	2♏	3♑	13♉	1♎	22♒	23♊	5♏	22♓
27	26♋	4♐	25♈	14♏	16♑	26♉	16♎	4♓	5♋	19♏	6♈
28	9♌	18♐	9♉	26♏	28♑	10♊	0♏	16♓	18♋	3♐	20♈
29			23♉				14♏				4♉

MARCH

	1890	1891	1892	1893	1894	1895	1896	1897	1898	1899	1900	1901	1902
1	12♋	13♏	14♈	27♌	2♑	4♉	5♎	18♒	22♊	25♎	11♐	26♋	29♏
2	24♋	26♏	29♈	10♍	14♑	17♉	20♎	0♓	4♋	8♍	26♐	8♌	11♐
3	6♌	9♐	13♉	23♍	26♑	0♊	5♍	13♐	16♋	21♍	11♈	21♌	23♐
4	18♌	22♐	27♉	5♎	8♒	13♊	19♍	25♐	28♋	5♐	26♈	3♏	5♑
5	0♍	5♑	11♊	18♎	20♒	27♊	3♐	8♈	10♌	19♐	10♉	16♏	17♑
6	12♍	19♑	25♊	0♏	3♓	11♋	16♐	20♈	23♌	3♑	24♉	28♏	0♒
7	25♍	4♒	8♋	12♍	15♓	25♋	0♑	2♉	6♏	17♑	7♊	10♏	13♒
8	8♎	19♒	21♋	24♍	28♓	10♌	12♑	14♉	19♏	1♒	20♊	22♏	26♒
9	20♎	4♓	4♌	6♎	11♈	25♌	25♑	25♉	3♎	16♒	3♋	4♏	10♓
10	4♏	19♓	16♌	17♎	25♈	10♏	7♒	7♊	16♎	1♓	15♋	15♏	24♓
11	17♏	5♈	28♌	29♎	8♉	25♏	19♒	19♊	0♏	16♓	27♋	27♏	8♈
12	0♐	20♈	11♍	12♑	22♉	10♎	1♓	1♋	14♍	1♈	9♌	9♌	22♈
13	14♐	4♉	23♍	24♑	6♊	24♎	13♓	14♋	29♍	15♈	21♌	21♐	6♉
14	28♐	18♉	5♎	7♒	20♊	8♍	25♓	27♋	13♐	29♈	3♍	4♑	21♉
15	12♑	2♊	16♎	20♒	4♋	22♍	6♈	10♌	27♐	12♉	15♍	17♑	5♊
16	26♑	15♊	28♎	4♓	19♋	5♐	18♈	24♌	11♑	25♉	27♍	0♒	19♊
17	11♒	28♊	10♍	18♓	3♌	18♐	0♉	8♍	25♑	8♊	9♎	14♒	3♋
18	25♒	10♋	22♍	2♈	17♌	0♑	12♉	22♍	9♒	21♊	21♎	29♒	17♋
19	10♓	22♋	4♐	16♈	1♍	13♑	24♉	7♎	23♒	2♋	3♍	13♓	1♌
20	24♓	4♌	16♐	1♉	16♍	24♑	7♊	22♎	6♓	14♋	15♍	28♓	14♌
21	9♈	16♌	28♐	16♉	29♍	6♒	19♊	7♏	20♐	26♋	28♍	14♈	28♌
22	23♈	28♌	11♑	0♊	13♎	18♒	2♋	22♍	3♐	8♌	10♎	29♈	11♏
23	6♉	10♍	24♑	14♊	26♎	0♓	15♋	7♐	16♈	20♌	23♐	14♉	24♏
24	19♉	22♍	8♒	29♊	9♍	12♐	29♋	21♐	29♈	2♏	6♌	28♉	7♐
25	2♊	4♎	22♒	13♋	22♍	24♐	13♌	5♑	12♉	14♏	20♑	12♊	19♎
26	15♊	16♎	7♓	26♋	4♌	6♈	28♌	18♑	24♉	26♏	4♒	26♊	2♍
27	27♊	28♎	22♓	8♌	16♐	18♈	6♊	6♒	9♏	19♒	10♋	10♎	14♍
28	9♋	10♍	7♈	23♌	28♐	1♉	28♍	14♒	18♊	22♒	4♏	23♎	26♍
29	20♋	23♍	22♈	6♏	10♑	14♉	13♎	27♒	0♓	5♍	19♐	6♑	7♐
30	2♌	5♐	8♉	19♏	22♑	27♉	28♎	10♓	11♎	18♐	4♈	18♌	19♐
31	14♌	18♐	22♉	1♎	4♒	10♊	13♍	22♐	23♋	2♐	19♈	0♍	1♑

MARCH

	1903	1904	1905	1906	1907	1908	1909	1910	1911	1912	1913	1914	1915
1	4♈	1♏	17♑	19♉	24♏	22♒	8♋	9♍	15♐	13♌	29♐	29♈	6♏
2	17♈	17♏	0♒	1♊	8♎	7♐	20♋	21♍	29♐	28♌	11♑	10♉	20♏
3	0♉	2♎	12♒	13♊	21♎	22♐	2♌	3♐	13♈	13♍	23♑	22♉	4♎
4	13♉	16♎	24♒	25♊	5♍	7♈	14♌	15♐	27♈	27♍	5♒	5♊	19♎
5	27♉	1♏	6♓	7♋	19♍	21♈	26♌	27♐	11♉	11♎	17♒	17♊	3♏
6	11♊	14♏	18♐	20♋	3♐	5♉	8♏	10♑	25♉	25♎	29♒	0♋	18♏
7	25♊	28♏	0♈	3♌	17♐	18♉	20♏	23♑	9♊	8♍	10♒	13♋	2♐
8	9♋	11♐	12♈	16♌	1♑	1♊	2♎	6♒	24♊	21♍	22♒	27♋	16♐
9	23♋	23♐	23♈	0♍	16♑	14♊	14♎	20♒	8♋	3♐	4♈	11♌	0♑
10	8♌	6♑	5♉	14♍	0♒	26♊	26♎	5♐	22♋	16♐	16♈	25♌	14♑
11	23♌	18♑	17♉	29♍	14♒	8♋	8♍	20♐	6♌	28♐	28♈	10♍	28♑
12	7♍	0♒	29♉	13♎	28♒	20♋	20♍	5♈	19♌	9♑	11♉	25♍	11♒
13	21♍	12♒	12♊	28♎	12♐	1♌	2♐	20♈	3♍	21♑	23♉	10♎	24♒
14	5♎	23♒	24♊	13♍	26♐	13♌	15♐	4♉	16♍	3♒	6♊	26♎	7♐
15	19♎	5♐	7♋	27♍	9♈	25♌	28♐	19♉	0♎	15♒	19♊	10♍	20♐
16	2♏	17♐	21♋	12♌	22♈	7♍	12♑	3♊	12♎	27♒	3♐	25♏	2♈
17	15♏	29♐	5♌	26♌	5♉	19♍	25♑	17♊	25♎	10♐	17♐	9♎	15♈
18	28♏	11♈	19♌	9♑	17♉	2♎	10♒	1♋	7♍	22♐	1♎	23♐	27♈
19	10♐	23♈	4♍	23♑	0♊	14♎	25♒	14♋	19♍	5♐	16♑	6♑	9♉
20	22♐	6♉	19♍	6♒	12♊	27♎	10♐	27♋	1♐	18♈	1♏	19♑	21♉
21	4♑	18♉	4♎	19♒	23♊	10♏	25♐	10♌	13♐	1♉	16♏	2♒	3♊
22	16♑	1♊	19♎	2♓	5♋	23♏	10♈	23♌	25♐	15♉	1♎	14♒	15♊
23	28♑	15♊	4♍	15♐	17♋	7♐	25♈	5♍	7♑	28♉	16♎	26♒	27♊
24	10♒	28♊	19♍	27♐	29♋	20♐	10♉	18♍	19♑	12♊	1♍	8♐	9♋
25	22♒	12♋	4♌	9♈	11♌	4♑	24♉	0♎	1♒	26♊	15♍	20♐	21♋
26	4♐	26♋	18♌	21♈	24♌	18♑	8♊	12♎	14♒	10♋	29♍	2♈	4♌
27	17♐	10♌	1♑	3♉	7♏	2♒	22♊	24♎	27♒	24♋	12♐	14♈	17♌
28	0♈	25♌	14♑	15♉	20♏	17♒	5♋	6♍	10♐	9♌	25♐	26♈	0♍
29	13♈	10♍	27♑	27♉	3♎	1♐	17♋	17♍	24♐	23♌	7♑	7♉	14♏
30	26♈	25♍	9♒	9♊	17♎	16♐	29♋	29♍	8♈	7♍	20♑	19♉	28♏
31	10♉	10♎	21♒	21♊	1♍	0♈	11♌	11♐	22♈	22♏	2♒	1♊	13♎

	1916	1917	1918	1919	1920	1921	1922	1923	1924	1925	1926	1927	1928
1	5♒	19♊	19♎	27♒	26♋	9♐	9♈	17♌	19♑	29♋	0♎	7♒	10♋
2	19♒	1♋	1♏	11♓	11♌	21♐	21♈	2♍	2♒	11♊	12♎	22♒	24♋
3	4♓	13♋	13♍	26♓	25♌	3♑	3♉	17♍	16♒	23♊	24♎	7♓	7♌
4	18♓	25♋	25♍	10♈	8♏	15♑	16♉	2♎	29♒	5♋	7♏	22♓	20♌
5	1♈	7♌	8♐	25♈	22♏	27♑	28♉	17♎	12♓	17♋	20♏	8♈	3♍
6	15♈	19♌	20♐	10♉	5♎	9♒	11♊	1♏	25♓	29♋	3♐	23♈	16♍
7	28♈	0♍	4♑	24♉	18♎	21♒	24♊	16♏	8♈	11♌	16♐	8♉	28♍
8	11♉	12♍	17♑	8♊	1♏	3♓	8♋	0♐	20♈	23♌	0♑	22♉	10♎
9	23♉	25♍	1♒	22♊	13♏	15♓	22♋	14♐	2♉	5♍	14♑	6♊	22♎
10	5♊	7♎	16♒	6♋	25♏	28♓	7♌	28♐	14♉	18♍	28♑	19♊	4♏
11	17♊	19♎	1♓	19♋	7♐	10♈	22♌	11♑	26♉	1♎	13♒	2♋	16♏
12	29♊	2♏	16♓	2♌	19♐	23♈	7♍	24♑	8♊	14♎	28♒	15♋	28♏
13	11♋	15♏	1♈	15♌	0♑	6♉	22♍	6♒	20♊	28♎	13♓	27♋	10♐
14	23♋	28♍	17♈	28♌	12♑	19♉	7♎	19♒	2♋	11♏	28♓	9♌	22♐
15	5♌	11♎	2♉	10♍	25♑	3♊	22♎	1♓	14♋	25♏	13♈	21♌	4♑
16	17♌	25♎	16♉	23♍	7♒	17♊	7♏	13♓	27♋	9♐	27♈	3♍	16♑
17	0♍	9♑	0♊	5♎	20♒	0♋	21♏	25♓	10♌	23♐	11♉	15♍	29♑
18	12♍	23♑	14♊	17♎	3♓	15♋	4♐	7♈	23♌	7♑	25♉	27♍	13♒
19	25♍	7♒	27♊	29♎	16♓	29♋	18♐	19♈	6♍	21♑	8♊	9♎	27♒
20	9♎	22♒	10♋	11♍	0♈	14♌	0♑	1♉	20♍	6♒	21♊	21♎	11♓
21	23♎	7♓	22♋	23♍	14♈	28♌	13♑	12♉	4♎	20♒	3♋	3♏	25♓
22	6♏	22♓	4♌	4♎	28♈	13♍	25♑	24♉	19♎	4♓	15♏	10♈	10♈
23	20♏	6♈	16♌	16♎	12♉	27♍	7♒	6♊	4♍	18♓	27♋	27♏	25♈
24	4♐	21♈	28♌	28♎	26♉	12♎	19♒	19♊	18♍	2♈	9♌	9♐	10♉
25	19♐	5♉	10♍	11♏	11♊	25♎	1♓	1♋	1♎	16♈	21♌	22♐	25♉
26	3♑	19♉	22♍	24♏	25♊	9♍	12♓	14♋	17♐	29♈	2♏	5♑	9♊
27	17♑	2♊	4♎	7♒	9♋	22♍	24♓	27♋	2♑	12♉	14♏	18♑	23♊
28	1♒	15♊	16♎	20♒	24♋	5♌	6♈	11♌	16♑	24♉	26♏	2♒	7♋
29	15♒	27♊	28♎	4♓	7♌	17♐	18♌	25♌	29♑	7♊	9♎	16♓	21♋
30	29♒	10♋	10♍	19♓	21♌	29♐	0♎	10♏	13♒	19♊	21♎	0♒	4♌
31	13♓	21♋	22♍	4♈	4♏	11♑	13♉	25♏	26♒	1♋	4♏	15♓	17♌

	1929	1930	1931	1932	1933	1934	1935	1936	1937	1938	1939	1940	1941
1	19♍	20♐	28♋	2♑	8♉	11♏	19♑	24♊	28♎	1♐	10♋	15♐	18♈
2	1♐	3♐	13♌	16♑	20♉	23♏	4♒	7♋	10♍	14♐	25♋	28♐	29♈
3	12♐	15♐	28♌	29♑	2♊	6♒	19♒	20♋	22♍	27♐	10♋	11♑	11♉
4	24♐	28♐	13♍	11♒	14♊	19♒	4♓	2♌	4♐	11♈	25♋	23♑	23♉
5	6♑	11♑	29♍	24♒	26♊	2♍	19♓	14♌	15♐	24♈	10♍	5♒	5♊
6	18♑	24♑	14♎	6♓	8♋	16♍	4♈	27♌	27♐	8♉	25♍	17♒	17♊
7	0♒	7♊	28♎	18♓	20♋	0♐	19♈	9♍	10♑	22♉	10♎	29♒	0♋
8	13♒	21♊	13♏	0♈	3♌	14♐	3♉	21♍	22♑	6♊	24♎	11♓	12♋
9	26♒	5♋	27♏	12♈	16♌	28♐	17♉	2♎	5♒	20♊	8♏	23♓	26♋
10	9♓	20♋	10♐	24♈	29♌	12♑	1♊	14♎	19♒	4♋	21♏	5♈	9♌
11	22♓	4♌	23♐	6♉	12♍	26♑	14♊	26♎	3♓	18♋	4♐	16♈	23♌
12	5♈	19♌	6♑	18♉	26♍	11♒	26♊	8♏	17♓	2♌	16♐	28♈	8♍
13	19♈	4♍	18♑	0♊	10♎	25♒	8♋	20♏	2♈	17♌	28♐	10♉	22♍
14	3♉	19♍	0♒	12♊	25♎	10♓	20♋	2♐	16♈	1♍	10♑	23♉	7♎
15	17♉	3♎	12♒	24♊	9♏	24♓	2♌	14♐	1♉	15♍	22♑	5♊	22♎
16	1♊	18♎	24♒	7♋	23♏	8♈	14♌	27♐	16♉	28♍	4♒	18♊	7♏
17	15♊	2♏	6♓	20♋	8♐	21♈	26♌	10♑	0♊	12♎	16♒	1♋	22♏
18	29♊	15♏	18♓	3♌	22♐	5♉	8♏	23♑	14♊	25♎	28♒	14♋	6♐
19	14♋	28♏	29♓	17♌	6♑	18♉	20♏	7♒	28♊	8♏	10♓	28♋	20♐
20	28♋	10♐	11♈	1♍	20♑	0♊	2♒	22♒	12♋	20♏	22♓	13♌	4♑
21	12♌	23♐	23♈	16♍	4♒	13♊	14♒	7♓	25♋	2♐	4♈	28♌	17♑
22	26♌	5♑	5♉	1♎	17♒	25♊	26♒	22♓	9♌	14♐	17♈	13♍	0♒
23	9♍	17♑	18♉	16♎	0♓	6♋	9♍	7♈	22♌	26♐	0♉	28♍	13♒
24	23♍	29♑	0♊	1♏	14♓	18♋	21♍	22♈	5♏	8♑	13♉	13♎	26♒
25	6♎	11♒	13♊	16♏	27♓	0♌	4♐	7♉	17♏	20♑	26♉	28♎	8♓
26	19♎	23♒	26♊	1♐	9♈	12♌	17♐	22♉	0♐	2♒	9♊	13♏	20♓
27	2♏	5♓	9♋	15♐	22♈	24♌	1♑	6♊	12♐	14♒	23♊	27♏	2♈
28	14♏	17♓	23♋	29♐	4♉	7♍	15♑	20♊	24♐	27♒	6♋	11♐	14♈
29	26♏	29♓	7♌	13♑	16♉	19♍	29♑	4♋	6♍	9♓	21♋	24♐	26♈
30	8♐	12♈	22♌	26♑	28♉	2♎	13♒	18♋	18♍	23♓	5♌	7♑	8♉
31	20♐	25♈	7♏	8♒	10♊	15♎	28♒	29♋	0♐	6♈	20♌	20♑	20♉

	1942	1943	1944	1945	1946	1947	1948	1949	1950	1951	1952
1	21♌	2♑	6♊	8♎	11♒	24♊	27♏	28♐	2♌	17♐	17♉
2	5♏	17♑	19♊	20♎	25♒	9♋	9♐	10♈	15♌	1♑	29♉
3	18♏	2♒	1♋	1♍	9♓	23♋	22♌	22♈	29♌	15♑	12♊
4	2♎	16♒	14♋	13♍	23♐	8♌	4♑	3♉	14♏	0♒	24♊
5	16♎	1♐	26♋	25♍	7♈	22♌	16♑	15♉	28♏	14♒	6♋
6	0♏	16♐	7♌	7♐	22♈	6♏	28♑	28♉	13♎	28♒	18♋
7	14♏	0♈	19♌	20♐	6♉	21♏	9♒	10♊	28♎	11♐	29♋
8	28♏	14♈	1♏	3♑	21♉	4♎	21♒	23♊	13♍	25♐	11♌
9	12♐	28♈	13♏	16♑	5♊	18♎	3♓	6♋	27♍	8♈	23♌
10	27♐	11♉	25♏	29♑	19♊	1♏	15♐	20♋	11♐	20♈	5♏
11	11♑	24♉	7♎	13♒	3♋	13♍	27♐	4♌	25♐	3♉	18♏
12	25♑	6♊	19♎	28♒	17♋	26♏	10♑	19♌	9♑	15♉	0♎
13	9♒	18♊	1♍	13♐	0♌	8♌	22♈	4♏	22♑	27♉	13♎
14	22♒	0♋	14♍	28♐	13♌	20♌	5♉	19♏	5♒	9♊	26♎
15	6♓	12♋	26♍	13♈	27♌	2♑	17♉	4♎	18♒	21♊	9♍
16	19♓	24♋	9♌	28♈	10♏	13♑	0♊	19♎	1♓	3♋	22♍
17	2♈	6♌	22♌	13♉	22♏	25♑	14♊	4♏	13♐	15♋	6♐
18	15♈	18♌	6♑	28♉	5♎	7♒	27♊	19♏	25♐	27♋	20♐
19	27♈	0♏	20♑	12♊	17♎	20♒	11♋	3♐	8♈	10♌	4♑
20	10♉	12♏	4♒	25♊	0♍	2♓	25♋	16♐	20♈	22♌	18♑
21	22♉	25♏	19♒	9♋	12♍	15♓	10♌	0♑	1♉	5♏	2♒
22	4♊	8♎	3♓	22♋	24♍	28♓	25♌	12♑	13♉	19♏	17♒
23	15♊	21♎	19♓	4♌	5♐	12♈	10♏	3♑	25♉	2♎	1♐
24	27♊	4♍	4♈	16♌	17♐	25♐	25♏	7♒	7♊	16♎	16♐
25	9♋	17♍	19♈	29♌	29♐	9♌	9♎	19♒	19♊	1♍	0♈
26	21♋	1♐	3♉	11♏	11♑	23♌	24♎	1♓	1♌	15♏	14♎
27	4♌	15♐	18♉	23♏	23♑	7♊	8♍	13♐	14♋	29♏	28♈
28	16♌	29♐	1♊	5♎	6♒	21♊	22♍	25♐	26♋	14♌	11♉
29	29♌	13♑	15♊	16♎	19♒	5♋	5♐	7♈	10♌	28♐	25♉
30	13♏	27♑	28♊	28♎	3♓	19♋	17♐	19♈	23♌	12♑	7♊
31	27♏	12♒	10♋	10♍	17♓	4♌	0♑	0♉	7♏	26♑	20♊

APRIL

	1890	1891	1892	1893	1894	1895	1896	1897	1898	1899	1900	1901	1902
1	26♌	2♑	7♊	14♎	16♒	23♊	28♍	4♈	6♌	15♐	4♉	13♏	13♑
2	8♏	15♑	21♊	26♎	28♒	7♋	12♐	16♈	18♌	29♐	18♉	25♏	25♑
3	21♏	29♑	4♒	8♍	11♋	21♋	26♐	28♈	1♏	13♑	2♊	7♎	8♒
4	4♎	13♒	18♒	20♍	24♋	5♌	9♑	10♉	14♍	27♑	16♊	19♎	21♒
5	17♎	28♒	1♌	2♐	7♈	20♌	22♑	22♉	27♍	12♒	29♊	0♏	4♓
6	0♏	13♓	13♌	14♐	21♈	4♍	4♒	4♊	11♎	26♒	12♋	12♏	18♓
7	13♏	28♓	26♌	26♐	4♉	19♍	16♒	16♊	26♎	10♓	24♋	24♏	2♈
8	27♏	13♈	8♏	8♑	18♉	4♎	28♒	28♊	10♏	25♓	6♌	6♐	16♈
9	11♐	28♈	20♏	20♑	2♊	18♎	10♓	10♋	25♏	9♈	18♌	18♐	1♉
10	25♐	12♉	2♒	2♒	17♊	2♏	22♓	22♋	9♐	23♈	0♏	0♑	16♉
11	9♑	26♉	13♒	15♒	1♋	16♏	3♈	5♌	24♐	7♉	12♏	13♑	1♊
12	23♑	10♊	25♒	28♒	15♋	0♐	15♈	18♌	8♑	20♉	24♏	26♑	15♊
13	7♒	23♊	7♍	12♓	0♌	13♐	27♈	2♏	22♑	3♊	6♎	9♎	0♋
14	21♒	6♋	19♍	26♓	14♌	26♐	9♉	16♏	6♒	16♊	18♎	23♒	14♋
15	5♓	18♋	1♐	10♈	28♌	8♑	21♉	1♎	19♒	28♊	0♏	7♓	28♋
16	20♓	1♌	13♐	25♈	11♍	21♑	4♊	16♎	3♓	10♋	12♏	22♒	11♌
17	4♈	13♌	25♐	10♉	25♍	3♒	16♊	1♏	16♓	22♋	25♏	7♈	25♌
18	17♈	25♌	8♑	25♉	8♎	15♒	29♊	16♏	29♓	4♌	7♐	22♈	8♏
19	1♉	6♏	20♑	10♊	22♎	26♒	12♋	1♐	12♈	16♌	20♐	7♉	21♏
20	14♉	18♏	4♒	24♊	5♍	8♓	25♋	16♐	25♈	28♌	3♑	22♉	3♎
21	27♉	0♐	17♒	9♋	17♍	20♓	9♌	1♑	8♉	10♏	17♑	7♊	16♎
22	10♊	12♐	1♓	23♋	0♐	2♈	22♌	15♑	20♉	22♏	0♒	21♊	28♎
23	22♊	25♐	16♓	7♌	12♐	15♈	7♍	28♑	2♊	5♎	14♒	5♋	10♍
24	4♋	7♍	0♈	20♌	24♐	27♈	21♍	11♒	14♊	18♎	28♒	19♋	22♍
25	16♋	20♏	15♈	3♍	6♑	10♉	6♎	24♒	26♊	1♍	13♓	2♌	4♐
26	28♋	2♐	1♉	16♍	18♑	23♉	21♎	7♓	8♋	14♍	28♓	15♌	16♐
27	10♌	15♐	16♉	28♍	0♒	7♊	6♍	19♓	19♋	28♍	13♈	27♌	27♐
28	22♌	28♐	1♊	10♎	12♒	20♊	21♍	1♈	1♌	12♐	27♈	10♏	9♑
29	4♏	12♑	15♊	23♎	24♒	4♋	6♐	13♈	13♌	26♐	12♉	22♏	21♑
30	16♏	26♑	0♋	5♍	6♓	18♋	20♐	25♈	26♌	10♑	26♉	4♎	4♒

APRIL

	1903	1904	1905	1906	1907	1908	1909	1910	1911	1912	1913	1914	1915
1	23♉	24♎	3♐	3♋	15♏	15♈	23♌	23♐	7♉	6♎	14♒	14Ⅱ	28♎
2	7Ⅱ	9♏	15♐	15♋	0♌	29♈	5♏	5♑	21♉	19♏	25♒	26Ⅱ	13♏
3	21Ⅱ	22♏	27♐	28♋	14♐	13♉	17♏	18♑	6Ⅱ	3♏	7♒	9♋	28♏
4	6♋	6♐	9♈	11♌	28♐	26♉	29♏	1♒	20Ⅱ	16♏	19♒	22♋	12♐
5	20♋	19♐	20♈	24♌	12♑	9Ⅱ	11♎	15♒	4♋	29♏	1♈	5♌	27♐
6	4♌	2♑	2♉	8♏	26♑	22Ⅱ	23♎	28♒	19♋	11♌	13♈	19♌	11♑
7	18♌	14♑	14♉	22♏	10♒	4♋	5♏	13♐	2♌	23♐	25♈	4♏	25♑
8	2♏	26♑	26♉	7♎	24♒	16♋	17♏	28♐	16♌	5♑	8♉	18♏	8♒
9	16♏	8♒	9Ⅱ	22♎	8♐	28♋	0♐	13♈	29♌	17♑	20♉	3♎	21♒
10	0♎	20♒	21Ⅱ	7♏	21♐	10♌	12♐	28♈	13♏	29♑	3Ⅱ	19♎	4♓
11	14♎	2♓	4♋	22♏	4♈	21♌	25♐	13♉	26♏	11♒	16Ⅱ	4♏	16♓
12	27♎	14♓	17♋	7♐	18♈	3♏	8♑	28♉	8♒	23♒	0♋	19♏	29♓
13	10♏	26♓	0♌	22♐	0♉	15♏	21♑	13Ⅱ	21♎	5♓	13♋	4♐	11♈
14	23♏	8♉	14♌	6♑	13♉	28♏	5♒	27Ⅱ	3♏	18♓	27♋	18♐	23♈
15	5♐	20♈	28♌	20♑	25♉	10♎	19♒	11♋	15♏	1♈	11♋	2♑	5♉
16	18♐	3♉	12♏	3♒	8Ⅱ	23♎	4♏	24♋	27♏	14♈	26♋	15♒	17♉
17	0♑	15♉	27♏	16♒	20Ⅱ	6♏	19♐	7♌	9♌	27♏	10♏	28♒	29♉
18	12♑	28♉	12♎	29♒	1♋	20♏	4♈	20♌	21♐	11♉	25♏	11Ⅱ	11Ⅱ
19	24♑	12Ⅱ	27♎	12♓	13♋	3♐	19♈	2♏	3♑	24♉	9♎	23♒	23Ⅱ
20	6♒	25Ⅱ	13♏	24♓	25♋	17♐	4♉	15♏	15♑	8Ⅱ	24♎	5♏	5♋
21	18♒	9♋	28♏	6♈	7♌	1♑	18♉	27♏	27♑	23Ⅱ	9♏	17♏	17♋
22	0♓	22♋	12♐	18♈	19♌	15♑	3Ⅱ	9♒	9♒	7♋	23♏	29♐	29♋
23	12♓	6♌	26♐	0♉	2♏	29♑	16Ⅱ	21♎	22♒	21♋	7♒	11♈	12♌
24	25♓	21♌	10♑	12♉	14♏	13♒	0♋	2♏	5♓	5♌	20♒	23♈	25♌
25	8♈	5♏	23♑	24♉	28♏	27♒	13♋	14♏	18♓	20♌	3♑	4♉	8♏
26	21♈	19♏	6♒	6Ⅱ	12♎	11♓	26♋	26♏	2♈	4♏	16♑	16♉	22♏
27	5♉	4♐	18♒	18Ⅱ	26♎	26♓	8♌	8♐	16♈	18♏	28♑	28♉	6♎
28	19♉	18♐	0♓	0♋	10♏	10♈	20♌	20♐	1♉	1♎	10♒	11Ⅱ	21♎
29	3Ⅱ	3♑	12♓	12♋	25♏	24♈	2♏	2♑	16♉	15♎	22♒	23Ⅱ	6♏
30	18Ⅱ	17♏	24♓	24♋	10♐	8♉	14♏	14♑	1Ⅱ	28♎	4♓	6♋	22♏

APRIL

	1916	1917	1918	1919	1920	1921	1922	1923	1924	1925	1926	1927	1928
1	26♐	3♌	4♐	19♈	18♏	23♑	25♉	10♎	9♐	13♋	17♏	1♈	0♏
2	10♈	15♌	17♐	4♉	1♎	5♏	8♊	25♎	21♐	24♋	0♐	16♈	12♏
3	23♈	27♌	0♑	19♉	14♏	17♒	21♊	10♏	4♈	6♌	13♐	18♉	25♏
4	6♉	9♏	13♑	4♊	26♏	29♒	4♋	25♏	16♈	18♌	26♐	16♉	7♎
5	19♉	21♏	26♑	18♊	9♏	11♓	18♋	10♐	29♈	1♏	10♑	1♊	19♎
6	1♊	3♎	10♒	2♋	21♏	24♓	2♌	24♐	11♉	13♏	24♑	15♊	1♏
7	13♊	16♎	25♒	16♋	3♐	6♈	16♌	7♑	23♉	26♏	8♒	28♊	13♏
8	25♊	29♎	9♓	29♋	15♐	19♈	1♏	21♑	4♊	10♎	22♒	11♋	25♏
9	7♋	12♏	24♓	12♌	27♐	2♉	16♏	3♒	16♊	23♎	7♓	24♋	6♐
10	19♋	25♏	10♈	25♌	8♑	16♉	1♎	16♒	28♊	7♏	22♓	6♌	18♐
11	1♌	8♐	25♈	7♏	20♑	0♊	15♎	28♒	10♋	21♏	6♈	18♌	0♑
12	13♌	22♐	10♉	20♏	2♒	13♊	0♏	10♐	22♋	5♐	21♈	0♏	12♑
13	25♌	5♑	25♉	2♎	15♒	27♊	15♏	22♐	5♌	20♐	5♉	12♏	25♑
14	8♏	19♑	9♊	14♎	28♒	11♋	29♏	4♈	17♌	4♑	19♉	24♏	8♒
15	20♏	3♒	22♊	26♎	11♓	26♋	13♐	16♈	1♏	18♑	3♊	6♎	21♒
16	4♎	17♒	6♋	8♏	24♓	10♌	26♐	28♈	14♏	2♒	16♊	18♎	5♓
17	18♎	2♓	19♋	19♏	8♈	24♌	9♑	9♉	28♏	16♒	29♊	0♏	19♓
18	2♏	16♓	1♌	1♐	22♈	8♏	21♑	21♉	13♎	0♓	11♋	12♏	4♈
19	16♏	1♈	13♌	13♐	7♉	22♏	3♒	3♊	28♎	14♓	23♋	24♏	19♈
20	0♐	15♈	25♌	25♐	22♉	6♎	15♒	16♊	28♓	28♓	5♌	6♉	4♉
21	15♐	29♈	7♏	7♑	6♊	20♎	27♒	28♊	28♏	11♈	17♌	19♐	19♉
22	29♐	13♉	19♏	20♑	21♊	4♏	9♐	10♋	13♐	24♈	29♌	1♒	4♊
23	14♑	27♉	1♒	2♒	5♋	17♏	21♐	23♋	28♐	7♉	11♏	14♒	19♊
24	28♑	10♊	13♒	15♒	20♋	0♐	3♈	6♌	12♑	20♉	23♏	28♒	3♋
25	12♒	23♊	25♒	29♒	4♌	12♐	15♈	20♌	26♑	2♊	5♎	11♒	17♋
26	26♒	5♋	7♏	13♓	18♌	25♐	27♈	4♏	10♒	15♊	17♎	25♒	1♌
27	9♓	17♋	19♏	27♓	1♏	7♑	9♉	18♏	23♒	27♊	0♏	10♓	14♌
28	23♓	29♋	1♐	12♈	14♏	19♑	22♉	3♎	6♐	9♋	13♏	24♓	27♌
29	6♈	11♌	14♐	27♈	27♏	1♒	5♊	18♎	18♐	21♋	26♏	9♈	9♏
30	19♈	23♌	27♐	13♉	10♎	13♒	18♊	3♏	1♈	2♌	10♐	24♈	22♏

	1929	1930	1931	1932	1933	1934	1935	1936	1937	1938	1939	1940	1941
1	2♑	8♉	22♍	21♒	22♊	29♎	13♐	11♌	12♐	20♈	4♏	2♒	2♊
2	14♑	21♉	7♎	3♓	4♋	12♍	27♐	24♌	24♐	4♉	19♏	14♒	14♊
3	26♑	4♊	22♎	15♐	16♋	26♍	12♈	6♏	6♑	18♉	3♐	26♒	26♊
4	8♒	18♊	7♍	27♐	28♋	10♎	27♈	18♏	18♑	2♊	18♐	8♐	8♋
5	21♒	2♋	21♍	9♈	10♌	25♎	11♉	29♏	0♒	17♊	2♑	20♐	21♋
6	4♓	16♋	5♐	21♈	23♌	9♑	25♉	11♎	13♒	1♋	15♑	2♈	4♌
7	17♓	0♌	19♐	3♉	7♍	23♑	9♊	23♎	27♒	15♋	29♑	13♈	17♌
8	0♈	15♌	2♑	15♉	20♍	7♒	22♊	5♍	11♐	29♋	12♒	25♈	1♏
9	14♈	29♌	14♑	26♉	4♎	21♒	4♋	17♍	25♐	13♌	24♒	7♉	16♏
10	28♈	13♍	27♑	8♊	19♎	5♐	17♋	29♍	10♑	27♌	6♓	20♉	0♎
11	13♉	28♍	9♒	21♊	4♏	19♐	29♋	11♎	25♑	11♍	18♓	2♊	15♎
12	27♉	12♎	21♒	3♋	19♏	3♈	11♌	24♎	10♒	24♍	0♈	15♊	1♏
13	12♊	26♎	3♓	15♋	3♐	16♈	22♌	6♏	25♒	7♎	12♈	27♊	16♏
14	26♊	9♏	15♓	28♋	18♐	0♉	4♍	19♏	10♊	20♎	24♈	11♋	1♐
15	10♋	23♏	26♓	12♌	3♑	13♉	16♍	3♎	24♊	3♏	6♉	24♋	16♐
16	25♋	6♐	8♈	25♌	17♑	26♉	28♍	16♎	8♋	16♏	18♉	8♌	0♑
17	8♌	18♐	20♈	10♍	1♒	8♊	10♎	0♐	22♋	28♏	1♈	22♌	14♑
18	22♌	1♑	2♉	24♍	14♒	20♊	23♎	15♐	6♌	10♐	13♈	7♍	27♑
19	6♍	13♑	15♉	9♎	28♒	2♋	5♏	0♈	19♌	32♐	26♈	21♍	10♒
20	19♍	25♑	27♉	24♎	11♐	14♋	18♏	15♈	2♍	4♑	9♉	6♎	23♒
21	2♎	7♒	10♊	10♏	23♐	26♋	1♐	1♉	14♍	16♑	22♉	21♎	5♐
22	15♎	19♒	23♊	25♏	6♈	8♌	14♐	16♉	27♍	28♑	6♊	6♏	17♐
23	28♎	0♓	6♋	10♐	18♈	20♌	28♐	1♊	9♎	10♒	19♊	21♏	29♐
24	10♏	13♓	19♋	24♐	0♉	2♍	11♑	15♊	21♎	22♒	3♋	5♐	11♈
25	22♏	25♓	3♌	8♑	13♉	14♍	25♑	29♊	3♍	4♐	17♋	19♐	23♈
26	5♐	7♈	17♌	22♑	25♉	27♍	9♒	12♋	15♍	17♐	2♌	3♑	5♉
27	16♐	20♈	1♍	5♒	6♊	10♎	23♒	25♋	27♍	1♑	16♌	16♑	17♉
28	28♐	3♉	16♍	18♒	18♊	24♎	8♐	8♌	8♎	14♈	0♍	28♑	29♉
29	10♑	17♉	1♎	0♓	0♋	8♏	22♐	20♌	20♎	28♈	14♍	11♒	11♊
30	22♑	1♊	15♎	12♐	12♋	22♏	7♈	3♍	2♑	13♉	28♍	23♒	23♊

APRIL

	1942	1943	1944	1945	1946	1947	1948	1949	1950	1951	1952
1	11♎	26♒	22♋	22♍	1♈	18♌	12♑	12♉	22♏	10♒	2♋
2	25♎	10♓	4♌	4♐	16♈	2♏	24♑	25♉	7♎	24♒	14♋
3	9♏	24♓	16♌	16♐	1♉	16♏	6♒	7♊	22♎	7♓	26♋
4	24♏	8♈	28♌	29♐	16♉	29♏	18♒	19♊	7♍	20♓	7♌
5	9♐	22♈	10♍	11♑	1♊	3♎	0♓	2♋	22♍	3♈	19♌
6	23♐	5♉	22♏	24♑	15♊	26♎	12♓	16♋	7♐	16♈	1♍
7	8♑	19♉	4♎	8♒	29♊	9♍	24♓	29♋	21♐	29♈	14♍
8	22♑	1♊	16♎	22♒	13♋	21♍	6♈	13♌	5♑	11♉	26♍
9	5♒	14♊	28♎	6♓	27♋	4♐	19♈	28♌	19♑	23♉	9♎
10	19♒	26♊	11♍	21♓	10♌	16♐	1♉	12♍	2♒	5♊	22♎
11	2♓	8♋	23♍	6♈	24♌	28♐	14♉	27♍	15♒	17♊	5♏
12	15♓	20♋	6♐	22♈	6♍	9♑	27♉	12♎	28♒	29♊	19♍
13	28♓	2♌	19♐	7♉	19♍	21♑	11♊	27♎	10♓	11♋	2♐
14	11♈	14♌	3♑	22♉	2♎	3♒	24♊	12♍	22♓	23♋	16♐
15	23♈	26♌	16♑	7♊	14♎	15♒	8♋	27♍	4♈	5♌	0♑
16	6♉	8♏	0♒	21♊	26♎	28♒	22♋	11♐	16♈	17♌	15♑
17	18♉	20♏	14♒	5♋	8♍	10♓	6♌	25♐	28♈	0♏	29♑
18	0♊	3♎	28♒	18♋	20♍	23♓	20♌	8♑	10♉	13♏	13♒
19	12♊	16♎	13♓	1♌	2♐	7♈	5♏	21♑	22♉	27♏	27♒
20	24♊	0♍	27♓	13♌	14♐	20♈	19♍	4♒	4♊	11♎	11♓
21	6♋	13♍	12♈	26♌	25♐	4♉	4♎	16♒	16♊	25♎	25♓
22	17♋	27♍	27♈	8♏	7♑	19♉	18♎	28♒	28♊	9♍	9♈
23	29♋	12♐	11♉	20♏	19♑	3♊	2♏	10♓	10♋	24♍	23♈
24	12♌	26♐	26♉	2♎	2♒	17♊	16♏	22♓	22♋	9♐	6♉
25	24♌	10♑	9♊	13♎	15♒	2♋	29♍	4♈	5♌	24♐	20♉
26	7♍	24♑	23♊	25♎	28♒	16♋	13♐	15♈	18♌	9♑	3♊
27	21♍	8♒	6♋	7♍	11♓	0♌	25♐	27♈	2♏	23♑	15♊
28	4♎	22♒	18♋	19♍	25♓	14♌	8♑	9♉	16♏	7♒	28♊
29	19♎	6♓	0♌	1♐	10♈	28♌	20♑	22♉	0♎	21♒	10♋
30	3♏	20♓	12♌	13♐	24♈	12♏	2♒	4♊	15♎	4♓	22♋

MAY

	1890	1891	1892	1893	1894	1895	1896	1897	1898	1899	1900	1901	1902
1	29♏	9♒	13♋	17♍	19♐	2♌	4♑	7♉	9♏	24♑	10♊	16♎	16♒
2	12♎	24♒	27♋	29♍	2♈	16♌	17♑	19♉	22♏	8♒	24♊	27♎	29♒
3	25♎	8♓	10♌	10♌	15♈	0♍	0♒	1♊	5♎	23♒	7♋	9♍	12♐
4	9♏	23♓	22♌	22♌	29♈	14♏	13♒	13♊	20♎	7♋	20♋	21♍	26♐
5	23♏	7♈	5♏	4♑	13♉	29♏	25♒	25♊	4♏	21♓	2♋	3♌	10♈
6	7♐	22♈	17♏	16♑	28♉	13♎	7♐	7♋	19♍	5♈	14♌	15♌	25♈
7	21♌	6♉	29♍	28♓	12♊	27♎	18♐	19♋	4♐	18♈	26♌	27♌	9♉
8	5♑	20♉	10♎	11♎	27♊	11♏	0♈	1♌	19♌	2♉	8♏	10♑	24♉
9	20♑	4♊	22♎	23♎	12♋	25♍	12♈	14♌	3♑	15♉	20♍	22♌	10♊
10	4♒	18♊	4♏	7♓	26♋	8♌	24♈	27♌	18♑	28♉	2♎	5♎	25♊
11	18♒	1♋	16♏	20♓	10♌	21♌	6♉	11♏	2♒	11♊	14♎	18♒	9♋
12	2♓	14♋	28♏	4♈	24♌	4♑	18♉	25♏	16♒	24♊	26♎	2♓	24♋
13	16♓	26♋	10♌	18♈	8♏	16♑	1♊	9♎	0♐	6♋	9♍	16♓	8♌
14	0♈	9♌	22♌	3♉	22♏	29♑	13♊	24♎	13♐	18♋	21♍	0♈	22♌
15	13♈	21♌	5♑	18♉	5♎	11♒	26♊	9♍	26♐	0♌	4♌	15♈	5♏
16	27♈	3♍	17♑	3♊	18♎	22♒	9♋	24♍	9♈	12♌	17♌	0♉	18♏
17	10♉	15♍	0♒	19♊	1♍	4♐	22♒	10♌	22♈	24♌	0♑	15♉	0♎
18	23♉	27♏	14♒	4♋	13♍	16♐	5♌	25♌	4♉	6♏	13♑	0♊	13♎
19	6♊	9♎	27♒	18♋	26♍	28♐	19♋	9♑	17♉	18♏	27♑	15♊	25♎
20	18♊	21♌	11♐	3♌	8♌	10♈	3♍	24♑	29♉	0♎	11♒	0♋	7♍
21	0♋	3♍	25♓	16♋	20♌	23♈	17♍	7♎	11♊	13♎	25♒	14♋	19♍
22	12♋	16♍	10♈	0♍	2♑	6♉	1♎	21♒	23♊	26♏	9♓	28♌	1♐
23	24♋	28♍	24♈	13♍	14♑	19♉	16♎	3♐	4♋	9♍	8♉	11♌	13♌
24	6♌	12♌	9♉	25♍	26♑	2♊	0♍	16♐	16♋	23♍	8♈	24♌	24♐
25	18♌	25♌	24♉	8♎	8♒	16♊	15♍	28♐	28♋	7♌	22♍	6♏	6♑
26	0♍	9♊	9♌	20♎	20♒	0♋	0♌	10♈	10♌	21♌	7♉	19♏	18♑
27	12♍	22♑	23♊	2♏	2♓	14♋	12♌	22♍	22♌	6♑	21♉	1♎	0♒
28	24♍	6♒	8♌	14♏	14♐	28♋	28♌	4♉	4♏	20♑	5♊	12♎	13♒
29	7♎	20♒	22♋	26♍	27♐	13♑	12♑	16♉	17♏	5♒	19♊	24♎	25♒
30	20♎	5♓	5♌	7♐	10♈	27♌	25♑	28♉	0♎	19♒	2♋	6♏	8♐
31	3♍	19♐	18♌	19♌	23♈	11♏	8♒	10♊	14♎	3♐	15♋	18♍	21♐

MAY

	1903	1904	1905	1906	1907	1908	1909	1910	1911	1912	1913	1914	1915
1	2♋	0♐	6♈	6♌	24♐	21♉	26♏	27♑	15Ⅱ	11♎	15♐	18♋	7♐
2	17♋	14♐	17♈	19♌	9♑	4Ⅱ	8♎	10♒	0♎	24♏	27♐	1♌	22♐
3	1♌	27♐	29♈	2♍	23♑	17Ⅱ	20♎	23♒	15♎	7♐	9♈	15♌	7♑
4	15♌	10♑	11Ⅱ	16♍	7♒	29Ⅱ	2♍	7♐	29♎	19♐	22♈	29♌	21♑
5	29♌	22♑	23♋	0♎	21♒	12♋	14♍	22♐	13♏	1♑	4♉	13♍	5♒
6	13♍	4♒	6Ⅱ	15♎	5♓	24♋	26♍	6♐	26♑	13♑	17♉	27♍	18♒
7	26♍	16♒	18Ⅱ	0♏	18♓	6♌	9♐	21♈	10♍	25♑	0Ⅱ	12♎	1♓
8	10♎	28♒	1♋	15♏	1♈	17♌	22♐	6♉	23♍	7♒	13Ⅱ	27♎	14♓
9	23♎	10♓	14♋	1♐	14♈	29♌	5♑	21♉	5♎	19♒	26Ⅱ	12♍	26♓
10	6♏	22♓	27♋	16♐	27♈	11♍	18♑	6Ⅱ	18♎	1♓	10♋	27♍	8♈
11	19♍	4♈	10♌	1♑	9♉	23♍	2♒	21♈	0♍	13♐	24♋	12♌	20♈
12	1♐	16♈	24♌	15♑	22♉	6♎	15♒	6♋	12♍	26♐	8♌	26♐	2♉
13	14♐	29♈	7♍	29♑	4Ⅱ	19♎	0♓	20♋	24♍	9♈	22♌	10♑	14♉
14	26♐	11♉	22♍	13♒	16Ⅱ	2♏	14♓	3♌	6♎	22♈	6♍	24♑	26♉
15	8♑	24♉	6♎	26♒	28Ⅱ	15♍	28♓	16♌	18♐	5♉	20♍	7♒	8Ⅱ
16	20♑	8Ⅱ	21♎	9♓	10♋	29♍	13♈	29♌	0♑	19♉	5♎	20♒	20Ⅱ
17	2♒	21Ⅱ	6♍	21♓	21♋	13♐	28♈	12♍	11♑	4Ⅱ	19♎	2♓	2♋
18	14♒	5♋	21♍	3♈	3♌	27♐	12♉	24♍	23♑	18Ⅱ	3♏	14♓	14♋
19	25♒	19♋	6♐	15♈	15♌	11♑	27♉	6♎	5♒	3♋	17♍	26♓	26♋
20	8♓	3♌	20♐	27♈	27♌	25♑	11Ⅱ	18♎	18♒	17♋	1♐	8♈	8♌
21	20♓	17♌	4♑	9♉	10♍	10♒	24Ⅱ	29♎	0♓	2♌	15♐	19♈	21♌
22	3♈	2♍	18♑	21♉	23♍	24♒	8♎	11♍	13♓	16♌	28♐	1♉	4♏
23	16♈	16♍	1♒	3Ⅱ	6♎	8♓	21♎	23♍	26♓	0♏	11♑	13♉	17♍
24	29♈	0♎	14♒	15Ⅱ	20♎	22♓	4♌	5♎	10♈	14♍	23♑	25♉	1♎
25	13♉	14♎	26♒	27Ⅱ	4♍	6♈	16♌	17♎	24♐	28♍	6♒	8Ⅱ	15♎
26	28♉	28♎	8♓	9♋	18♍	20♈	28♌	29♎	9♑	11♎	18♒	20Ⅱ	0♍
27	12Ⅱ	12♍	20♓	21♋	3♐	3♉	10♍	12♑	24♌	25♎	0♓	3♋	15♍
28	27Ⅱ	25♍	2♈	3♌	18♐	17♌	22♍	24♑	9Ⅱ	8♍	12♐	15♋	0♐
29	12♋	9♐	14♈	16♌	3♑	0Ⅱ	4♎	7♒	24Ⅱ	20♍	23♐	28♋	15♐
30	27♋	22♐	26♈	29♌	18♑	13Ⅱ	16♎	20♒	9♋	3♐	5♈	12♌	0♑
31	11♌	5♑	8♉	12♍	3♒	25Ⅱ	28♎	3♓	24♋	15♐	17♈	25♌	15♑

MAY

	1916	1917	1918	1919	1920	1921	1922	1923	1924	1925	1926	1927	1928
1	2♉	5♏	10♑	28♉	23♌	25♒	1♋	18♏	13♈	14♌	23♈	9♌	4♎
2	15♉	17♏	23♑	13Ⅱ	5♏	7♐	15♋	3♐	25♈	26♌	7♑	24♉	16♎
3	27♉	29♏	6♒	27Ⅱ	17♏	19♐	28♋	18♌	7♉	9♍	21♑	9Ⅱ	28♎
4	9Ⅱ	12♎	20♒	12♋	29♏	2♈	12♌	2♑	19♌	21♍	5♒	23Ⅱ	10♏
5	21Ⅱ	24♎	4♓	25♋	11♐	15♈	27♌	16♑	1Ⅱ	4♎	19♒	7♋	22♏
6	3♋	8♏	19♓	9♌	23♐	28♈	11♍	0♒	13Ⅱ	18♎	3♓	20♋	3♐
7	15♋	21♏	4♈	22♌	5♑	11♉	25♏	13♒	25Ⅱ	2♏	17♓	2♌	15♐
8	27♋	4♐	18♈	4♍	17♑	25♉	10♎	25♒	7♋	16♏	2♈	15♌	27♐
9	9♌	18♐	3♉	17♍	29♑	9Ⅱ	24♎	7♓	19♋	1♐	16♈	27♌	9♑
10	21♌	2♑	18♉	29♍	11♒	23Ⅱ	9♍	19♓	1♌	15♐	0♉	9♏	21♑
11	3♍	16♑	3Ⅱ	11♎	23♒	8♋	23♍	1♈	13♌	0♑	14♉	21♏	4♒
12	15♍	0♒	17Ⅱ	23♎	6♓	22♋	7♐	13♈	26♌	15♑	28♉	3♐	17♒
13	28♍	14♒	1♋	5♏	19♓	7♌	21♐	25♈	9♍	29♑	11Ⅱ	15♐	0♓
14	12♎	28♒	14♋	16♏	2♈	21♌	4♑	6♉	22♍	13♒	23Ⅱ	27♐	14♓
15	26♎	13♓	27♋	28♏	16♈	5♍	17♑	18♉	6♎	27♒	7♋	9♑	28♓
16	10♏	27♓	9♌	10♐	1♉	19♍	29♑	0Ⅱ	21♎	11♓	19♋	21♑	12♈
17	25♏	11♈	22♌	22♐	15♉	3♎	12♒	13Ⅱ	6♏	24♓	1♌	3♐	27♈
18	9♐	25♈	4♏	4♑	0Ⅱ	16♎	24♒	25Ⅱ	21♏	8♈	13♌	16♐	12♉
19	24♐	8♉	16♏	16♑	15Ⅱ	29♎	5♓	7♋	6♌	21♈	25♌	29♐	27♉
20	9♑	22♉	27♏	29♑	0♋	13♍	17♐	20♋	22♌	4♉	7♏	11♑	12Ⅱ
21	24♑	5Ⅱ	9♒	12♒	15♋	25♍	29♐	3♌	7♉	16♉	19♏	25♑	27Ⅱ
22	8♒	18Ⅱ	21♎	25♒	0♌	8♌	11♈	16♌	21♉	29♉	1♎	8♒	12♋
23	22♒	1♋	3♏	8♓	14♌	21♌	23♈	0♏	5♒	11Ⅱ	13♎	22♒	26♋
24	6♓	13♋	16♏	22♓	28♌	3♑	5♉	14♏	19♒	23Ⅱ	26♎	6♓	10♌
25	20♓	25♋	28♏	6♈	11♍	15♑	18♉	28♏	3♓	5♋	8♏	20♓	23♌
26	3♈	7♌	11♐	21♈	24♍	27♑	1Ⅱ	12♎	15♐	17♋	22♏	4♈	6♏
27	16♈	19♌	23♐	6♉	7♎	9♒	14Ⅱ	27♎	28♐	29♋	5♌	19♈	19♏
28	29♈	1♏	7♑	21♉	20♎	21♒	28Ⅱ	12♏	10♈	10♌	19♐	3♉	1♎
29	10♉	13♏	20♑	6Ⅱ	2♏	3♓	11♋	27♏	22♈	22♌	3♑	18♉	13♎
30	24♉	25♏	3♒	21Ⅱ	14♏	15♓	25♋	12♐	4♉	4♏	17♑	3Ⅱ	25♎
31	6Ⅱ	7♎	17♒	6♋	26♏	27♐	9♌	26♐	16♉	17♏	1♒	17Ⅱ	7♏

MAY

	1929	1930	1931	1932	1933	1934	1935	1936	1937	1938	1939	1940	1941
1	4♒	14♊	0♍	24♐	24♋	6♌	21♈	14♏	14♑	27♉	13♎	5♓	5♋
2	16♒	29♊	15♍	6♈	6♌	21♌	6♉	26♏	26♑	12♊	26♎	16♓	17♋
3	29♒	13♋	29♍	18♈	19♌	5♑	20♉	8♎	9♒	27♊	10♍	28♐	0♌
4	12♓	27♋	13♌	0♉	1♏	20♑	3♊	20♎	22♒	11♋	24♍	10♈	13♌
5	25♓	11♌	27♌	12♉	15♏	4♒	17♊	2♍	5♓	26♋	7♎	22♈	26♌
6	8♈	25♌	10♑	24♉	28♏	18♒	0♋	14♍	19♓	10♌	19♎	4♉	10♏
7	22♈	10♍	23♑	6♊	13♎	2♓	12♋	26♍	3♈	24♌	2♏	16♉	24♏
8	7♉	24♍	5♒	18♊	27♎	15♓	25♋	8♐	18♈	7♏	14♏	29♉	9♎
9	21♉	7♎	17♒	0♋	12♍	29♓	7♌	21♐	3♉	21♏	26♏	12♊	24♎
10	6♊	21♎	29♒	12♋	27♍	12♈	19♌	3♑	18♉	4♐	8♏	24♊	9♏
11	21♊	5♏	11♓	25♋	13♌	26♈	0♍	16♑	4♊	17♐	20♏	8♋	24♏
12	6♋	18♏	23♓	8♌	28♌	9♉	12♍	29♑	19♊	0♑	2♒	21♋	9♐
13	21♋	1♐	5♈	21♌	12♑	21♉	24♍	13♒	3♋	12♑	14♒	5♌	24♐
14	5♌	14♐	17♈	5♏	27♑	4♊	6♎	26♒	18♋	24♍	26♓	18♌	9♑
15	19♌	26♐	29♈	19♏	11♒	16♊	19♎	10♐	2♌	6♒	9♈	2♏	23♑
16	3♏	9♑	11♉	3♎	24♒	29♊	1♏	25♐	15♌	18♒	21♈	17♏	6♒
17	16♏	21♑	24♉	18♎	8♓	10♋	14♍	9♈	28♌	0♓	4♉	1♎	19♒
18	29♏	3♒	6♊	3♍	20♓	22♋	27♍	24♈	11♍	12♓	16♉	16♎	2♓
19	12♎	15♒	19♊	18♍	3♈	4♌	11♌	9♉	24♍	24♓	1♊	0♏	14♓
20	25♎	26♒	3♋	3♐	15♈	16♌	24♌	24♉	6♎	6♈	15♊	15♏	26♓
21	7♏	8♓	16♋	18♐	27♈	28♌	8♑	9♊	18♎	18♈	29♊	29♏	8♈
22	19♏	20♓	0♌	3♑	9♉	10♏	22♑	23♊	0♍	0♉	14♋	13♐	20♈
23	1♐	3♈	14♌	17♑	21♉	22♏	6♒	7♋	12♍	13♐	28♋	27♐	2♉
24	13♐	15♈	28♌	1♒	3♊	5♎	20♒	21♋	24♍	26♐	13♌	11♑	14♉
25	25♐	28♈	12♍	14♒	15♊	18♎	4♏	4♌	5♐	9♈	27♌	24♑	26♉
26	7♑	12♉	26♍	27♒	27♊	2♏	18♏	16♌	17♐	22♈	11♏	6♒	8♊
27	19♑	26♉	10♎	9♓	9♋	16♏	3♈	29♌	29♐	7♉	25♏	19♒	20♊
28	1♒	10♊	25♎	21♓	21♋	1♐	17♈	11♑	21♉	9♎	1♓	1♓	2♋
29	13♒	24♊	9♍	3♈	3♌	15♐	1♉	23♑	6♊	22♎	13♓	14♓	14♋
30	25♒	9♋	23♍	15♈	15♌	0♑	15♉	5♒	21♊	6♍	25♓	27♋	27♋
31	7♓	23♋	7♐	27♈	28♌	15♑	28♉	17♎	18♒	6♋	19♍	6♈	10♌

MAY

	1942	1943	1944	1945	1946	1947	1948	1949	1950	1951	1952
1	18♏	4♈	24♌	26♈	9♉	26♏	14♒	16♊	0♏	17♐	4♌
2	3♐	17♈	6♍	8♑	25♉	9♎	26♒	29♊	15♏	0♈	15♌
3	18♐	1♉	18♍	21♑	10♊	22♎	8♓	12♋	0♐	13♈	27♌
4	3♑	14♉	0♎	4♒	25♊	5♍	20♓	26♋	15♐	25♈	9♍
5	18♑	27♉	12♎	17♒	9♋	17♍	2♈	9♌	0♑	7♉	22♍
6	2♒	10♊	24♎	1♐	23♋	0♐	14♈	23♌	15♑	20♉	4♎
7	16♒	22♊	7♍	15♐	7♌	12♐	27♈	7♍	28♑	2♊	17♎
8	29♒	4♋	20♍	0♈	20♌	24♐	10♉	22♍	12♒	14♊	0♏
9	12♓	16♋	3♐	15♈	3♍	6♑	23♉	6♎	25♒	26♊	14♍
10	25♓	28♋	16♐	0♉	16♍	17♑	7♊	21♎	7♓	7♋	28♍
11	8♈	10♌	29♐	15♉	29♍	29♑	21♊	6♏	19♓	19♋	12♐
12	20♈	22♌	13♑	0♊	11♎	11♒	5♋	21♏	1♈	1♌	27♐
13	2♉	4♍	27♑	15♊	23♎	23♒	19♋	5♐	13♈	13♌	11♑
14	15♉	16♍	11♒	29♊	5♍	6♓	3♌	19♐	25♈	26♌	25♑
15	27♉	28♍	25♒	13♋	17♍	18♓	17♌	3♑	7♉	8♍	10♒
16	9♊	11♎	9♓	26♋	29♍	1♈	1♍	17♑	19♉	21♍	24♒
17	20♊	24♎	23♓	9♌	11♐	15♈	16♍	0♒	1♊	5♎	8♓
18	2♋	8♍	7♈	22♌	22♐	29♈	0♎	12♒	13♊	19♎	22♓
19	14♋	22♍	22♈	4♍	4♑	13♉	14♎	24♒	25♊	3♏	5♈
20	26♋	7♐	6♉	16♍	16♑	27♉	27♎	6♓	7♋	18♏	19♈
21	8♌	21♐	20♉	28♍	28♑	12♊	11♍	18♓	19♋	3♐	2♉
22	20♌	6♑	4♊	10♎	11♒	27♊	25♍	0♈	2♌	18♐	15♉
23	3♍	20♑	18♊	22♎	23♒	12♋	8♐	12♈	14♌	3♑	28♉
24	16♍	5♒	1♋	4♍	6♓	26♋	21♐	24♈	28♌	18♑	11♊
25	29♍	19♒	14♋	16♍	20♓	11♌	3♑	6♉	11♍	3♒	23♊
26	13♎	3♓	26♋	28♍	4♈	25♌	16♑	18♉	25♍	17♒	6♋
27	27♎	17♓	8♌	10♐	18♈	9♍	28♑	0♊	9♎	1♓	18♋
28	12♏	1♈	20♌	23♐	3♉	23♍	10♒	13♊	23♎	14♓	0♌
29	27♏	14♈	2♍	5♑	18♉	6♎	22♒	26♊	8♍	27♓	11♌
30	12♐	27♈	14♍	18♑	3♊	19♎	4♓	9♋	24♍	10♈	23♌
31	27♐	10♉	26♍	1♒	18♊	1♍	16♓	23♋	9♐	22♈	5♍

JUNE

	1890	1891	1892	1893	1894	1895	1896	1897	1898	1899	1900	1901	1902
1	17♍	3♈	1♏	1♑	7♉	25♏	21♒	22♊	28♎	18♐	28♋	0♐	4♈
2	1♐	17♈	13♏	13♑	21♉	9♎	3♐	4♋	12♍	1♈	10♌	12♐	18♈
3	16♐	1♉	25♏	25♑	6♊	23♎	15♐	16♋	27♍	15♈	22♌	24♐	3♉
4	0♑	15♉	7♎	8♒	21♊	7♍	27♐	28♋	12♌	28♈	4♏	7♑	18♉
5	15♑	29♉	19♎	20♒	6♋	20♍	9♈	11♌	27♌	12♉	16♏	19♑	3♊
6	0♒	13♊	1♏	3♓	21♋	4♌	20♈	24♌	13♑	25♉	28♏	2♒	18♊
7	14♒	26♊	13♏	16♓	6♌	17♌	2♉	7♍	27♑	7♊	10♎	15♒	3♋
8	29♒	9♋	25♏	29♓	21♌	29♌	15♉	20♍	12♒	20♊	22♎	29♒	18♋
9	13♓	22♋	7♐	13♈	5♍	12♑	27♉	4♎	26♒	2♋	4♏	12♓	3♌
10	27♓	4♌	19♐	27♈	19♍	24♑	9♊	18♎	10♓	14♋	17♍	26♓	17♌
11	10♈	17♌	1♑	11♉	2♎	7♒	22♊	3♍	23♐	26♋	0♐	10♈	1♏
12	24♈	29♌	14♑	27♉	15♎	19♒	5♋	18♍	6♈	8♌	13♐	25♈	14♏
13	7♉	11♏	27♑	12♊	28♎	0♐	19♋	3♐	19♈	20♌	26♐	9♉	27♏
14	20♉	23♏	11♒	27♊	10♍	12♐	2♌	18♐	1♉	2♍	10♑	24♉	10♎
15	2♊	4♐	24♒	12♋	23♍	24♐	16♌	3♑	14♉	14♍	23♑	9♊	22♎
16	15♊	16♐	8♓	27♋	5♌	6♈	0♍	18♑	26♉	26♍	8♒	23♊	4♏
17	27♊	29♐	21♓	11♌	17♌	18♈	13♍	2♒	8♊	8♎	22♒	8♋	16♏
18	9♋	11♑	6♈	25♌	29♌	1♉	28♍	16♒	20♊	21♎	6♓	22♋	28♏
19	21♋	24♑	20♈	9♍	11♎	14♉	12♎	29♒	1♋	4♏	20♓	6♌	10♐
20	3♌	7♐	4♉	22♍	23♎	27♉	26♎	12♐	13♋	17♍	4♈	19♌	21♐
21	15♌	20♐	19♉	4♎	5♏	11♊	10♍	25♐	25♋	1♐	19♈	2♏	3♑
22	26♌	4♑	3♊	17♎	17♏	25♊	25♍	7♈	7♌	16♐	3♉	15♏	15♑
23	8♍	18♑	18♊	29♎	29♏	9♋	9♌	19♈	19♌	0♑	17♉	27♏	27♑
24	20♍	2♒	2♋	11♏	11♐	24♋	23♌	1♉	1♏	15♑	0♊	9♎	10♒
25	3♎	17♒	16♋	23♏	23♐	9♌	7♑	13♉	13♏	0♒	14♊	21♎	22♒
26	15♎	1♐	0♌	4♐	5♑	23♌	20♑	25♉	26♏	15♒	27♊	3♍	5♐
27	28♎	16♐	13♌	16♐	18♈	8♏	3♒	7♊	9♎	29♒	10♋	14♍	17♐
28	11♍	0♈	26♌	28♐	2♉	22♏	16♒	19♊	23♎	14♐	23♋	26♍	0♈
29	25♍	14♈	9♏	10♑	15♉	6♎	29♒	1♋	7♍	28♐	6♌	8♐	14♈
30	9♌	28♈	21♏	22♑	0♊	20♎	11♐	13♋	21♍	12♈	18♑	21♐	28♈

JUNE

	1903	1904	1905	1906	1907	1908	1909	1910	1911	1912	1913	1914	1915
1	26♌	18♑	20♉	25♏	17♒	8♋	10♏	17♐	9♌	28♐	0♉	9♏	0♒
2	10♏	0♒	2♊	9♎	1♐	20♋	23♏	1♈	23♌	10♑	12♉	23♏	14♒
3	23♏	12♒	15♊	24♎	15♐	2♌	5♐	15♈	6♏	22♑	25♉	7♎	27♒
4	7♎	24♒	28♊	9♍	28♐	14♌	18♐	0♉	19♏	3♒	9♊	21♎	10♓
5	20♎	6♓	10♋	24♍	11♑	25♌	1♑	15♉	2♎	15♒	22♊	6♍	23♐
6	3♏	18♓	24♋	9♌	24♑	7♍	15♑	0♊	15♎	27♒	6♋	21♍	5♈
7	15♏	0♈	7♌	24♐	6♉	19♍	29♑	15♊	27♎	9♓	20♋	6♐	17♈
8	28♏	12♈	20♌	9♑	19♉	1♎	12♒	0♋	9♍	21♓	4♌	20♐	29♈
9	10♐	24♈	4♏	24♑	1♊	14♎	26♒	14♋	21♍	4♈	19♌	5♑	11♉
10	22♐	7♉	18♏	8♒	13♊	27♎	10♓	28♋	3♌	17♈	3♏	19♑	23♉
11	4♑	20♉	2♎	22♒	25♊	10♍	25♓	12♌	15♌	0♉	17♏	2♒	5♊
12	16♑	3♊	16♎	5♓	6♋	23♍	9♈	25♌	27♌	13♉	1♎	15♒	17♊
13	28♑	17♊	1♍	18♓	18♋	7♐	23♈	8♏	8♑	28♉	15♎	28♒	29♊
14	10♒	1♋	15♍	0♈	0♌	22♐	7♉	20♏	20♑	12♊	29♎	10♓	11♋
15	22♒	15♋	0♌	12♈	12♌	6♑	22♉	2♎	2♒	27♊	13♍	22♓	23♋
16	4♓	29♋	14♌	24♈	24♌	21♑	6♊	14♎	15♒	12♋	27♍	4♈	5♌
17	16♓	14♌	29♌	6♉	6♍	5♒	19♊	26♎	27♒	27♋	10♐	16♈	18♌
18	28♓	28♌	13♑	18♉	18♍	20♒	3♋	8♏	9♐	12♌	23♐	28♈	0♏
19	11♈	13♏	26♑	0♊	1♎	5♓	16♋	20♏	22♐	27♌	6♑	10♉	13♏
20	24♈	27♏	9♒	12♊	14♎	19♓	29♋	2♐	5♈	11♏	19♑	22♉	26♏
21	7♉	11♎	22♒	24♊	28♎	3♈	11♌	14♐	19♈	25♏	2♒	4♊	10♎
22	21♉	24♎	4♓	6♋	12♍	17♈	24♌	26♐	3♉	8♎	14♒	16♊	24♎
23	6♊	8♏	16♓	18♋	27♍	0♉	6♏	8♑	18♉	22♎	26♒	29♊	9♍
24	21♊	22♏	28♓	0♌	12♐	13♉	18♏	21♑	2♊	5♍	8♐	12♋	24♍
25	6♋	5♌	10♈	13♌	27♐	26♉	0♎	4♒	17♊	17♍	20♐	25♋	9♐
26	21♋	18♐	22♈	26♌	12♑	9♊	12♎	17♒	3♋	0♐	1♈	8♌	24♐
27	6♌	1♑	4♉	8♏	27♑	22♊	24♎	0♐	18♋	12♐	13♈	22♌	9♑
28	21♌	14♑	16♉	22♏	12♒	4♋	6♏	14♐	3♌	24♐	25♈	6♏	24♑
29	6♍	26♑	28♉	5♎	27♒	16♋	18♏	28♐	18♌	6♑	8♉	19♏	8♒
30	20♍	8♒	11♊	19♎	11♐	28♋	1♐	11♈	2♏	18♑	21♉	3♎	22♒

JUNE

	1916	1917	1918	1919	1920	1921	1922	1923	1924	1925	1926	1927	1928
1	18♊	20♎	1♐	20♋	8♉	10♈	23♌	11♑	28♉	29♍	16♒	1♋	19♍
2	0♋	3♏	15♐	4♌	20♐	22♈	7♏	25♑	10♊	12♎	0♋	15♋	0♐
3	12♋	16♏	29♐	18♌	2♑	6♉	22♏	8♒	22♊	26♎	14♋	28♋	12♐
4	23♋	29♏	14♑	1♏	13♑	20♉	6♎	21♒	4♋	10♍	28♋	11♌	24♐
5	5♌	13♐	28♈	13♏	25♑	4♊	20♎	3♐	16♋	24♍	12♈	23♋	6♑
6	17♌	27♐	13♉	26♏	7♒	18♊	4♏	16♐	28♋	9♎	26♈	5♏	18♑
7	29♌	12♑	27♉	8♎	20♒	3♋	18♏	28♐	10♌	24♌	10♋	17♏	1♒
8	11♏	26♑	11♊	20♎	2♐	18♋	2♐	10♈	22♌	9♎	23♋	29♏	14♒
9	24♏	11♒	25♊	2♍	15♐	3♌	15♐	21♈	5♏	24♑	6♊	11♎	26♒
10	7♎	25♒	9♋	13♍	28♐	17♌	29♐	3♉	18♏	9♒	19♊	23♎	10♐
11	20♎	9♓	22♋	25♍	11♈	2♏	12♑	15♉	2♎	23♒	2♋	5♍	23♐
12	4♏	24♓	5♌	7♎	25♈	16♏	25♑	27♉	15♎	7♐	15♋	17♍	7♈
13	18♏	8♈	17♌	19♐	9♋	0♎	7♒	9♊	0♍	21♐	27♋	0♐	21♈
14	3♐	21♈	0♍	1♑	23♉	13♎	19♒	22♊	14♍	5♈	9♌	12♐	6♉
15	18♐	5♉	12♍	13♑	8♊	26♎	1♐	4♋	0♎	18♈	21♌	25♐	21♉
16	3♑	18♉	24♍	26♑	24♊	9♏	13♐	17♋	15♎	1♉	3♏	8♑	6♊
17	18♑	1♊	6♎	9♒	9♋	22♏	25♐	0♌	0♑	13♉	15♏	21♑	21♊
18	3♒	14♊	17♎	22♒	24♋	5♐	7♈	13♌	15♑	26♉	27♏	5♒	5♋
19	18♒	27♊	29♎	5♐	9♌	17♐	19♈	27♌	0♒	8♊	9♎	18♒	20♋
20	2♐	9♋	12♏	18♐	23♌	29♐	1♉	10♏	14♒	20♊	21♎	2♐	4♌
21	16♐	21♋	24♏	2♈	7♏	11♑	14♉	24♏	28♒	2♋	4♍	16♐	18♌
22	0♈	3♌	6♐	16♈	21♏	24♑	26♉	8♎	11♐	14♋	17♍	1♈	2♏
23	13♈	15♌	19♐	1♉	4♎	5♒	10♊	22♎	24♐	25♋	0♎	15♈	15♏
24	26♈	27♌	3♑	15♉	17♎	17♒	23♊	7♍	7♈	7♌	14♐	29♈	27♏
25	8♉	9♏	16♑	0♊	29♎	29♒	7♋	21♍	19♈	19♌	28♐	13♉	10♎
26	21♉	21♏	0♒	15♊	11♍	11♐	21♋	6♌	1♉	1♏	12♑	28♉	22♎
27	3♊	3♐	14♒	29♊	23♍	23♐	5♌	20♐	13♉	13♏	27♑	12♊	3♏
28	15♊	15♎	28♒	14♋	5♐	5♈	20♌	5♑	25♉	25♏	11♒	26♊	15♏
29	27♊	28♎	12♓	28♋	17♐	18♈	4♏	19♑	7♊	8♐	26♒	9♋	27♍
30	9♋	11♍	26♐	12♌	29♐	1♉	18♏	3♒	19♊	21♎	10♐	23♋	9♐

JUNE

	1929	1930	1931	1932	1933	1934	1935	1936	1937	1938	1939	1940	1941
1	20♐	8♌	21♐	9♉	10♍	0♎	12♊	29♎	1♓	21♋	2♌	18♈	23♌
2	3♈	22♌	5♑	20♉	23♏	14♎	25♊	11♍	15♐	6♌	15♌	0♉	6♏
3	17♈	6♏	18♑	2♊	7♎	28♎	8♋	23♍	28♐	20♌	28♌	13♉	20♏
4	1♉	20♏	1♒	15♊	21♎	12♐	20♋	5♌	12♈	4♏	10♑	25♉	4♎
5	15♉	4♎	13♒	27♊	6♏	26♐	3♌	17♐	27♈	18♏	22♑	8♊	18♎
6	0♊	18♎	25♒	9♋	20♏	9♑	15♌	0♑	12♉	1♎	4♒	21♊	3♏
7	15♊	1♏	7♐	22♋	6♐	23♈	27♌	13♑	27♉	14♎	16♒	4♋	18♏
8	0♋	14♏	19♐	5♌	21♐	5♉	8♏	26♑	12♊	27♎	28♒	18♋	3♐
9	15♋	27♏	1♈	18♌	6♑	18♉	20♏	10♒	27♊	9♏	10♐	1♌	18♐
10	0♌	10♐	13♈	1♏	21♑	1♊	2♎	23♒	12♋	21♏	22♐	15♌	2♑
11	15♌	22♐	25♈	15♏	6♒	13♊	14♎	7♐	26♋	3♌	4♈	29♌	17♑
12	29♌	5♑	7♉	29♏	20♒	25♊	27♎	21♐	10♌	15♐	17♈	13♍	1♒
13	13♍	17♑	19♉	13♎	4♓	7♋	9♍	5♐	24♌	27♐	29♈	27♍	15♒
14	26♍	29♑	2♊	27♎	17♓	19♋	22♍	20♈	7♏	9♑	12♉	12♎	28♒
15	9♎	11♒	15♊	12♏	0♈	1♌	6♐	4♉	20♏	21♑	26♉	26♎	10♓
16	22♎	23♒	29♊	27♏	12♈	12♌	20♐	19♉	3♎	3♒	10♊	10♏	23♓
17	4♏	5♓	12♋	12♐	25♈	24♌	4♑	3♊	15♎	15♒	24♊	24♏	5♈
18	16♏	16♓	26♋	26♐	7♉	6♏	18♑	17♊	27♎	27♒	9♋	8♐	17♈
19	28♏	29♓	10♌	11♑	19♉	18♏	2♒	1♋	9♏	9♓	24♋	22♐	29♈
20	10♐	11♈	25♌	25♑	0♊	1♎	17♒	15♋	21♏	21♏	8♌	5♑	10♉
21	22♐	23♈	9♏	9♒	12♊	13♎	1♓	29♋	2♌	4♈	23♌	19♑	22♉
22	4♑	6♉	23♏	22♒	24♊	27♎	15♓	12♌	14♌	17♈	8♏	2♒	4♊
23	16♑	20♉	7♎	5♓	6♋	10♍	29♓	24♌	26♌	1♉	22♏	14♒	16♊
24	27♑	4♊	21♎	17♓	18♋	24♍	14♈	7♏	8♑	15♉	6♎	27♒	29♊
25	9♒	18♊	5♏	29♓	0♌	9♎	27♈	19♏	20♑	29♉	19♎	9♐	11♋
26	22♒	3♋	19♏	11♈	12♌	24♎	11♉	1♎	3♒	14♊	3♏	21♐	24♋
27	4♓	18♋	3♐	23♈	24♌	9♑	25♉	13♎	15♒	29♊	16♏	3♈	7♌
28	16♓	3♌	16♐	5♉	7♍	24♑	8♊	25♎	28♒	15♋	29♏	14♈	20♌
29	29♓	18♌	0♑	17♉	20♍	9♒	21♊	7♏	11♓	0♌	12♐	26♈	3♏
30	12♈	2♏	13♑	29♉	3♎	24♒	4♋	19♍	25♓	15♌	24♐	8♉	16♏

JUNE

	1942	1943	1944	1945	1946	1947	1948	1949	1950	1951	1952
1	12♑	23♉	8♎	14≈	3♋	14♏	28♐	6♌	24♐	4♉	17♏
2	27♑	6♊	20♎	28≈	18♋	26♏	10♈	20♌	9♑	17♉	29♏
3	12≈	18♊	3♏	12♐	2♌	8♐	22≈	4♏	23♑	29♉	12♎
4	26≈	0♋	15♏	26♐	16♌	20♐	5♉	18♏	7≈	11♊	25♎
5	9♓	12♋	28♏	10♈	0♏	2♑	18♉	2♎	20≈	22♊	9♏
6	22♓	24♋	12♐	25♈	13♏	14♑	2♊	16♎	3♓	4♋	22♏
7	5♈	6♌	25♐	9♉	25♏	26♑	16♊	1♏	16♓	16♋	7♐
8	17♈	18♌	9♑	24♉	8♎	8≈	0♋	15♏	28♓	28♋	21♐
9	0♉	0♍	23♑	9♊	20♎	20≈	14♋	29♏	10♈	10♌	6♑
10	12♉	12♍	7≈	23♊	2♏	2♓	29♋	14♐	22♈	22♌	21♑
11	24♉	24♍	21≈	7♋	14♏	14♓	14♌	28♐	4♉	4♍	6≈
12	6♊	6♎	6♓	21♋	26♏	27♓	28♌	11♑	16♉	17♍	20≈
13	17♊	19♎	20♓	4♌	8♐	10♈	12♍	25♑	28♉	0♎	4♓
14	29♊	3♏	4♈	17♌	19♐	23♈	26♏	7≈	10♊	13♎	18♓
15	11♋	16♏	18♈	0♍	1♑	7♉	10♎	20≈	22♊	27♎	2♈
16	23♋	1♐	2♉	12♍	13♑	21♉	24♎	2♓	4♋	11♍	16♈
17	5♌	15♐	16♉	25♍	25♑	6♊	7♏	14♓	16♋	26♍	29♈
18	17♌	0♑	0♊	7♎	8≈	21♊	21♏	26♓	29♋	11♐	12♉
19	29♌	15♑	13♊	18♎	20≈	6♋	4♐	8♈	12♌	27♐	25♉
20	12♍	0≈	26♊	0♍	3♓	21♋	17♐	20♈	24♌	12♑	8♊
21	25♍	15≈	9♋	12♍	16♓	6♌	29♐	2♉	8♍	27♑	20♊
22	8♎	29≈	22♋	24♍	0♈	21♌	12♑	14♉	21♏	12≈	2♋
23	22♎	13♓	4♌	6♏	13♈	5♍	24♑	26♉	5♎	26≈	14♋
24	6♏	27♓	16♌	19♏	27♈	19♍	6≈	9♊	19♎	10♓	26♋
25	20♏	11♈	28♌	2♑	12♉	3♎	18≈	22♊	3♍	24♓	8♌
26	5♐	24♈	10♍	15♑	26♉	16♎	0♓	5♋	18♍	7♈	20♌
27	20♐	7♉	22♍	28♑	11♊	28♎	12♓	19♋	3♐	19♈	2♍
28	6♑	20♉	4♎	11≈	26♊	11♏	24♓	3♌	17♐	2♉	13♍
29	21♑	3♊	16♎	25≈	11♋	23♏	6♈	17♌	2♑	14♉	25♍
30	6≈	15♊	28♎	8♓	26♋	5♐	18♈	1♏	17♑	26♉	8♎

JULY

	1890	1891	1892	1893	1894	1895	1896	1897	1898	1899	1900	1901	1902
1	24♐	12♉	3♎	5♒	15♊	3♏	23♐	25♋	6♌	25♈	0♏	3♑	12♉
2	9♑	25♉	15♎	17♒	0♋	17♏	5♈	8♌	21♌	9♉	12♏	16♑	26♉
3	24♑	9♊	27♎	0♓	15♋	0♐	16♈	21♌	6♑	22♉	24♏	29♑	11♊
4	9♒	22♊	9♏	13♓	0♌	13♐	28♈	4♏	21♑	4♊	6♎	12♒	26♊
5	24♒	5♋	21♏	26♓	15♌	26♐	10♉	17♏	6♒	17♊	18♎	26♒	12♋
6	9♓	18♋	3♐	9♈	0♏	8♑	23♉	1♎	21♒	29♊	0♏	9♓	27♋
7	23♓	0♌	15♐	23♈	14♏	21♑	5♊	14♎	5♓	11♋	12♏	23♓	11♌
8	7♈	13♌	28♐	7♉	28♏	3♒	18♊	29♎	19♓	23♋	25♏	7♈	26♌
9	21♈	25♌	10♑	21♉	12♎	15♒	1♋	13♏	2♈	5♌	8♐	21♈	10♏
10	4♉	7♏	24♑	6♊	25♎	27♒	14♋	27♏	16♈	17♌	21♐	5♉	23♏
11	17♉	19♏	7♒	21♊	7♏	9♓	28♋	12♐	28♈	28♌	5♑	19♉	6♎
12	29♉	1♎	21♒	6♋	20♏	20♓	12♌	27♐	11♉	10♏	19♑	4♊	18♎
13	12♊	12♎	4♓	20♋	2♐	2♈	26♌	11♑	23♉	22♏	3♒	18♊	1♏
14	24♊	24♎	18♓	5♌	14♐	14♈	10♏	26♑	5♊	4♎	17♒	2♋	13♏
15	6♋	7♏	2♈	20♌	26♐	26♈	24♏	10♒	17♊	17♎	2♓	16♋	25♏
16	18♋	19♏	16♈	4♏	8♑	9♉	9♎	24♒	28♊	29♎	17♓	0♌	6♐
17	0♌	2♐	1♉	17♏	20♑	22♉	23♎	7♓	10♋	12♏	1♈	14♌	18♐
18	11♌	15♐	15♉	0♎	2♒	5♊	7♏	20♓	22♋	26♏	15♈	27♌	0♑
19	23♌	29♐	29♉	13♎	14♒	19♊	21♏	3♈	4♌	9♐	0♉	10♏	12♑
20	5♏	13♑	13♊	25♎	26♒	3♋	5♐	15♈	16♌	24♐	13♉	23♏	24♑
21	17♏	27♑	27♊	7♏	8♓	18♋	19♐	27♈	28♌	8♑	27♉	5♎	7♒
22	29♏	12♒	11♋	19♏	20♐	3♌	2♑	9♉	10♏	23♑	10♊	17♎	19♒
23	11♎	27♒	25♋	1♐	2♈	18♌	16♑	21♉	23♏	9♒	24♊	29♎	2♓
24	24♎	11♓	8♌	13♐	15♈	3♏	29♑	3♊	6♎	24♒	6♋	11♏	14♐
25	7♏	26♓	21♌	25♐	28♈	18♏	12♒	15♊	19♎	9♓	19♋	22♏	27♐
26	20♏	11♈	4♏	7♑	11♉	2♎	24♒	27♊	2♏	24♐	2♌	4♐	11♑
27	4♐	25♈	17♏	19♑	24♉	16♎	7♓	9♋	16♏	8♈	14♌	16♐	24♈
28	18♐	9♉	29♏	1♒	9♊	0♏	19♓	22♋	0♐	22♈	26♌	29♐	8♉
29	2♑	22♉	11♎	14♒	23♊	14♏	1♈	4♌	14♐	5♉	9♏	12♑	22♉
30	17♑	6♊	23♎	27♒	8♋	27♏	13♈	17♌	29♐	18♉	21♏	25♑	6♊
31	2♒	19♊	5♏	10♓	23♋	10♐	24♈	0♏	14♑	1♊	2♎	8♒	21♊

JULY

	1903	1904	1905	1906	1907	1908	1909	1910	1911	1912	1913	1914	1915
1	3♎	20♒	24♊	3♍	25♐	10♌	14♐	26♈	15♏	0♎	4♊	18♎	6♐
2	17♎	2♓	7♋	18♍	8♈	22♌	27♐	10♉	29♏	12♎	17♊	2♍	19♐
3	0♏	14♓	20♋	3♐	21♈	4♍	10♑	24♉	11♐	24♎	1♋	16♍	2♈
4	12♏	26♓	3♌	18♐	3♉	16♍	24♑	9♊	24♊	6♐	15♋	1♐	14♈
5	25♏	8♈	17♌	3♑	16♉	28♍	8♒	24♊	6♏	18♐	0♌	15♐	26♈
6	7♐	20♈	1♍	17♑	28♉	10♎	23♒	8♋	18♏	0♐	14♌	29♐	8♉
7	19♐	2♉	15♍	2♒	10♊	22♎	7♓	22♋	0♐	12♐	29♌	13♑	20♉
8	1♑	15♉	29♍	16♒	22♊	5♍	21♓	6♌	12♐	25♈	14♍	27♑	2♊
9	13♑	28♉	13♎	0♓	3♋	18♍	6♈	20♌	23♐	8♉	28♍	10♒	14♊
10	25♑	11♊	27♎	13♓	15♋	2♌	20♈	3♍	5♑	22♉	12♎	23♒	26♊
11	7♒	25♊	11♍	26♓	27♋	15♐	4♉	16♍	17♑	6♊	26♎	6♓	8♋
12	19♒	9♋	26♍	8♈	9♌	0♑	18♉	28♍	29♑	20♊	10♍	18♓	20♋
13	1♓	24♋	10♐	21♈	21♌	15♑	2♊	10♎	12♒	5♋	23♍	0♈	2♌
14	13♓	9♌	24♐	3♉	3♍	0♒	15♊	23♎	24♒	21♋	7♎	12♈	15♌
15	25♓	24♌	8♑	15♉	15♍	15♒	29♊	4♍	6♓	6♌	20♎	24♈	27♌
16	7♈	8♍	21♑	27♉	28♍	0♓	12♋	16♍	19♓	21♌	3♏	6♉	10♍
17	20♈	23♍	4♒	8♊	11♎	15♓	25♋	28♍	2♈	6♏	15♐	18♉	23♍
18	3♉	7♎	17♒	20♊	24♎	29♓	7♌	10♐	15♈	20♏	28♐	0♊	7♎
19	16♉	21♎	0♓	2♋	7♍	13♈	20♌	22♐	29♈	5♐	10♑	12♊	20♎
20	0♊	5♏	12♓	15♋	21♍	27♈	2♍	5♑	13♉	18♐	22♑	25♊	4♏
21	14♊	19♏	24♓	27♋	6♌	10♉	14♍	17♑	27♉	1♏	4♒	8♋	19♏
22	29♊	2♐	6♈	10♌	20♐	28♉	26♍	0♒	11♊	14♏	16♒	21♋	3♐
23	14♌	15♐	18♈	22♌	5♑	6♊	8♎	13♒	26♊	27♏	28♐	4♌	18♐
24	0♍	28♐	0♉	5♍	20♑	19♊	20♎	27♒	11♋	9♐	9♈	18♌	3♑
25	15♍	10♑	12♉	19♍	5♒	1♋	2♍	11♓	26♋	21♐	21♈	2♍	17♑
26	0♎	23♑	24♉	2♎	20♒	13♋	14♍	24♒	11♌	3♑	3♉	16♍	2♒
27	15♎	5♒	6♊	16♎	5♓	25♋	26♍	8♈	26♌	15♑	16♉	0♎	16♒
28	29♎	17♒	19♊	0♏	19♓	7♌	9♐	22♈	10♍	27♑	29♉	14♎	0♓
29	13♏	29♒	2♋	14♍	3♈	19♌	22♐	6♉	24♍	9♒	12♊	29♎	14♓
30	26♏	11♓	15♋	28♍	17♈	0♏	5♑	21♉	7♎	21♒	25♊	13♍	27♓
31	9♍	22♓	29♋	13♐	0♉	12♏	19♑	5♊	20♎	3♓	9♋	27♍	10♈

JULY

	1916	1917	1918	1919	1920	1921	1922	1923	1924	1925	1926	1927	1928
1	20♋	24♍	10♈	26♌	10♑	14♌	3♎	16♒	1♋	4♍	25♐	6♌	21♐
2	2♌	8♐	25♈	9♏	22♑	28♌	17♎	29♒	13♋	18♍	9♈	19♌	3♑
3	14♌	22♐	9♉	22♏	4♎	12♊	1♏	11♎	25♋	3♐	23♈	1♏	15♑
4	26♌	6♑	23♉	4♎	17♎	27♊	14♏	24♎	7♌	18♐	6♉	13♏	28♑
5	8♍	21♑	7♊	16♎	29♎	12♋	28♏	6♐	20♌	3♑	20♉	25♏	11♒
6	20♍	6♒	20♊	28♎	11♐	27♋	11♐	18♐	2♏	18♑	3♊	7♎	23♒
7	3♎	20♒	4♋	10♏	24♐	12♌	25♐	29♐	15♏	3♒	16♊	19♎	7♐
8	16♎	5♐	17♋	22♍	7♈	27♋	8♑	11♉	28♍	18♒	28♊	1♏	20♐
9	29♎	20♐	0♌	4♐	20♈	12♍	21♑	23♉	11♎	3♐	11♋	13♏	4♈
10	13♍	4♈	13♌	16♐	4♉	26♍	3♎	5♊	25♎	17♐	23♋	25♏	17♈
11	27♍	18♈	25♌	28♐	18♉	10♎	15♎	18♊	9♍	1♈	5♌	8♌	2♉
12	11♐	2♉	8♏	10♑	2♊	23♎	28♎	0♋	24♍	14♈	17♌	20♐	16♉
13	26♐	15♉	20♏	23♑	17♊	6♏	9♐	13♋	9♐	27♈	29♌	3♑	0♊
14	11♑	28♉	2♎	5♒	2♋	19♍	21♐	26♋	24♐	10♉	11♏	17♑	15♊
15	27♑	11♊	13♎	19♒	17♋	2♐	3♐	10♌	9♑	23♉	23♏	1♒	29♊
16	12♒	23♊	25♎	2♐	2♌	14♐	15♐	23♌	23♑	5♊	5♎	15♒	14♋
17	26♒	6♋	7♏	15♐	17♌	26♐	27♐	7♏	8♒	17♊	17♎	29♒	28♋
18	11♓	18♋	19♏	29♐	2♏	8♑	9♉	21♏	22♒	29♊	29♎	13♐	13♌
19	25♓	0♌	2♐	13♈	16♏	20♑	21♉	5♎	6♓	11♋	12♍	27♐	26♌
20	9♈	12♌	15♐	27♈	0♎	2♒	4♊	19♎	20♐	23♋	25♍	12♈	10♍
21	22♈	24♌	28♐	11♉	13♎	14♒	18♊	3♏	3♏	4♌	8♐	26♈	23♍
22	5♉	6♏	11♑	25♉	25♎	26♒	1♋	17♏	15♏	16♌	22♐	10♉	5♎
23	18♉	17♏	25♑	10♊	8♍	8♓	16♋	2♐	28♏	28♌	6♑	24♉	18♎
24	0♊	29♏	9♒	24♊	20♍	20♐	0♌	16♐	10♌	10♍	21♑	8♊	0♏
25	12♊	11♎	23♒	8♋	2♐	2♈	15♌	0♑	22♌	22♍	5♒	22♊	12♏
26	24♊	24♎	8♓	23♋	14♐	14♈	29♌	14♑	4♎	5♎	20♒	5♋	23♏
27	6♋	6♍	22♓	7♌	26♐	27♈	14♏	28♑	16♎	17♎	5♓	18♋	5♐
28	17♋	19♍	7♈	20♌	7♑	9♉	29♏	11♒	28♎	0♐	20♓	1♌	17♐
29	29♋	2♐	21♈	4♏	19♑	23♉	13♎	24♒	10♎	14♏	5♈	14♌	29♐
30	11♌	16♐	5♉	17♏	1♒	6♊	27♎	7♓	22♎	27♏	19♈	27♌	12♑
31	23♌	0♑	19♉	0♎	14♒	20♊	11♍	19♓	4♌	12♐	3♉	9♏	24♑

	1929	1930	1931	1932	1933	1934	1935	1936	1937	1938	1939	1940	1941
1	25♈	17♏	26♑	11♊	16♎	8♓	16♋	1♐	8♈	29♌	6♑	21♉	0♎
2	9♉	1♎	9♒	23♊	0♏	22♐	29♋	13♐	22♈	14♏	19♑	3♊	14♎
3	23♉	15♎	21♒	6♋	15♏	6♈	11♋	26♐	6♉	27♏	1♒	16♊	28♎
4	8♊	28♎	3♓	19♋	29♏	19♈	23♋	9♑	21♉	11♎	13♒	0♋	13♏
5	23♊	11♏	15♓	2♌	14♐	2♉	5♏	22♑	6♊	23♎	25♒	13♋	27♏
6	8♋	24♏	27♓	15♌	29♐	15♉	16♏	6♒	20♊	6♏	6♓	27♋	12♐
7	24♋	7♐	9♈	28♌	15♑	0♊	28♏	20♒	5♋	18♏	18♓	11♌	26♐
8	9♌	19♐	21♈	12♏	0♒	10♊	10♎	4♓	20♋	0♐	0♈	26♌	11♑
9	24♌	1♑	3♉	26♏	14♒	22♊	22♎	18♓	4♌	12♐	12♈	10♏	25♑
10	8♏	13♑	15♉	9♎	28♒	4♋	5♏	2♈	19♌	24♐	25♈	24♏	9♒
11	22♏	25♑	27♉	23♎	12♓	16♋	17♏	16♈	2♏	6♑	7♉	8♎	23♒
12	5♎	7♒	10♊	8♏	26♓	28♋	1♐	0♉	16♏	18♑	21♉	23♎	6♓
13	18♎	19♒	24♊	22♏	9♈	9♌	14♐	15♉	29♏	0♒	4♊	7♏	19♓
14	1♏	1♓	7♋	7♐	21♈	21♌	28♐	29♉	11♎	12♒	18♊	20♏	1♈
15	13♏	13♓	22♋	21♐	3♉	3♏	12♑	13♊	23♎	24♒	3♋	4♐	13♈
16	25♏	25♓	6♌	5♑	15♉	15♏	27♑	27♊	5♏	6♓	17♋	18♐	25♈
17	7♐	7♈	20♌	19♑	27♉	27♏	11♒	10♋	17♏	18♓	3♌	1♑	7♉
18	19♐	19♈	5♏	3♒	9♊	10♎	26♒	24♋	29♏	1♈	18♌	14♑	19♉
19	1♑	2♉	19♏	17♒	21♊	22♎	11♓	7♌	11♐	14♈	3♏	27♑	1♊
20	13♑	15♉	4♎	0♓	3♋	5♏	26♓	20♌	23♐	27♈	18♏	10♒	13♊
21	25♑	28♉	18♎	13♓	15♋	19♏	10♈	2♏	5♑	10♉	2♎	23♒	25♊
22	7♒	12♊	2♏	25♓	27♋	3♐	24♈	15♏	17♑	24♉	16♎	5♓	7♋
23	19♒	26♊	16♏	7♈	9♌	17♐	8♉	27♏	0♏	8♊	0♏	17♓	20♋
24	1♓	11♋	0♐	19♈	22♌	2♑	22♉	9♎	12♐	23♊	13♏	29♓	3♌
25	13♓	26♋	13♐	1♉	4♏	17♑	5♊	21♎	25♐	8♋	26♏	10♈	16♌
26	26♓	12♌	26♐	13♉	17♏	2♒	18♊	3♏	8♑	23♋	9♐	22♈	0♏
27	9♈	27♌	9♑	25♉	0♎	18♒	0♋	15♏	22♑	8♌	21♐	4♉	13♏
28	22♈	12♏	22♑	7♊	13♎	3♓	13♋	27♏	5♒	23♌	3♑	16♉	27♏
29	5♉	26♏	5♒	19♊	27♎	17♓	25♋	9♐	19♈	8♏	15♑	29♉	11♎
30	19♉	11♎	17♒	2♋	10♏	2♈	7♌	21♐	3♉	22♏	27♑	11♊	25♎
31	3♊	25♎	29♒	14♋	25♏	15♈	19♌	4♑	17♉	6♎	9♒	24♊	9♏

JULY

	1942	1943	1944	1945	1946	1947	1948	1949	1950	1951	1952
1	20♒	27♊	11♍	22♐	11♌	17♐	0♋	15♏	1♎	8♊	20♎
2	4♓	9♋	23♍	6♈	25♌	29♐	13♉	29♏	15♒	20♊	3♏
3	18♓	21♋	7♐	21♈	8♍	11♑	26♉	13♎	29♒	1♋	17♏
4	1♈	3♌	20♐	5♉	21♍	23♑	10♊	27♎	12♓	13♋	1♐
5	14♈	15♌	4♑	19♉	4♎	5♒	24♊	11♍	24♓	25♋	15♐
6	26♈	26♌	18♑	4♊	17♎	17♒	9♋	25♏	7♈	7♌	0♑
7	9♉	8♍	3♒	18♊	29♎	29♒	24♋	9♐	19♈	19♌	15♑
8	21♉	20♏	17♒	2♋	11♍	11♓	8♌	23♐	1♉	1♏	0♒
9	3♊	2♎	2♓	16♋	23♍	23♓	23♌	6♑	12♉	14♏	15♒
10	14♊	15♎	16♓	29♋	4♐	6♈	8♍	20♑	24♉	26♏	0♓
11	26♊	28♎	1♈	13♌	16♐	18♈	23♍	3♒	6♊	9♎	14♓
12	8♋	11♏	15♈	25♌	28♐	2♉	7♎	16♒	18♊	23♎	29♓
13	20♋	25♏	29♈	8♍	10♑	15♉	21♎	28♒	0♋	6♏	12♈
14	2♌	9♐	13♉	20♍	22♑	0♊	4♍	10♓	13♋	21♏	26♈
15	14♌	23♐	26♉	3♎	5♒	14♊	18♍	22♓	25♋	5♐	9♉
16	27♌	8♑	10♊	15♎	17♒	29♊	1♐	4♈	8♌	20♐	22♉
17	9♍	23♑	23♊	26♎	0♓	14♋	13♐	16♈	21♌	5♑	5♊
18	22♍	9♒	5♋	8♏	13♓	29♋	26♐	28♈	5♏	20♑	17♊
19	5♎	24♒	18♋	20♏	26♓	14♌	8♑	10♉	18♏	5♒	29♊
20	18♎	9♓	0♌	2♐	10♈	29♌	21♑	22♉	1♎	20♒	11♋
21	1♏	23♓	12♌	15♐	24♈	14♍	3♒	4♊	15♎	5♓	23♋
22	15♏	7♈	24♌	27♐	8♉	28♍	15♒	17♊	29♎	19♓	5♌
23	0♐	21♈	6♍	10♑	22♉	12♎	27♒	0♋	14♏	2♈	17♌
24	14♐	4♉	18♍	23♑	6♊	25♎	8♓	14♋	28♏	15♈	28♌
25	29♐	17♉	0♎	7♒	21♊	8♏	20♓	28♋	12♐	28♈	10♍
26	14♑	0♊	12♎	21♒	5♋	20♏	2♈	12♌	27♐	10♉	22♍
27	29♑	12♊	24♎	5♓	20♋	2♐	14♈	26♌	11♑	23♉	4♎
28	14♒	24♊	6♍	19♓	5♌	14♐	26♈	11♍	26♑	5♊	17♎
29	28♒	6♋	19♍	3♈	19♌	26♐	9♉	25♏	10♒	16♊	29♎
30	13♓	18♋	1♐	17♈	3♏	8♑	21♉	10♎	23♒	28♊	12♍
31	26♓	0♌	15♐	2♉	16♏	20♑	5♊	24♎	7♓	10♋	25♍

AUGUST

	1890	1891	1892	1893	1894	1895	1896	1897	1898	1899	1900	1901	1902
1	18♒	2♋	17♍	23♓	9♌	23♐	6♉	14♏	29♑	14♊	14♎	22♒	6♋
2	3♓	14♋	29♍	6♈	24♌	5♑	18♊	27♏	14♎	26♊	26♎	5♓	20♋
3	18♓	27♋	11♐	19♈	9♍	17♑	1♊	11♎	29♎	8♋	8♍	20♓	5♌
4	2♈	9♌	23♐	3♉	23♍	0♒	13♊	25♎	13♓	20♋	20♍	4♈	20♌
5	17♈	21♌	6♑	17♉	7♎	12♒	26♊	9♍	27♓	2♌	3♐	18♈	4♍
6	0♉	3♍	19♑	1♊	21♎	24♒	9♋	24♍	11♈	14♌	16♐	2♉	18♍
7	13♉	15♍	2♒	16♊	4♍	5♓	23♋	8♌	24♈	25♌	29♐	16♉	1♎
8	26♉	27♍	16♒	0♋	16♍	17♓	7♌	22♐	7♉	7♍	13♑	0♊	14♎
9	9♊	9♎	0♓	15♋	29♍	29♓	21♌	6♑	19♉	19♍	27♑	14♊	27♎
10	21♊	21♎	14♓	29♋	11♐	11♈	5♍	21♑	1♊	1♎	12♒	28♊	9♍
11	3♋	3♍	29♓	14♌	23♐	23♈	20♍	5♒	13♊	13♎	26♒	12♋	21♍
12	15♋	15♍	13♈	28♌	5♑	5♉	5♎	18♒	25♊	26♎	11♓	26♋	3♐
13	27♋	27♍	27♈	12♏	17♑	18♉	19♎	2♓	7♊	8♍	26♓	9♌	15♐
14	8♌	10♐	12♉	25♏	29♑	0♊	4♍	15♓	19♊	21♍	11♈	22♌	27♐
15	20♌	23♐	26♉	8♎	11♒	14♊	18♍	28♓	1♌	4♐	26♈	5♍	9♑
16	2♍	7♑	10♊	21♎	23♒	27♊	2♐	11♈	13♌	18♐	10♉	18♍	21♑
17	14♍	21♑	23♊	3♍	5♓	12♋	16♐	23♈	25♌	2♒	24♉	1♎	3♒
18	26♍	5♒	7♋	15♍	17♓	26♋	29♐	5♉	7♍	17♑	7♊	13♎	15♒
19	8♎	20♒	21♋	27♍	29♓	11♌	12♑	17♉	20♍	2♒	21♊	25♎	28♒
20	21♎	5♓	4♌	9♐	12♈	26♌	25♑	29♉	3♎	17♒	3♋	7♍	11♓
21	3♍	21♓	17♌	21♐	24♈	11♍	8♒	11♊	16♎	2♓	16♋	18♍	24♓
22	16♍	6♈	0♍	3♑	7♉	26♍	20♒	23♊	29♎	17♓	29♋	0♐	7♈
23	29♍	20♈	13♍	15♑	21♉	11♎	3♓	5♋	13♍	2♈	11♌	12♐	21♈
24	13♐	5♉	25♍	27♑	4♊	26♎	15♓	17♋	26♍	17♈	23♌	24♐	5♉
25	27♐	19♉	7♎	10♒	18♊	10♍	27♓	0♌	10♐	1♉	5♍	7♑	18♉
26	11♑	3♊	19♎	23♒	3♋	24♍	9♈	13♌	25♐	15♉	17♍	20♑	2♊
27	26♑	16♊	1♍	6♓	17♋	7♐	21♈	26♌	9♑	28♉	29♍	3♒	17♊
28	11♒	29♊	13♍	19♓	2♌	20♐	3♉	10♍	23♑	10♊	11♎	17♒	1♋
29	26♒	11♋	25♍	2♈	17♌	2♑	15♉	23♍	8♒	23♊	23♎	1♐	15♋
30	11♓	24♋	7♐	16♈	2♍	15♑	27♉	8♎	23♒	5♋	5♍	15♐	0♌
31	26♓	6♌	19♐	0♉	17♍	27♑	9♊	22♎	7♒	17♋	17♍	29♓	14♌

	1903	1904	1905	1906	1907	1908	1909	1910	1911	1912	1913	1914	1915
1	22♏	4♈	13♌	27♐	12♉	24♏	3♒	19♊	2♏	15♐	24♋	11♐	22♈
2	4♐	16♈	27♌	12♑	25♉	6♏	18♒	3♋	15♏	27♐	9♌	25♐	4♉
3	16♐	28♈	11♍	26♑	7♊	18♎	2♓	17♋	27♏	9♈	24♌	9♑	16♌
4	28♐	10♉	25♍	10♒	19♊	1♏	17♓	1♌	8♐	21♈	9♏	22♑	28♉
5	10♑	23♉	10♎	24♒	0♋	13♏	2♈	15♌	20♐	4♉	23♏	5♒	10♊
6	22♑	6♊	24♎	8♓	12♋	26♏	16♈	28♌	2♑	17♉	8♎	18♒	22♊
7	4♒	19♊	8♏	21♓	24♋	10♐	1♉	11♏	14♑	1♊	22♎	1♓	4♋
8	16♒	3♋	22♏	4♈	6♌	24♐	15♉	24♏	26♑	15♊	6♏	14♓	16♋
9	28♒	18♋	6♐	16♈	18♌	8♑	29♉	6♎	8♒	29♊	20♏	26♓	29♋
10	10♓	2♌	20♐	29♈	0♍	23♑	12♊	18♎	21♒	14♋	4♐	8♈	11♌
11	22♓	17♌	4♑	10♉	12♍	8♒	25♊	0♏	3♓	29♋	17♐	20♈	24♌
12	4♈	3♍	17♑	23♉	25♍	23♒	8♋	12♏	16♓	14♌	29♐	2♉	7♏
13	17♈	18♍	0♒	5♊	8♎	8♓	21♋	24♏	29♓	0♏	12♑	14♉	20♏
14	29♈	3♎	13♒	16♊	21♎	24♓	4♌	6♐	12♈	15♏	24♑	26♉	4♐
15	12♉	17♎	26♒	28♊	4♍	8♈	16♌	18♐	26♈	29♏	7♒	8♊	17♎
16	26♉	1♍	8♏	11♋	17♏	23♈	28♌	0♑	9♒	13♎	19♎	20♊	1♍
17	9♊	15♍	20♏	23♋	1♐	7♉	10♍	13♑	23♉	27♎	1♐	3♎	15♍
18	24♊	29♍	2♈	6♌	15♐	20♉	22♍	26♑	7♊	10♏	13♐	16♎	29♍
19	8♋	12♐	14♈	18♌	0♑	3♊	4♎	9♒	21♊	23♏	24♐	29♎	14♌
20	23♋	25♐	26♈	2♍	14♑	16♊	16♎	22♒	6♋	6♐	6♑	13♌	28♌
21	8♌	7♑	8♉	15♍	29♑	28♊	28♎	6♓	21♋	18♐	18♑	27♌	12♑
22	23♌	20♑	20♉	29♍	14♒	10♋	10♏	20♓	5♌	0♑	0♒	11♏	27♑
23	8♍	2♒	2♊	13♎	29♒	22♋	22♏	5♈	20♌	12♑	12♉	26♏	11♒
24	23♍	14♒	14♊	27♎	13♓	4♌	4♐	19♈	4♏	24♑	24♉	10♎	25♒
25	7♎	26♒	27♊	11♏	28♓	16♌	17♐	3♉	18♏	6♒	7♊	25♎	8♓
26	21♎	7♓	10♋	25♏	12♈	28♌	0♑	17♉	2♎	18♒	20♊	9♏	22♓
27	5♏	19♓	23♋	9♐	25♈	9♍	13♑	2♊	15♎	0♓	4♋	24♏	5♈
28	18♏	1♈	7♌	23♐	8♉	21♍	27♑	16♊	28♎	12♓	18♋	8♐	18♈
29	1♐	13♈	21♌	8♑	21♉	3♎	11♒	0♋	10♏	24♓	2♌	22♐	0♉
30	13♐	25♈	5♏	22♑	3♊	15♎	26♒	13♋	23♏	6♈	17♌	5♑	12♉
31	25♐	7♉	20♏	5♒	15♊	28♎	11♓	27♋	5♐	19♈	2♏	19♑	24♉

AUGUST

	1916	1917	1918	1919	1920	1921	1922	1923	1924	1925	1926	1927	1928
1	5♏	14♑	3♊	12♎	26♒	5♋	25♍	2♈	16♌	26♐	17♉	21♏	7♒
2	17♏	29♑	17♊	24♎	8♓	20♋	8♐	14♈	29♌	11♑	0♊	3♎	20♒
3	0♎	14♒	0♋	6♍	21♓	5♌	21♐	26♈	12♍	26♑	13♊	15♎	3♓
4	12♎	29♒	13♋	18♍	4♈	21♌	4♑	7♉	25♏	11♒	25♊	27♎	17♓
5	25♎	14♓	26♋	0♐	17♈	6♍	17♑	19♉	8♐	26♒	8♋	9♍	1♈
6	9♏	29♓	9♌	12♐	0♉	21♍	0♒	1♊	22♐	11♓	20♋	21♍	14♈
7	22♏	14♈	21♌	24♐	14♉	5♎	12♒	13♊	6♍	26♐	2♌	3♐	28♈
8	6♐	28♈	4♍	6♑	28♉	19♎	24♒	26♊	20♍	10♈	14♌	16♐	12♉
9	20♐	12♉	16♍	18♑	12♊	3♍	6♓	9♋	4♎	23♈	26♌	28♐	27♉
10	5♑	25♉	28♍	1♒	27♊	16♍	18♓	22♋	19♐	7♉	8♏	12♑	11♊
11	20♑	8♊	10♎	15♒	11♋	29♍	0♈	5♌	3♑	19♉	20♏	25♑	25♊
12	5♒	21♊	22♎	28♒	26♋	11♐	11♈	19♌	18♑	2♊	1♎	9♒	9♋
13	20♒	3♋	3♍	12♓	11♌	23♐	23♈	3♍	2♒	14♊	13♎	24♒	23♋
14	5♓	15♋	15♍	26♓	26♌	5♑	5♉	17♍	16♒	26♊	25♎	8♓	7♌
15	20♓	27♋	27♍	10♈	10♍	17♑	17♉	1♎	1♓	8♋	8♍	23♓	21♌
16	4♈	9♌	10♐	24♈	24♍	29♑	0♊	16♎	14♓	20♋	20♍	8♈	5♏
17	18♈	21♌	22♐	8♉	8♎	11♒	13♊	0♏	28♓	1♌	3♐	22♈	18♏
18	1♉	3♍	6♑	22♉	21♎	23♒	26♊	14♏	11♈	13♌	16♐	7♉	1♎
19	14♉	14♍	19♑	6♊	4♍	5♓	10♋	28♏	23♈	25♌	0♑	21♉	13♎
20	26♉	26♍	3♒	20♊	16♍	17♓	24♋	12♐	6♉	7♍	14♑	5♊	26♎
21	9♊	8♎	18♒	4♋	28♍	29♓	8♌	26♐	18♉	19♍	29♑	18♊	8♍
22	21♊	20♎	2♓	18♋	10♐	11♈	23♌	10♑	0♊	2♎	14♒	2♋	20♍
23	2♋	3♍	17♓	2♌	22♐	23♈	8♍	24♑	12♊	14♎	29♒	15♋	1♐
24	14♋	15♍	2♈	16♌	4♑	6♉	23♍	7♒	24♊	27♎	14♓	28♋	13♐
25	26♋	28♍	17♈	29♌	16♑	19♉	8♎	20♒	6♋	10♍	29♓	10♌	25♐
26	8♌	11♐	2♉	12♏	28♑	2♊	23♎	3♓	18♋	24♍	14♈	23♌	7♑
27	20♌	24♐	16♉	25♏	10♒	15♊	7♍	15♓	0♌	7♐	29♈	5♏	20♑
28	2♍	8♑	0♊	8♎	22♒	29♊	21♍	28♓	12♌	21♐	13♉	18♏	2♒
29	14♍	23♑	14♊	20♎	5♓	14♋	5♏	10♈	25♌	5♑	27♉	0♎	15♒
30	27♍	7♒	27♊	2♍	18♓	29♋	18♐	22♈	8♍	20♑	10♊	12♎	29♒
31	9♎	23♒	10♋	14♍	1♈	14♌	1♑	4♉	21♏	5♒	22♊	23♎	13♓

AUGUST

	1929	1930	1931	1932	1933	1934	1935	1936	1937	1938	1939	1940	1941
1	17♊	8♍	11♐	28♋	9♐	29♈	1♏	18♑	1♊	20♎	21♒	8♋	23♍
2	2♋	21♍	23♐	11♌	24♐	12♉	13♏	1♒	16♊	2♍	3♐	22♋	8♐
3	17♋	4♐	5♈	24♌	9♑	25♉	25♍	15♒	0♋	15♍	15♐	6♌	22♐
4	2♌	16♐	17♈	8♍	23♑	7♊	7♎	29♒	14♋	27♍	27♐	21♌	6♑
5	17♌	28♐	29♈	22♍	8♒	19♊	19♎	14♓	29♋	9♐	9♈	5♍	20♑
6	2♍	10♑	11♉	6♎	22♒	1♋	1♏	28♓	13♋	21♐	21♈	20♍	4♒
7	16♍	22♑	23♉	20♎	7♐	13♋	13♏	13♈	27♓	3♑	3♉	5♎	18♒
8	0♎	4♒	5♊	5♍	20♐	25♋	26♏	27♈	10♍	15♑	16♉	19♎	1♐
9	14♎	16♒	18♊	19♍	4♈	6♌	9♐	10♉	24♍	27♑	29♉	3♍	14♐
10	27♎	28♒	2♋	3♐	17♈	18♌	22♐	25♉	7♎	9♒	9♊	17♍	26♐
11	9♍	10♐	16♋	17♐	29♈	0♍	6♑	9♊	19♎	21♒	26♊	1♐	9♈
12	22♍	22♐	0♌	1♑	12♉	12♍	20♑	23♊	1♍	3♐	11♋	15♐	21♈
13	4♐	4♈	15♌	15♑	24♉	24♍	5♒	6♋	13♍	15♐	26♋	28♐	3♉
14	16♐	16♈	29♌	29♑	6♊	7♎	20♒	20♋	25♍	28♐	11♌	11♑	15♉
15	28♐	28♈	14♍	12♒	18♊	19♎	5♓	3♌	7♐	11♐	26♌	24♑	27♉
16	9♑	10♉	29♍	25♒	29♊	2♍	20♓	16♌	19♐	23♐	12♍	6♒	9♊
17	21♑	24♉	14♎	8♓	11♋	15♍	5♈	28♌	1♑	7♈	27♍	19♒	21♊
18	3♒	7♊	28♎	21♓	23♋	28♍	20♈	11♏	13♑	20♉	11♎	1♐	3♋
19	15♒	21♊	13♍	3♈	6♌	12♐	4♉	23♏	25♑	4♒	25♎	13♐	16♋
20	28♒	5♋	26♍	15♈	18♌	26♐	18♉	5♎	8♒	18♊	9♍	25♐	28♋
21	10♓	20♋	10♐	27♈	1♍	11♑	2♊	17♎	21♒	2♋	23♍	7♈	12♌
22	23♓	5♌	23♐	9♉	14♍	26♑	15♊	29♎	4♓	17♐	5♐	19♈	25♌
23	6♈	20♌	6♑	21♉	27♍	11♒	27♊	11♏	18♓	2♑	18♐	1♉	9♍
24	19♈	5♍	19♑	3♊	10♎	26♒	10♋	23♏	2♈	17♑	0♑	12♉	23♍
25	2♉	20♍	1♒	15♊	24♎	11♓	22♋	5♐	16♈	2♍	13♑	24♉	7♎
26	15♉	5♎	14♒	27♊	7♍	26♐	4♌	17♐	0♉	16♍	25♑	7♊	21♎
27	29♉	20♎	26♒	10♋	21♍	10♈	16♌	29♐	14♉	1♎	7♒	19♊	6♍
28	13♊	4♍	8♓	23♋	5♐	24♈	28♌	12♑	28♉	14♎	18♒	2♋	20♍
29	27♊	17♍	20♓	6♌	20♐	8♉	10♏	26♑	12♊	28♎	0♐	16♋	4♐
30	12♋	0♐	2♈	19♌	4♑	21♉	22♍	9♒	26♊	11♍	12♐	0♌	18♐
31	26♋	13♐	13♈	3♍	18♑	3♊	4♎	24♒	10♋	23♍	24♐	14♌	2♑

AUGUST

	1942	1943	1944	1945	1946	1947	1948	1949	1950	1951	1952
1	10♈	12♌	28♐	16♉	0♎	2♒	18♊	8♍	20♐	22♋	9♐
2	22♈	23♌	12♑	0♊	12♎	14♒	2♋	22♍	2♈	4♌	23♐
3	5♉	5♍	27♑	14♊	25♎	26♒	17♋	6♌	15♈	16♌	8♑
4	17♉	17♍	11♒	28♊	7♍	8♓	2♌	19♌	27♈	28♌	23♑
5	29♉	29♍	26♒	11♋	19♍	20♓	17♌	3♑	9♉	11♍	8♒
6	11♊	12♎	11♓	25♋	1♐	3♈	2♍	16♑	20♉	24♍	23♒
7	23♊	24♎	26♓	8♌	13♐	15♈	15♍	29♑	2♊	6♎	8♓
8	5♋	7♍	11♈	21♌	25♐	28♈	2♎	12♒	14♊	19♎	23♓
9	17♋	20♍	25♈	4♍	7♑	11♉	17♎	24♒	26♊	3♍	8♈
10	29♋	4♐	9♉	16♍	19♑	25♉	1♍	6♓	9♋	17♍	22♈
11	11♌	18♐	23♉	28♍	1♒	9♊	14♍	19♓	21♋	1♐	5♉
12	23♌	2♑	7♊	11♎	14♒	23♊	28♍	1♈	4♌	15♐	19♉
13	6♍	17♑	20♊	23♎	27♒	8♋	10♐	12♈	17♌	29♐	1♊
14	19♍	2♒	2♋	4♍	10♓	23♋	23♐	24♈	1♍	14♑	14♊
15	2♎	17♒	15♋	16♍	23♓	8♌	5♑	6♉	14♍	29♑	26♊
16	15♎	2♓	27♋	28♍	7♈	23♌	18♑	18♉	28♍	14♒	8♋
17	28♎	17♓	9♌	10♐	20♈	8♍	0♒	0♊	12♎	29♒	20♋
18	12♍	2♈	21♌	23♐	4♉	22♍	12♒	12♊	26♎	13♓	2♌
19	26♍	16♈	3♍	5♑	18♉	7♎	24♒	25♊	10♍	27♓	14♌
20	10♐	0♉	15♍	18♑	2♊	20♎	5♓	8♋	25♍	10♈	26♌
21	24♐	13♉	27♍	2♒	17♊	4♍	17♓	22♋	9♌	24♈	7♍
22	9♑	26♉	9♎	15♒	1♋	16♍	29♓	6♌	23♌	6♉	19♍
23	24♑	9♊	21♎	0♓	15♋	29♍	11♈	21♌	7♑	19♉	1♎
24	8♒	21♊	3♍	14♓	29♋	11♐	23♈	5♍	21♑	1♊	14♎
25	23♒	3♋	15♍	29♓	13♌	23♐	5♉	20♍	5♒	13♊	26♎
26	7♓	15♋	27♍	13♈	27♌	5♑	18♉	5♎	18♒	25♊	9♍
27	21♓	27♋	10♐	28♈	11♍	17♑	0♊	20♎	2♓	7♋	21♍
28	4♈	9♌	23♐	13♉	25♍	29♑	13♊	4♍	15♓	19♋	5♐
29	18♈	20♌	6♑	27♉	8♎	11♒	27♊	19♍	28♓	1♌	18♐
30	0♉	2♍	20♑	11♊	20♎	23♒	11♋	3♐	10♈	13♌	2♑
31	13♉	14♍	5♒	25♊	3♍	5♓	26♋	16♐	22♈	25♌	17♑

SEPTEMBER

	1890	1891	1892	1893	1894	1895	1896	1897	1898	1899	1900	1901	1902
1	11♈	18♌	1♑	14♉	1♎	9♒	21♊	6♍	22♐	29♋	29♍	14♈	28♌
2	25♈	0♍	14♑	28♉	15♎	20♒	4♋	20♍	6♈	11♌	11♐	28♈	12♏
3	9♉	12♏	27♑	12♊	29♎	2♓	17♋	5♐	19♈	22♌	24♐	13♉	26♏
4	22♉	24♏	10♒	26♊	12♍	14♓	1♌	19♐	2♉	4♏	7♑	27♉	9♎
5	5♊	6♎	24♒	11♋	25♍	26♓	15♌	3♑	15♉	16♏	21♑	11♊	22♎
6	18♊	18♎	9♓	25♋	7♐	8♈	29♌	17♑	27♉	28♏	5♒	25♊	5♍
7	0♋	29♎	23♓	9♌	20♐	20♈	14♏	1♒	10♊	10♎	20♒	9♋	17♍
8	12♋	11♏	8♈	23♌	2♑	2♉	29♏	14♒	21♊	23♎	5♓	22♋	29♍
9	24♋	24♏	23♈	7♍	14♑	14♉	14♎	27♒	3♋	5♏	20♓	6♌	11♐
10	5♌	6♐	8♉	20♍	25♑	27♉	29♎	11♓	15♋	18♏	5♈	19♌	23♐
11	17♌	19♐	22♉	3♎	7♒	10♊	14♍	24♓	27♋	1♐	21♈	2♏	5♑
12	29♌	2♑	6♊	16♎	19♒	23♊	28♍	6♈	9♌	14♐	5♉	14♏	17♑
13	11♏	15♑	20♊	29♎	1♓	6♋	12♐	19♈	21♌	28♐	20♉	27♏	29♑
14	23♏	29♑	4♋	11♍	14♓	20♋	26♐	1♉	4♍	12♑	4♊	9♎	11♒
15	5♎	14♒	18♋	23♍	26♓	5♌	9♑	13♉	16♍	26♑	17♊	21♎	24♒
16	18♎	29♒	1♌	5♐	9♈	20♌	22♑	25♉	29♍	11♒	0♋	3♍	7♓
17	0♏	14♓	14♌	17♐	21♈	5♍	5♒	7♊	12♎	25♒	13♋	15♍	20♓
18	13♏	29♓	26♌	29♐	4♉	20♍	17♒	19♊	26♎	11♓	26♋	26♍	4♈
19	26♏	14♈	9♏	11♑	18♉	5♎	0♓	1♋	10♏	26♓	8♌	8♐	17♈
20	9♐	29♈	21♏	23♑	1♊	20♎	12♓	13♋	23♍	11♈	3♌	20♐	1♉
21	23♐	14♉	4♎	5♒	15♊	4♏	24♓	25♋	7♐	25♈	2♍	2♑	15♉
22	7♑	28♉	16♎	18♒	29♊	19♏	6♈	8♌	21♐	9♉	14♍	15♑	29♉
23	21♑	12♊	28♎	1♓	13♋	2♐	18♈	21♌	5♑	23♉	26♍	28♑	13♊
24	5♒	25♊	9♏	14♓	27♋	16♐	29♈	4♍	19♑	6♊	8♎	11♒	28♊
25	20♒	8♋	21♏	28♓	12♌	29♐	11♉	18♍	4♒	19♊	20♎	25♒	12♋
26	5♓	21♋	3♐	12♈	26♌	11♑	23♉	2♎	18♒	1♋	2♏	9♓	26♋
27	20♓	3♌	15♐	26♈	11♍	24♑	5♊	17♎	2♓	14♋	14♏	23♓	10♌
28	4♈	15♌	27♐	10♉	25♍	6♒	17♊	2♏	16♓	25♋	26♏	8♈	24♌
29	19♈	27♌	9♑	24♉	9♎	17♒	0♋	16♏	0♈	7♌	8♐	23♈	8♏
30	3♉	9♏	22♑	9♊	23♎	29♒	12♋	1♐	14♈	19♌	20♐	8♉	21♏

SEPTEMBER

	1903	1904	1905	1906	1907	1908	1909	1910	1911	1912	1913	1914	1915
1	7♑	19♉	5♎	19♒	27♊	10♍	26♐	10♌	17♐	1♉	17♏	2♒	6♊
2	19♑	2♊	20♎	3♓	9♋	23♍	11♈	24♌	28♐	14♉	2♎	15♒	18♊
3	1♒	15♊	4♍	16♓	21♋	6♐	26♈	7♏	10♑	27♉	17♎	27♒	0♋
4	13♒	28♊	19♍	29♓	2♌	19♐	10♉	20♏	22♑	11♊	2♍	10♐	12♋
5	25♒	12♋	3♐	12♈	14♌	3♑	25♉	2♎	4♒	24♊	16♍	22♐	24♋
6	7♓	26♋	17♐	24♈	27♌	17♑	9♊	14♎	17♒	9♋	0♌	4♈	7♌
7	19♓	11♌	1♑	7♉	9♏	1♒	22♊	26♎	0♓	23♋	13♐	16♈	20♌
8	1♈	26♌	14♑	19♉	22♏	16♒	5♋	8♏	12♓	8♌	26♐	28♈	3♍
9	14♈	11♏	27♑	1♊	4♎	2♓	18♋	20♏	26♐	23♌	9♑	10♉	16♏
10	26♈	26♏	10♒	12♊	18♎	17♓	1♌	2♐	9♈	8♏	22♑	22♉	0♎
11	9♉	11♎	22♒	24♊	1♍	2♈	13♌	14♐	22♐	23♏	4♒	4♊	14♎
12	22♉	26♎	5♓	6♋	14♍	17♈	25♌	26♐	6♑	7♎	16♒	16♊	28♎
13	6♊	10♏	17♓	19♋	1♍	1♉	7♏	8♑	20♐	22♎	28♒	28♊	12♏
14	20♊	24♍	29♓	1♌	12♎	15♋	19♍	21♒	4♊	5♍	10♐	11♒	26♏
15	4♋	8♐	11♈	14♌	26♐	29♋	1♎	4♒	18♊	19♍	21♐	24♋	11♐
16	18♋	21♐	23♈	27♌	10♑	12♊	13♎	17♒	2♋	2♐	3♈	7♌	25♐
17	2♌	4♑	5♉	10♏	24♑	25♊	1♓	16♌	14♐	15♈	21♌	21♌	9♑
18	17♌	17♑	16♉	24♏	9♎	7♋	7♍	15♓	1♌	27♐	27♈	5♏	23♑
19	2♍	29♑	28♉	8♎	23♒	19♋	19♍	29♓	15♌	9♑	9♉	20♏	7♒
20	17♍	11♒	10♊	23♎	7♓	1♌	1♓	14♈	29♌	21♑	21♉	5♎	20♒
21	1♎	23♒	23♊	7♍	22♎	13♌	13♐	29♈	13♏	3♒	4♊	20♎	4♓
22	15♎	4♓	5♋	22♍	6♈	24♌	25♐	13♉	27♏	15♒	16♊	5♍	17♓
23	29♎	16♓	18♋	6♐	20♈	6♍	8♑	28♉	10♎	27♒	29♊	20♍	0♈
24	13♍	28♓	1♌	20♐	3♉	18♍	21♑	12♊	23♎	9♓	13♋	4♐	13♈
25	26♍	10♈	15♌	4♑	16♉	0♎	5♒	26♊	6♍	21♐	26♋	18♐	26♈
26	9♐	22♈	29♌	18♑	29♉	12♎	20♒	10♋	18♍	3♈	11♌	2♑	8♉
27	21♐	4♉	14♍	2♒	11♊	25♎	4♓	24♋	0♐	15♈	25♌	16♑	20♉
28	3♑	16♉	29♍	16♒	23♊	7♍	19♓	7♌	12♐	28♈	10♏	29♑	2♊
29	15♑	29♉	14♎	29♒	5♋	20♍	5♈	20♌	24♐	11♉	25♏	12♒	14♊
30	27♑	11♊	29♎	12♓	17♋	3♐	20♈	3♏	6♑	24♉	11♎	24♒	26♊

SEPTEMBER

	1916	1917	1918	1919	1920	1921	1922	1923	1924	1925	1926	1927	1928
1	22♎	8♐	23♋	26♍	14♈	29♌	14♌	15♌	5♎	20♒	5♋	5♍	26♐
2	6♍	23♐	5♌	8♐	27♋	14♍	26♑	27♉	19♎	5♐	17♋	17♍	11♈
3	19♍	8♈	18♌	19♐	11♌	29♍	9♒	9♊	3♍	19♐	29♋	29♍	25♈
4	2♐	23♈	0♍	2♑	25♌	14♎	21♒	21♊	17♍	4♈	11♌	11♐	9♉
5	16♐	7♉	12♍	14♑	8♊	28♎	3♐	4♋	1♐	18♈	23♌	24♐	23♉
6	0♑	21♉	24♍	27♑	23♊	11♍	15♐	17♋	15♐	2♉	5♍	6♑	8♊
7	15♑	4♊	6♎	10♒	7♋	25♍	26♐	0♌	29♐	15♉	17♍	20♑	22♊
8	29♑	17♊	18♎	23♒	21♋	7♐	8♈	13♌	13♑	28♉	28♍	3♒	6♋
9	14♒	0♋	0♍	7♐	6♌	20♐	20♈	27♌	28♑	10♊	10♎	17♒	19♋
10	29♒	12♋	12♍	21♐	20♌	2♑	2♉	11♍	12♒	22♊	22♎	2♐	3♌
11	13♐	24♋	24♍	5♈	4♍	14♑	14♉	26♍	26♒	4♋	5♍	17♐	17♌
12	28♐	6♌	6♐	20♈	19♍	26♑	26♉	11♎	9♐	16♋	17♍	2♈	0♍
13	12♈	18♌	18♐	4♉	2♎	8♒	9♊	25♎	23♐	28♋	29♍	17♈	13♍
14	26♈	0♍	1♑	19♉	16♎	20♒	21♊	10♍	6♈	10♌	12♐	2♉	26♍
15	9♉	12♍	14♑	3♊	29♎	2♓	5♋	25♍	19♈	22♌	25♐	17♉	9♎
16	22♉	23♍	27♑	17♊	12♍	14♎	18♋	9♐	1♉	4♍	9♑	1♊	21♎
17	5♊	5♎	11♒	1♋	24♍	26♎	2♌	23♐	14♉	16♍	23♑	15♊	4♍
18	17♊	17♎	26♒	15♋	6♌	8♐	17♌	7♑	26♉	28♍	7♒	29♊	16♍
19	29♊	0♍	11♐	28♋	18♐	20♈	1♍	20♑	8♊	11♎	22♒	12♋	28♍
20	11♋	12♍	26♐	12♌	0♑	3♉	17♍	4♒	20♊	24♎	7♒	25♋	9♐
21	22♋	25♍	11♈	25♌	12♑	16♉	2♎	16♒	2♋	7♍	22♐	7♌	21♐
22	4♌	7♐	26♈	8♍	24♑	29♉	17♎	29♒	14♋	21♍	8♈	20♌	3♑
23	16♌	20♐	11♉	21♍	6♒	12♊	2♍	12♐	26♋	4♐	23♈	2♍	15♑
24	28♌	4♑	26♉	4♎	18♒	26♊	17♍	24♐	8♌	18♐	7♉	14♍	28♑
25	11♍	18♑	10♊	16♎	1♐	9♋	1♐	6♈	21♌	2♑	22♉	26♍	10♒
26	23♍	2♒	24♊	28♎	14♐	24♋	15♐	18♈	3♍	16♑	5♊	8♎	23♒
27	6♎	16♒	7♋	10♍	27♐	8♌	28♐	0♉	17♍	0♒	19♊	20♎	7♐
28	19♎	1♐	20♋	22♍	10♈	23♌	11♑	12♉	0♎	14♒	1♋	2♍	21♐
29	2♍	16♐	3♌	4♐	23♈	8♍	23♑	24♉	14♎	29♒	14♋	14♍	5♈
30	16♍	1♈	15♌	16♐	7♉	23♍	6♒	6♊	28♎	13♐	26♋	26♍	20♈

SEPTEMBER

	1929	1930	1931	1932	1933	1934	1935	1936	1937	1938	1939	1940	1941
1	11♌	25♐	25♈	17♏	3≈	16♊	15≏	8♓	24♋	6♐	6♈	29♌	16♑
2	26♌	7♑	7♉	2≏	17≈	28♊	27≏	23♓	8♌	18♐	18♈	14♏	0≈
3	10♏	20♑	19♉	16♏	1♓	10♋	10♏	8♈	22♌	29♐	0♉	29♏	13≈
4	25♏	1≈	1♊	1♏	15♓	22≏	22♏	23♈	6♏	11♑	13♉	14≏	26≈
5	8≏	13♑	14♊	15♏	28♓	3♌	5♐	8♉	19♏	23♑	25♉	29≏	9♓
6	22≏	25≈	27♊	0♐	12♈	15♌	17♐	22♉	2≏	5≈	8♊	13♏	22♓
7	5♏	7♓	10♋	14♐	25♈	27♌	1♑	6♊	15≏	17≈	22♊	28♏	5♈
8	18♏	19♓	24♋	28♐	7♉	9♏	14♑	20♊	27≏	29≈	6♋	11♐	17♈
9	0♐	1♈	8♌	12♑	20♉	21♏	29♑	3♋	9♏	12♓	20♋	25♐	29♈
10	12♐	13♈	23♌	25♑	2♊	4≏	13≈	17♋	21♏	25♓	4♌	8♑	11♉
11	24♐	25♈	8♏	8≈	14♊	16≏	28≈	0♌	3♐	7♈	19♌	21♑	23♉
12	6♑	8♉	23♏	21≈	26♊	29≏	13♓	12♌	15♐	20♈	5♏	3≈	5♊
13	18♑	21♉	8≏	4♓	7♋	12♏	29♓	25♌	27♐	4♉	20♏	16≈	17♊
14	0≈	3♊	23≏	17♓	19♋	25♏	14♈	7♏	9♑	17♉	5≏	28≈	29♊
15	12≈	17♊	8♏	29♓	1♌	9♐	29♈	19♏	21♑	1♊	20≏	10♓	11♋
16	24≈	0♋	22♏	11♈	14♌	22♐	13♉	2≏	3≈	14♊	4♏	22♓	23♋
17	6♓	14♋	6♐	23♈	26♌	6♑	28♉	14≏	16≈	28♊	18♏	4♈	6♌
18	19♓	29♋	20♐	5♉	9♏	21♑	11♊	25≏	29≈	13♋	1♐	16♈	20♌
19	2♈	14♌	3♑	17♉	22♏	5≈	24♊	7♏	13♓	27♋	14♐	27♈	3♏
20	15♈	29♌	16♑	29♉	6≏	20≈	7♋	19♏	27♓	12♌	27♐	9♉	18♏
21	29♈	14♏	28♑	11♊	20≏	4♓	19♋	1♐	11♈	26♌	9♑	21♉	2≏
22	12♉	29♏	11≈	23♊	4♏	19♓	1♌	13♐	26♈	11♏	21♑	3♊	17≏
23	26♉	13≏	23≈	5♋	18♏	4♈	13♌	25♐	10♉	25♏	3≈	15♊	1♏
24	10♊	28≏	5♓	18♋	2♐	18♈	25♌	8♑	24♉	9≏	15≈	28♊	16♏
25	24♊	12♏	17♓	0♌	16♐	2♉	7♏	20♑	9♊	22≏	27≈	11♋	1♐
26	8♋	25♏	29♓	14♌	1♑	16♉	19♏	4≈	23♊	6♏	9♓	24♋	15♐
27	22♋	9♐	10♈	27♌	15♑	29♉	1≏	17≈	7♋	19♏	21♓	8♌	29♐
28	7♌	21♐	22♈	11♏	29♑	12♊	13≏	2♓	21♋	1♐	3♈	23♌	13♑
29	21♌	4♑	4♉	26♏	13≈	24♊	25≏	16♓	5♌	13♐	15♈	7♏	27♑
30	5♏	16♑	16♉	11≏	27≈	6♋	7♏	1♈	18♌	26♐	27♈	22♏	10≈

SEPTEMBER

	1942	1943	1944	1945	1946	1947	1948	1949	1950	1951	1952
1	25♉	26♍	20♒	8♋	14♍	17♐	11♌	0♑	4♌	8♍	2♒
2	7♊	9♎	5♓	21♋	26♍	29♐	26♌	13♑	16♌	20♍	16♒
3	19♊	21♎	20♓	4♌	9♐	12♈	11♍	26♑	28♌	3♎	2♓
4	1♋	4♏	5♈	17♌	21♐	25♈	26♍	8♒	10♊	16♎	17♓
5	13♋	17♏	20♈	0♍	3♑	8♉	11♎	21♒	22♊	0♍	1♈
6	25♋	0♐	5♉	12♍	15♑	22♉	26♎	3♓	4♋	13♍	16♈
7	7♌	13♐	19♉	25♍	27♑	5♊	10♍	15♐	17♋	27♍	0♉
8	19♌	27♐	3♊	7♎	9♒	19♊	24♍	27♐	29♋	11♐	14♉
9	2♍	11♑	16♊	19♎	22♒	3♋	7♐	9♈	12♌	25♐	27♉
10	15♍	26♑	29♊	1♏	5♓	17♋	20♐	21♈	26♌	10♑	10♊
11	28♍	11♒	12♋	13♏	19♓	2♌	2♑	3♉	9♏	24♑	23♊
12	11♎	25♒	24♋	24♏	3♈	17♌	15♑	14♉	23♏	9♒	5♋
13	25♎	10♓	6♌	6♐	17♈	2♍	27♑	26♉	8♎	23♒	17♋
14	9♍	25♓	18♌	18♐	1♉	16♍	9♒	8♊	22♍	7♓	29♋
15	23♍	10♈	0♍	1♑	15♉	1♎	21♒	21♊	7♍	21♐	11♌
16	7♐	24♈	12♍	13♑	29♉	15♎	2♓	4♋	21♍	5♈	22♌
17	21♐	8♉	24♍	26♑	13♊	28♎	14♐	17♋	6♐	18♈	4♍
18	5♑	22♉	6♎	10♒	27♊	12♍	26♐	0♌	20♐	1♉	16♍
19	19♑	5♊	18♎	24♒	12♋	25♍	8♈	14♌	4♑	14♉	28♍
20	4♒	17♊	0♍	8♓	25♋	7♐	20♈	29♌	18♑	27♉	11♎
21	18♒	0♋	12♍	23♓	9♌	19♐	2♉	14♍	1♒	9♊	23♎
22	2♓	12♋	24♍	8♈	23♌	1♑	15♉	29♍	15♒	21♊	6♏
23	16♓	24♋	6♐	23♈	6♍	13♑	27♉	14♎	28♒	3♋	18♏
24	29♓	5♌	19♐	8♉	20♍	25♑	10♊	29♎	11♓	15♋	2♐
25	13♈	17♌	2♑	23♉	3♎	7♒	23♊	14♍	24♓	27♋	15♐
26	26♈	29♌	15♑	7♊	16♎	19♒	7♋	28♍	6♈	9♌	28♐
27	8♉	11♏	29♑	21♊	29♎	1♐	20♋	12♐	18♈	21♌	12♑
28	21♉	23♏	13♒	5♋	11♍	13♐	5♌	26♐	1♉	3♏	26♑
29	3♊	5♎	28♒	18♋	23♍	26♐	19♌	10♑	13♉	16♏	11♒
30	15♊	18♎	13♓	1♌	5♐	9♈	4♍	23♑	25♉	29♍	25♒

	1890	1891	1892	1893	1894	1895	1896	1897	1898	1899	1900	1901	1902
1	17♉	21♏	5♒	23♊	7♍	11♒	25♋	15♐	27♈	1♏	3♑	23♉	4♎
2	0♊	3♎	19♒	7♋	22♍	23♓	9♌	0♑	10♉	13♏	16♑	7♊	17♎
3	13♊	15♎	3♓	21♋	3♐	5♈	23♌	14♑	23♉	25♏	0♒	22♊	0♍
4	26♊	27♎	17♓	5♌	15♐	17♈	7♍	27♑	5♊	7♎	14♒	6♋	13♍
5	8♋	9♏	2♈	19♌	28♐	29♈	22♍	11♒	17♊	20♎	28♒	19♋	25♍
6	20♋	21♏	17♈	3♏	10♑	11♉	7♎	24♒	29♊	2♏	13♓	3♌	7♐
7	2♌	3♐	2♉	16♏	22♑	24♉	23♎	7♓	11♋	15♏	28♓	16♌	19♐
8	14♌	15♐	17♉	29♏	3♒	7♊	8♍	20♓	23♋	28♏	14♈	28♌	1♑
9	26♌	28♐	2♊	12♐	15♒	20♊	23♍	2♈	5♌	11♐	29♈	11♏	12♑
10	8♏	11♑	16♊	25♐	27♒	3♋	8♐	15♈	17♌	24♐	14♉	23♏	24♑
11	20♏	24♑	0♋	7♍	10♓	16♋	22♐	27♈	29♌	8♑	28♉	6♎	7♒
12	2♎	8♒	14♋	19♍	22♓	0♌	6♑	9♉	12♏	22♑	13♊	18♎	19♒
13	14♎	22♒	28♋	1♐	5♈	14♌	19♑	21♉	25♏	6♒	26♊	0♍	2♓
14	27♎	7♓	11♌	13♐	17♈	29♌	2♒	3♊	8♎	20♒	10♋	11♍	15♓
15	10♍	22♓	24♌	25♐	1♉	13♏	14♒	15♊	22♎	5♓	22♋	23♍	28♓
16	23♍	7♈	6♏	7♑	14♉	28♏	21♒	27♊	5♍	20♓	5♌	5♐	12♈
17	6♐	22♈	18♏	19♑	28♉	13♓	9♓	9♋	19♍	4♈	17♌	17♐	26♈
18	20♐	7♉	0♎	1♒	12♊	28♓	21♋	21♋	4♐	19♈	29♌	29♐	11♉
19	3♑	22♉	12♎	13♒	26♊	13♍	3♈	3♌	18♐	3♉	11♏	11♑	25♉
20	17♑	7♊	24♎	26♒	10♋	27♍	14♈	16♌	2♑	17♉	23♏	23♑	10♊
21	1♒	20♊	6♍	9♓	24♋	11♎	26♈	29♌	16♑	1♊	5♎	6♒	24♊
22	15♒	4♋	18♍	22♓	8♌	24♎	8♉	12♏	0♒	14♊	17♎	19♒	9♋
23	0♓	17♋	0♐	6♈	22♌	7♏	20♉	26♏	14♒	27♊	29♎	3♓	23♋
24	14♓	29♋	12♐	20♈	6♏	20♏	2♊	11♎	28♒	9♋	11♏	17♓	7♌
25	29♓	12♌	24♐	5♉	20♏	2♐	14♊	25♎	12♓	22♋	23♏	1♈	21♌
26	13♈	24♌	6♑	19♉	4♎	14♐	27♊	10♍	26♓	4♌	5♐	16♈	4♏
27	27♈	6♏	18♑	4♊	18♎	26♐	9♋	26♍	9♈	15♌	17♐	1♉	18♏
28	11♉	18♏	1♒	19♊	2♍	8♑	22♋	11♐	23♈	27♌	0♑	16♉	1♎
29	25♉	0♎	14♒	4♋	15♍	19♑	5♌	25♐	6♉	9♍	13♑	2♊	14♎
30	8♊	12♎	27♒	18♋	28♍	1♈	18♌	10♑	18♉	21♏	26♑	16♊	26♎
31	21♊	23♎	11♓	2♌	11♐	13♈	2♏	24♑	1♊	3♎	9♒	1♋	9♍

OCTOBER

	1903	1904	1905	1906	1907	1908	1909	1910	1911	1912	1913	1914	1915
1	9♒	24♊	14♍	25♒	29♋	16♐	5♌	16♏	18♑	7♊	26♎	7♓	8♋
2	21♒	8♋	29♍	8♈	11♌	29♐	20♌	28♏	0♒	21♊	10♍	19♓	20♋
3	3♓	21♋	13♐	20♈	23♌	13♑	4♊	11♎	12♒	5♋	25♍	1♈	2♌
4	15♓	5♌	27♐	3♉	5♏	27♑	18♊	23♎	25♒	19♋	9♐	13♈	15♌
5	28♓	20♌	11♑	15♉	18♏	11♒	2♋	5♏	8♓	3♌	22♐	25♈	27♌
6	10♈	4♍	24♑	27♉	0♎	25♒	15♋	17♏	21♓	18♌	6♑	7♉	11♍
7	23♈	19♍	7♒	9♊	14♎	10♓	28♋	28♏	4♈	2♍	18♑	18♉	24♍
8	6♉	4♎	19♒	20♊	27♎	25♓	10♌	10♐	18♈	17♍	1♒	0♊	8♎
9	19♉	19♎	2♓	2♋	11♍	10♈	22♌	22♐	2♉	1♎	13♒	12♊	23♎
10	3♊	4♏	14♓	14♋	25♍	25♈	4♍	4♑	16♉	16♎	25♒	24♊	7♍
11	16♊	19♏	26♓	26♋	9♐	9♉	16♍	16♑	0♊	0♍	6♓	7♋	22♍
12	0♋	3♐	8♈	9♌	23♐	23♉	28♍	29♑	15♊	13♍	18♓	19♋	7♐
13	14♋	17♐	20♈	21♌	7♑	7♊	10♎	12♒	29♊	27♍	0♈	2♌	21♐
14	28♋	0♑	1♉	5♍	21♑	20♊	22♎	25♒	13♊	10♐	12♒	15♌	6♑
15	13♌	13♒	13♉	18♍	5♒	3♋	4♍	9♓	27♋	22♐	24♈	29♌	20♑
16	27♌	25♑	25♉	2♎	19♒	15♋	16♍	23♓	11♌	5♑	6♉	13♍	4♎
17	11♍	7♒	7♊	17♎	3♓	27♋	28♍	8♈	25♌	17♑	18♉	28♍	17♎
18	26♍	19♒	19♊	2♏	17♓	9♌	10♐	23♈	9♍	29♑	1♊	13♎	0♐
19	10♎	1♓	1♋	16♏	1♈	21♌	22♐	8♉	22♍	11♒	13♊	28♎	14♐
20	24♎	13♓	14♋	1♐	15♈	3♍	5♑	23♉	6♎	23♒	26♊	13♍	26♐
21	7♏	25♓	27♋	16♐	28♈	15♍	17♑	8♊	19♎	5♓	9♋	29♍	9♑
22	21♏	7♈	10♌	1♑	11♉	27♍	1♒	22♊	1♍	17♓	22♋	14♐	22♑
23	4♐	19♈	23♌	15♑	24♉	9♎	14♒	7♋	14♍	29♓	6♌	28♐	4♉
24	17♐	1♉	7♍	29♑	7♊	21♎	28♒	21♋	26♍	11♈	20♌	12♑	16♉
25	29♐	13♉	22♍	12♒	19♊	4♏	13♓	4♌	8♐	24♈	4♍	25♑	29♉
26	11♑	26♉	7♎	26♒	1♋	17♏	28♓	17♌	20♐	7♉	19♍	9♒	10♊
27	23♑	8♊	22♎	9♓	13♋	0♐	13♈	0♍	2♑	20♉	4♎	21♒	22♊
28	5♒	21♊	7♏	22♓	25♋	13♐	28♈	13♍	14♑	4♊	19♎	4♓	4♋
29	17♒	4♋	22♏	4♈	6♌	26♐	13♉	25♍	26♑	18♊	4♍	16♓	16♋
30	29♒	18♋	7♐	17♈	18♌	10♑	28♉	8♎	8♒	2♋	18♍	28♓	28♋
31	11♓	1♌	22♐	29♈	0♏	23♑	13♊	20♎	20♒	16♋	3♐	10♈	10♌

OCTOBER

	1916	1917	1918	1919	1920	1921	1922	1923	1924	1925	1926	1927	1928
1	29♏	16♈	27♌	27♐	21♉	7♎	18♒	17Ⅱ	13♍	28♓	8♌	8♐	5♋
2	13♐	1♉	9♍	9♑	5Ⅱ	22♎	0♓	0♋	27♍	12♈	20♌	20♐	19♉
3	27♐	16♉	21♏	22♑	19Ⅱ	6♍	12♓	12♋	12♐	26♈	2♏	2♑	4Ⅱ
4	11♑	0Ⅱ	3♎	4♒	4♋	19♍	23♓	25♋	26♐	10♉	14♏	15♑	18Ⅱ
5	25♑	13Ⅱ	15♎	17♒	18♋	3♐	5♈	8♌	10♑	23♉	25♏	28♑	2♋
6	9♒	26Ⅱ	27♎	1♓	2♌	16♐	17♈	21♌	24♑	6Ⅱ	7♎	12♒	16♋
7	24♒	8♋	9♍	15♓	16♌	28♐	29♈	5♏	8♒	18Ⅱ	20♎	26♒	0♌
8	8♓	21♋	21♍	29♓	0♏	11♑	11♉	20♍	22♒	0♋	2♏	10♓	14♌
9	22♓	3♌	3♐	14♈	14♏	23♑	23♉	4♎	5♓	12♋	14♏	25♓	27♌
10	6♈	15♌	15♐	29♈	28♏	5♒	5Ⅱ	19♎	18♓	24♋	27♏	10♈	10♍
11	20♈	26♌	27♐	14♉	11♎	16♒	18Ⅱ	4♏	2♈	6♌	9♎	26♈	23♍
12	4♉	8♏	10♑	28♉	24♎	28♒	1♋	20♍	14♈	18♌	22♎	11♓	5♎
13	17♉	20♏	23♑	13Ⅱ	7♍	10♓	14♋	5♐	27♈	0♍	5♏	26♓	18♎
14	0Ⅱ	2♎	6♒	28Ⅱ	20♍	22♓	27♋	19♐	10♉	12♍	19♏	10♈	0♏
15	12Ⅱ	14♎	20♒	12♋	2♐	5♈	11♌	3♑	22♉	24♍	2♏	26Ⅱ	12♏
16	24Ⅱ	27♎	4♓	25♋	14♐	17♈	25♌	17♑	4Ⅱ	7♎	17♏	8♋	24♏
17	7♋	9♏	19♓	9♌	26♐	0♉	10♍	1♒	16Ⅱ	20♎	1♓	22♋	6♐
18	19♋	23♏	4♈	22♌	8♑	12♉	25♍	13♒	28Ⅱ	3♍	16♓	4♌	17♐
19	0♌	4♐	19♈	5♏	20♑	26♉	10♎	26♒	10♋	17♍	1♈	17♌	29♐
20	12♌	17♐	5♉	18♏	2♒	9Ⅱ	25♎	9♓	22♋	1♐	16♈	29♌	11♑
21	24♌	1♑	20♉	0♎	14♒	23Ⅱ	10♏	21♓	4♌	15♐	1♉	11♏	23♑
22	6♍	14♑	4♎	13♎	26♒	6♋	25♏	3♈	16♌	29♐	16♉	23♏	6♒
23	19♍	28♑	19Ⅱ	25♎	9♓	20♋	9♐	15♈	28♌	13♑	0Ⅱ	5♎	18♒
24	1♎	12♒	3♓	7♍	22♓	4♌	23♐	27♈	11♍	27♑	14Ⅱ	17♎	1♓
25	14♎	26♒	16♓	19♍	5♈	19♌	7♑	9♉	25♍	11♒	27Ⅱ	29♎	15♓
26	28♎	11♓	29♓	0♎	18♈	3♏	20♑	21♉	8♎	25♒	10♋	11♍	29♓
27	12♏	25♓	12♈	12♎	2♉	17♏	2♒	2Ⅱ	23♎	9♓	22♋	23♍	13♈
28	26♏	10♈	24♈	24♐	16♉	2♎	15♒	14Ⅱ	7♏	23♓	4♌	5♐	28♈
29	10♐	25♈	6♍	6♑	1Ⅱ	16♎	27♒	26Ⅱ	22♏	7♈	16♌	17♐	13♑
30	24♐	9♉	18♍	18♑	15Ⅱ	0♏	9♓	8♋	7♐	21♈	28♌	29♐	28♉
31	8♑	24♉	0♎	0♒	0♋	14♍	20♓	21♋	22♐	4♉	10♏	11♑	13Ⅱ

	1929	1930	1931	1932	1933	1934	1935	1936	1937	1938	1939	1940	1941
1	19♏	28♑	28♉	25♎	10♓	18♋	19♍	17♈	2♏	7♑	10♌	7♎	23♒
2	3♎	10♒	10♊	10♍	24♓	0♌	1♐	2♉	15♏	19♑	22♉	23♎	6♓
3	17♎	22♒	23♊	25♍	7♈	12♌	14♐	17♉	28♏	1♒	5♊	8♍	18♓
4	0♏	4♓	6♋	10♐	20♈	23♌	27♐	2♊	11♎	13♒	18♊	22♍	1♈
5	13♏	16♓	19♋	24♐	3♉	5♏	10♑	16♊	23♎	25♒	2♋	7♐	13♈
6	25♏	28♓	3♌	8♑	15♉	18♏	24♑	0♋	5♏	8♒	16♋	21♐	25♈
7	8♐	10♈	17♌	22♑	27♉	0♎	8♒	13♋	17♏	20♓	0♌	4♑	7♉
8	20♐	22♈	1♏	5♒	10♊	13♎	22♒	27♋	29♏	3♈	14♌	18♑	19♉
9	2♑	5♉	16♏	18♒	22♊	26♎	7♓	9♌	11♐	16♈	29♌	0♒	1♊
10	14♑	18♉	1♎	1♓	3♋	9♍	22♓	22♌	23♐	0♉	13♏	13♒	13♊
11	25♑	0♊	16♎	14♓	15♋	22♍	7♈	4♏	5♐	13♉	28♏	25♒	25♊
12	7♒	14♊	1♍	26♓	27♋	6♐	22♈	16♏	17♐	27♉	13♎	7♓	7♋
13	20♒	27♊	16♍	8♈	9♌	19♐	7♉	28♏	29♐	11♊	28♎	19♓	19♋
14	2♓	11♋	1♐	20♈	22♌	3♑	22♉	10♐	11♑	25♊	12♍	1♈	2♌
15	15♓	25♋	15♐	2♉	4♏	17♑	6♊	22♐	24♑	9♋	26♍	13♈	14♌
16	27♓	9♌	29♐	14♉	17♏	1♒	20♊	4♑	7♒	24♋	9♐	24♈	28♌
17	11♈	23♌	12♑	26♉	1♎	15♒	3♋	16♍	21♏	8♌	23♎	6♉	11♍
18	24♈	8♏	25♑	8♊	15♎	0♓	15♋	28♍	5♐	22♌	5♒	18♉	26♍
19	8♉	23♏	8♒	19♊	29♎	14♓	28♋	10♐	20♈	6♍	18♑	0♊	10♎
20	22♉	7♐	20♒	1♋	13♏	28♓	10♌	22♐	5♉	20♍	0♒	12♊	25♎
21	6♊	22♐	2♓	14♋	28♏	12♈	22♌	4♑	19♉	4♎	12♒	25♊	10♍
22	21♊	6♑	14♓	26♋	13♐	26♈	4♍	16♑	4♊	17♎	24♒	7♋	25♍
23	5♋	20♑	26♓	9♌	27♐	10♉	16♍	29♑	19♊	1♍	6♓	20♋	10♏
24	19♋	3♒	7♈	22♌	12♑	24♉	27♍	12♒	3♋	14♍	17♓	4♌	25♏
25	3♌	17♒	19♈	5♍	26♑	7♊	9♎	26♒	18♋	27♍	29♓	17♌	9♐
26	17♌	29♒	1♉	19♍	10♒	19♊	21♎	10♓	2♌	9♎	12♈	1♍	23♐
27	1♍	12♑	13♉	4♎	23♒	2♋	4♏	25♓	15♌	21♐	24♈	16♍	7♑
28	15♍	24♑	25♉	19♎	7♓	14♋	16♍	10♈	29♌	3♑	6♉	1♎	20♑
29	29♍	6♒	7♊	4♏	20♓	26♋	28♍	25♈	12♏	15♑	19♉	16♎	3♒
30	12♎	18♒	20♊	19♏	3♈	8♌	11♐	10♉	25♏	27♑	2♊	1♍	15♒
31	25♎	0♓	3♌	4♐	16♈	19♌	24♐	25♉	7♎	9♒	15♊	16♍	28♓

	1942	1943	1944	1945	1946	1947	1948	1949	1950	1951	1952
1	27♊	1♏	28♐	14♌	17♐	22♈	19♏	5♒	6♊	12♎	10♐
2	9♋	14♏	13♈	27♌	28♐	5♉	4♎	18♒	18♊	26♎	25♐
3	21♋	27♏	29♈	9♏	10♑	18♉	19♎	0♓	0♋	10♏	10♈
4	3♌	10♐	13♉	21♏	22♑	2♊	4♏	12♓	12♋	24♏	24♈
5	15♌	24♐	28♉	4♎	5♒	16♊	18♏	24♓	25♋	8♌	8♉
6	27♌	8♑	12♊	16♎	17♒	0♋	2♐	6♈	7♌	22♐	22♉
7	10♏	22♑	25♊	27♎	0♓	14♋	15♐	18♈	20♌	6♑	6♊
8	23♏	6♒	8♋	9♏	14♓	28♋	28♐	29♈	4♏	21♑	19♊
9	7♎	20♒	21♋	21♏	27♓	12♌	11♑	11♉	18♏	5♒	1♋
10	20♎	5♓	3♌	3♐	11♈	27♌	23♑	23♉	2♎	19♒	13♋
11	4♏	19♓	15♌	15♐	26♈	11♏	5♒	5♊	16♎	3♓	25♋
12	19♏	4♈	27♌	27♐	10♉	25♏	17♒	17♊	1♏	16♓	7♌
13	3♐	18♈	9♏	9♑	25♉	9♎	29♒	0♋	16♏	0♈	19♌
14	18♐	2♉	21♏	22♑	10♊	23♎	11♓	12♋	1♐	13♈	1♏
15	2♑	16♉	3♎	5♒	24♊	6♏	23♓	25♋	16♐	27♈	13♏
16	16♑	0♊	15♎	18♒	8♋	20♏	5♈	9♌	0♑	10♉	25♏
17	0♒	13♊	27♎	2♓	22♋	2♐	17♈	23♌	14♑	22♉	7♎
18	14♒	25♊	9♏	16♓	6♌	15♐	29♈	7♏	28♑	5♊	20♎
19	28♒	8♋	21♏	1♈	20♌	27♐	12♉	22♏	12♒	17♊	2♏
20	12♓	20♋	3♐	16♈	3♏	9♑	24♉	7♎	25♒	29♊	15♏
21	25♓	2♌	16♐	1♉	16♏	21♑	7♊	22♎	8♓	11♋	28♏
22	8♈	13♌	29♐	17♉	29♏	3♒	20♊	7♏	20♓	23♋	12♎
23	21♈	25♌	12♑	2♊	12♎	15♒	3♋	22♏	3♈	4♌	25♎
24	4♉	7♏	25♑	16♊	25♎	27♒	17♉	7♐	15♈	16♌	9♑
25	17♉	19♏	9♒	1♋	7♏	9♓	1♌	21♐	27♈	29♌	23♑
26	29♉	1♎	23♒	15♋	19♏	21♓	15♌	5♑	9♉	11♏	7♒
27	11♊	14♎	7♓	28♋	1♐	4♈	29♌	19♑	21♉	24♏	21♒
28	23♊	27♎	22♓	11♌	13♐	17♈	14♏	2♒	3♊	7♎	5♓
29	5♋	10♏	7♈	24♌	25♐	1♉	28♏	15♒	15♊	21♎	20♓
30	17♋	23♏	22♈	6♏	7♑	14♉	13♎	27♒	27♊	5♏	4♈
31	29♋	7♐	7♉	19♏	18♑	28♉	28♎	9♓	9♋	19♏	18♈

	1890	1891	1892	1893	1894	1895	1896	1897	1898	1899	1900	1901	1902
1	4♋	5♍	25♎	16♌	25♐	26♈	16♏	8♒	13♊	16♎	23♎	15♋	21♍
2	16♋	18♍	10♏	0♍	6♑	8♉	0♎	21♒	25♊	28♎	7♏	29♋	3♐
3	28♋	0♎	25♏	13♏	18♑	21♉	15♎	4♓	7♋	11♍	22♏	12♌	15♐
4	10♌	12♎	10♐	26♏	29♑	3♊	1♍	17♓	19♋	24♍	7♐	25♌	27♐
5	22♌	25♎	25♐	9♎	11♒	16♊	16♍	29♓	1♌	8♐	22♐	8♍	9♑
6	4♏	8♑	10♊	21♎	23♒	0♋	1♐	12♈	13♌	21♐	7♑	20♍	21♑
7	16♏	21♑	25♊	3♍	5♓	13♋	16♐	24♈	25♌	5♑	22♑	3♎	2♒
8	28♏	4♒	10♋	16♍	17♓	27♋	0♑	6♉	7♍	19♑	7♒	15♎	15♒
9	10♎	18♒	24♋	28♍	0♈	11♌	14♑	18♉	20♍	3♒	21♊	26♎	27♒
10	23♎	2♓	7♌	10♐	13♈	25♌	28♑	0♊	3♎	17♒	5♊	8♍	10♓
11	6♏	17♓	20♌	21♐	26♈	9♍	11♒	12♊	16♎	1♓	18♊	20♍	23♓
12	19♏	1♈	3♏	3♑	9♉	23♍	23♒	24♊	0♍	15♓	1♌	2♐	6♈
13	2♐	16♈	15♏	15♑	23♉	7♎	6♓	5♋	14♍	29♓	13♌	14♐	20♈
14	16♐	1♉	28♏	27♑	7♊	22♎	17♓	17♋	28♍	14♈	26♌	26♐	4♉
15	0♑	16♉	10♎	9♒	22♊	6♏	0♈	29♋	13♐	28♈	8♏	8♑	19♉
16	14♑	0♊	21♎	21♒	6♋	21♏	11♈	12♌	28♐	12♉	20♏	20♑	4♊
17	28♑	14♊	3♍	4♓	21♋	5♐	23♈	24♌	12♑	26♉	2♎	2♒	19♊
18	12♒	28♊	15♍	17♓	5♌	19♐	5♉	7♍	27♑	9♊	13♎	15♒	4♋
19	26♒	12♋	27♍	0♈	19♌	2♑	17♉	20♍	11♒	22♊	25♎	28♒	19♋
20	11♓	25♋	9♌	14♈	3♍	15♑	29♉	4♎	25♒	5♍	7♏	11♓	3♌
21	25♓	8♌	21♌	28♈	17♍	28♑	11♊	19♎	9♓	17♍	19♏	25♓	17♌
22	9♈	20♌	3♑	13♉	1♎	10♒	24♊	3♏	23♓	29♍	2♐	10♈	1♏
23	23♈	2♍	15♑	28♉	14♎	22♒	6♋	18♏	6♈	11♎	14♐	24♈	15♏
24	6♉	14♍	27♑	13♊	28♎	4♓	19♋	4♐	19♈	23♎	27♐	9♉	28♏
25	20♉	26♍	10♒	28♊	11♏	16♓	1♌	19♐	2♉	5♏	10♑	24♉	10♎
26	3♊	8♎	23♒	13♋	24♏	27♓	14♌	4♑	15♉	17♏	23♑	10♊	23♎
27	16♊	20♎	6♓	28♋	6♐	9♈	28♌	19♑	27♉	29♏	6♒	25♊	5♍
28	29♊	2♏	20♓	12♌	19♐	21♈	11♍	3♒	9♊	11♐	20♒	10♋	18♍
29	11♋	14♏	4♈	26♌	1♑	4♉	25♍	17♒	22♊	24♐	4♓	24♋	0♐
30	24♋	26♏	18♈	10♏	14♑	16♉	10♎	1♓	4♋	7♍	18♓	8♌	12♐

NOVEMBER

	1903	1904	1905	1906	1907	1908	1909	1910	1911	1912	1913	1914	1915
1	23♐	15♌	6♑	11♉	13♏	7♒	27♊	2♏	3♐	0♌	17♐	22♈	23♌
2	5♈	29♌	20♑	23♉	26♏	21♒	10♋	13♏	16♐	14♌	1♑	4♉	5♏
3	18♈	14♏	3♒	5♊	9♎	6♓	24♋	25♏	29♐	28♌	14♑	15♉	19♏
4	2♉	28♏	16♒	17♊	22♎	20♓	6♌	7♐	12♈	12♏	27♑	27♉	2♎
5	15♉	13♎	29♒	29♊	6♏	5♈	19♌	19♐	26♈	26♏	9♒	9♊	17♎
6	29♉	28♎	11♓	11♋	20♏	19♈	1♏	1♑	11♉	10♎	21♒	21♊	1♏
7	13♊	12♏	23♓	23♋	4♐	3♉	13♏	13♑	25♉	24♎	3♓	3♋	16♏
8	27♊	27♏	5♈	5♌	19♐	18♉	25♏	25♑	10♊	8♏	15♓	16♋	1♐
9	11♋	11♐	17♈	17♌	3♑	1♊	7♎	7♒	25♊	22♏	27♓	28♋	16♌
10	25♋	25♐	28♈	0♏	17♑	15♊	19♎	20♒	9♋	5♐	9♈	11♌	1♑
11	10♌	8♑	10♉	13♏	2♒	28♊	1♏	3♐	24♋	18♐	21♈	24♌	16♑
12	24♌	21♑	22♉	26♏	16♒	11♋	13♏	17♐	8♌	0♑	3♉	8♏	0♒
13	8♏	3♒	4♊	10♎	0♓	23♋	25♏	1♈	22♌	13♑	15♉	22♏	14♒
14	22♏	16♒	16♊	25♎	14♓	5♌	7♐	16♈	6♏	25♑	27♉	6♎	27♒
15	5♎	28♒	29♊	10♍	27♓	17♌	19♐	0♉	19♏	7♒	10♊	21♎	11♓
16	19♎	9♓	11♋	25♍	11♈	29♌	2♑	16♉	2♎	19♒	23♊	6♏	23♓
17	3♏	21♓	23♋	10♐	24♈	11♏	14♑	1♊	15♎	0♓	6♋	22♏	6♈
18	16♏	3♈	6♌	25♐	7♉	23♏	27♑	16♊	28♎	12♓	19♋	7♐	19♈
19	29♏	15♈	19♌	10♑	20♉	5♒	11♒	1♋	10♏	24♓	3♌	22♐	1♉
20	12♐	27♈	3♏	25♑	2♊	17♒	24♒	16♋	23♏	7♈	17♌	7♑	13♉
21	25♐	9♉	16♏	9♒	15♊	0♓	8♓	0♌	5♐	19♈	0♏	21♑	25♉
22	7♑	22♉	1♎	22♒	27♊	12♓	22♓	14♌	17♐	2♉	15♏	4♒	7♊
23	19♑	5♊	15♎	6♓	9♋	25♏	7♈	27♌	29♐	15♉	29♏	17♒	19♊
24	1♒	18♊	0♏	19♓	21♋	9♐	22♈	10♏	11♑	29♉	13♎	0♓	1♋
25	13♒	1♋	15♏	1♈	3♌	22♐	7♉	22♏	22♑	13♊	28♎	13♓	13♋
26	25♒	15♋	0♌	14♈	14♌	6♑	21♉	5♎	4♒	28♊	12♏	25♓	25♋
27	7♓	28♋	15♌	26♈	26♌	20♑	6♏	17♎	16♒	12♋	27♏	7♈	6♌
28	19♓	12♌	0♑	8♉	8♏	4♒	21♊	29♎	28♒	26♋	11♐	19♈	19♌
29	1♈	26♌	15♑	20♉	21♏	18♒	5♋	10♏	11♓	11♌	25♐	0♉	1♏
30	13♈	10♏	28♑	2♊	3♎	2♓	18♋	22♏	23♐	25♌	9♑	12♉	14♏

NOVEMBER

	1916	1917	1918	1919	1920	1921	1922	1923	1924	1925	1926	1927	1928
1	22♑	7♊	12♎	13♒	14♋	27♍	2♈	3♌	7♑	18♉	22♍	24♑	28♊
2	6♒	21♋	24♎	26♒	29♋	11♐	14♈	16♌	21♑	1♊	4♎	7♒	13♋
3	20♒	4♋	6♍	9♓	13♌	24♐	26♈	0♍	5♎	14♊	16♎	21♒	27♋
4	4♓	16♋	18♍	23♓	27♌	6♑	8♉	13♍	19♒	26♊	28♎	4♓	10♌
5	18♓	29♋	0♐	7♈	10♍	18♑	20♉	28♍	2♐	8♋	11♍	19♓	24♌
6	2♈	11♌	12♐	22♈	24♍	1♒	2♊	12♎	15♐	20♋	23♍	3♈	7♍
7	16♈	23♌	24♐	7♉	7♎	12♒	15♊	27♎	28♐	2♌	6♐	19♈	20♍
8	29♈	5♍	7♑	22♉	20♎	24♒	28♊	13♍	11♈	14♌	19♐	4♉	2♎
9	12♉	17♍	19♑	7♊	3♍	6♓	11♋	28♍	24♈	26♌	2♑	19♐	15♎
10	25♉	28♍	2♒	22♊	16♍	18♓	24♋	13♐	6♉	8♏	16♑	4♊	27♎
11	8♊	11♎	15♒	7♋	28♍	0♈	7♌	28♐	18♉	20♏	29♑	19♊	9♍
12	20♊	23♎	29♒	21♋	10♐	13♈	21♌	13♑	0♊	2♎	13♑	3♋	21♍
13	3♋	5♍	13♓	5♌	22♐	25♈	5♍	26♑	12♊	15♎	27♎	17♓	2♐
14	15♋	18♍	28♓	19♌	4♑	8♉	19♍	10♒	24♊	29♎	11♏	0♌	14♐
15	26♋	1♐	13♈	2♍	16♑	21♉	4♎	23♒	6♋	12♍	26♏	13♌	26♐
16	8♌	14♐	28♈	15♍	28♑	5♊	19♎	6♓	18♋	26♍	10♈	26♌	8♑
17	20♌	27♐	13♉	27♍	10♒	19♊	3♍	18♓	0♌	10♐	25♈	8♍	20♑
18	2♍	11♑	28♉	10♎	22♒	3♋	18♍	0♈	12♌	25♐	9♉	20♏	2♒
19	14♍	25♑	12♊	22♎	4♓	17♋	3♐	12♈	24♌	9♑	24♉	2♎	14♒
20	26♍	9♒	27♊	4♏	16♓	1♌	17♐	24♈	6♍	23♑	8♊	14♎	27♒
21	9♎	23♒	11♋	16♍	29♓	15♌	1♑	6♉	19♍	8♒	21♊	26♎	10♓
22	22♎	7♓	24♋	27♍	12♈	0♍	15♑	18♉	2♎	22♒	5♋	8♍	23♓
23	6♍	21♓	8♌	9♐	26♈	14♍	28♑	29♉	16♎	6♓	18♋	20♍	7♈
24	20♍	5♈	20♌	21♐	10♉	28♍	10♒	11♊	1♍	20♓	0♌	2♐	21♈
25	4♐	20♈	3♍	3♑	25♉	12♎	23♒	23♊	15♍	3♈	12♌	14♐	6♉
26	19♐	4♉	15♍	15♑	10♊	25♎	5♓	6♋	1♐	17♈	24♌	26♐	21♉
27	3♑	18♉	27♍	27♑	25♊	9♍	17♓	18♋	16♐	0♉	6♏	8♑	6♊
28	18♑	2♊	9♎	9♒	10♋	22♍	29♓	0♌	1♑	14♉	18♏	21♑	21♊
29	3♒	15♊	21♎	22♒	24♋	6♐	10♈	13♌	16♑	27♉	0♎	4♒	7♋
30	17♒	29♊	3♍	5♓	9♌	19♐	22♈	26♌	1♒	9♊	12♎	17♒	22♋

NOVEMBER

	1929	1930	1931	1932	1933	1934	1935	1936	1937	1938	1939	1940	1941
1	8♏	12♓	16♋	19♐	29♈	1♏	7♑	10♊	20♎	21♒	29♊	1♐	10♈
2	21♏	24♓	29♋	4♑	11♉	13♏	20♑	25♊	2♏	3♓	12♋	15♐	22♈
3	3♐	6♈	12♌	18♑	24♉	26♏	4♒	9♋	14♏	16♓	26♋	29♐	4♉
4	15♐	18♈	26♌	2♒	6♊	8♐	18♒	23♋	26♏	28♓	10♌	13♑	16♉
5	28♐	1♉	10♏	15♒	18♊	21♐	2♓	6♌	8♐	11♈	24♌	26♑	28♉
6	10♑	14♉	25♏	28♒	0♋	4♏	16♓	19♌	19♐	25♈	9♏	9♒	10♊
7	21♑	27♉	10♎	11♓	11♋	18♏	1♈	1♏	1♑	8♉	23♏	22♒	22♊
8	3♒	10♊	24♎	23♓	23♋	2♐	16♈	13♏	13♑	23♉	7♎	4♓	4♋
9	15♒	24♊	9♏	5♈	5♌	16♐	1♉	26♏	25♑	7♊	22♎	16♓	16♋
10	27♒	8♋	24♏	17♈	17♌	0♑	15♉	8♎	7♒	21♊	6♏	28♓	28♋
11	10♓	22♋	9♐	29♈	29♌	14♑	0♊	19♎	20♒	6♋	20♏	9♈	10♌
12	22♓	6♌	23♐	11♉	12♏	28♑	14♊	1♏	2♓	20♋	4♐	21♈	23♌
13	5♈	20♌	7♑	23♉	25♏	12♒	27♊	13♏	15♓	5♌	17♐	3♉	6♏
14	19♈	4♏	21♑	5♊	9♐	26♒	11♋	25♏	29♓	19♌	0♑	15♉	20♏
15	2♉	18♏	4♒	16♊	23♐	10♓	23♋	7♐	13♈	3♏	13♑	27♉	4♎
16	17♉	2♎	16♒	28♊	7♏	24♓	6♌	19♐	28♈	17♏	26♑	9♊	18♎
17	1♊	16♎	28♒	10♋	22♏	8♈	18♌	1♑	13♉	0♎	8♒	22♊	3♏
18	16♊	0♏	10♓	23♋	7♐	22♈	0♏	13♑	28♉	14♎	20♒	5♋	18♏
19	0♋	14♏	22♓	5♌	22♐	5♉	12♏	26♑	13♊	27♎	2♓	17♋	4♐
20	15♋	28♏	4♈	18♌	7♑	19♉	24♏	9♒	28♊	10♏	13♓	0♌	19♐
21	0♌	11♐	16♈	1♏	22♑	2♊	6♐	22♒	13♋	22♏	25♓	14♌	4♑
22	14♌	24♐	28♈	14♏	6♒	15♊	18♎	5♓	27♋	5♐	7♈	27♌	19♑
23	28♌	7♑	10♉	28♏	20♒	27♊	0♏	19♓	11♌	17♐	20♈	11♏	3♒
24	12♏	20♑	22♉	12♎	4♓	10♋	12♏	4♈	25♌	29♐	2♉	25♏	16♒
25	25♏	2♒	4♊	27♎	17♓	22♋	25♏	18♈	9♏	11♑	15♉	10♎	0♓
26	9♎	14♒	17♊	12♏	0♈	4♌	8♐	3♉	22♏	23♑	28♉	24♎	12♓
27	22♎	26♒	0♋	27♏	13♈	16♌	21♐	18♉	4♎	5♒	11♊	9♏	25♓
28	5♏	8♓	13♋	12♐	25♈	27♌	4♑	3♊	17♎	17♒	25♊	24♏	7♈
29	17♏	20♓	26♋	28♐	8♉	9♏	17♑	18♊	29♎	29♒	9♋	9♐	19♈
30	0♐	2♈	9♌	12♑	20♉	21♏	1♒	3♋	11♏	11♓	23♋	23♐	1♉

NOVEMBER

	1942	1943	1944	1945	1946	1947	1948	1949	1950	1951	1952
1	11♌	21♐	22♉	1♎	0♒	12♊	12♏	21♐	21♋	4♌	3♉
2	23♌	5♑	6♊	13♎	13♒	26♊	26♏	3♈	3♌	18♌	17♉
3	5♏	19♑	20♊	24♎	25♒	11♋	10♐	15♈	15♌	3♑	0♊
4	18♏	3♒	4♋	6♏	8♐	25♋	23♐	26♈	28♌	17♑	13♊
5	1♎	17♒	17♋	18♏	21♐	9♌	6♑	8♉	12♏	2♒	26♊
6	15♎	1♓	29♋	0♐	5♈	23♌	19♑	20♉	25♏	16♒	9♋
7	29♎	15♓	12♌	12♐	20♈	7♏	1♒	2♊	10♎	29♒	21♋
8	13♏	29♓	24♌	24♐	4♉	21♏	13♒	14♊	24♎	13♐	3♌
9	28♏	13♈	6♏	6♑	19♉	5♎	25♒	27♊	9♏	26♐	15♌
10	13♐	27♈	17♏	18♑	4♊	18♎	7♓	9♋	25♏	10♈	27♌
11	27♐	11♉	29♏	1♒	19♊	2♏	19♓	22♋	10♐	23♈	9♏
12	12♑	24♉	11♎	14♒	4♋	15♏	1♈	5♌	25♐	5♉	21♏
13	27♑	8♊	23♎	27♒	18♋	28♏	13♈	18♌	10♑	18♉	3♎
14	11♒	21♊	5♏	11♐	3♌	10♐	25♈	2♏	24♑	1♊	15♎
15	25♒	3♋	18♏	25♐	17♌	23♐	8♉	16♏	8♒	13♊	28♎
16	8♓	15♋	0♐	9♈	0♏	5♑	21♉	1♎	22♒	25♊	11♏
17	22♓	27♋	13♐	24♈	13♏	17♑	3♊	15♎	5♓	7♋	24♏
18	5♈	9♌	26♐	9♉	26♏	29♑	17♊	0♏	17♓	19♋	8♌
19	18♈	21♌	9♑	25♉	9♎	11♒	0♋	15♏	0♈	1♌	22♐
20	0♉	3♏	22♑	10♊	21♎	23♒	14♋	0♐	12♈	12♌	6♑
21	13♉	15♏	5♒	25♊	4♏	5♓	28♋	15♐	24♈	24♌	20♑
22	25♉	27♏	19♒	9♋	16♏	17♓	12♌	29♐	6♉	6♏	4♒
23	7♊	9♎	3♓	23♋	28♏	29♓	26♌	14♑	18♉	19♏	18♒
24	20♊	22♎	17♓	7♌	10♐	12♈	10♏	27♑	0♊	2♎	2♓
25	2♋	5♏	2♈	20♌	21♐	25♈	24♏	10♒	12♊	15♎	16♓
26	13♋	18♏	16♈	3♏	3♑	9♉	8♎	23♒	24♊	29♎	0♈
27	25♋	2♐	1♉	15♏	15♑	23♉	22♎	6♓	6♋	13♏	14♏
28	7♌	16♐	15♉	28♏	27♑	7♊	7♏	18♓	18♋	28♏	28♈
29	19♌	0♑	0♊	10♎	9♒	21♊	21♏	0♈	0♌	13♐	12♉
30	1♏	15♑	14♊	21♎	21♒	6♋	4♐	11♈	12♌	28♐	25♉

	1890	1891	1892	1893	1894	1895	1896	1897	1898	1899	1900	1901	1902
1	6♌	9♐	3♉	23♍	26♑	29♉	24♎	14♐	15♐	20♍	2♈	21♌	23♐
2	18♌	22♐	18♉	6♎	7♒	13♊	9♍	26♐	27♐	3♐	16♈	5♏	5♑
3	29♌	5♑	3♊	18♎	19♒	26♊	24♍	9♈	9♌	17♐	18♈	17♏	17♑
4	11♍	18♑	18♊	0♍	1♐	10♋	9♌	21♈	21♌	1♑	16♈	29♏	29♑
5	23♍	1♒	9♋	12♍	13♐	23♋	24♌	3♉	3♏	15♑	0♊	11♎	11♒
6	5♎	15♒	18♋	24♍	25♐	7♌	8♑	15♉	15♏	29♑	14♊	23♎	23♒
7	18♎	29♒	2♌	6♐	7♈	21♌	22♑	27♉	28♏	13♒	28♊	5♍	5♐
8	1♏	13♓	16♌	18♐	20♈	5♏	6♒	9♊	10♐	28♒	12♋	17♍	18♐
9	14♏	27♓	29♌	0♑	3♉	20♏	19♒	21♊	24♎	12♐	26♋	29♍	1♈
10	27♏	11♈	12♍	12♑	17♉	4♎	2♐	2♋	8♍	26♐	9♌	11♐	14♈
11	11♐	26♈	24♍	24♑	1♊	18♎	14♐	14♋	22♍	10♐	21♌	23♐	28♈
12	25♐	10♉	6♎	6♒	16♊	2♍	26♐	26♋	6♐	24♐	4♍	5♑	12♉
13	9♑	24♉	18♎	18♒	1♋	16♍	8♈	8♌	21♐	8♑	16♍	17♑	27♉
14	24♑	8♊	0♏	0♐	15♋	0♌	20♈	21♌	6♑	21♉	28♍	29♑	12♊
15	8♒	22♊	12♍	13♐	0♌	13♐	2♉	3♏	21♑	4♒	10♎	12♒	27♊
16	23♒	6♋	24♍	25♐	15♌	27♐	14♉	16♏	6♒	17♊	21♎	25♒	13♋
17	7♐	20♋	5♐	8♈	0♍	10♑	26♉	29♏	21♒	0♊	3♍	8♐	28♋
18	22♐	3♌	17♐	22♈	14♍	23♑	8♊	13♎	5♐	13♑	15♍	21♐	13♌
19	6♈	15♌	0♑	6♉	28♍	5♒	20♊	27♎	19♐	25♑	28♍	5♈	27♌
20	19♈	28♌	12♑	21♉	11♎	18♒	3♋	12♍	3♈	7♑	10♎	19♈	11♍
21	3♉	10♏	24♑	5♊	25♎	0♓	15♋	27♍	16♈	19♌	23♎	3♉	24♍
22	16♉	22♏	7♒	21♊	8♍	12♐	20♋	12♎	29♈	1♏	6♌	18♉	7♎
23	29♉	4♐	20♒	6♋	20♍	23♐	11♌	27♐	12♑	13♏	19♌	3♊	20♎
24	12♊	16♐	3♓	21♋	3♐	5♈	25♌	12♑	24♉	25♏	3♒	18♊	2♏
25	25♊	20♐	16♓	6♌	15♐	17♈	8♍	27♑	6♊	7♐	16♒	3♋	15♏
26	7♋	10♍	0♈	21♌	28♐	29♈	22♍	12♒	18♊	19♐	0♓	17♋	27♏
27	20♋	22♍	14♈	5♏	10♑	12♉	6♎	26♒	0♋	2♑	14♐	2♌	9♐
28	2♌	4♐	28♈	19♏	22♑	24♉	20♎	9♐	12♋	14♑	28♐	16♌	20♐
29	14♌	17♐	12♉	2♎	4♒	7♊	4♍	22♐	24♋	27♑	13♈	0♍	2♑
30	26♌	0♑	27♉	15♎	16♒	21♊	19♍	5♈	6♌	11♐	27♈	13♏	14♑
31	7♍	14♑	12♊	27♎	27♒	5♋	3♐	18♈	18♌	25♐	11♉	26♏	26♑

DECEMBER

	1903	1904	1905	1906	1907	1908	1909	1910	1911	1912	1913	1914	1915
1	26♈	24♏	12♎	14♊	16♎	16♏	2♌	4♌	6♈	9♏	22♑	24♉	27♏
2	10♉	8♎	25♒	26♊	0♏	1♏	15♌	16♌	30♈	23♏	5♒	6♊	10♎
3	23♉	23♎	7♓	8♌	14♏	15♏	27♌	28♌	4♉	7♎	17♒	18♊	25♎
4	7♊	7♏	19♓	19♌	28♏	29♏	9♏	10♑	18♉	20♎	29♒	1♋	9♏
5	22♊	21♏	1♈	1♎	13♐	13♏	21♏	22♑	3♊	4♏	11♓	13♋	24♏
6	6♋	5♐	13♈	13♎	28♐	26♏	3♎	4♒	18♊	17♏	23♓	25♋	9♐
7	21♋	19♐	25♈	26♎	13♑	10♏	15♎	17♒	4♋	0♐	5♈	8♌	25♐
8	6♌	3♑	7♉	8♏	27♑	23♏	27♎	0♓	19♋	13♐	17♈	21♌	10♑
9	20♌	16♑	19♉	21♏	12♒	6♋	9♏	13♓	4♌	26♐	29♈	4♏	25♑
10	5♏	29♑	1♊	5♎	26♒	18♋	21♏	26♓	18♌	8♑	11♉	18♏	9♒
11	19♏	11♒	13♊	19♎	10♓	1♌	3♐	10♈	2♏	21♑	23♉	1♎	23♒
12	2♎	23♒	25♊	3♍	24♓	13♌	16♐	24♈	16♏	3♒	6♊	16♎	7♓
13	16♎	5♓	8♋	18♍	8♈	25♌	28♐	9♉	29♏	15♒	19♊	0♍	20♓
14	29♎	17♓	20♋	3♎	21♈	7♍	11♑	24♉	12♎	27♒	2♋	15♍	3♈
15	12♏	29♓	3♌	18♐	4♉	19♍	24♑	9♊	25♎	8♓	16♋	0♐	16♈
16	25♏	11♈	16♌	3♑	16♉	1♎	8♒	24♊	7♏	20♓	0♌	15♐	28♈
17	8♐	23♈	29♌	19♑	29♉	13♎	21♒	9♋	20♏	2♈	13♌	0♑	10♉
18	21♐	5♉	13♏	3♒	11♊	25♎	5♓	24♋	2♐	14♈	27♌	14♑	22♉
19	3♑	17♉	27♏	18♒	23♊	7♏	19♓	8♌	14♐	27♈	11♏	29♑	4♊
20	15♑	0♊	11♎	2♓	5♋	20♏	3♈	25♌	26♐	10♉	25♏	12♒	16♊
21	27♑	13♊	25♎	15♓	17♋	4♐	17♈	6♏	7♑	23♉	9♎	26♒	28♊
22	9♒	27♊	9♍	28♓	29♋	17♐	2♉	19♏	19♑	7♊	24♎	9♓	10♋
23	21♒	10♋	24♍	11♈	11♌	1♑	16♉	1♎	1♒	22♊	8♏	21♓	22♋
24	3♓	24♋	9♐	23♈	23♌	15♑	1♊	13♎	13♒	6♋	22♏	3♈	3♌
25	15♓	8♌	24♐	5♉	5♏	0♒	15♊	25♎	25♒	21♋	6♐	15♈	16♌
26	27♓	23♌	8♑	17♉	17♏	14♒	29♊	7♏	7♓	6♌	20♐	27♈	28♌
27	9♈	7♍	22♑	29♉	29♏	29♒	13♋	19♏	19♓	21♌	3♑	9♉	10♏
28	21♈	21♍	6♒	11♊	12♐	13♓	26♋	1♐	2♈	5♏	17♑	21♉	23♏
29	4♉	5♎	20♒	23♊	24♐	27♓	9♌	13♐	15♈	20♏	0♒	3♊	6♎
30	17♉	19♎	3♓	5♋	8♍	12♈	22♌	25♐	28♈	4♎	12♒	15♊	19♎
31	1♊	3♍	15♓	16♋	22♍	25♈	5♏	7♑	12♉	17♎	25♒	27♊	3♍

7 Q

DECEMBER

	1916	1917	1918	1919	1920	1921	1922	1923	1924	1925	1926	1927	1928
1	1♓	12♋	14♍	18♓	23♌	2♑	4♌	9♏	15♒	22♊	24♎	0♓	6♌
2	15♓	24♋	26♍	1♈	7♏	14♑	16♌	22♏	29♒	4♋	7♍	14♓	20♌
3	29♓	7♌	9♐	15♈	21♏	26♑	29♌	6♎	12♓	16♋	19♍	28♓	3♏
4	12♈	19♌	21♐	0♉	4♎	8♒	12♊	21♎	25♓	28♋	2♎	13♈	17♏
5	25♈	1♍	4♑	15♉	17♎	20♒	24♊	6♏	8♈	10♌	15♎	27♈	29♏
6	9♉	12♍	16♑	0♊	0♍	2♓	8♋	21♏	21♈	22♌	29♎	12♉	12♎
7	21♉	24♍	29♑	15♊	12♍	14♓	21♋	6♌	3♉	4♏	12♑	27♉	24♎
8	4♊	6♎	12♒	0♋	25♍	26♓	4♌	21♐	15♉	16♏	26♑	12♊	6♏
9	16♊	18♎	26♒	15♋	7♐	8♈	18♌	6♑	27♉	28♏	10♒	27♊	18♏
10	29♊	1♍	9♓	0♌	19♐	20♈	2♏	21♑	9♊	10♎	24♒	11♋	29♏
11	11♋	13♍	23♓	14♌	1♑	3♉	16♏	5♒	21♊	23♎	8♓	25♋	11♐
12	23♋	26♍	8♈	28♌	13♑	16♉	0♎	18♒	3♋	6♍	22♓	8♌	23♐
13	4♌	10♐	22♈	11♍	24♑	0♊	14♎	1♓	15♋	20♍	6♈	21♌	5♑
14	16♌	23♐	7♉	24♍	6♒	14♊	28♎	14♓	27♋	4♐	20♈	4♏	17♑
15	28♌	7♑	21♉	6♎	18♒	28♊	13♏	26♓	8♌	19♐	5♉	17♏	29♑
16	10♍	21♑	6♊	19♎	0♓	12♋	27♏	9♈	20♌	3♑	19♐	29♏	11♒
17	22♍	5♒	20♊	1♏	12♓	27♋	11♐	21♈	3♍	18♑	2♊	11♎	23♒
18	4♎	19♒	5♋	13♏	25♓	12♌	25♐	2♉	15♍	3♒	16♊	23♎	6♓
19	17♎	4♓	19♋	24♏	7♈	26♌	9♑	14♉	28♍	18♒	0♋	4♏	19♓
20	0♏	18♓	2♌	6♐	20♈	10♍	22♑	26♉	11♎	2♓	13♋	16♏	2♈
21	14♏	2♈	15♌	18♐	4♉	25♍	6♒	8♊	25♎	16♓	25♋	28♏	16♈
22	28♏	16♈	28♌	0♑	18♉	8♎	18♒	20♊	9♏	0♈	8♋	10♐	0♉
23	12♐	0♉	10♍	12♑	3♊	22♎	1♓	2♋	24♏	14♈	20♌	23♐	14♉
24	27♐	14♉	23♍	24♑	18♊	6♏	13♓	15♋	9♌	27♈	2♍	5♑	29♉
25	12♑	27♉	5♎	6♒	3♋	19♏	25♓	27♋	24♐	10♉	14♍	18♑	14♊
26	27♑	11♊	17♎	19♒	18♋	2♐	6♈	10♌	9♑	23♉	26♍	1♒	29♊
27	12♒	24♊	29♎	1♓	3♌	15♐	18♈	23♌	24♑	6♊	8♎	14♒	15♋
28	27♒	7♋	11♍	14♓	18♌	27♐	0♉	6♏	9♒	18♊	20♎	27♒	0♌
29	11♓	20♋	23♍	27♓	3♏	10♑	12♑	19♏	24♒	0♋	2♍	11♓	14♌
30	25♓	2♌	5♐	11♈	17♏	22♑	24♑	3♎	8♓	13♋	14♍	25♓	28♌
31	9♈	14♌	17♐	25♈	1♎	4♒	7♊	16♎	21♓	25♋	27♍	9♈	12♏

DECEMBER

	1929	1930	1931	1932	1933	1934	1935	1936	1937	1938	1939	1940	1941
1	12♐	14♈	23♌	27♑	2♊	3♎	15♒	17♋	23♍	23♐	7♌	7♑	13♉
2	24♐	26♈	6♏	11♒	14♊	16♎	28♒	1♌	5♐	6♈	21♌	21♑	25♉
3	6♑	9♉	20♏	24♒	26♊	29♎	13♐	14♌	16♐	19♈	5♏	5♒	7♊
4	18♑	22♉	5♎	7♓	8♋	12♍	27♐	27♌	28♐	3♉	19♏	17♒	19♊
5	0♒	6♊	19♎	20♓	20♋	26♍	11♈	10♏	10♑	16♉	4♎	0♋	1♋
6	12♒	19♊	3♏	2♈	2♌	10♐	25♈	22♏	22♑	1♊	18♎	12♋	13♋
7	23♒	3♋	18♏	14♈	14♌	25♐	10♉	4♎	4♒	15♊	1♏	24♋	25♋
8	5♓	18♋	3♐	26♈	26♌	9♑	24♉	16♎	16♒	0♋	15♏	6♌	7♌
9	18♓	2♌	17♐	8♉	8♏	24♑	8♊	28♎	28♒	15♋	29♏	18♌	20♌
10	0♈	17♌	1♑	20♉	20♏	8♒	22♊	10♍	11♐	0♌	12♏	29♌	2♍
11	13♈	1♏	15♑	1♊	3♎	23♒	5♋	22♍	24♐	15♌	25♐	11♉	15♏
12	26♈	15♏	28♑	13♊	17♎	7♓	18♋	4♌	8♈	29♌	8♑	23♉	29♏
13	10♉	29♏	11♒	25♊	1♍	21♓	1♌	16♎	21♈	13♏	21♑	6♊	12♐
14	24♉	13♎	24♒	8♋	15♏	5♈	14♌	28♐	6♉	27♏	3♒	18♊	27♎
15	9♊	27♎	6♓	20♋	0♌	19♈	26♌	10♑	20♉	11♐	16♒	1♋	11♍
16	24♊	10♍	18♓	2♌	15♐	2♉	8♏	23♑	6♊	24♎	28♒	14♋	26♍
17	9♋	24♍	0♈	15♌	0♑	15♉	20♏	6♒	21♊	6♏	9♓	27♋	12♐
18	24♋	7♐	12♈	27♌	15♑	28♉	2♎	19♒	6♓	19♏	21♐	11♌	27♐
19	9♌	20♐	24♈	10♏	0♒	11♊	14♎	2♓	21♓	1♐	3♈	24♌	12♑
20	24♌	3♑	6♉	24♏	15♒	23♊	26♎	16♓	6♈	14♐	15♈	8♏	27♑
21	8♍	15♑	18♉	7♎	0♓	6♋	8♍	29♓	20♈	26♐	27♈	22♏	11♒
22	22♍	28♑	0♊	21♎	13♐	18♋	20♍	13♈	4♏	8♑	15♉	6♎	25♒
23	6♎	10♒	13♊	6♏	27♐	0♌	3♐	28♈	18♏	20♑	23♉	20♎	8♓
24	19♎	22♒	26♊	21♏	10♈	12♌	16♐	12♉	1♎	2♒	6♊	4♍	21♓
25	2♏	4♓	9♋	5♐	23♈	24♌	29♐	27♉	13♎	14♒	20♊	19♍	4♈
26	14♏	16♓	22♋	21♐	5♉	5♏	13♑	12♊	26♎	25♒	4♋	3♐	16♈
27	27♏	27♓	6♌	6♑	17♉	17♏	27♑	26♊	8♏	7♓	18♋	17♐	28♈
28	9♐	9♈	19♌	20♑	29♉	29♏	11♒	11♋	20♏	19♓	3♌	1♑	10♉
29	21♐	22♈	3♏	5♒	11♊	14♎	25♒	25♋	2♐	2♈	17♌	15♑	22♉
30	3♑	4♉	17♏	19♒	23♊	24♎	9♓	9♌	13♐	14♈	2♏	29♑	3♊
31	15♑	17♉	1♎	2♓	5♋	7♍	24♓	22♌	25♐	27♈	16♏	12♒	15♊

DECEMBER

	1942	1943	1944	1945	1946	1947	1948	1949	1950	1951	1952
1	13♏	29♑	28♊	3♍	4♐	21♋	18♐	23♍	24♌	13♑	9♊
2	26♏	13♒	11♋	15♍	16♐	5♌	1♑	5♉	7♏	27♑	22♊
3	9♎	28♒	24♋	27♍	0♈	20♌	14♑	17♉	20♏	12♒	4♋
4	23♎	12♓	7♌	9♐	13♈	4♏	27♑	29♉	4♎	26♒	17♋
5	7♏	26♓	20♌	21♐	27♈	18♏	9♒	11♊	18♎	10♐	29♋
6	21♏	9♈	2♏	3♑	12♊	2♎	21♒	24♊	3♏	23♓	11♌
7	6♐	23♈	14♏	15♑	27♊	15♎	3♓	6♋	17♏	7♈	23♌
8	21♐	7♉	25♏	28♑	12♊	28♎	15♓	19♋	3♐	20♈	5♏
9	7♑	20♉	7♎	10♒	27♊	11♏	27♓	2♌	18♐	2♉	16♏
10	22♑	3♊	19♎	23♒	12♋	24♍	9♈	15♌	3♑	15♉	28♏
11	6♒	16♊	1♍	7♓	27♋	7♐	21♈	29♌	18♑	27♉	11♎
12	21♒	29♊	14♍	20♓	12♌	19♐	3♉	12♏	3♒	9♊	23♎
13	5♓	11♋	26♍	4♈	26♌	1♑	16♉	26♏	17♒	21♊	6♏
14	19♓	23♋	9♐	18♈	10♏	13♑	29♉	10♎	1♐	3♋	19♏
15	2♈	5♌	22♐	3♉	23♍	25♑	12♊	25♎	14♐	15♋	3♐
16	15♈	17♌	5♑	18♉	6♎	7♒	26♊	9♍	27♐	27♋	16♐
17	27♈	29♌	18♑	3♊	19♎	19♒	10♋	24♍	9♈	9♌	1♑
18	10♉	11♍	2♒	18♊	1♏	1♓	24♋	9♐	21♈	21♌	15♑
19	22♉	23♍	16♒	2♋	13♏	13♓	8♌	23♐	3♉	3♏	0♒
20	4♊	5♎	0♐	17♋	25♏	25♓	22♌	7♑	15♉	15♏	14♒
21	16♊	17♎	14♐	1♌	7♐	7♈	7♏	21♑	27♉	27♏	29♒
22	28♊	0♍	28♐	15♌	18♐	20♈	21♏	5♒	9♊	10♎	13♓
23	10♋	13♍	12♈	28♌	0♑	3♉	5♎	18♒	20♊	23♎	27♓
24	22♋	26♍	26♈	11♏	12♑	16♉	19♎	1♓	3♋	7♏	11♈
25	4♌	10♐	11♉	24♍	24♑	0♊	3♏	14♓	15♋	21♏	25♈
26	16♌	25♐	25♉	6♎	6♒	15♊	16♏	26♓	27♋	6♐	8♉
27	28♌	9♑	9♊	18♎	18♒	0♋	0♐	8♈	9♌	21♐	22♉
28	10♍	24♑	22♊	0♍	0♐	15♋	13♐	19♈	21♌	6♑	5♊
29	22♍	9♒	6♋	12♍	13♐	0♌	27♐	1♉	4♏	21♑	18♊
30	5♎	23♒	19♋	23♍	26♐	15♏	10♑	13♉	17♏	6♒	0♋
31	18♎	8♓	2♌	5♐	9♈	0♎	22♑	25♉	0♎	21♒	13♋